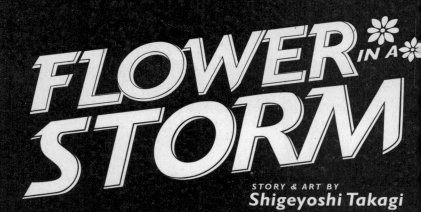

FLOWER IN A STORM

STORY & ART BY
Shigeyoshi Takagi

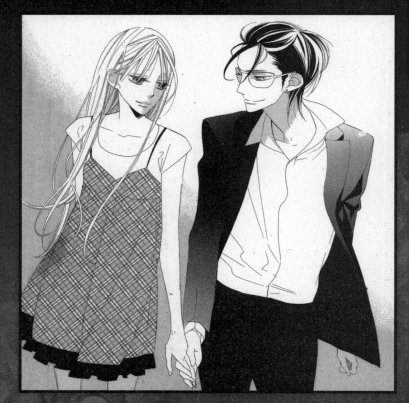

VOLUME TWO

CONTENTS

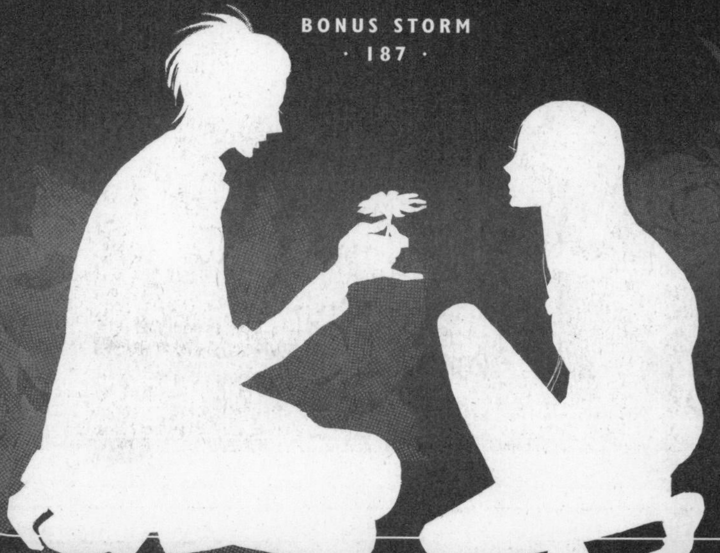

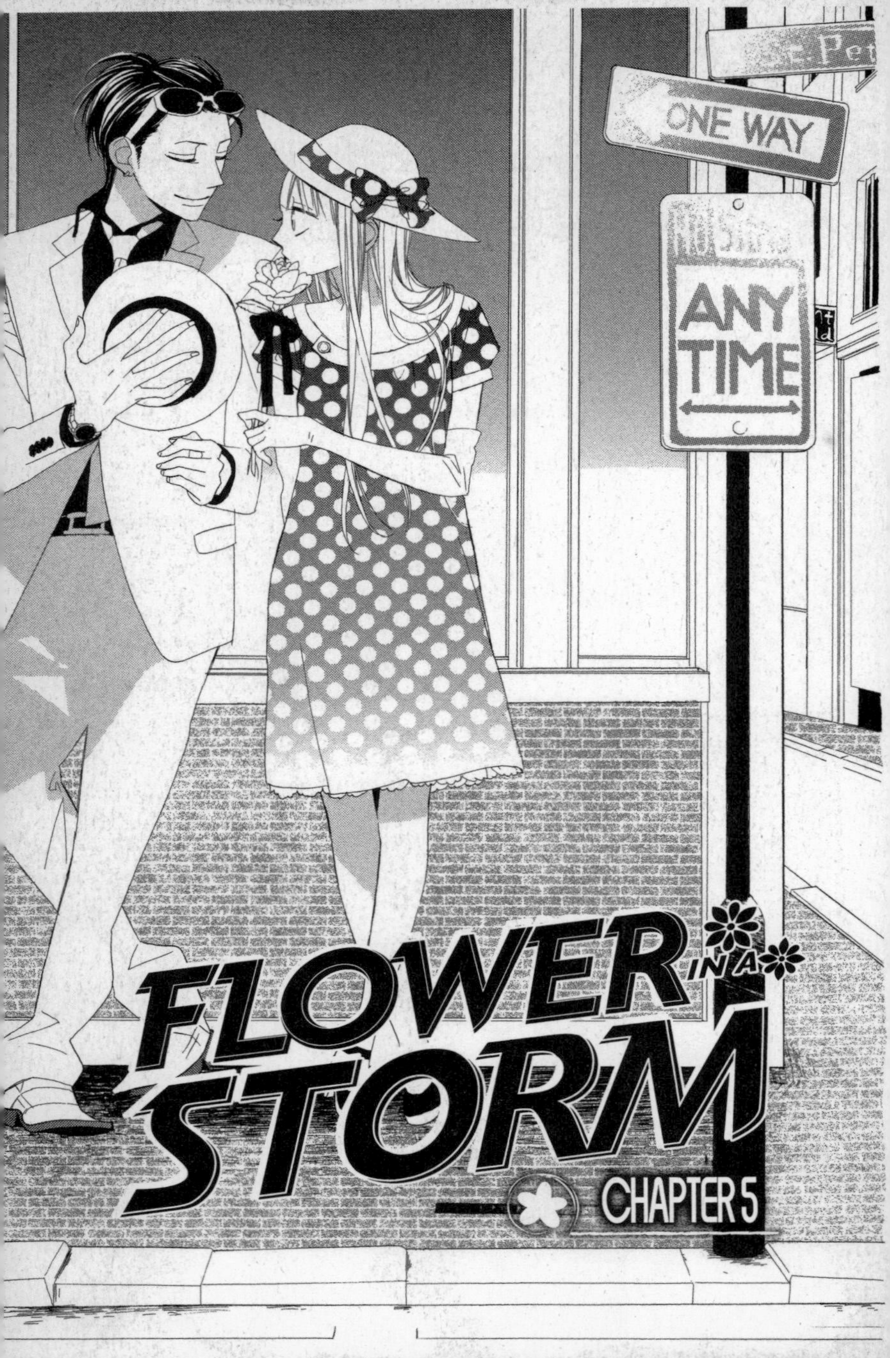
ONE WAY
ANY TIME
FLOWER IN A STORM
CHAPTER 5

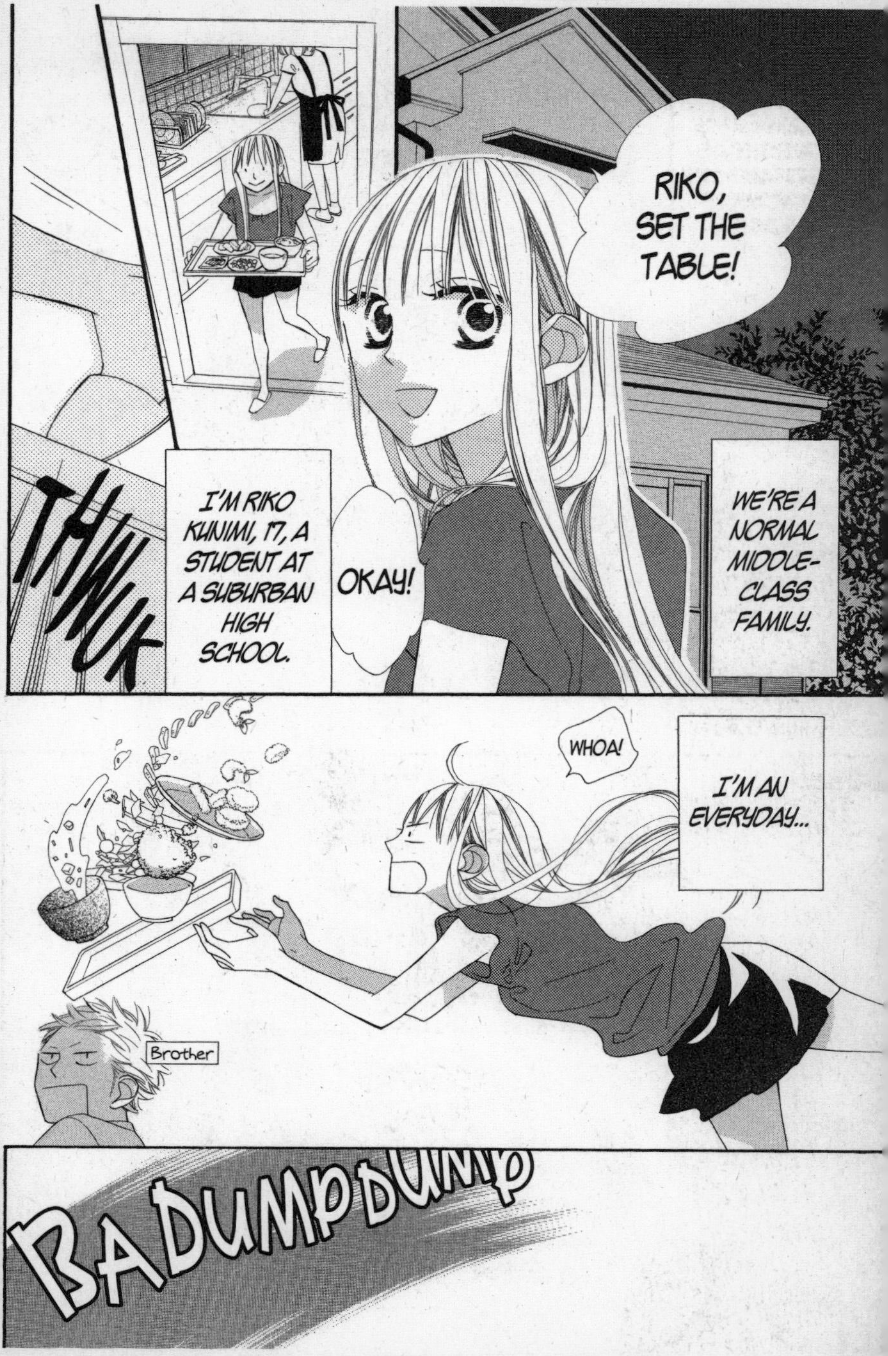
RIKO, SET THE TABLE!
WE'RE A NORMAL MIDDLE-CLASS FAMILY.
OKAY!
I'M RIKO KUNIMI, 17, A STUDENT AT A SUBURBAN HIGH SCHOOL.
THWUK
I'M AN EVERYDAY...
WHOA!
Brother
BADUMPDUMP

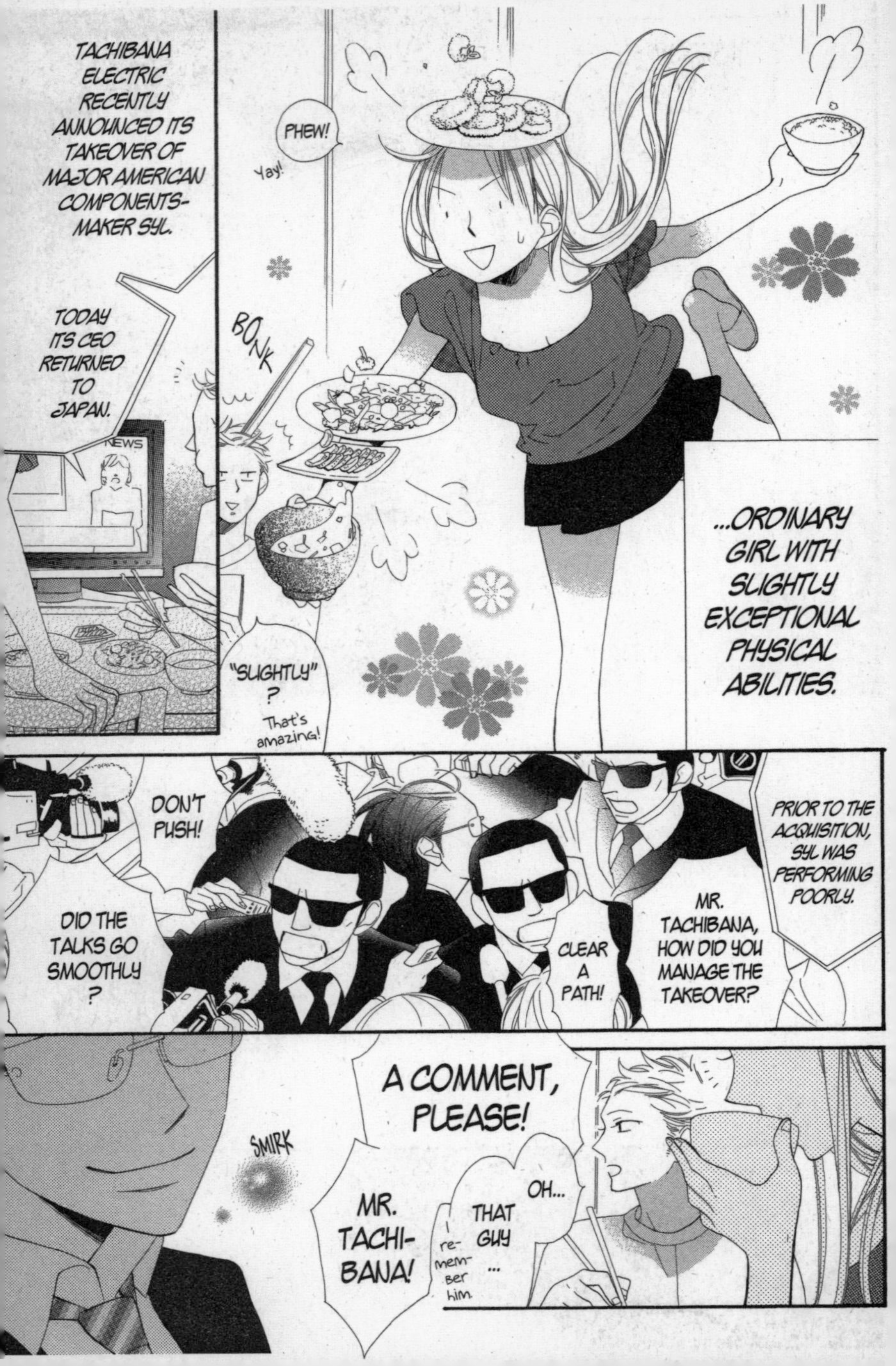
PHEW!
Yay!
BONK
...ORDINARY GIRL WITH SLIGHTLY EXCEPTIONAL PHYSICAL ABILITIES.
"SLIGHTLY"?
That's amazing!
TACHIBANA ELECTRIC RECENTLY ANNOUNCED ITS TAKEOVER OF MAJOR AMERICAN COMPONENTS-MAKER SYL.
TODAY ITS CEO RETURNED TO JAPAN.
NEWS
PRIOR TO THE ACQUISITION, SYL WAS PERFORMING POORLY.
MR. TACHIBANA, HOW DID YOU MANAGE THE TAKEOVER?
CLEAR A PATH!
DID THE TALKS GO SMOOTHLY?
DON'T PUSH!
A COMMENT, PLEASE!
OH...
THAT GUY...
I remember him.
MR. TACHIBANA!
SMIRK

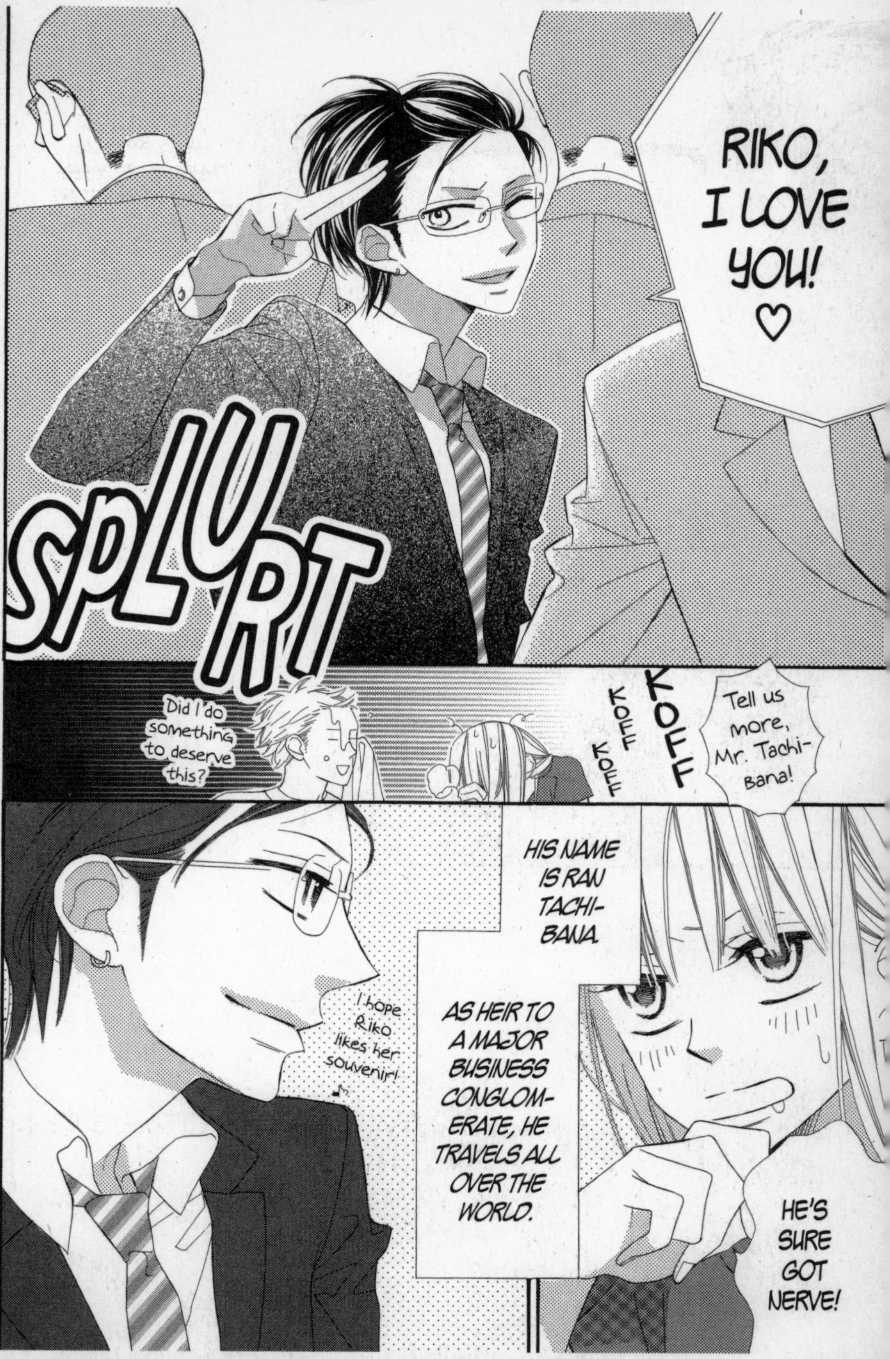
RIKO, I LOVE YOU! ♡
SPLURT
Tell us more, Mr. Tachi-bana!
KOFF
KOFF KOFF
Did I do something to deserve this?
HIS NAME IS RAN TACHI-BANA.
AS HEIR TO A MAJOR BUSINESS CONGLOM-ERATE, HE TRAVELS ALL OVER THE WORLD.
HE'S SURE GOT NERVE!
I hope Riko likes her souvenir! ♪

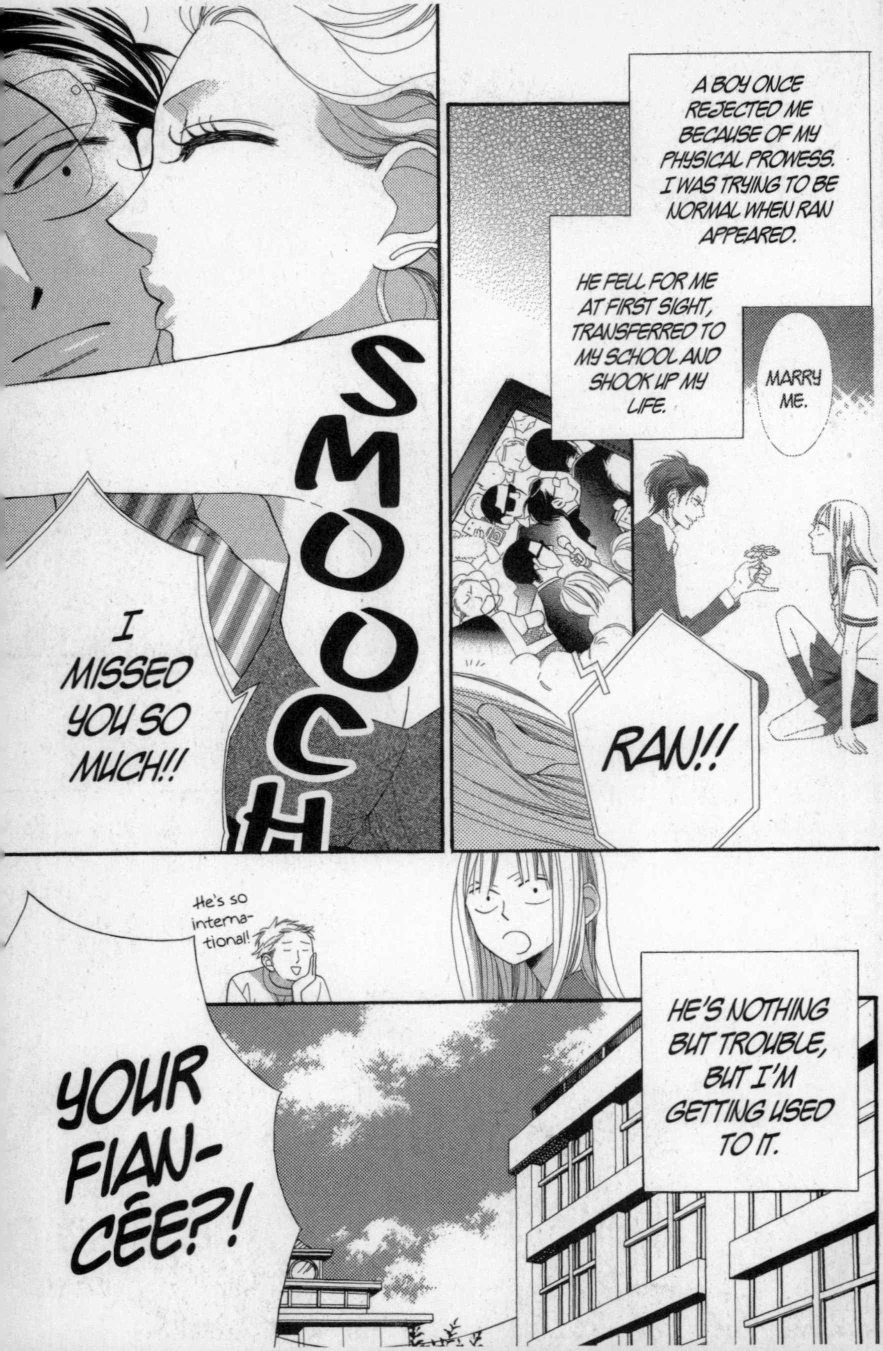
A BOY ONCE REJECTED ME BECAUSE OF MY PHYSICAL PROWESS. I WAS TRYING TO BE NORMAL WHEN RAN APPEARED.
HE FELL FOR ME AT FIRST SIGHT, TRANSFERRED TO MY SCHOOL AND SHOOK UP MY LIFE.
MARRY ME.
RAN!!
SMOOCH
I MISSED YOU SO MUCH!!
He's so interna-tional!
HE'S NOTHING BUT TROUBLE, BUT I'M GETTING USED TO IT.
YOUR FIAN-CÉE?!

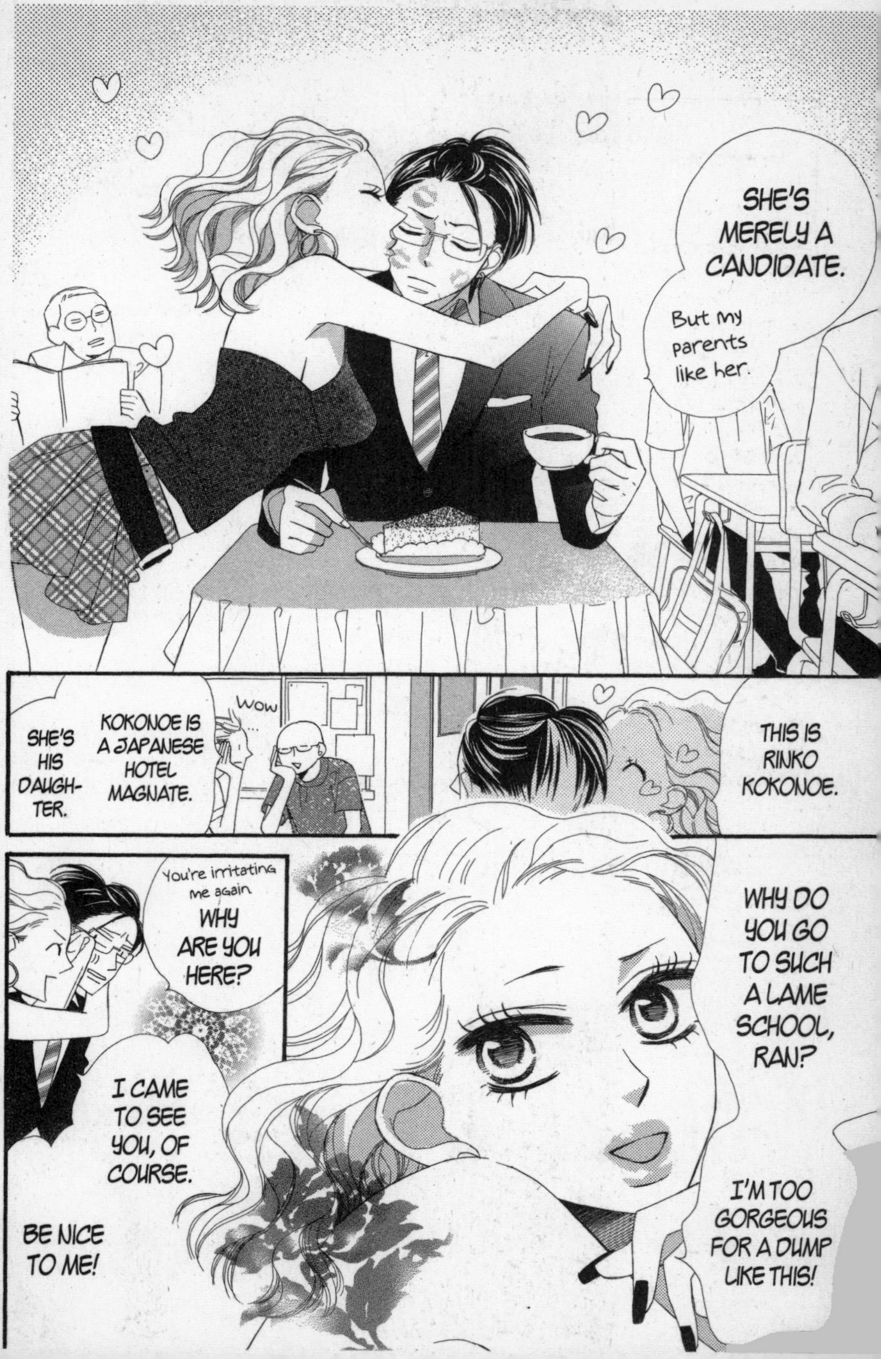
SHE'S MERELY A CANDIDATE.
But my parents like her.
THIS IS RINKO KOKONOE.
Wow
...
KOKONOE IS A JAPANESE HOTEL MAGNATE.
SHE'S HIS DAUGH-TER.
WHY DO YOU GO TO SUCH A LAME SCHOOL, RAN?
I'M TOO GORGEOUS FOR A DUMP LIKE THIS!
You're irritating me again
WHY ARE YOU HERE?
I CAME TO SEE YOU, OF COURSE.
BE NICE TO ME!

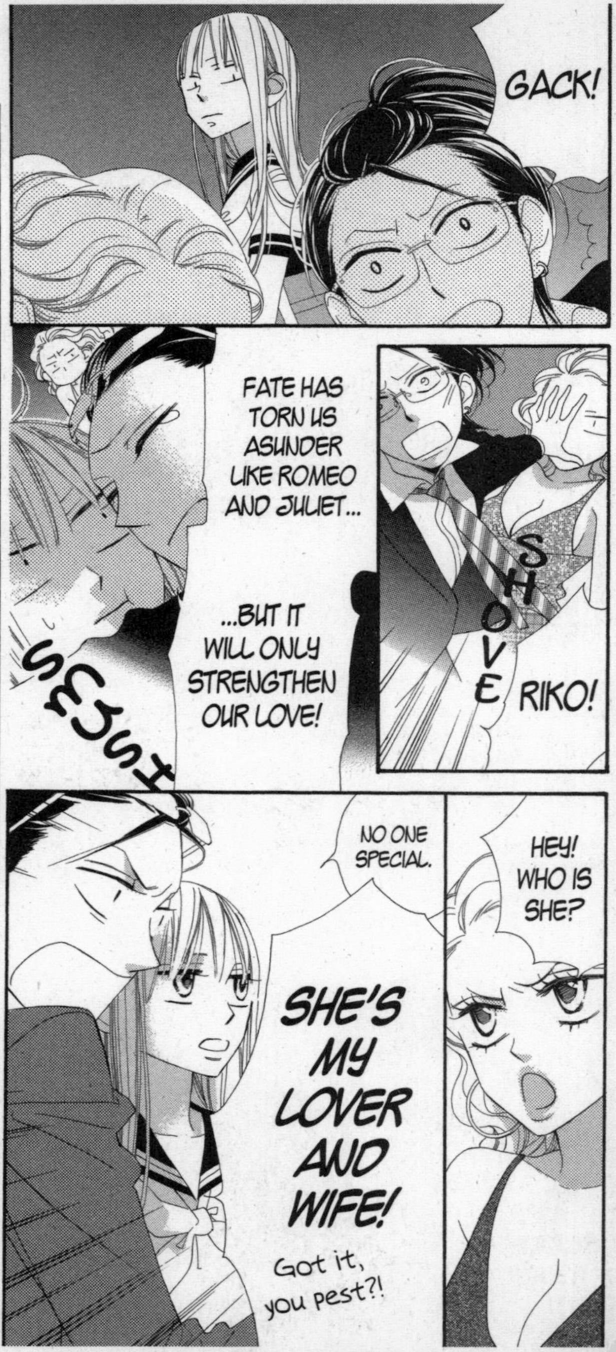
GACK!
RIKO!
SHOVE
FATE HAS TORN US ASUNDER LIKE ROMEO AND JULIET...
...BUT IT WILL ONLY STRENGTHEN OUR LOVE!
HEY! WHO IS SHE?
NO ONE SPECIAL.
SHE'S MY LOVER AND WIFE!
Got it, you pest?!

Greetings.

Hello, everyone. This is Shigeyoshi Takagi. Thank you very much for reading Flower in a Storm, volume 2. It's a humble work, but I'm glad you have stuck with me.

This volume has 11 sidebars. To tell the truth, I don't have much to write about, but I'll manage to fill them in with character info and behind-the-scenes chitchat.

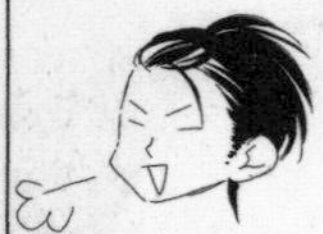

Well then.. Let's go!

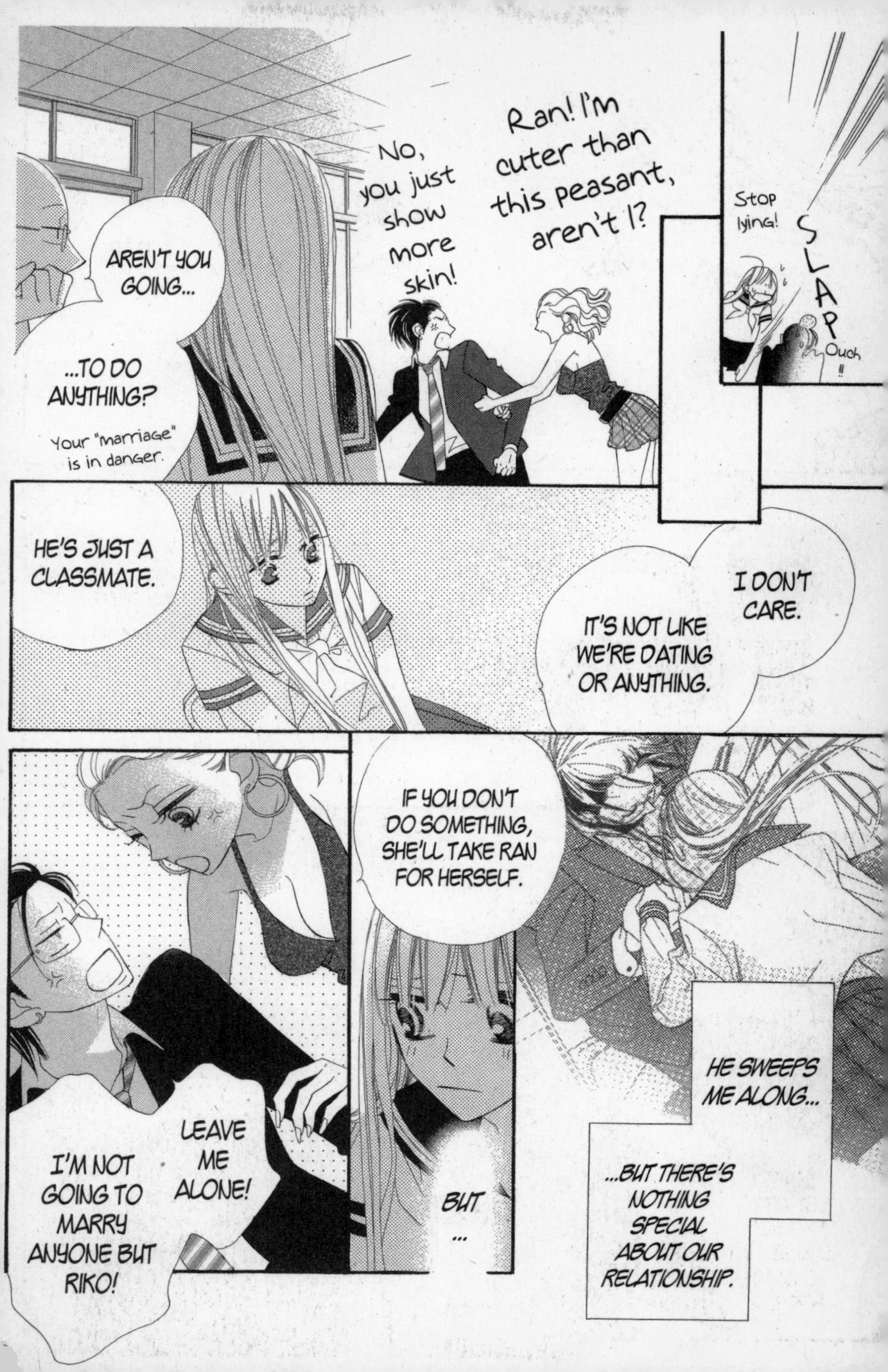
Stop lying!
SLAP
Ouch !!
Ran! I'm cuter than this peasant, aren't I?
No, you just show more skin!
AREN'T YOU GOING...
...TO DO ANYTHING?
Your "marriage" is in danger.
I DON'T CARE.
IT'S NOT LIKE WE'RE DATING OR ANYTHING.
HE'S JUST A CLASSMATE.
HE SWEEPS ME ALONG...
...BUT THERE'S NOTHING SPECIAL ABOUT OUR RELATIONSHIP.
IF YOU DON'T DO SOMETHING, SHE'LL TAKE RAN FOR HERSELF.
BUT ...
LEAVE ME ALONE!
I'M NOT GOING TO MARRY ANYONE BUT RIKO!

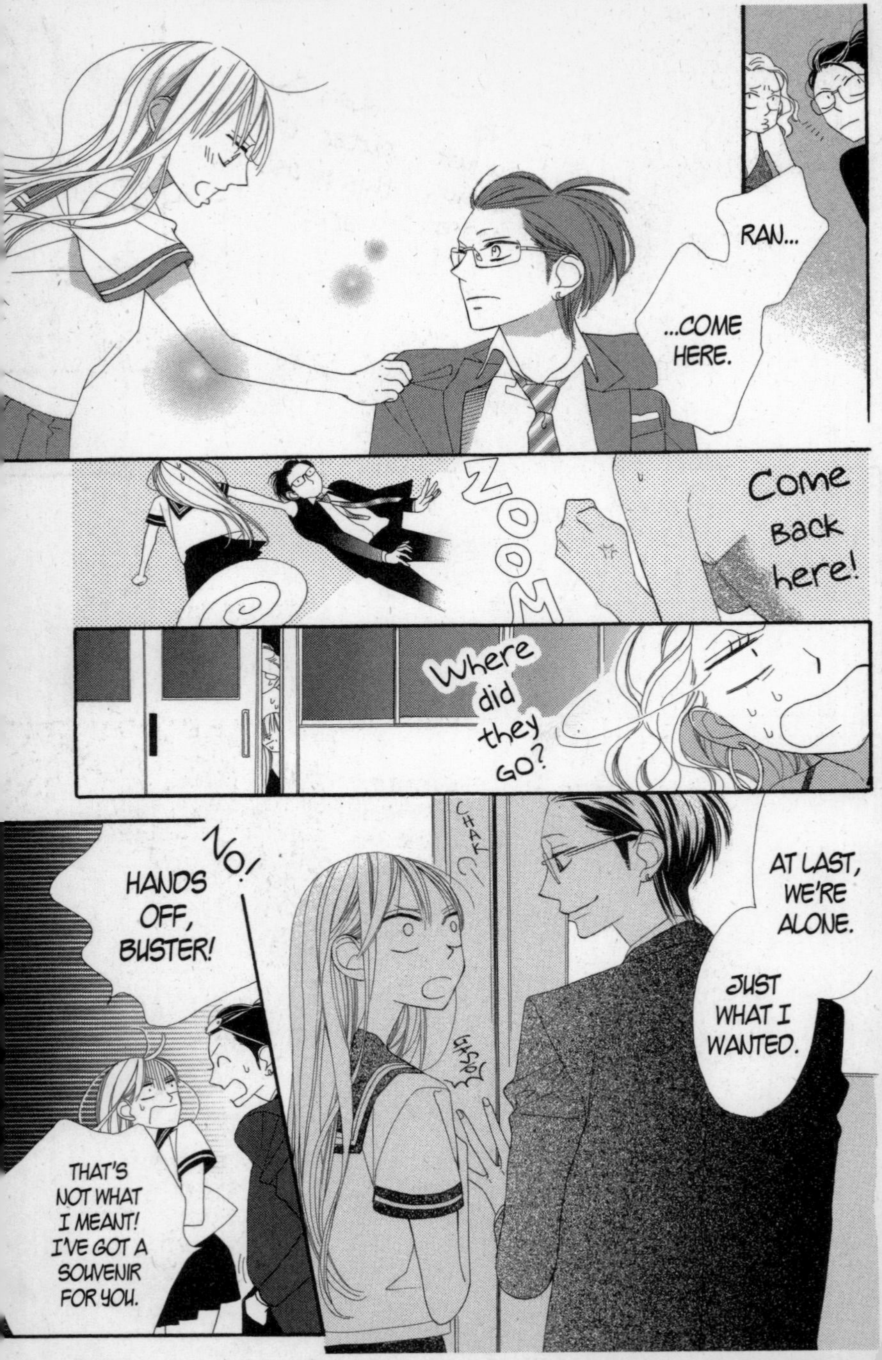
RAN...
...COME HERE.
Come back here!
ZOOM
Where did they go?
AT LAST, WE'RE ALONE.
JUST WHAT I WANTED.
CHAK
No!
HANDS OFF, BUSTER!
THAT'S NOT WHAT I MEANT! I'VE GOT A SOUVENIR FOR YOU.

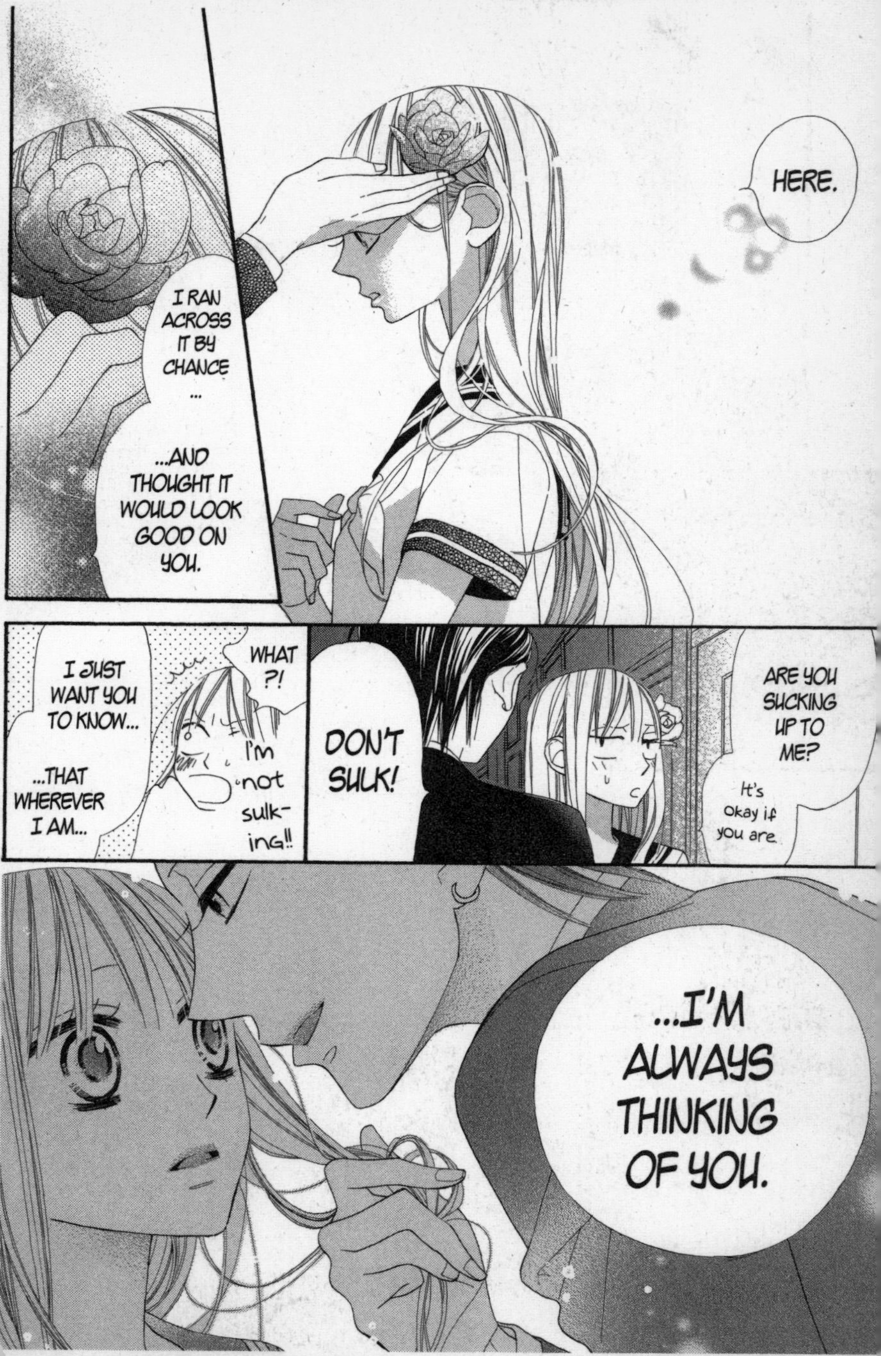
HERE.
I RAN ACROSS IT BY CHANCE...
...AND THOUGHT IT WOULD LOOK GOOD ON YOU.
ARE YOU SUCKING UP TO ME?
It's okay if you are.
DON'T SULK!
WHAT?!
I'm not sulk-ing!!
I JUST WANT YOU TO KNOW...
...THAT WHEREVER I AM...
...I'M ALWAYS THINKING OF YOU.

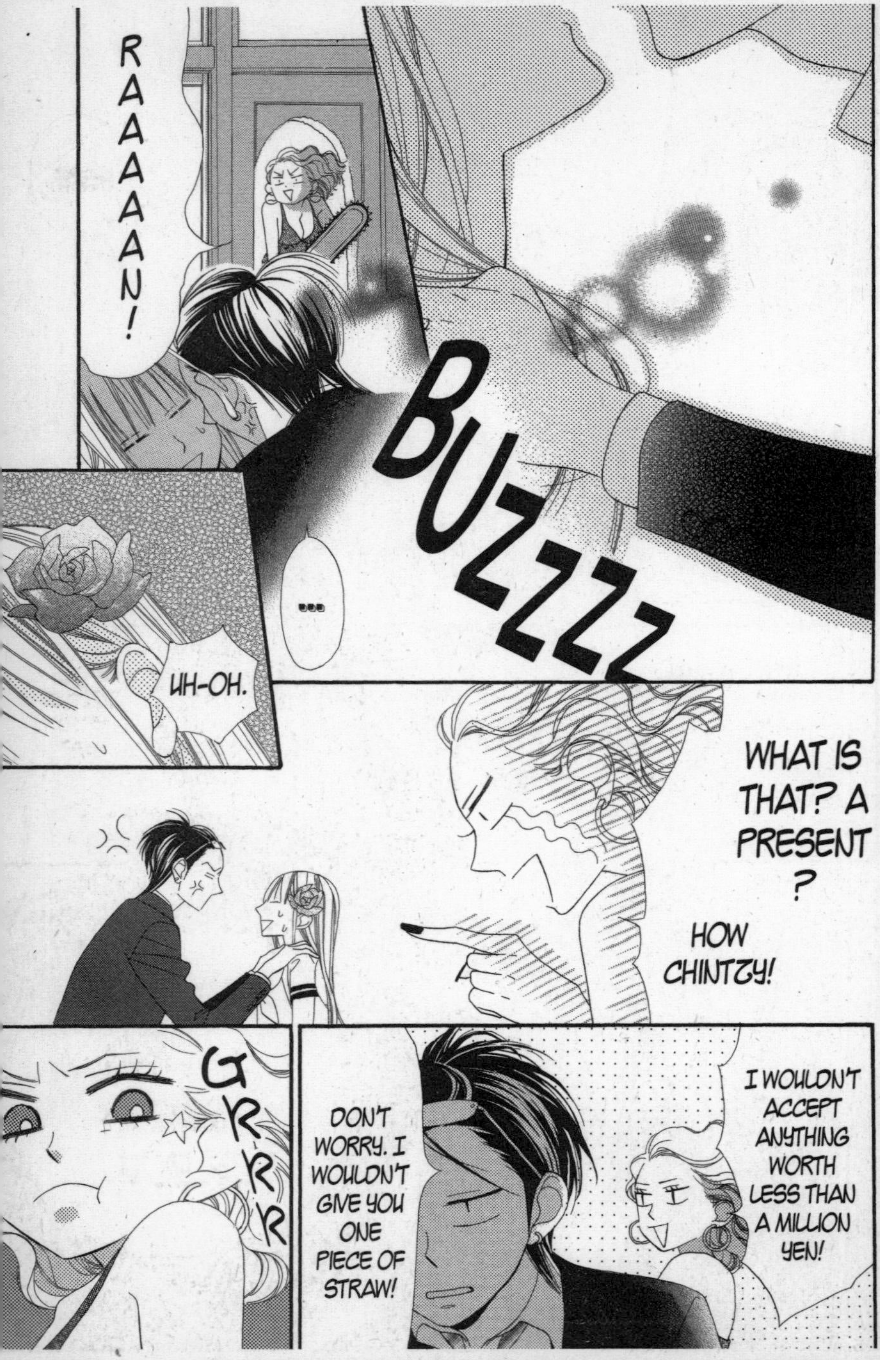
BUZZZZ
...
RAAAAAAN!
UH-OH.
WHAT IS THAT? A PRESENT?
HOW CHINTZY!
I WOULDN'T ACCEPT ANYTHING WORTH LESS THAN A MILLION YEN!
DON'T WORRY. I WOULDN'T GIVE YOU ONE PIECE OF STRAW!
GRRRR

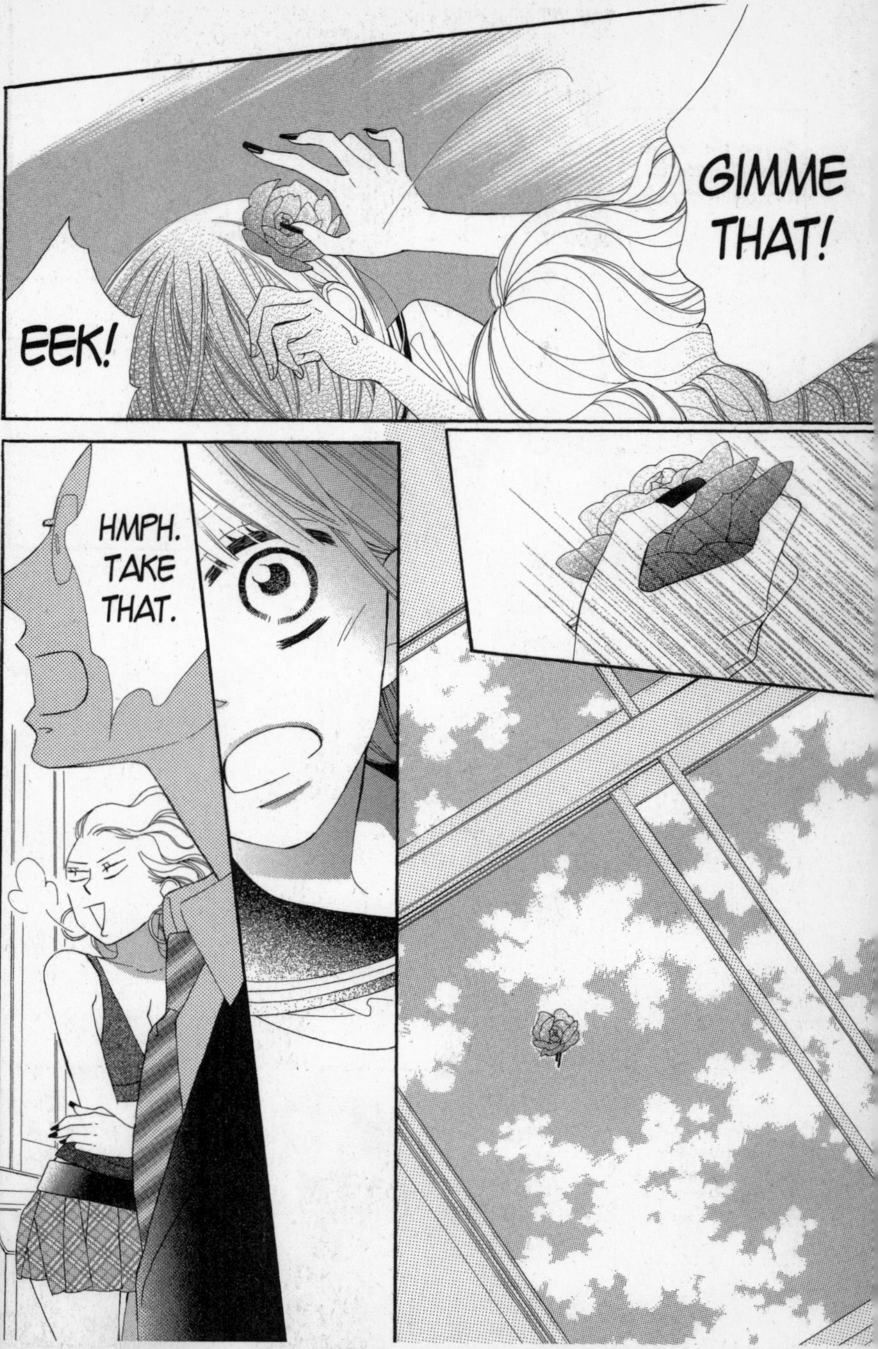
GIMME THAT!
EEK!
HMPH. TAKE THAT.

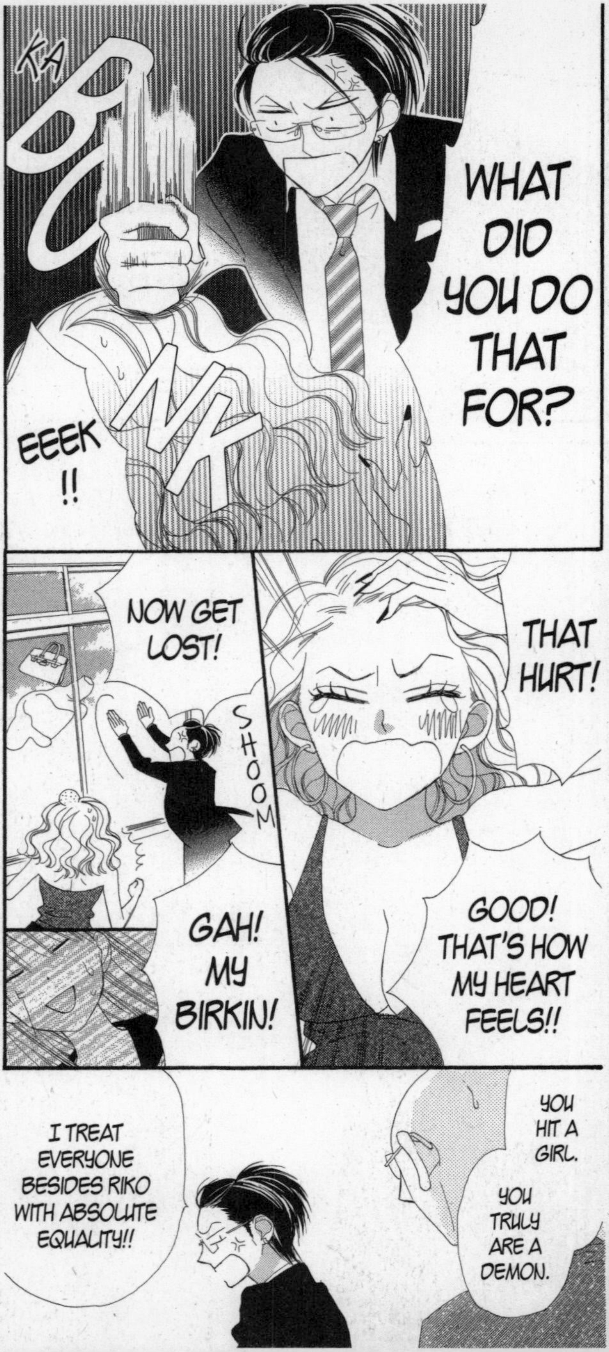
KABUNK
WHAT DID YOU DO THAT FOR?
EEEK!!
THAT HURT!
GOOD! THAT'S HOW MY HEART FEELS!!
NOW GET LOST!
SHOOOM
GAH! MY BIRKIN!
YOU HIT A GIRL.
YOU TRULY ARE A DEMON.
I TREAT EVERYONE BESIDES RIKO WITH ABSOLUTE EQUALITY!!

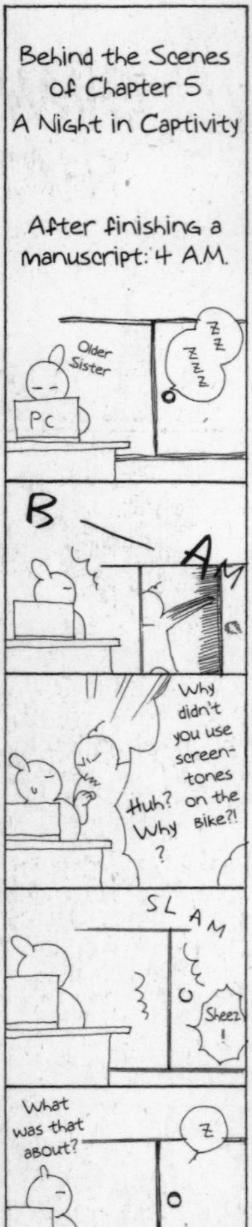
Behind the Scenes of Chapter 5 A Night in Captivity
After finishing a manuscript: 4 A.M.
Older Sister
ZZZ
PC
BAM
Why didn't you use screen-tones on the bike?!
Huh? Why?
SLAM
Sheez!
What was that about?
Z
I don't remember doing this. In any case, I had applied the screentones for the bike myself.

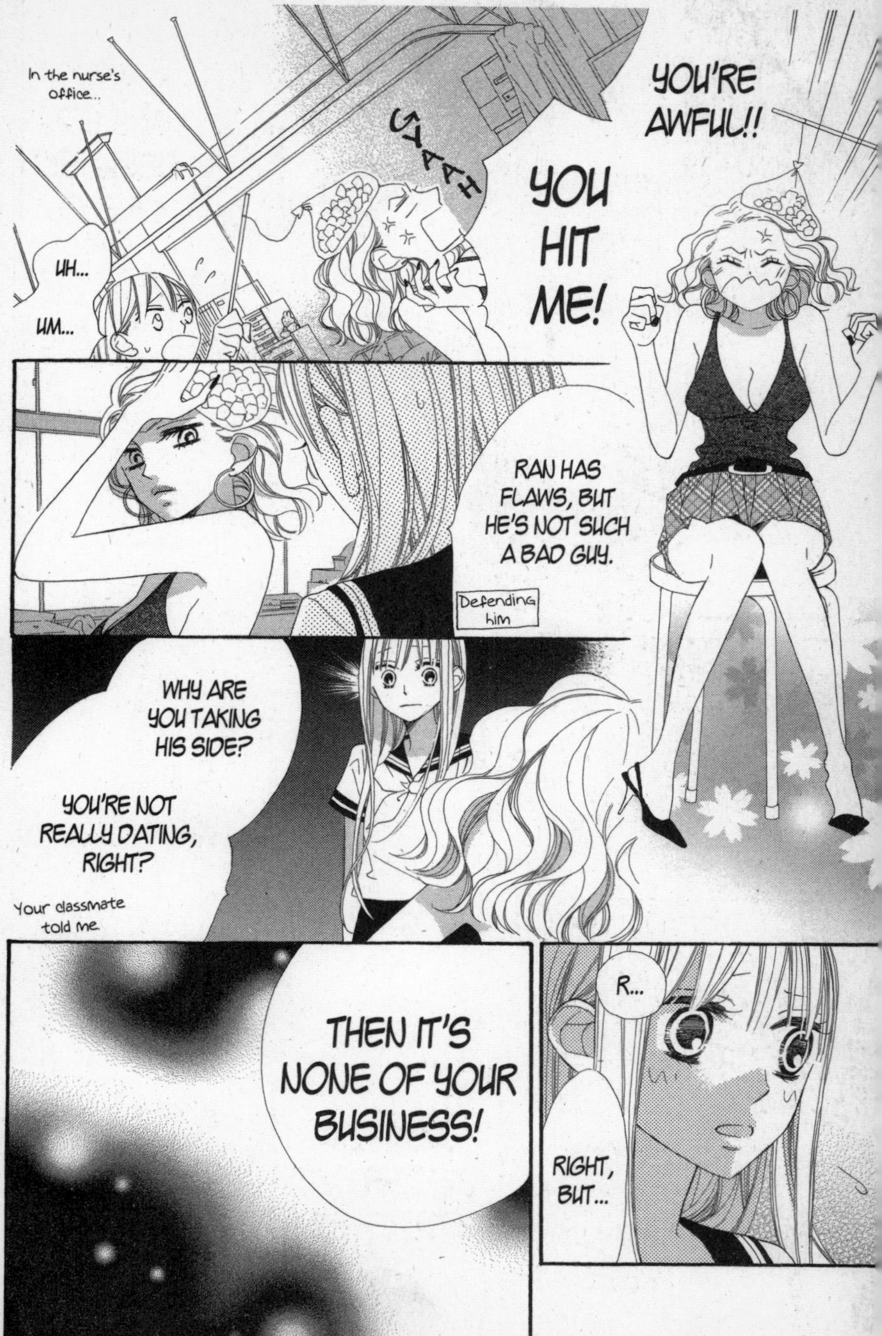

YOU'RE AWFUL!!
YOU HIT ME!
In the nurse's office...
UH...
UM...
RAN HAS FLAWS, BUT HE'S NOT SUCH A BAD GUY.
Defending him
WHY ARE YOU TAKING HIS SIDE?
YOU'RE NOT REALLY DATING, RIGHT?
Your classmate told me.
R...
RIGHT, BUT...
THEN IT'S NONE OF YOUR BUSINESS!

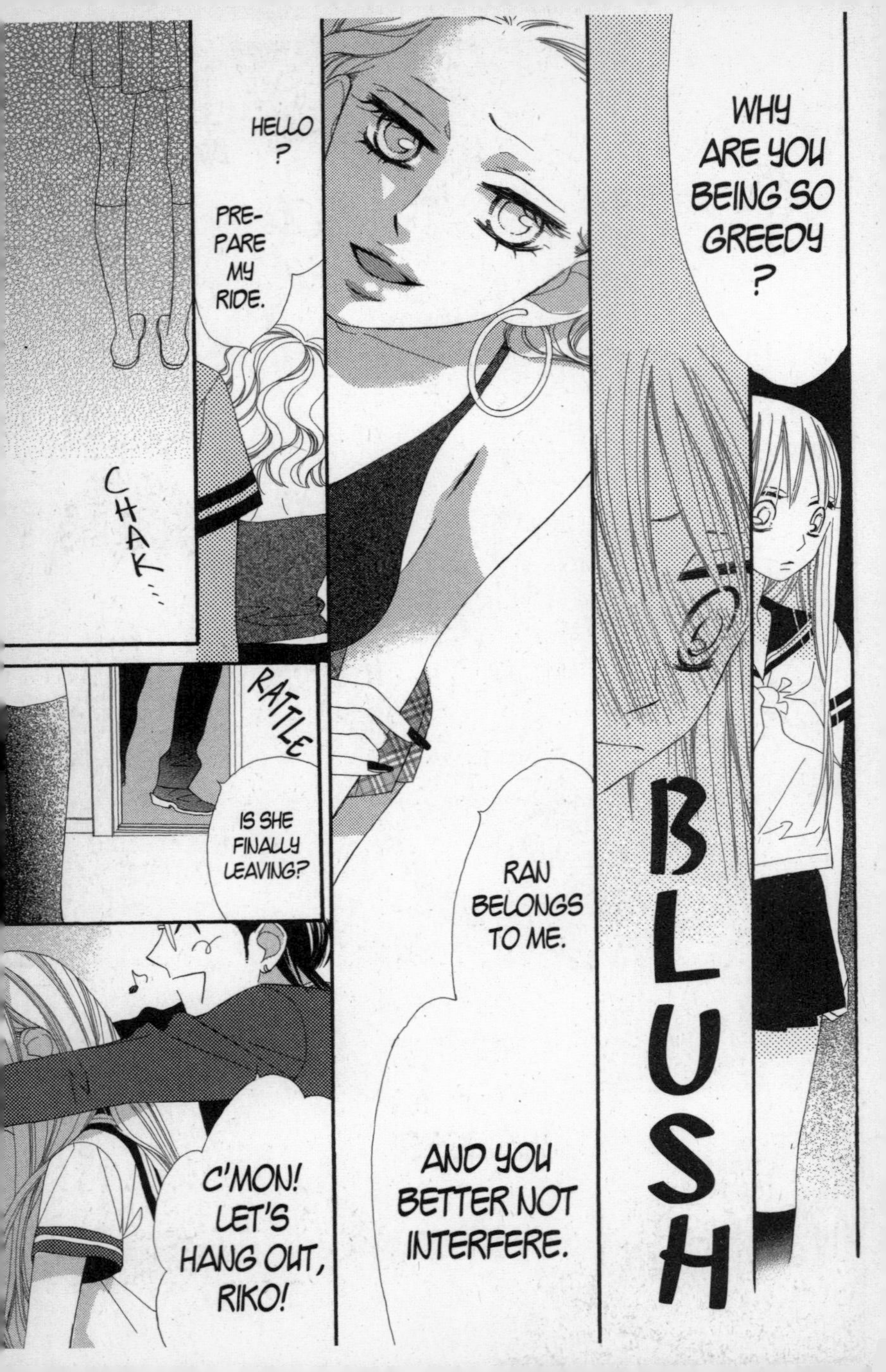
WHY ARE YOU BEING SO GREEDY?
BLUSH
HELLO?
PRE-PARE MY RIDE.
RAN BELONGS TO ME.
AND YOU BETTER NOT INTERFERE.
CHAK...
RATTLE
IS SHE FINALLY LEAVING?
C'MON! LET'S HANG OUT, RIKO!

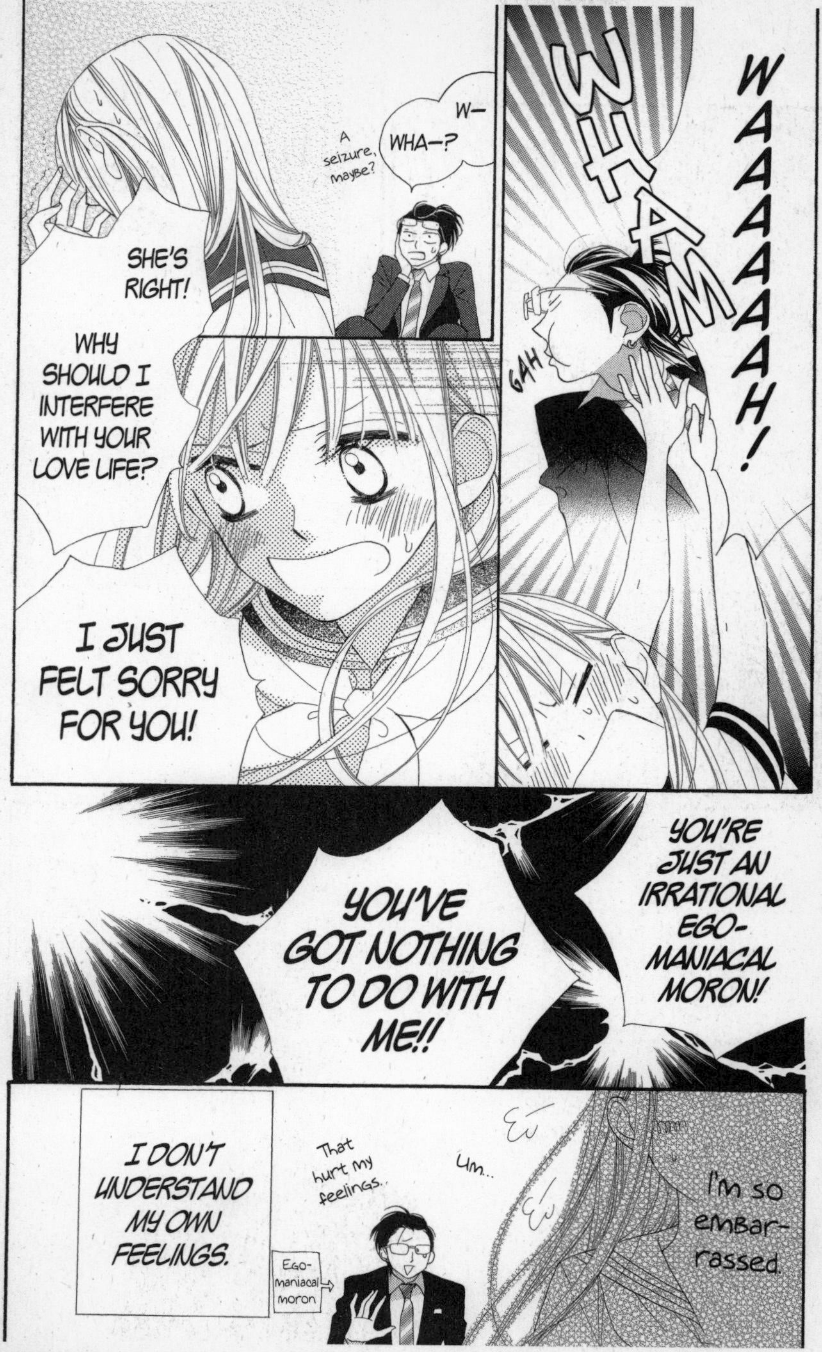
WHAM
WAAAAAAAH!
GAH
W—
WHA—?
A seizure, maybe?
SHE'S RIGHT!
WHY SHOULD I INTERFERE WITH YOUR LOVE LIFE?
I JUST FELT SORRY FOR YOU!
YOU'RE JUST AN IRRATIONAL EGO-MANIACAL MORON!
YOU'VE GOT NOTHING TO DO WITH ME!!
I'm so embar-rassed.
Um...
That hurt my feelings..
Ego-maniacal moron
I DON'T UNDERSTAND MY OWN FEELINGS.

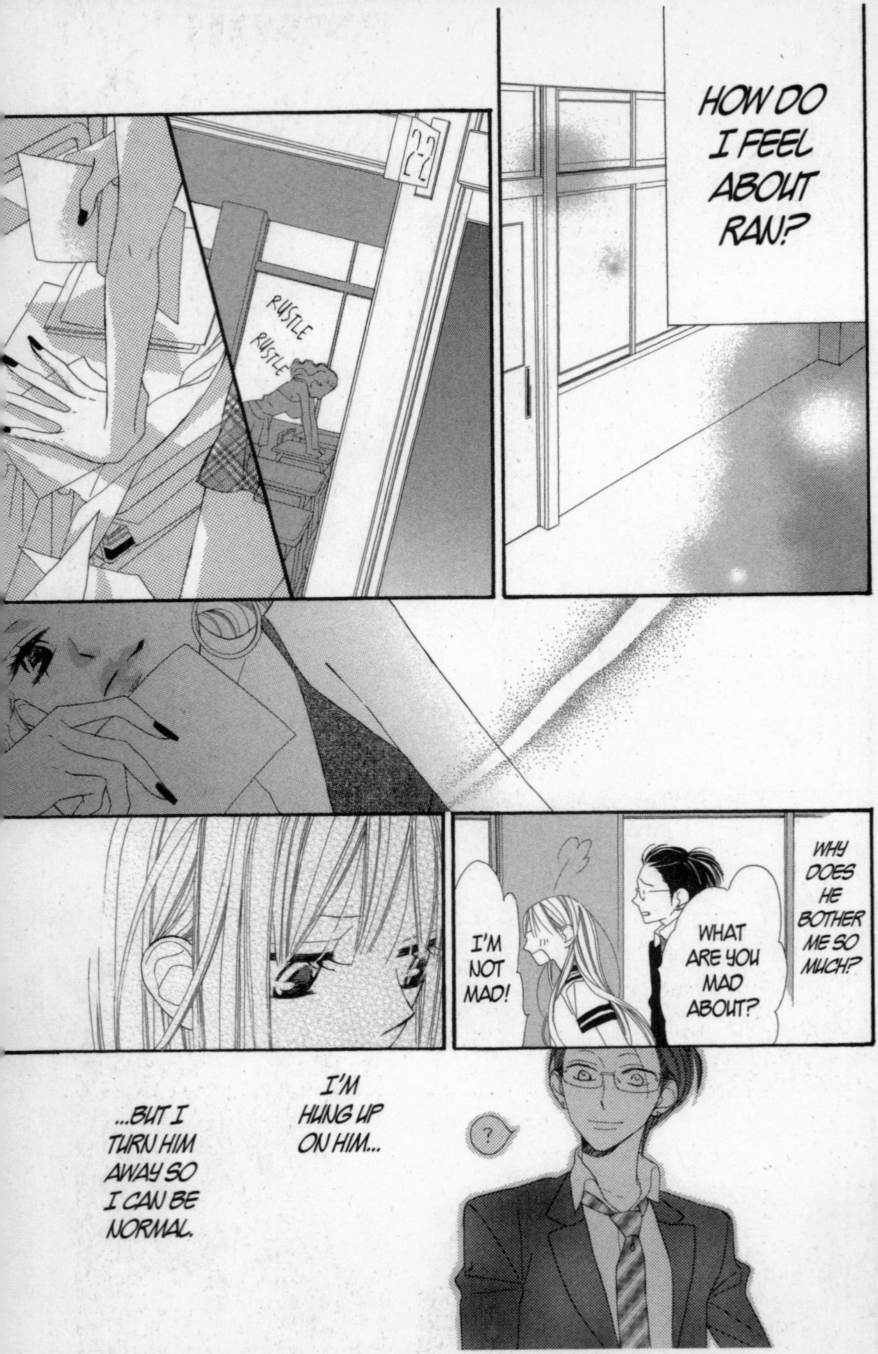

HOW DO I FEEL ABOUT RAN?
RUSTLE RUSTLE
WHY DOES HE BOTHER ME SO MUCH?
WHAT ARE YOU MAD ABOUT?
I'M NOT MAD!
?
I'M HUNG UP ON HIM...
...BUT I TURN HIM AWAY SO I CAN BE NORMAL.

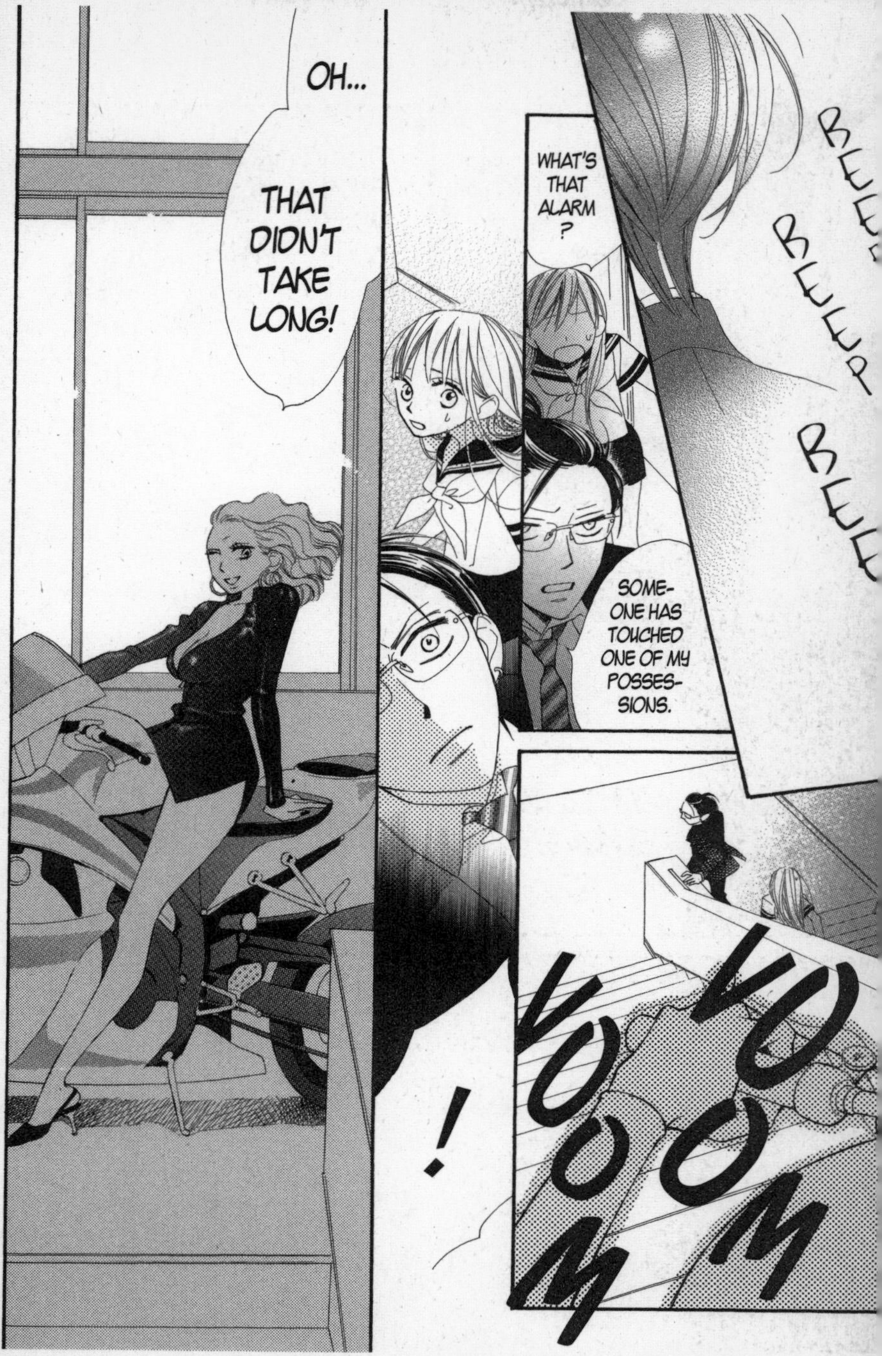
BEEE
BEEEP
BEEE
WHAT'S THAT ALARM?
SOME-ONE HAS TOUCHED ONE OF MY POSSES-SIONS.
VROOOM
VROOM
!
OH...
THAT DIDN'T TAKE LONG!

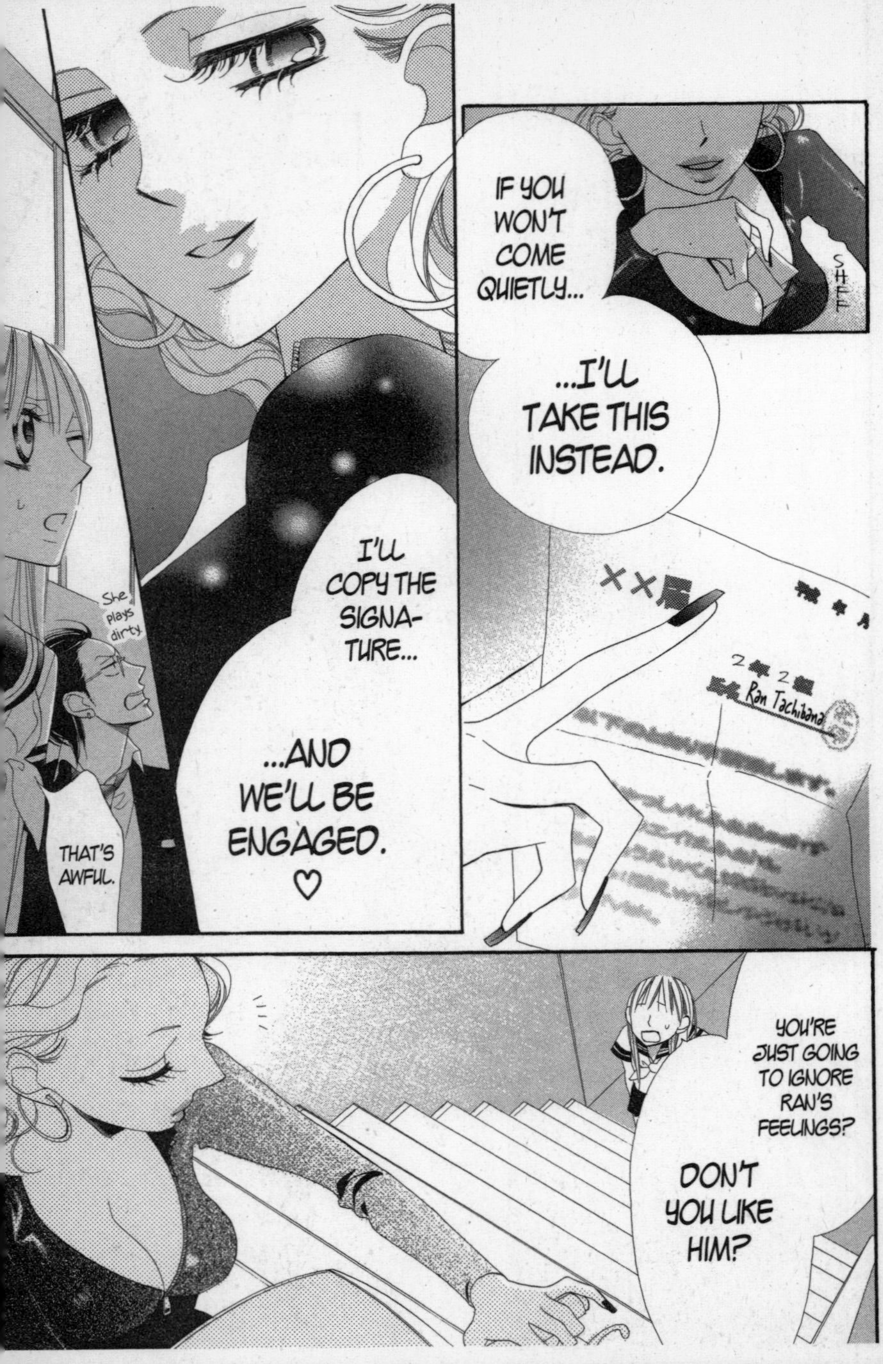
IF YOU WON'T COME QUIETLY...
SHFF
...I'LL TAKE THIS INSTEAD.
Ran Tachibana
I'LL COPY THE SIGNATURE...
...AND WE'LL BE ENGAGED. ♡
She plays dirty.
THAT'S AWFUL.
YOU'RE JUST GOING TO IGNORE RAN'S FEELINGS?
DON'T YOU LIKE HIM?

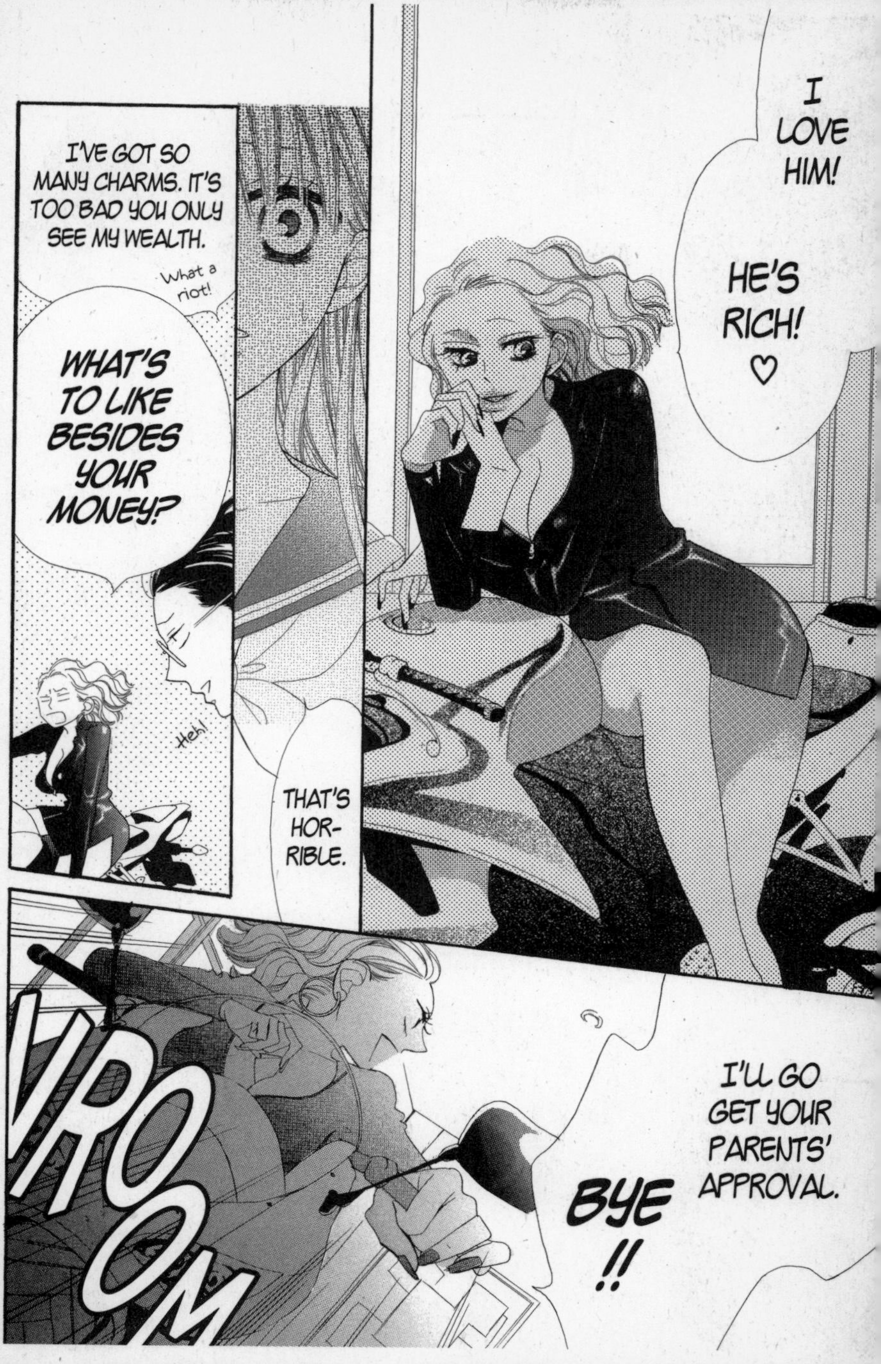
I LOVE HIM!
HE'S RICH! ♡
THAT'S HORRIBLE.
I'VE GOT SO MANY CHARMS. IT'S TOO BAD YOU ONLY SEE MY WEALTH.
What a riot!
WHAT'S TO LIKE BESIDES YOUR MONEY?
Heh!
I'LL GO GET YOUR PARENTS' APPROVAL.
BYE!!
VROOM

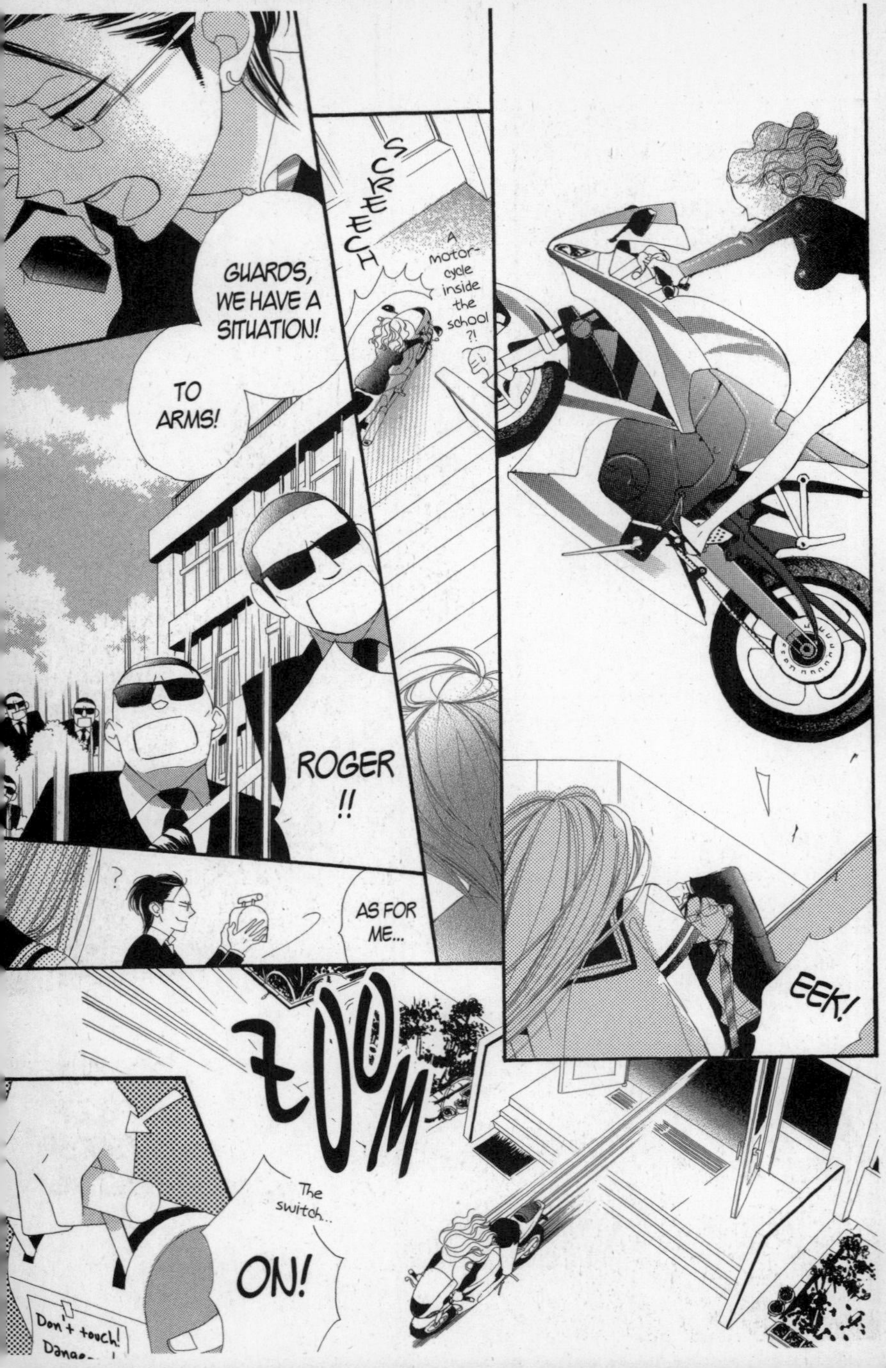
SCREECH
A motor-cycle inside the school?!
GUARDS, WE HAVE A SITUATION!
TO ARMS!
ROGER!!
EEK!
AS FOR ME...
ZOOM
The switch...
ON!
Don't touch!

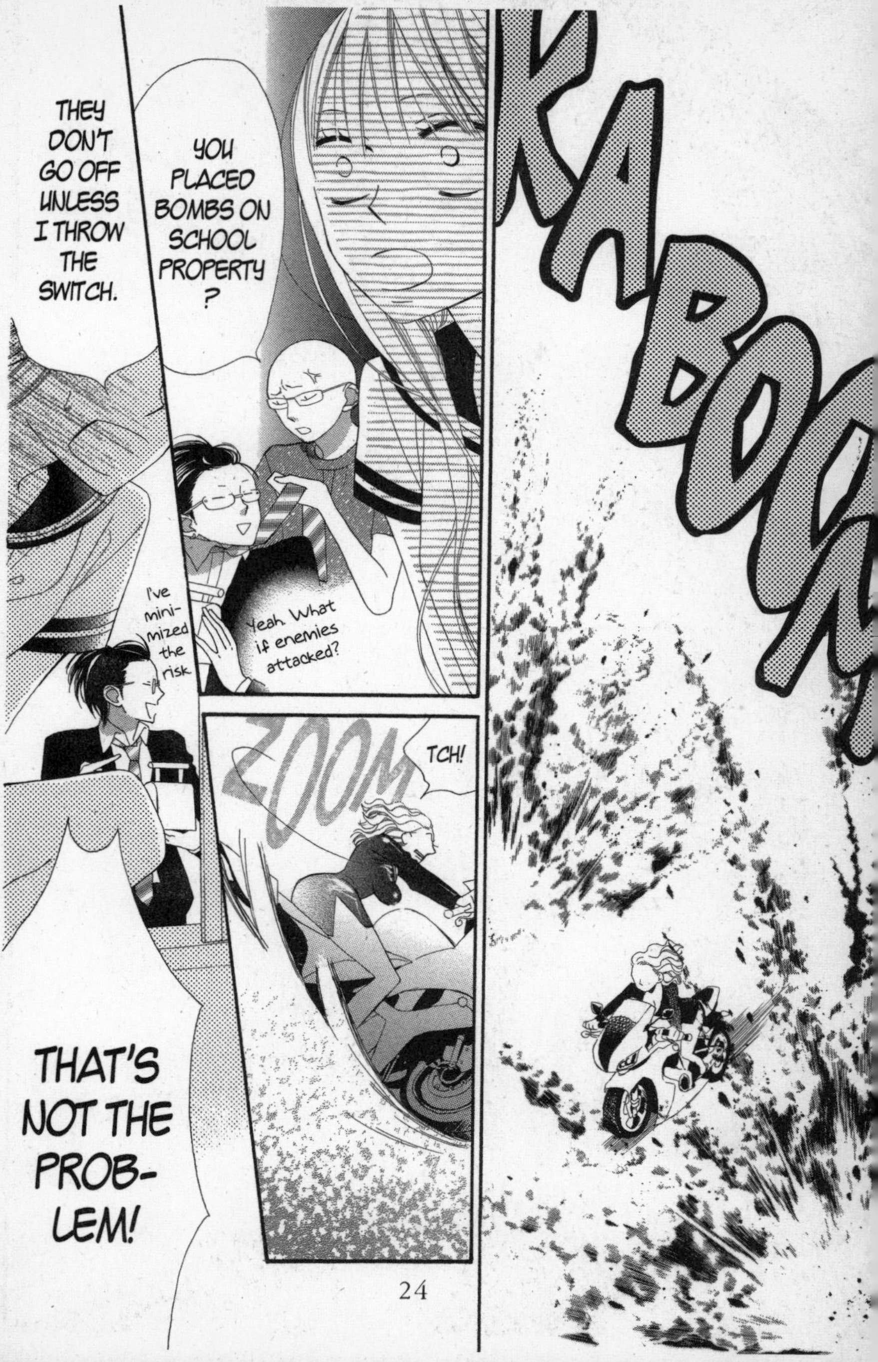
KABOOM
YOU PLACED BOMBS ON SCHOOL PROPERTY ?
Yeah. What if enemies attacked?
ZOOM
TCH!
THEY DON'T GO OFF UNLESS I THROW THE SWITCH.
I've minimized the risk.
THAT'S NOT THE PROBLEM!

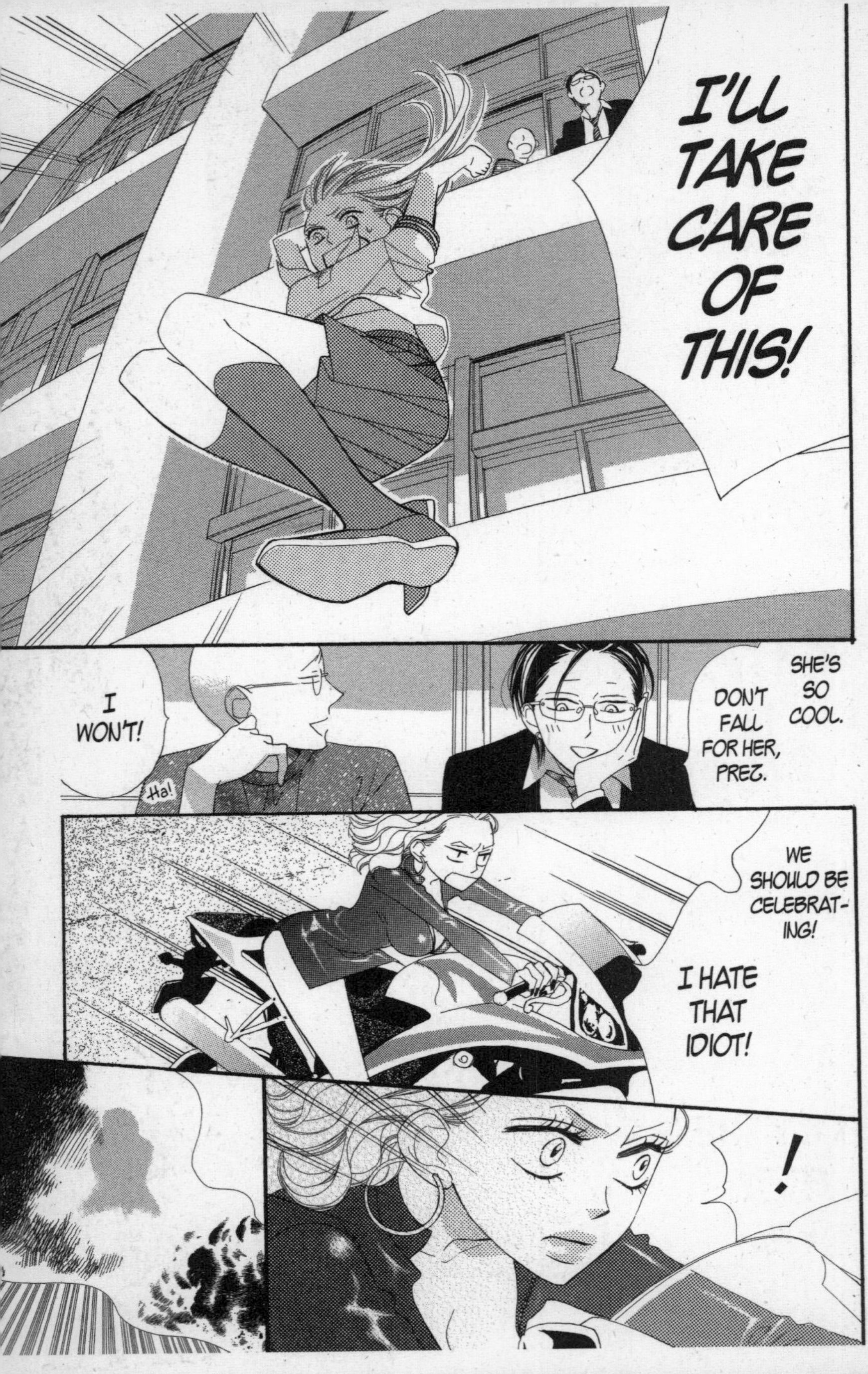
I'LL TAKE CARE OF THIS!
SHE'S SO COOL.
DON'T FALL FOR HER, PREZ.
I WON'T!
Ha!
WE SHOULD BE CELEBRAT-ING!
I HATE THAT IDIOT!
!

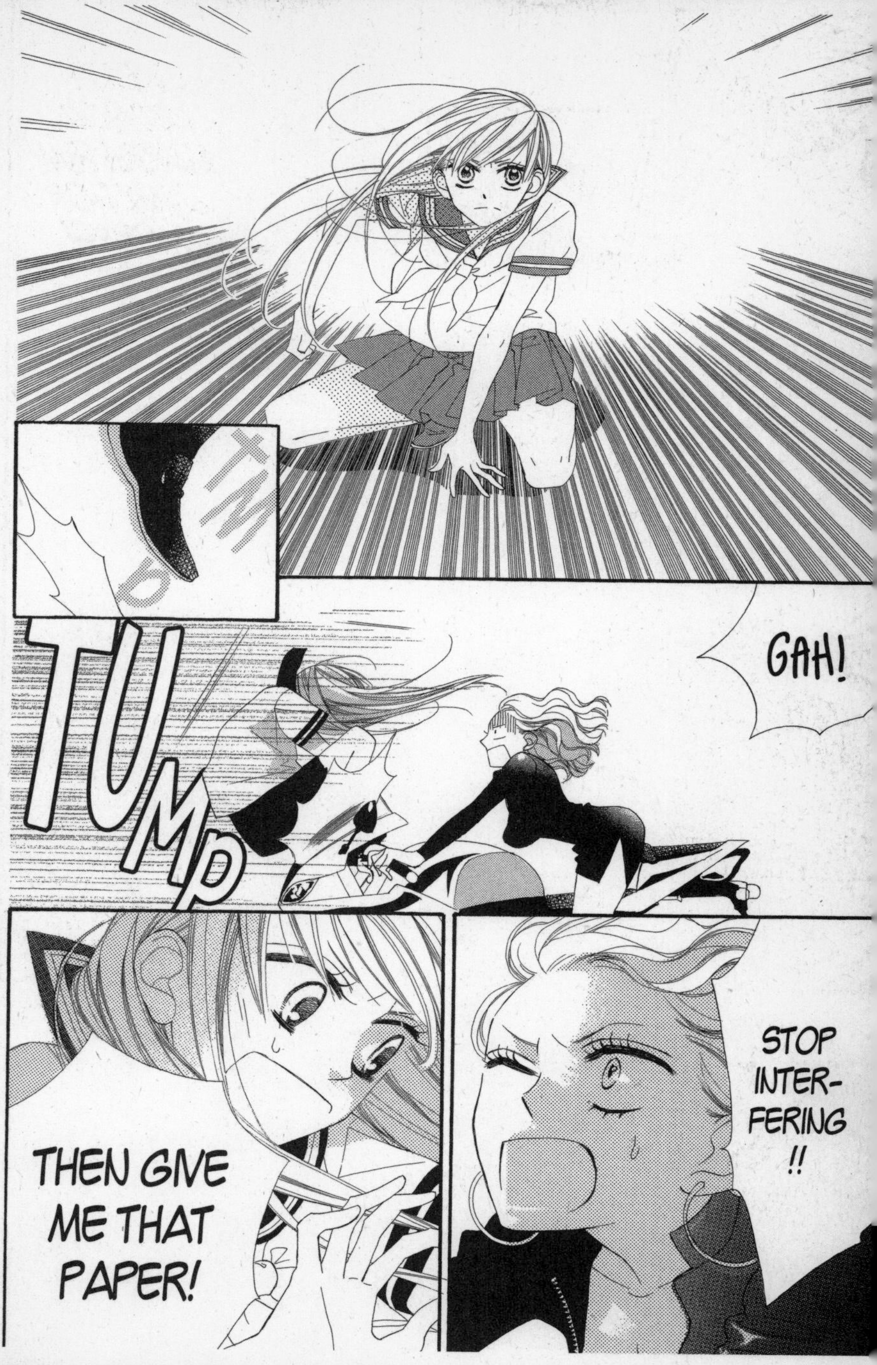
TMP
GAH!
TUMP
STOP INTER-FERING !!
THEN GIVE ME THAT PAPER!

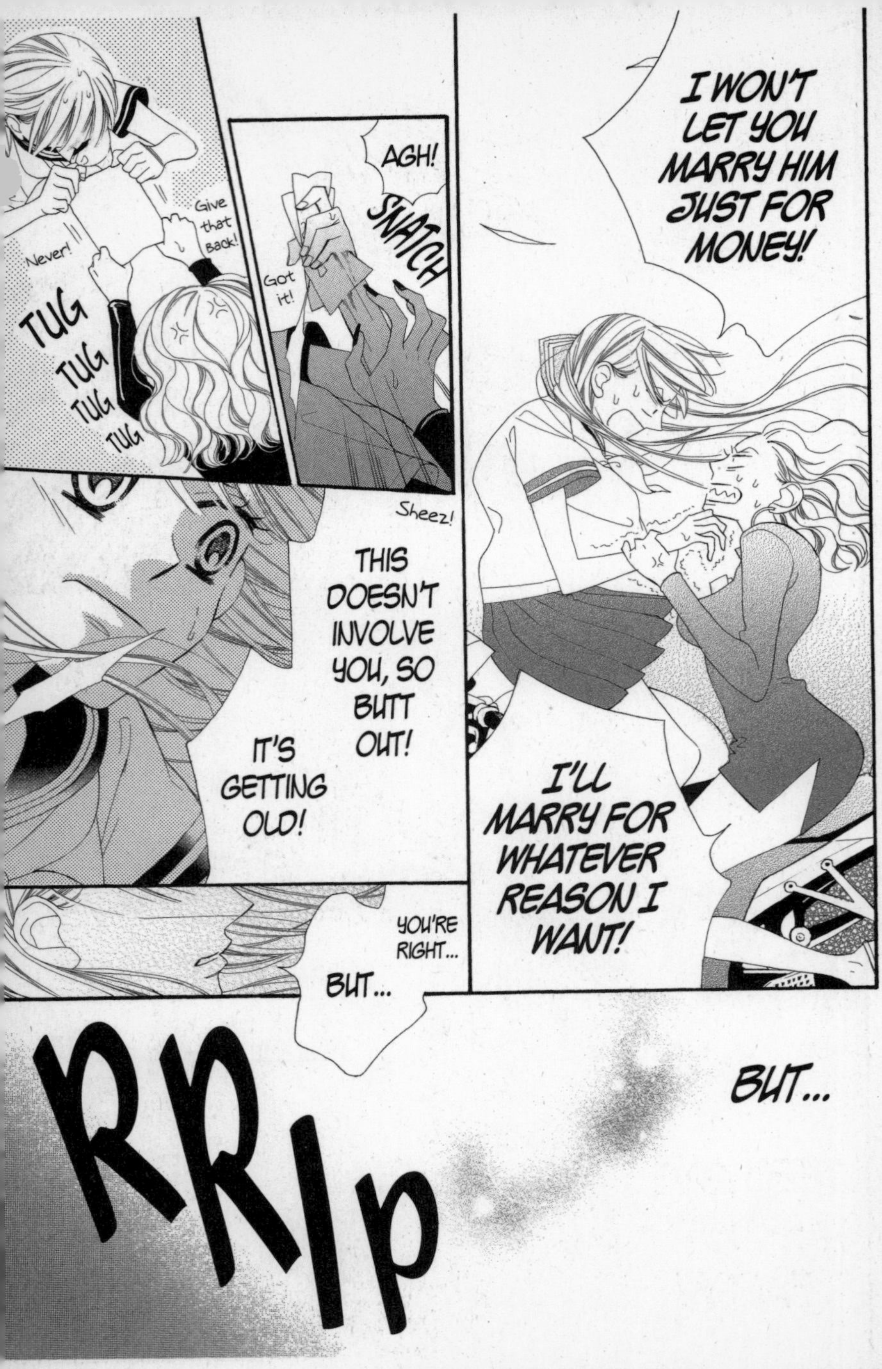
I WON'T LET YOU MARRY HIM JUST FOR MONEY!
I'LL MARRY FOR WHATEVER REASON I WANT!
AGH!
SNATCH
Got it!
Give that back!
Never!
TUG
TUG
TUG
TUG
Sheez!
THIS DOESN'T INVOLVE YOU, SO BUTT OUT!
IT'S GETTING OLD!
YOU'RE RIGHT...
BUT...
BUT...
RRIP

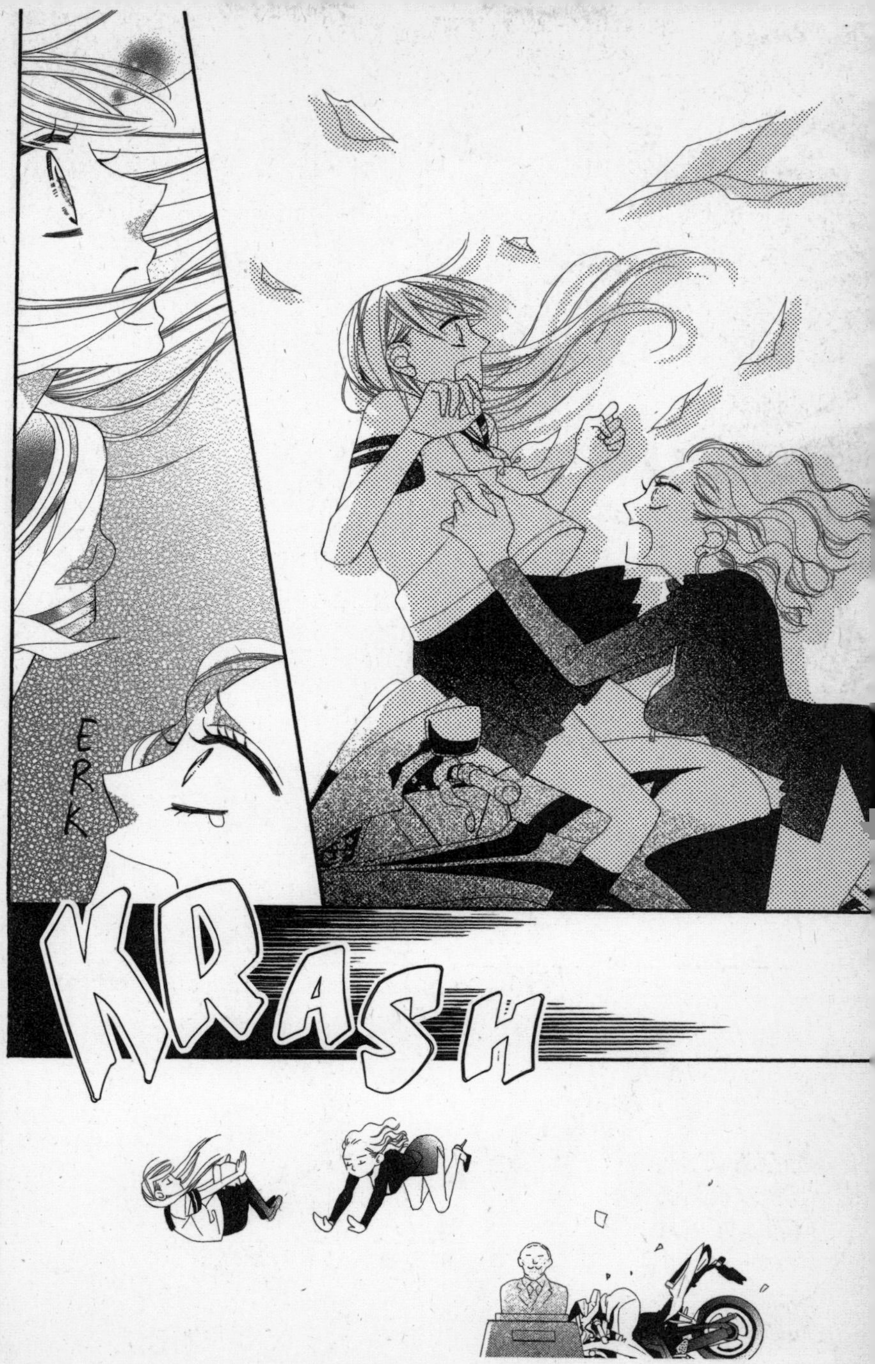
ERK
KRASH

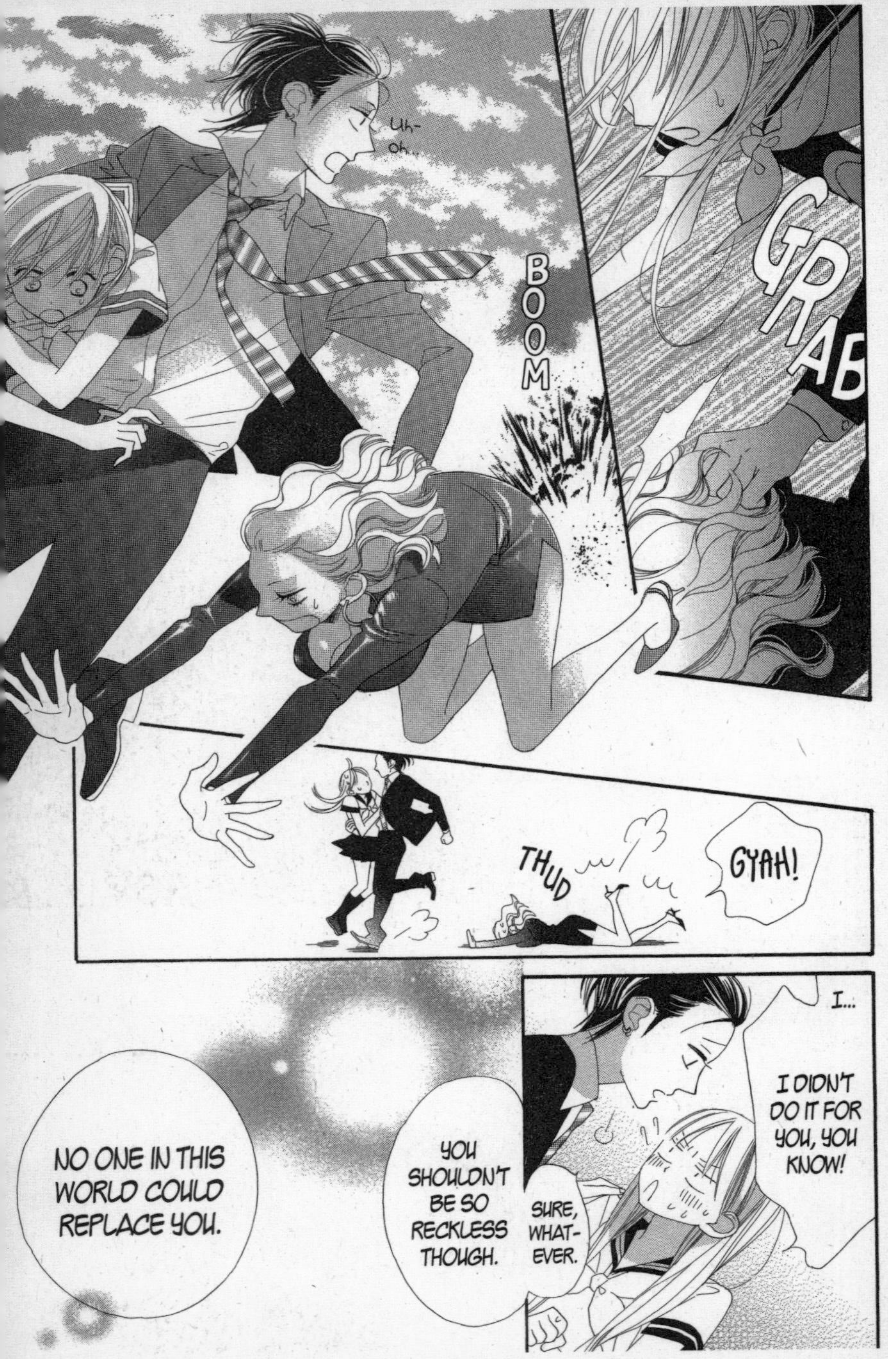
GRAB
Uh-oh...
BOOM
GYAH!
THUD
I...
I DIDN'T DO IT FOR YOU, YOU KNOW!
SURE, WHATEVER.
YOU SHOULDN'T BE SO RECKLESS THOUGH.
NO ONE IN THIS WORLD COULD REPLACE YOU.

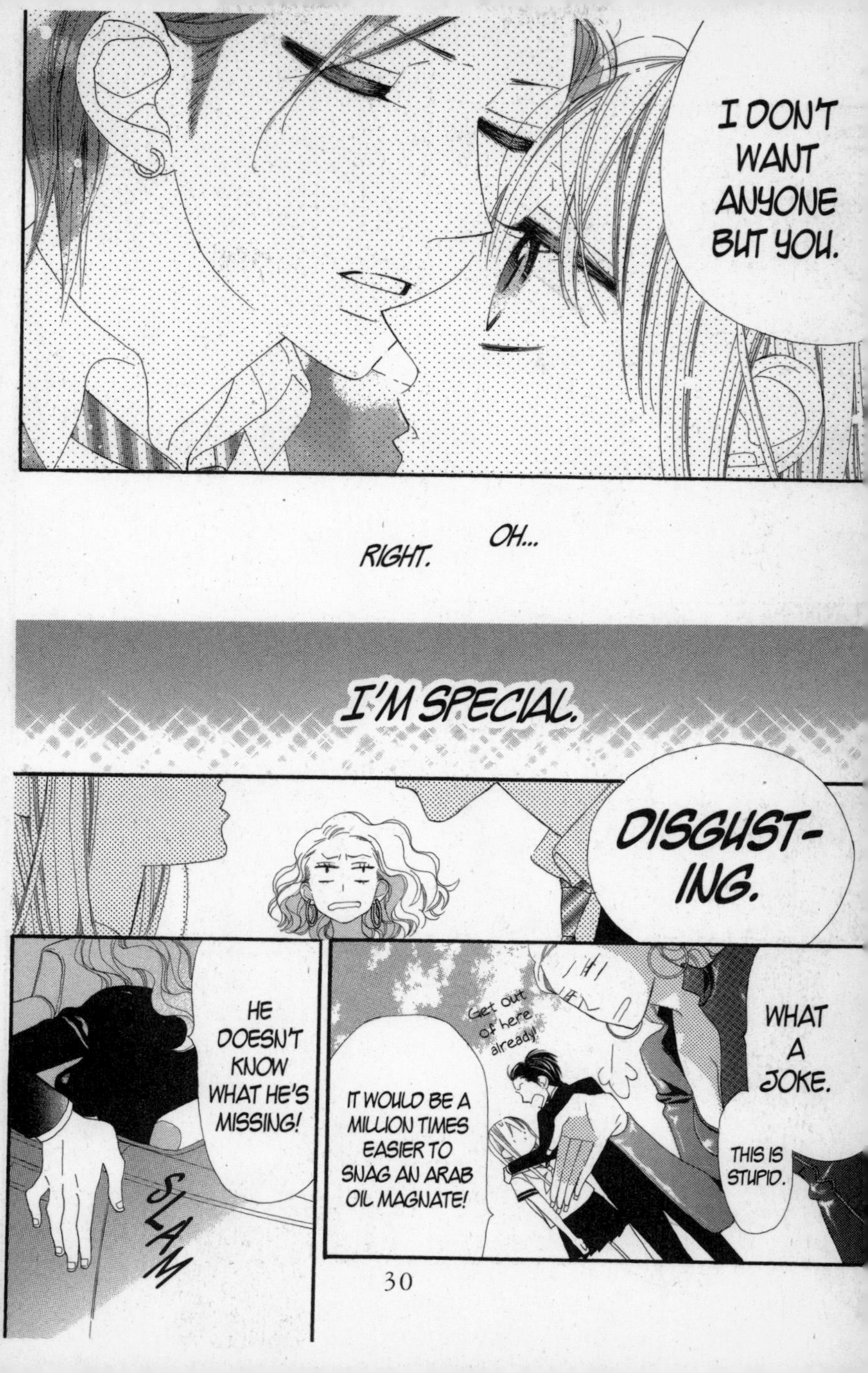
I DON'T WANT ANYONE BUT YOU.
OH...
RIGHT.
I'M SPECIAL.
DISGUST-ING.
WHAT A JOKE.
THIS IS STUPID.
Get out of here already!
IT WOULD BE A MILLION TIMES EASIER TO SNAG AN ARAB OIL MAGNATE!
HE DOESN'T KNOW WHAT HE'S MISSING!
SLAM

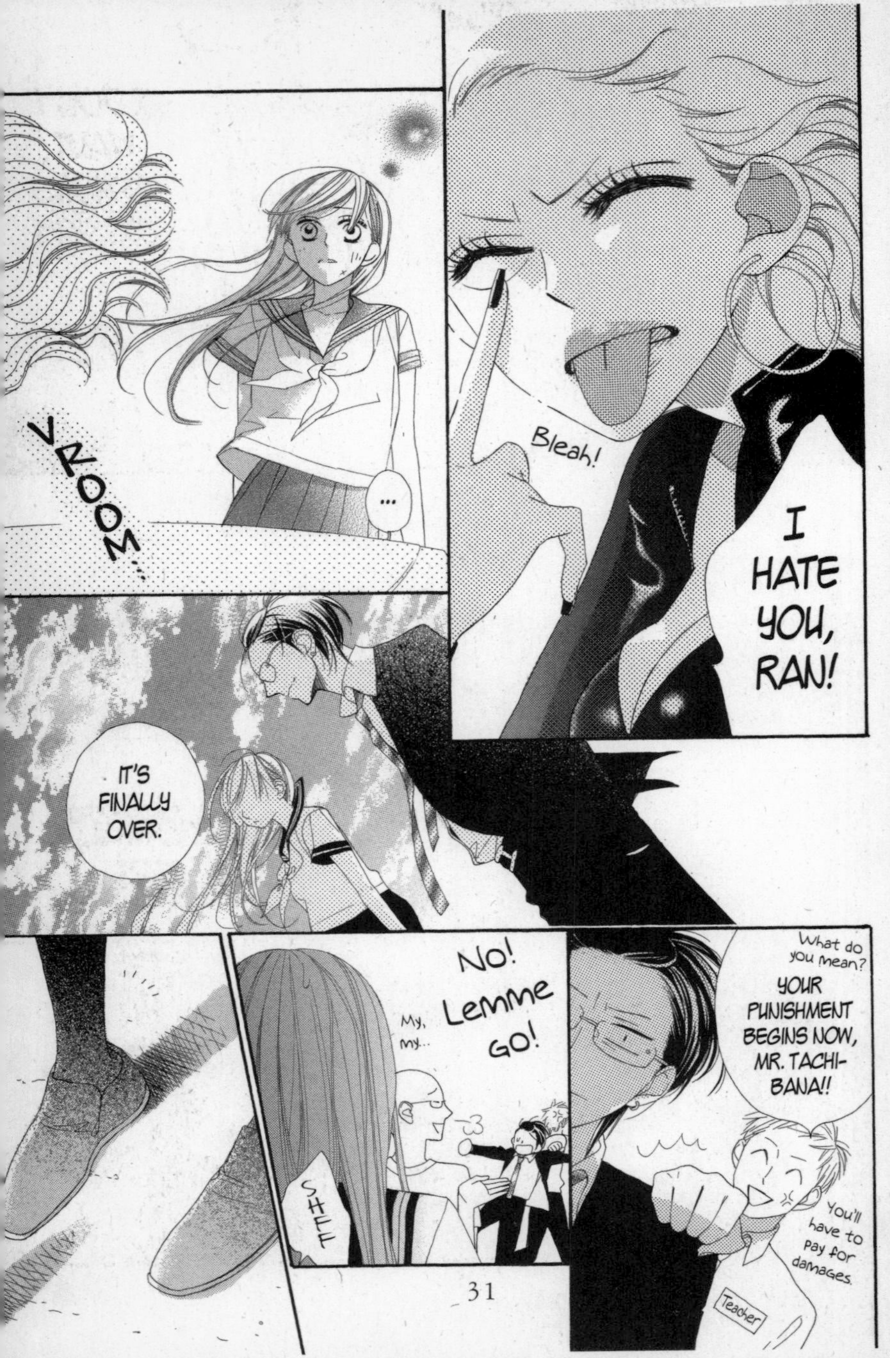
Bleah!
I HATE YOU, RAN!
VROOM...
...
IT'S FINALLY OVER.
What do you mean?
YOUR PUNISHMENT BEGINS NOW, MR. TACHIBANA!!
You'll have to pay for damages.
Teacher
No! Lemme go!
My, my...
SHFF

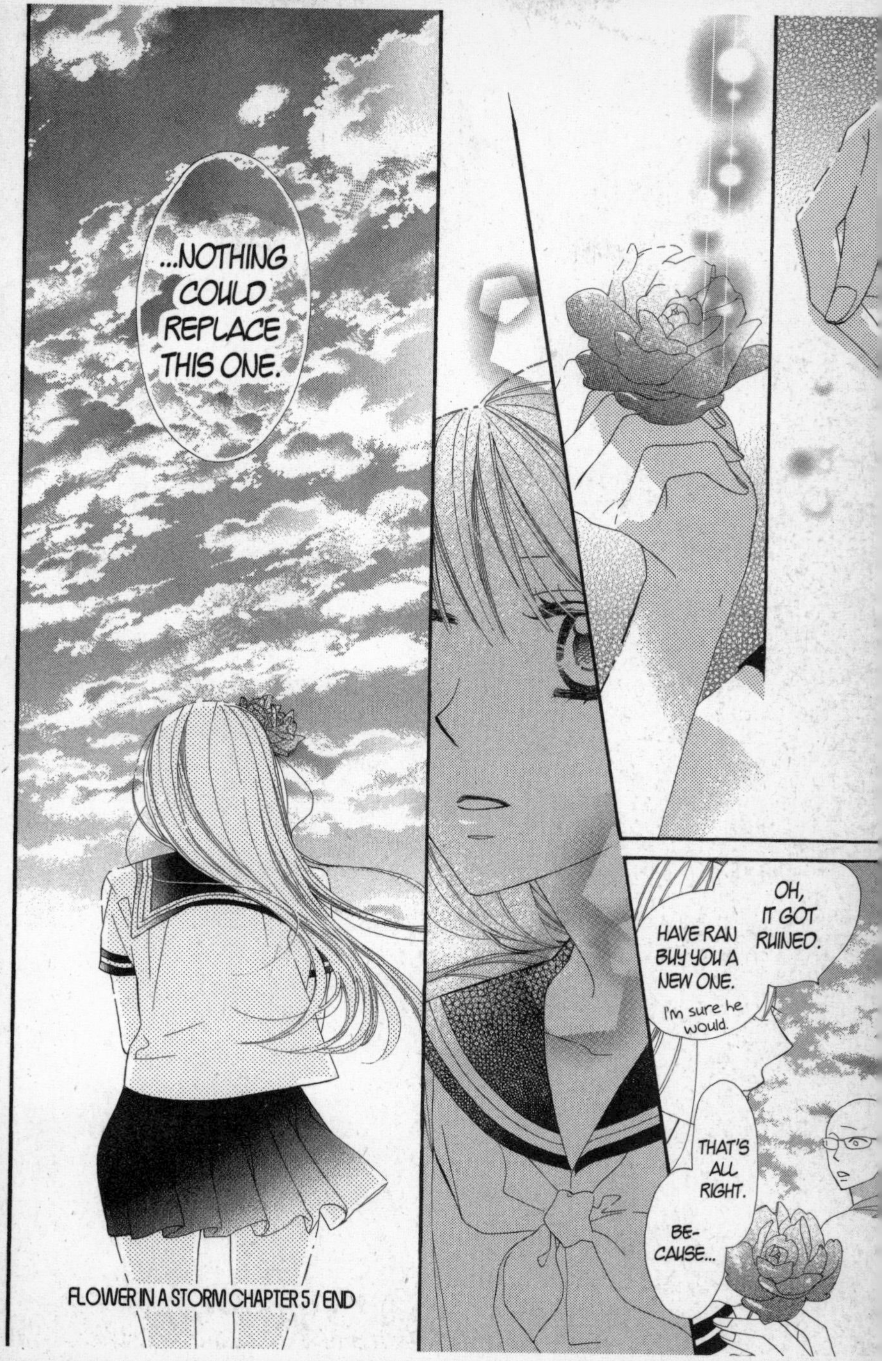
OH, IT GOT RUINED.
HAVE RAN BUY YOU A NEW ONE.
I'm sure he would.
THAT'S ALL RIGHT.
BE-CAUSE...
...NOTHING COULD REPLACE THIS ONE.
FLOWER IN A STORM CHAPTER 5 / END

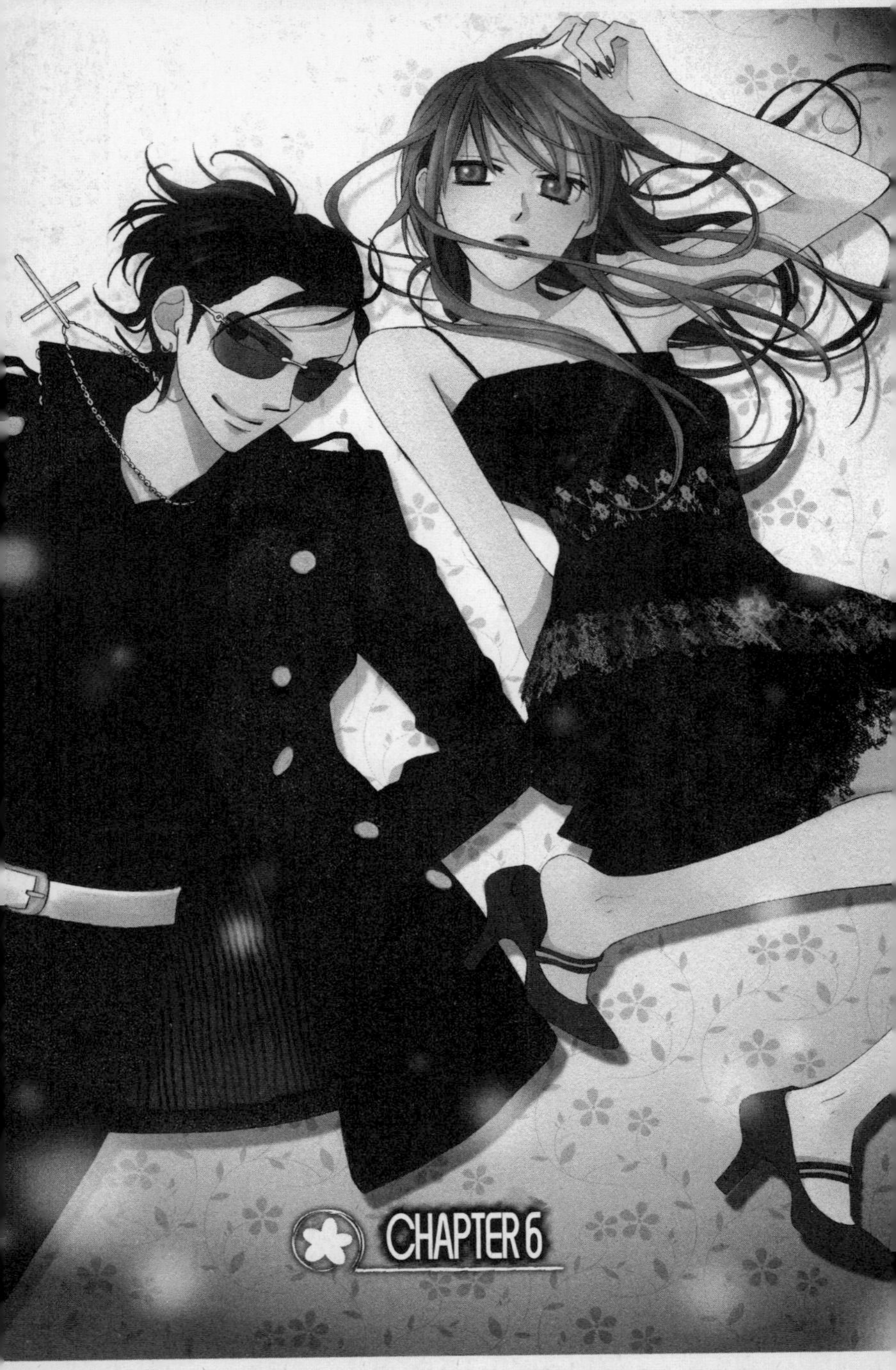
CHAPTER 6

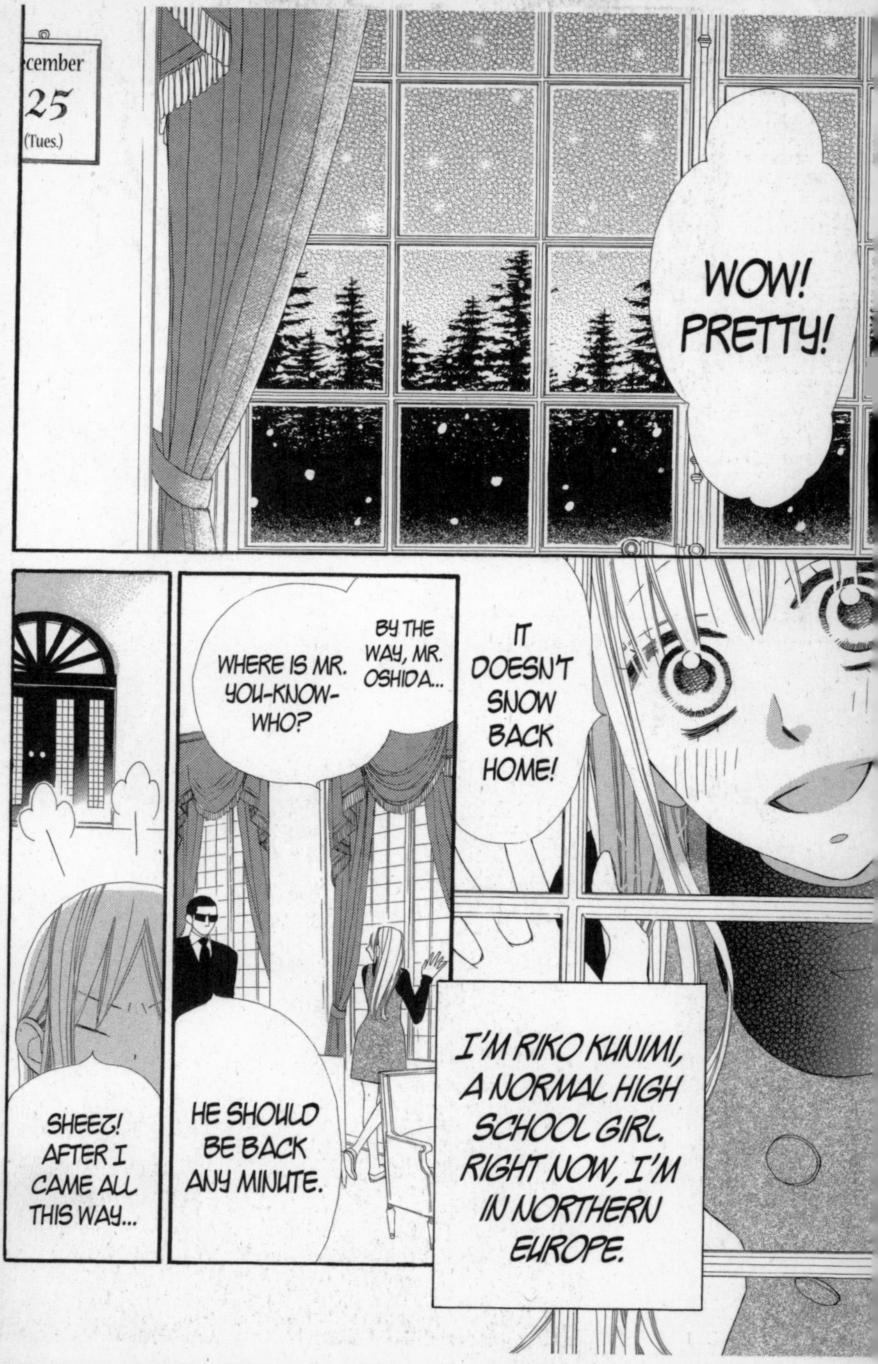
cember 25 (Tues.)
WOW! PRETTY!
IT DOESN'T SNOW BACK HOME!
I'M RIKO KUNIMI, A NORMAL HIGH SCHOOL GIRL. RIGHT NOW, I'M IN NORTHERN EUROPE.
BY THE WAY, MR. OSHIDA...
WHERE IS MR. YOU-KNOW-WHO?
HE SHOULD BE BACK ANY MINUTE.
SHEEZ! AFTER I CAME ALL THIS WAY...

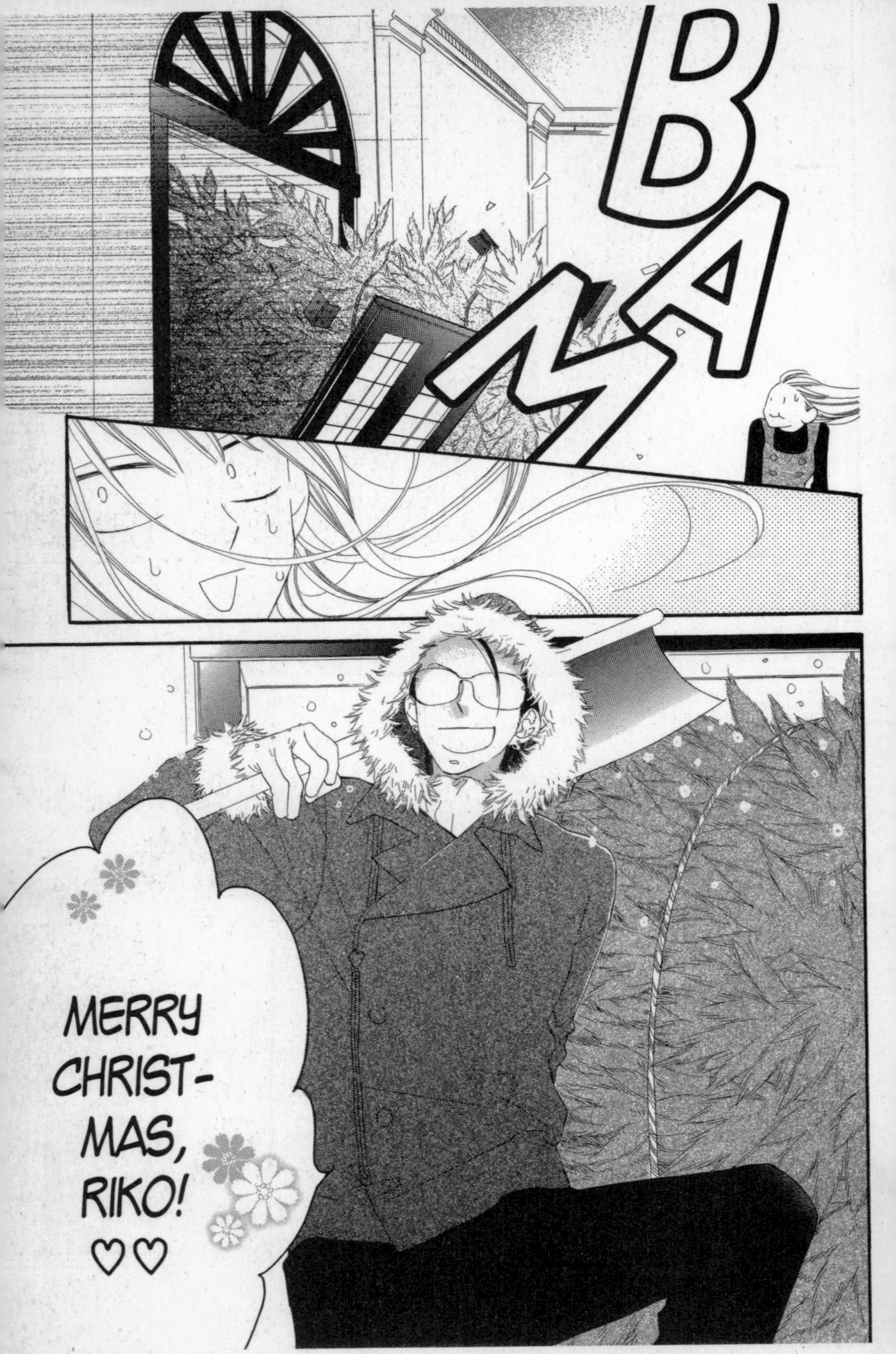
BAM
MERRY CHRIST-MAS, RIKO! ♡♡

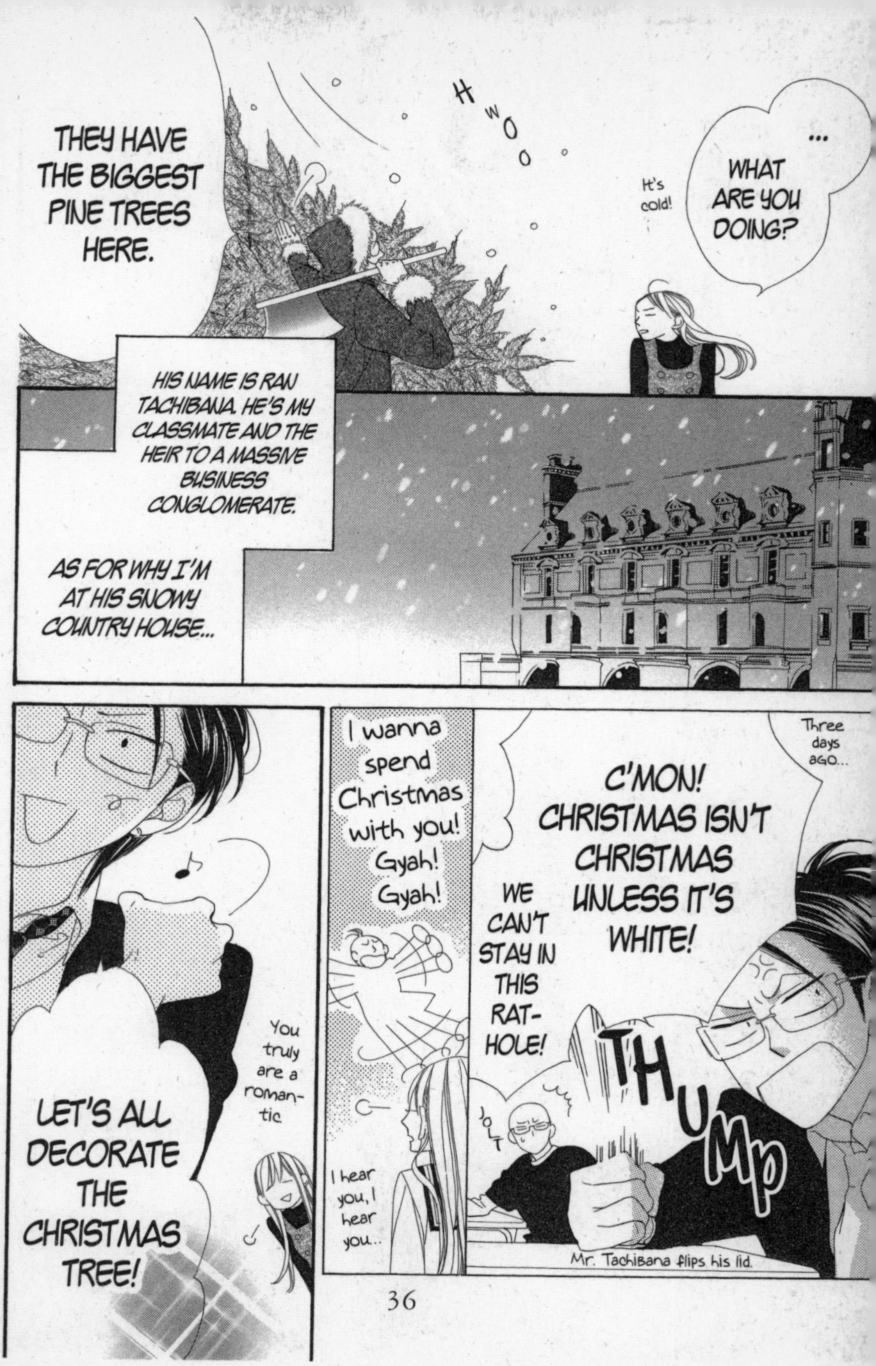

... WHAT ARE YOU DOING?
It's cold!
HWOOO
THEY HAVE THE BIGGEST PINE TREES HERE.
HIS NAME IS RAN TACHIBANA. HE'S MY CLASSMATE AND THE HEIR TO A MASSIVE BUSINESS CONGLOMERATE.
AS FOR WHY I'M AT HIS SNOWY COUNTRY HOUSE...
Three days ago...
C'MON! CHRISTMAS ISN'T CHRISTMAS UNLESS IT'S WHITE!
WE CAN'T STAY IN THIS RAT-HOLE!
THUMP
I wanna spend Christmas with you! Gyah! Gyah!
JOLT
I hear you, I hear you...
Mr. Tachibana flips his lid.
LET'S ALL DECORATE THE CHRISTMAS TREE!
You truly are a roman-tic.

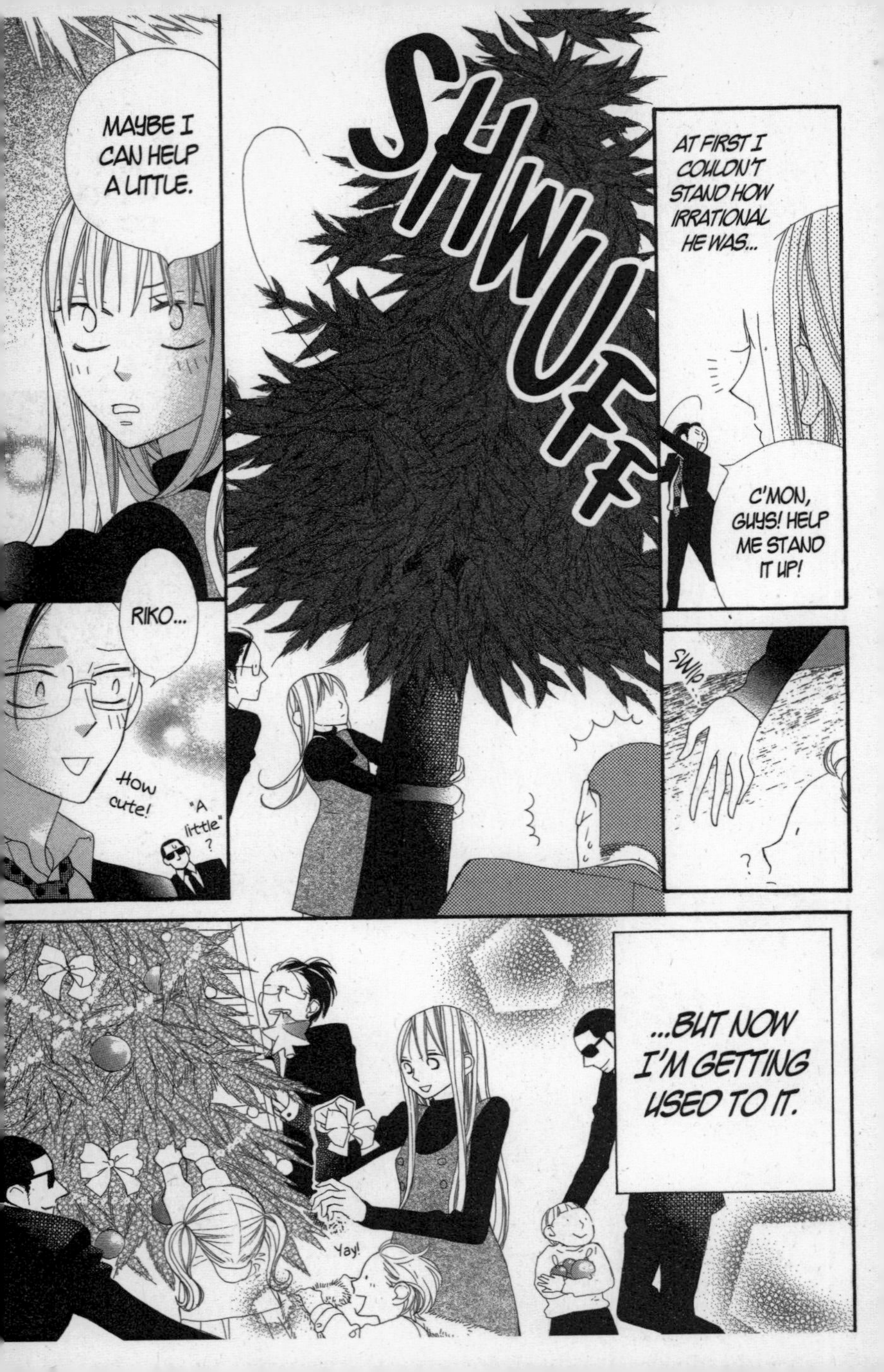
AT FIRST I COULDN'T STAND HOW IRRATIONAL HE WAS...
C'MON, GUYS! HELP ME STAND IT UP!
SHWUFF
MAYBE I CAN HELP A LITTLE.
RIKO...
How cute!
"A little"?
...BUT NOW I'M GETTING USED TO IT.
Yay!

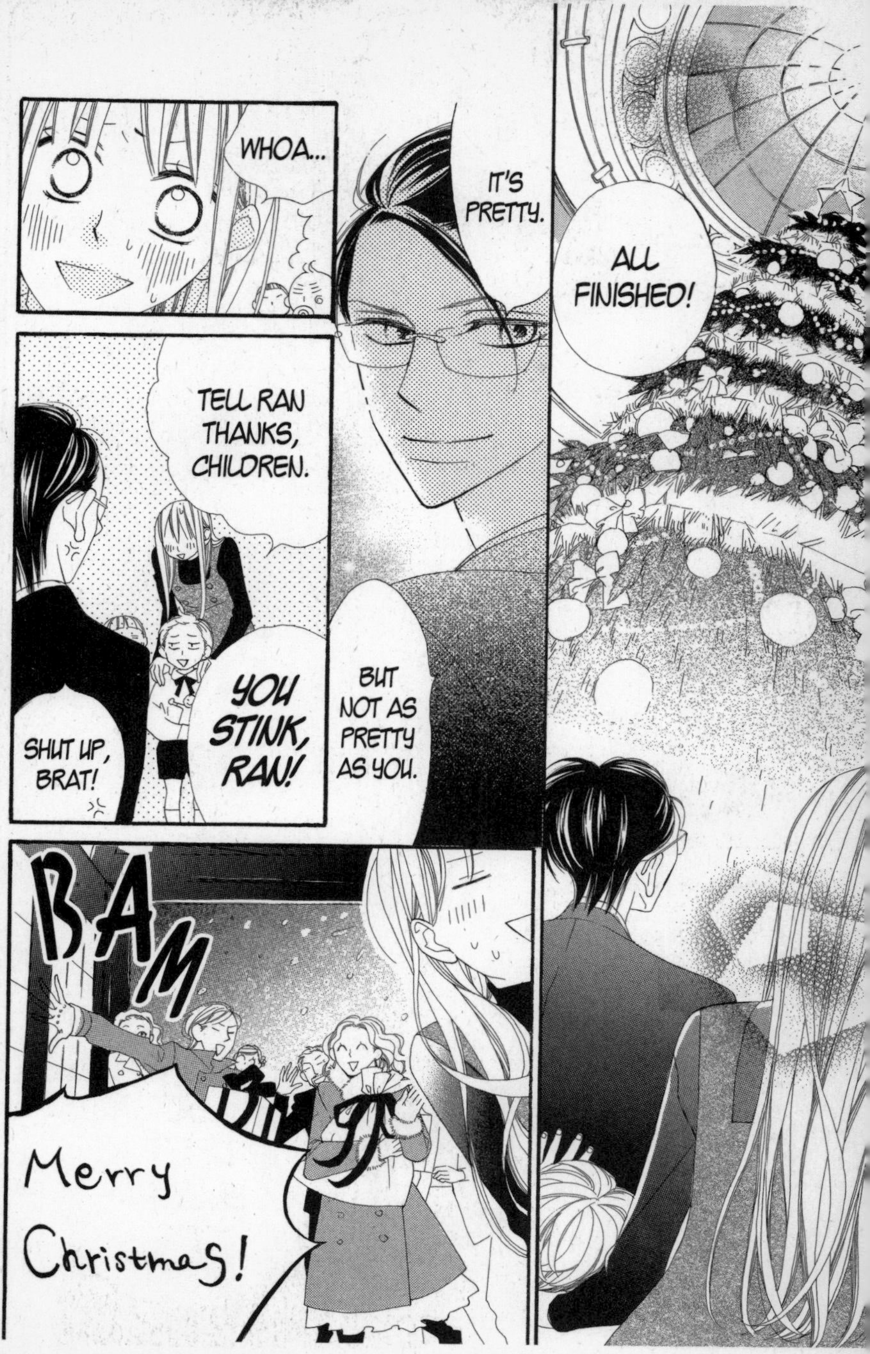
ALL FINISHED!
IT'S PRETTY.
BUT NOT AS PRETTY AS YOU.
WHOA...
TELL RAN THANKS, CHILDREN.
YOU STINK, RAN!
SHUT UP, BRAT!
BAM
Merry Christmas!

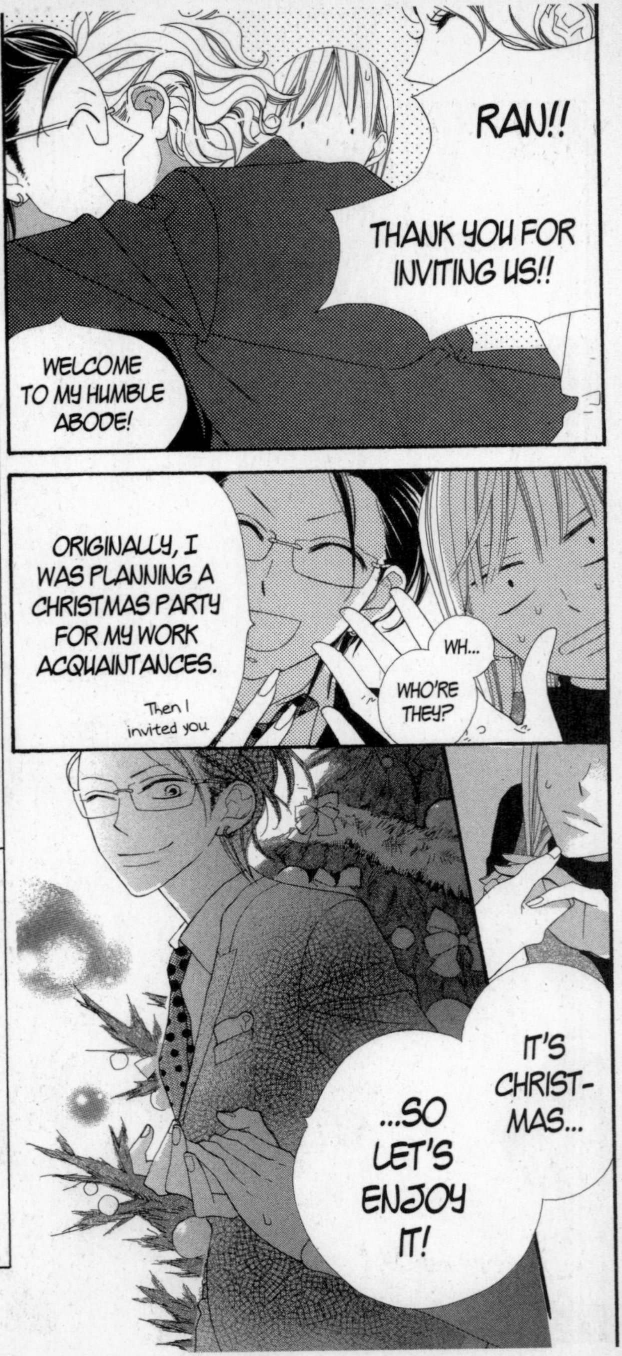
RAN!!
THANK YOU FOR INVITING US!!
WELCOME TO MY HUMBLE ABODE!
ORIGINALLY, I WAS PLANNING A CHRISTMAS PARTY FOR MY WORK ACQUAINTANCES.
Then I invited you
WH... WHO'RE THEY?
IT'S CHRISTMAS...
...SO LET'S ENJOY IT!

Continuing from last volume...

Supporting Character Profile

Rinko Kokonoe

17 years old, 5' 2"

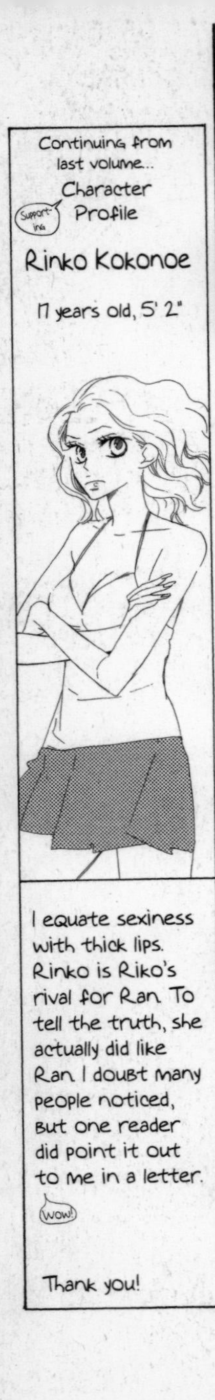

I equate sexiness with thick lips. Rinko is Riko's rival for Ran. To tell the truth, she actually did like Ran. I doubt many people noticed, but one reader did point it out to me in a letter. (wow!)

Thank you!

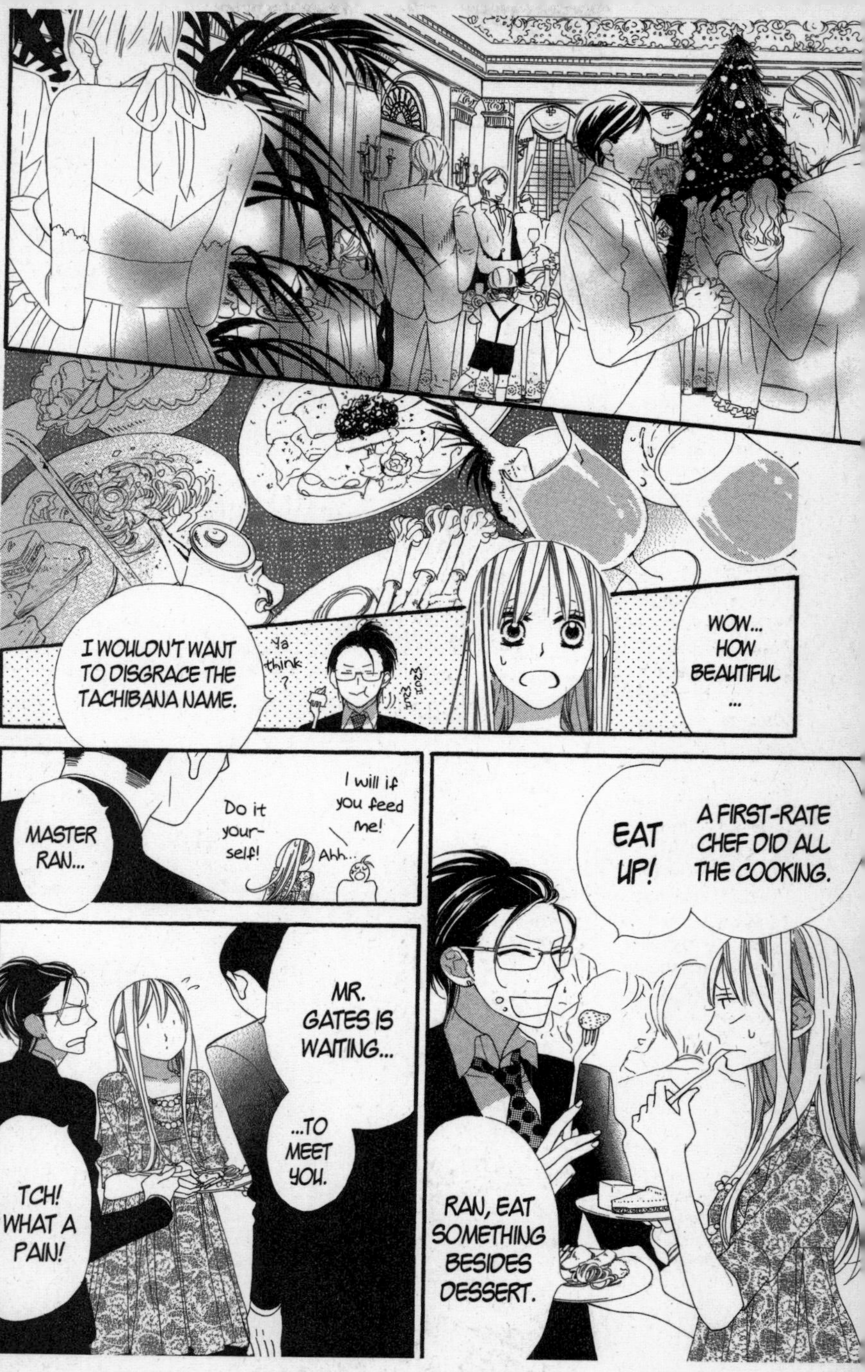
WOW... HOW BEAUTIFUL...
I WOULDN'T WANT TO DISGRACE THE TACHIBANA NAME.
Ya think?
A FIRST-RATE CHEF DID ALL THE COOKING.
EAT UP!
RAN, EAT SOMETHING BESIDES DESSERT.
Ahh...
Do it yourself!
I will if you feed me!
MASTER RAN...
MR. GATES IS WAITING...
...TO MEET YOU.
TCH! WHAT A PAIN!

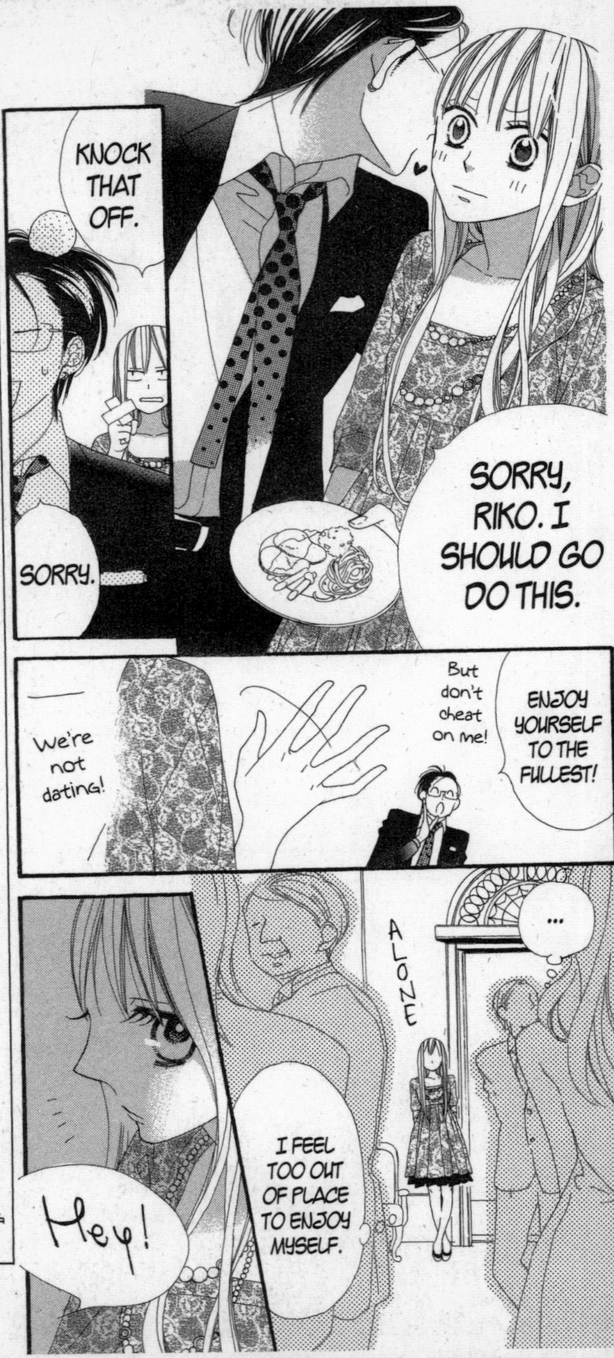
SORRY, RIKO. I SHOULD GO DO THIS.
KNOCK THAT OFF.
SORRY.
ENJOY YOURSELF TO THE FULLEST!
But don't cheat on me!
We're not dating!
...
ALONE
I FEEL TOO OUT OF PLACE TO ENJOY MYSELF.
Hey!

Behind the Scenes of Chapter 6

It was my first time to do a color title page, so I spent two weeks slaving over it. When I saw the printed version though, it hadn't turned out at all as I had imagined. I was shocked.

When I mentioned that, my editor said that I'm type A, but actually I'm type B. I'm negative about everything.

The end was in sight by this point, so I rushed the plot along, but the change in Riko's feelings might have been a little too sudden. That's more negative thinking... But in the end I'm the kind of person who can shrug and say, "Oh well."

By the way, the children who appear in the first half of the chapter all belong to Ran's servants.

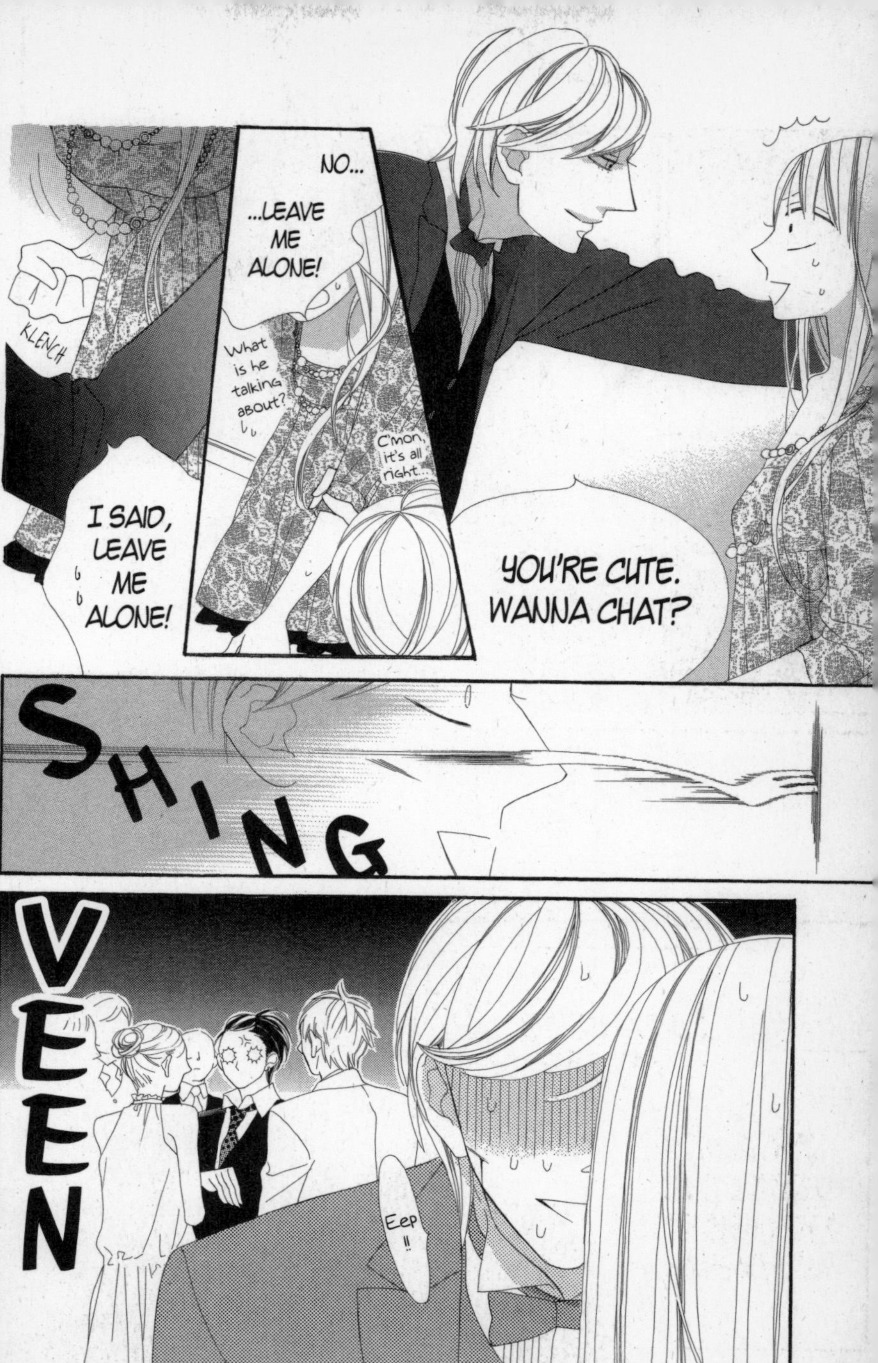
YOU'RE CUTE. WANNA CHAT?
NO...
...LEAVE ME ALONE!
C'mon, it's all right...
What is he talking about?
KLENCH
I SAID, LEAVE ME ALONE!
SHING
VEEN
Eep!!

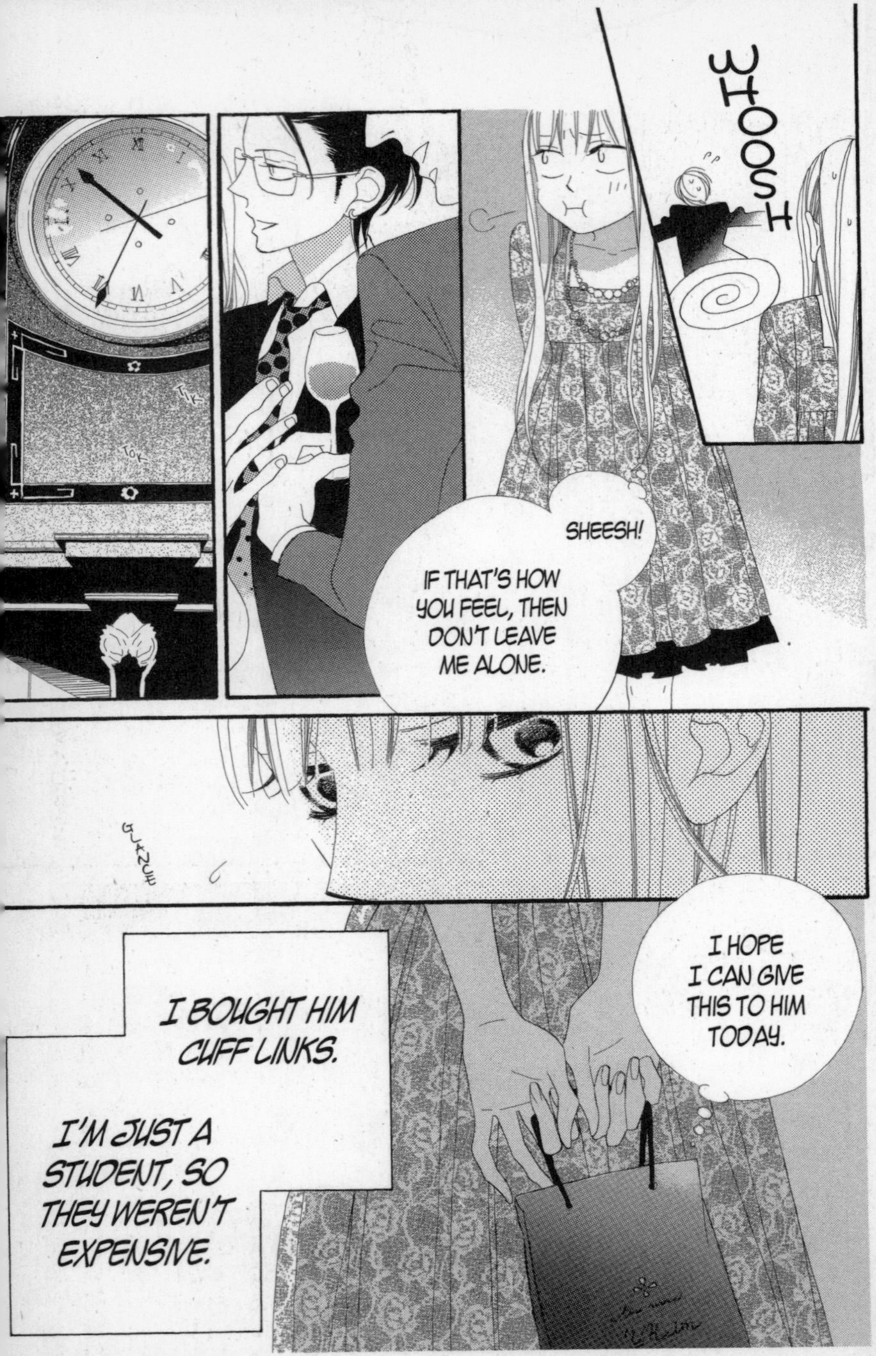
WHOOSH
SHEESH!
IF THAT'S HOW YOU FEEL, THEN DON'T LEAVE ME ALONE.
TIK
TOK
GLANCE
I HOPE I CAN GIVE THIS TO HIM TODAY.
I BOUGHT HIM CUFF LINKS.
I'M JUST A STUDENT, SO THEY WEREN'T EXPENSIVE.

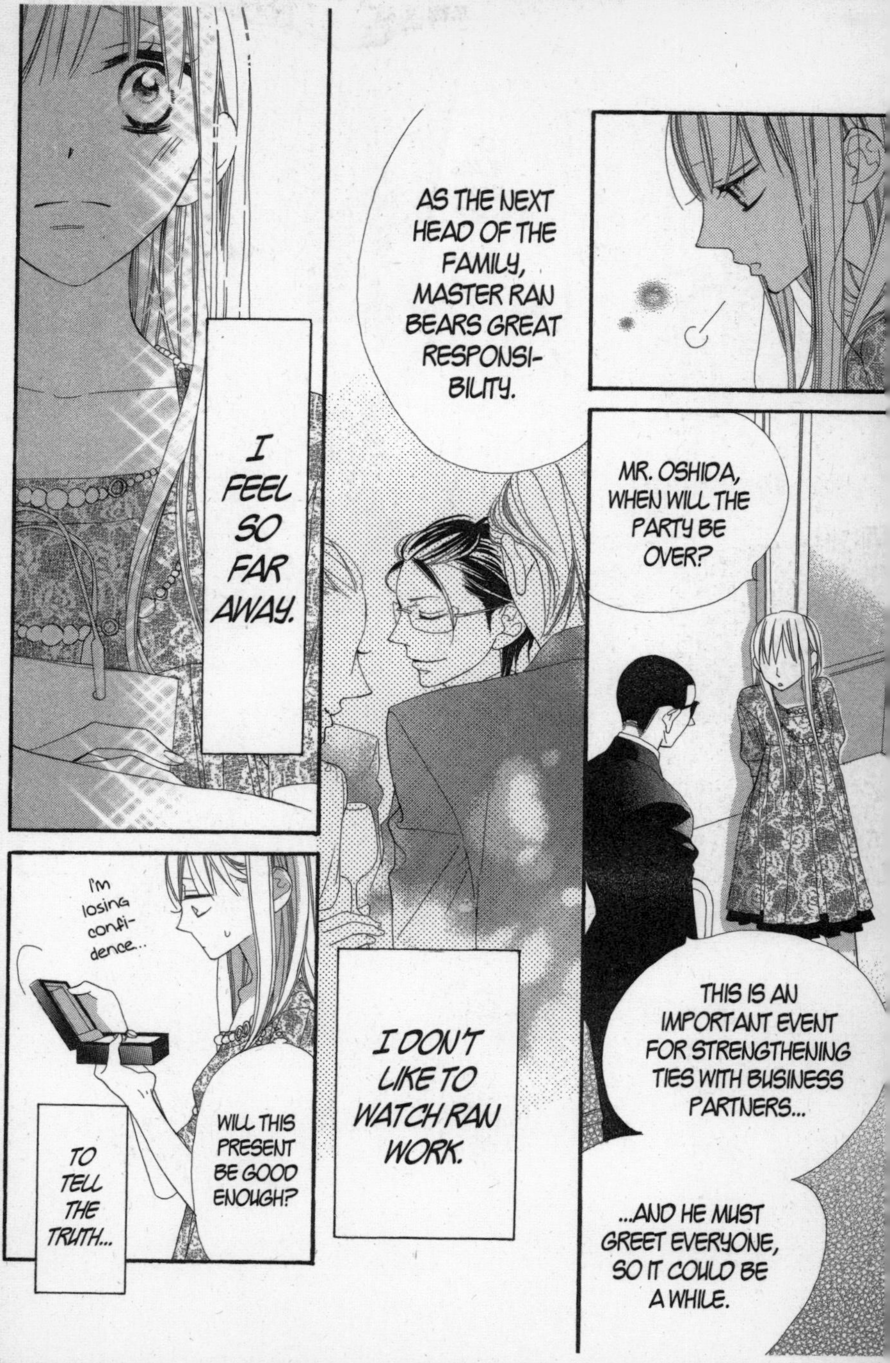
MR. OSHIDA, WHEN WILL THE PARTY BE OVER?
THIS IS AN IMPORTANT EVENT FOR STRENGTHENING TIES WITH BUSINESS PARTNERS...
...AND HE MUST GREET EVERYONE, SO IT COULD BE A WHILE.
AS THE NEXT HEAD OF THE FAMILY, MASTER RAN BEARS GREAT RESPONSI-BILITY.
I DON'T LIKE TO WATCH RAN WORK.
I FEEL SO FAR AWAY.
I'm losing confi-dence...
WILL THIS PRESENT BE GOOD ENOUGH?
TO TELL THE TRUTH...

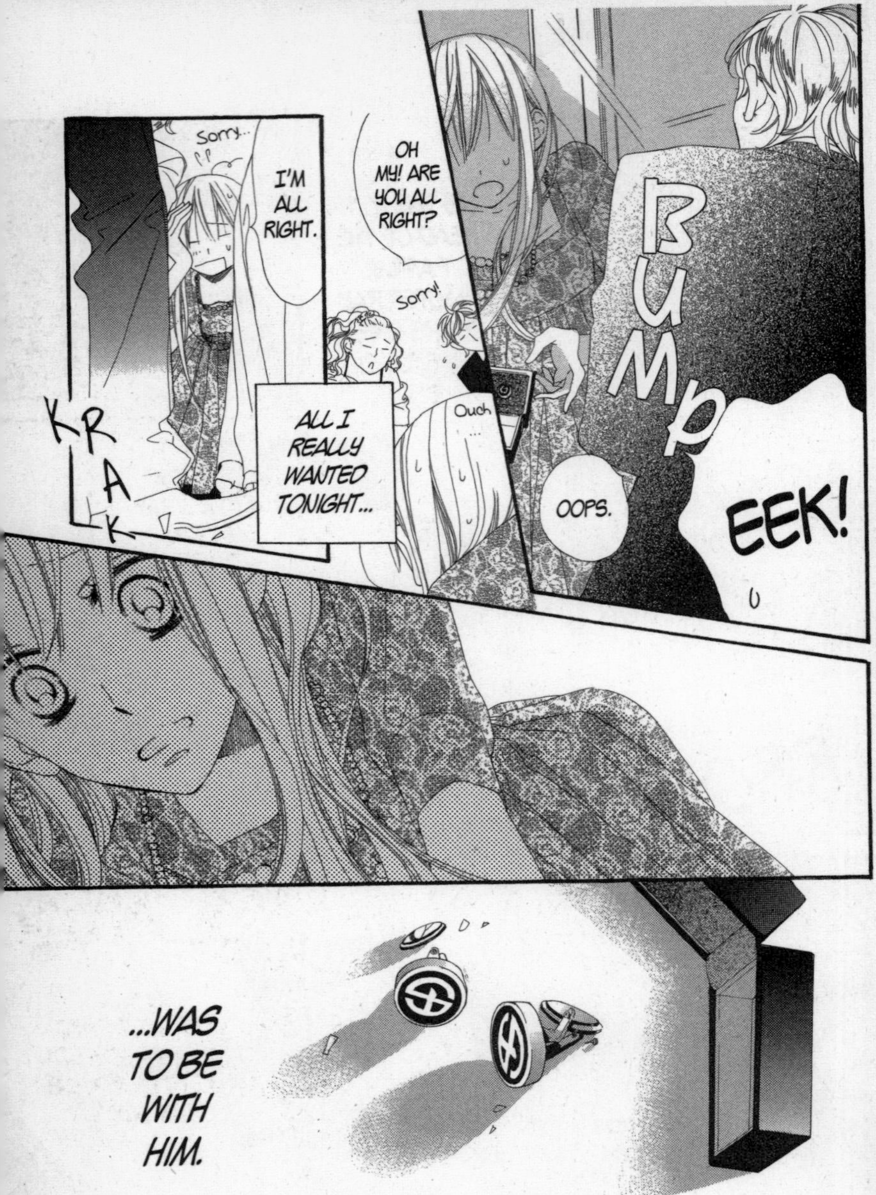
BUMP
EEK!
OOPS.
OH MY! ARE YOU ALL RIGHT?
Sorry!
Ouch...
Sorry...
I'M ALL RIGHT.
ALL I REALLY WANTED TONIGHT...
KRAK
...WAS TO BE WITH HIM.

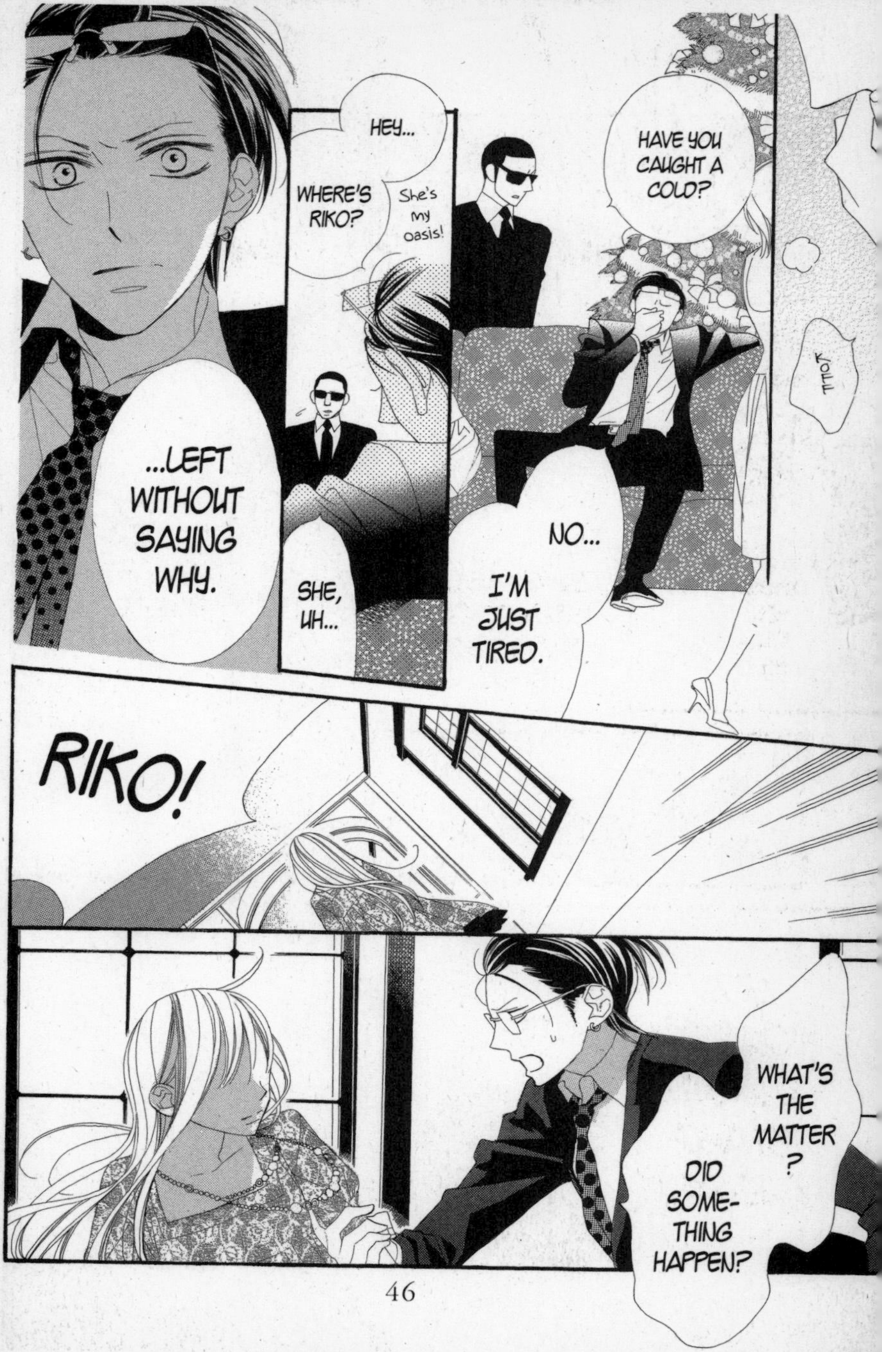
HAVE YOU CAUGHT A COLD?
KOFF
NO...
I'M JUST TIRED.
HEY...
WHERE'S RIKO?
She's my oasis!
SHE, UH...
...LEFT WITHOUT SAYING WHY.
RIKO!
WHAT'S THE MATTER?
DID SOMETHING HAPPEN?

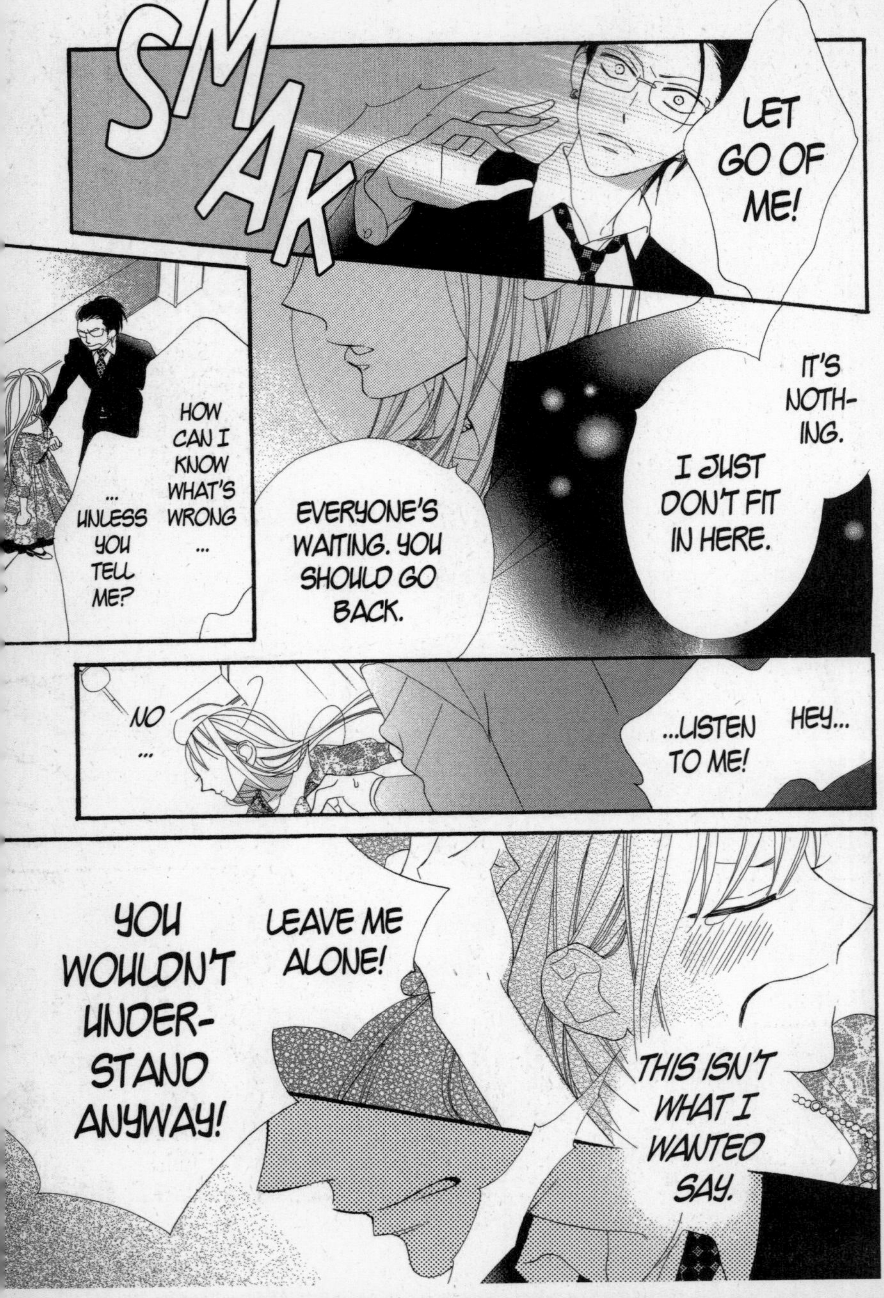
LET GO OF ME!
SMAK
IT'S NOTHING.
I JUST DON'T FIT IN HERE.
EVERYONE'S WAITING. YOU SHOULD GO BACK.
HOW CAN I KNOW WHAT'S WRONG ...
... UNLESS YOU TELL ME?
HEY...
...LISTEN TO ME!
NO ...
THIS ISN'T WHAT I WANTED SAY.
LEAVE ME ALONE!
YOU WOULDN'T UNDERSTAND ANYWAY!

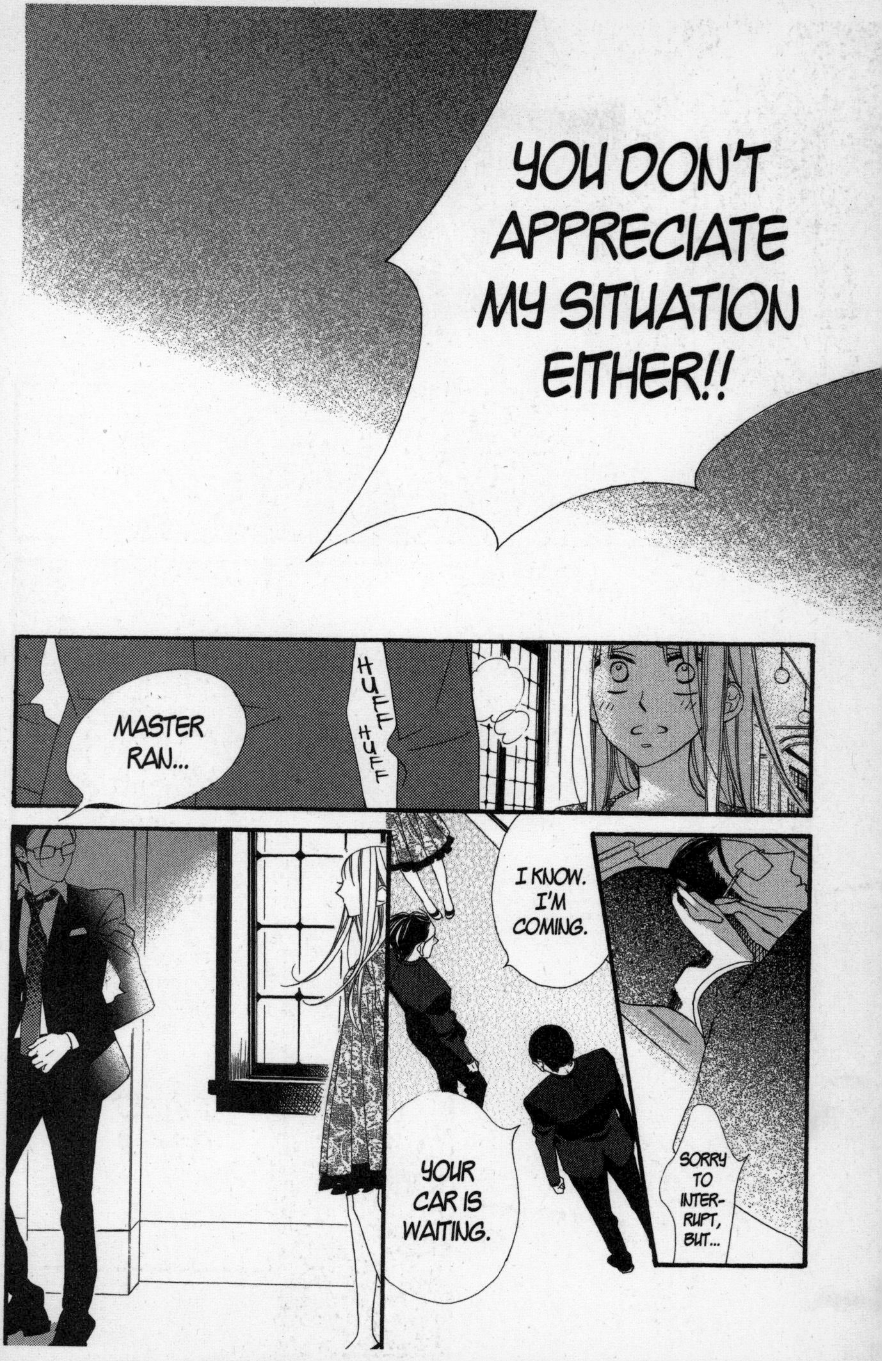
YOU DON'T APPRECIATE MY SITUATION EITHER!!
HUFF HUFF
MASTER RAN...
SORRY TO INTER-RUPT, BUT...
YOUR CAR IS WAITING.
I KNOW. I'M COMING.

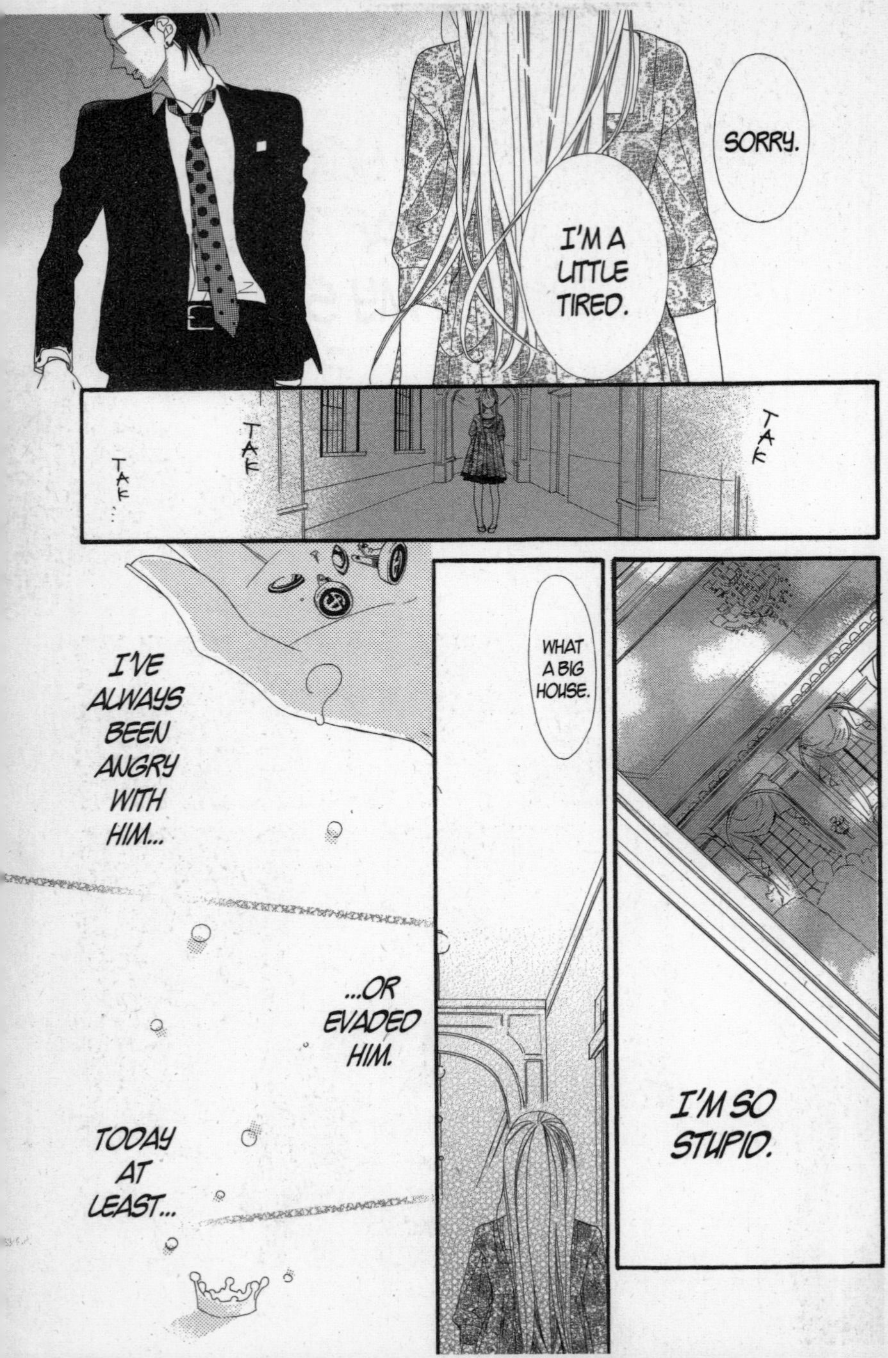
SORRY.
I'M A LITTLE TIRED.
TAK
TAK
TAK...
I'M SO STUPID.
WHAT A BIG HOUSE.
I'VE ALWAYS BEEN ANGRY WITH HIM...
...OR EVADED HIM.
TODAY AT LEAST...

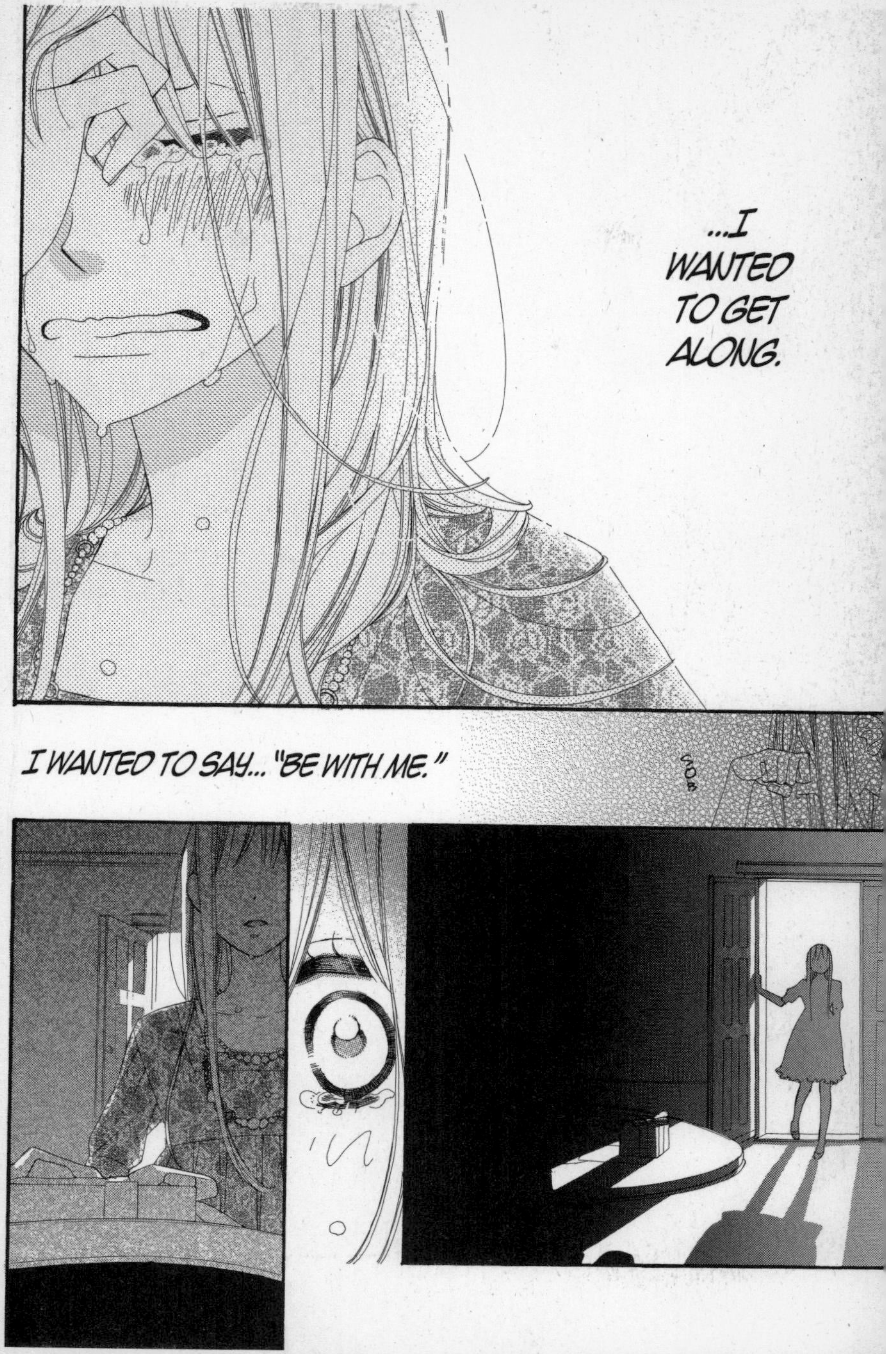
...I WANTED TO GET ALONG.
SOB
I WANTED TO SAY... "BE WITH ME."

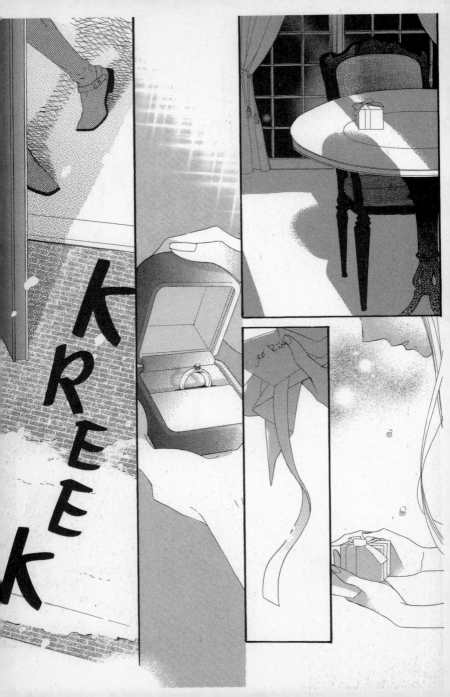

KREEK

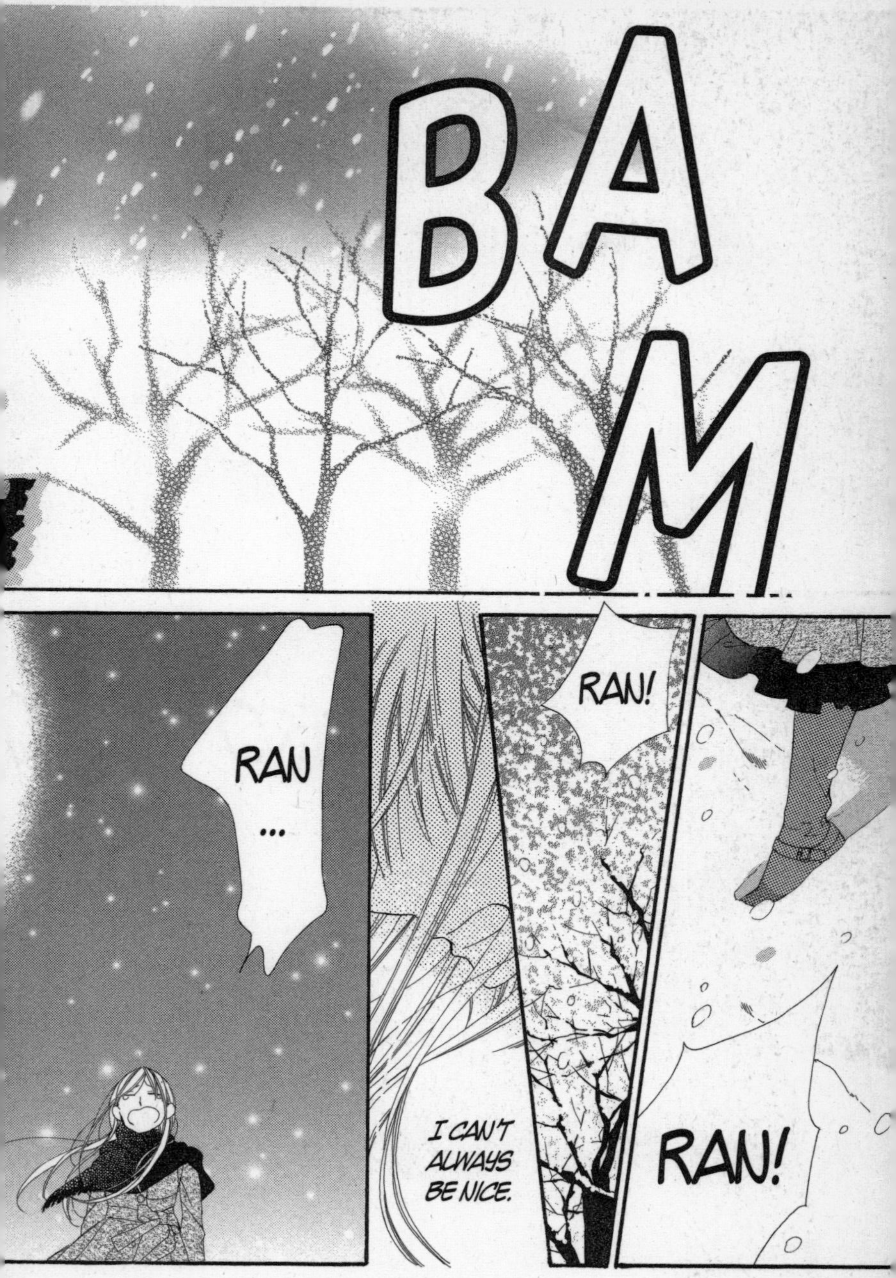
BAM
RAN!
RAN!
I CAN'T ALWAYS BE NICE.
RAN ...

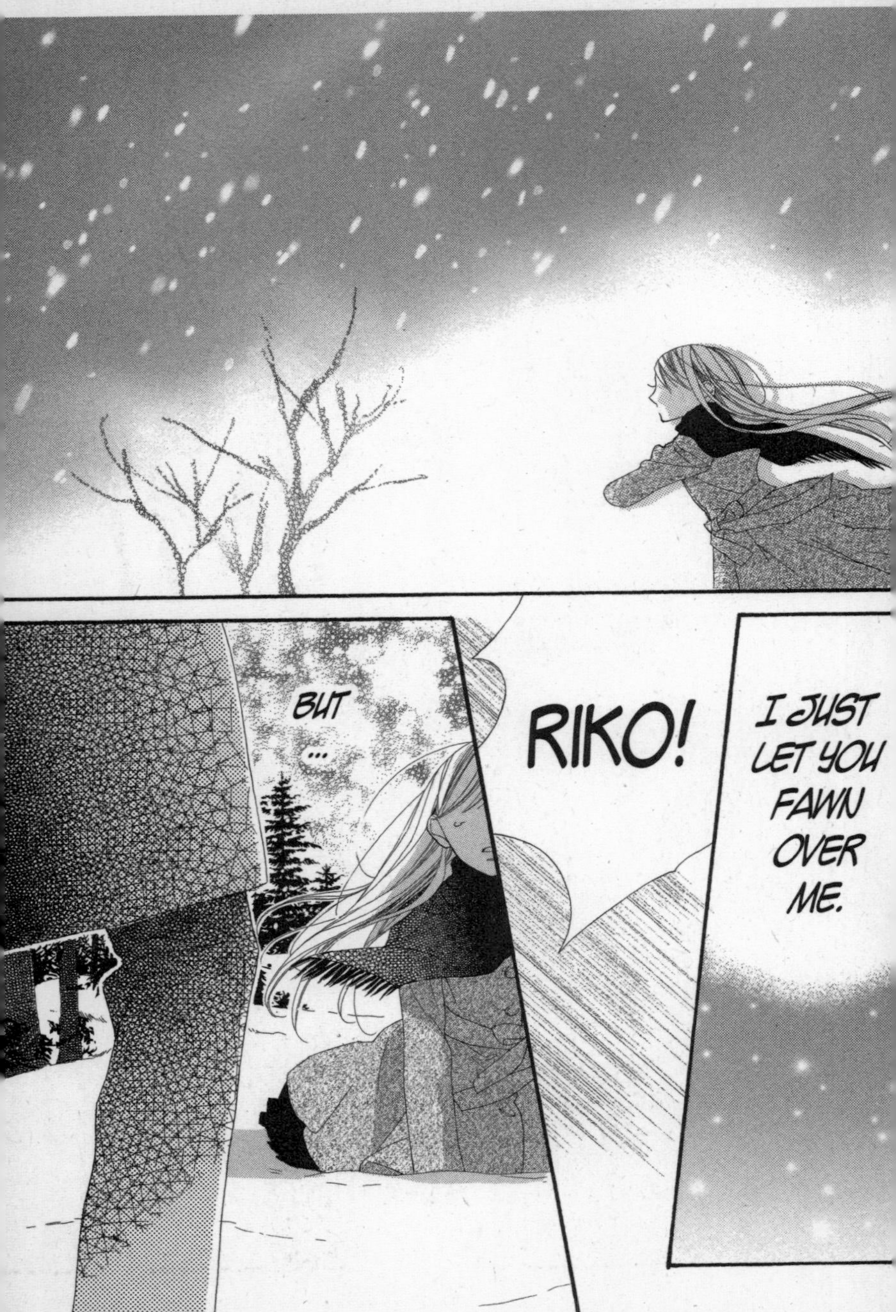
I JUST LET YOU FAWN OVER ME.
RIKO!
BUT ...

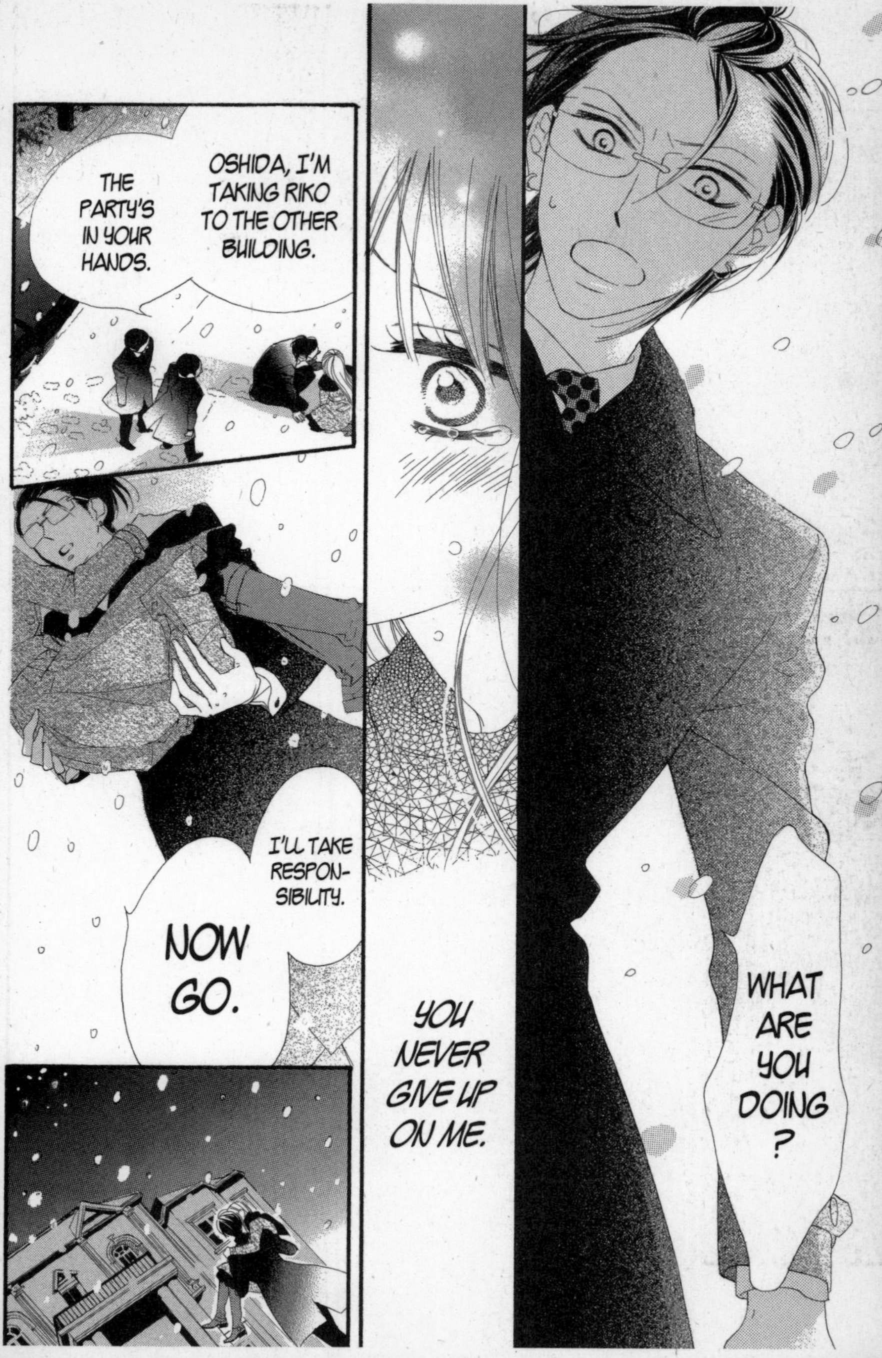
WHAT ARE YOU DOING?
YOU NEVER GIVE UP ON ME.
OSHIDA, I'M TAKING RIKO TO THE OTHER BUILDING.
THE PARTY'S IN YOUR HANDS.
I'LL TAKE RESPON-SIBILITY.
NOW GO.

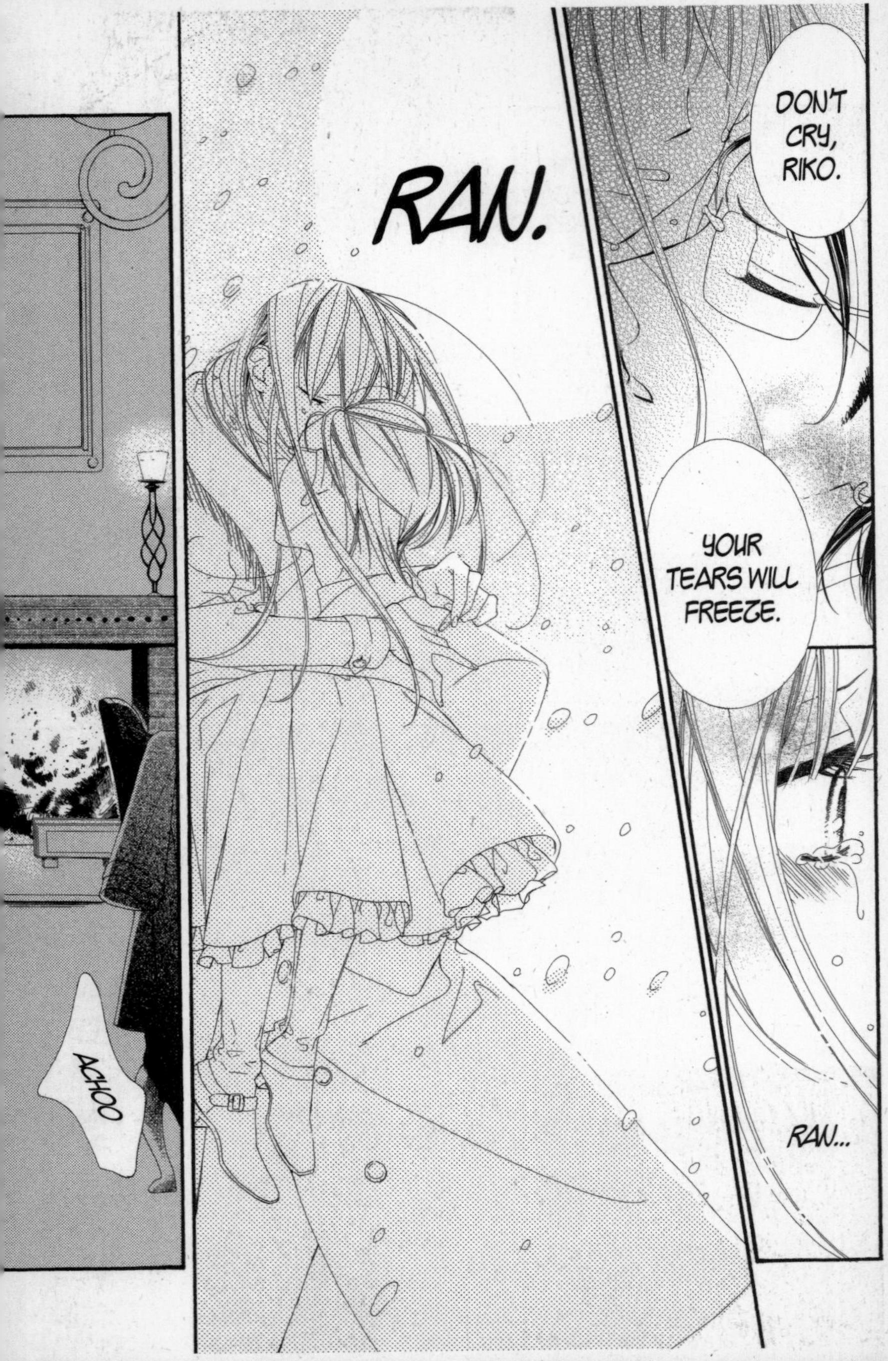
DON'T CRY, RIKO.
YOUR TEARS WILL FREEZE.
RAN...
RAN.
ACHOO

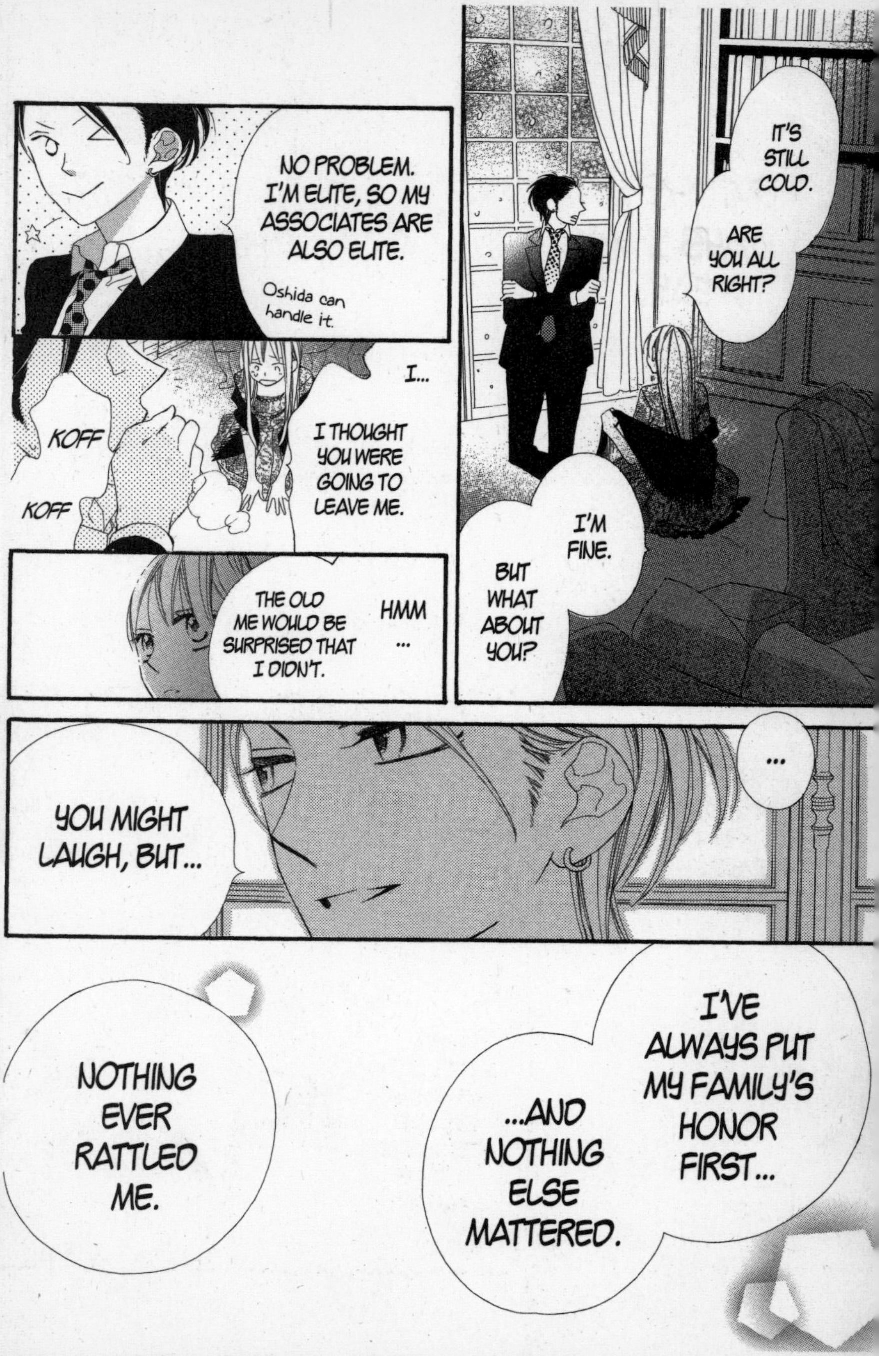
IT'S STILL COLD.
ARE YOU ALL RIGHT?
I'M FINE.
BUT WHAT ABOUT YOU?
NO PROBLEM. I'M ELITE, SO MY ASSOCIATES ARE ALSO ELITE.
Oshida can handle it.
I...
I THOUGHT YOU WERE GOING TO LEAVE ME.
KOFF
KOFF
HMM...
THE OLD ME WOULD BE SURPRISED THAT I DIDN'T.
...
YOU MIGHT LAUGH, BUT...
I'VE ALWAYS PUT MY FAMILY'S HONOR FIRST...
...AND NOTHING ELSE MATTERED.
NOTHING EVER RATTLED ME.

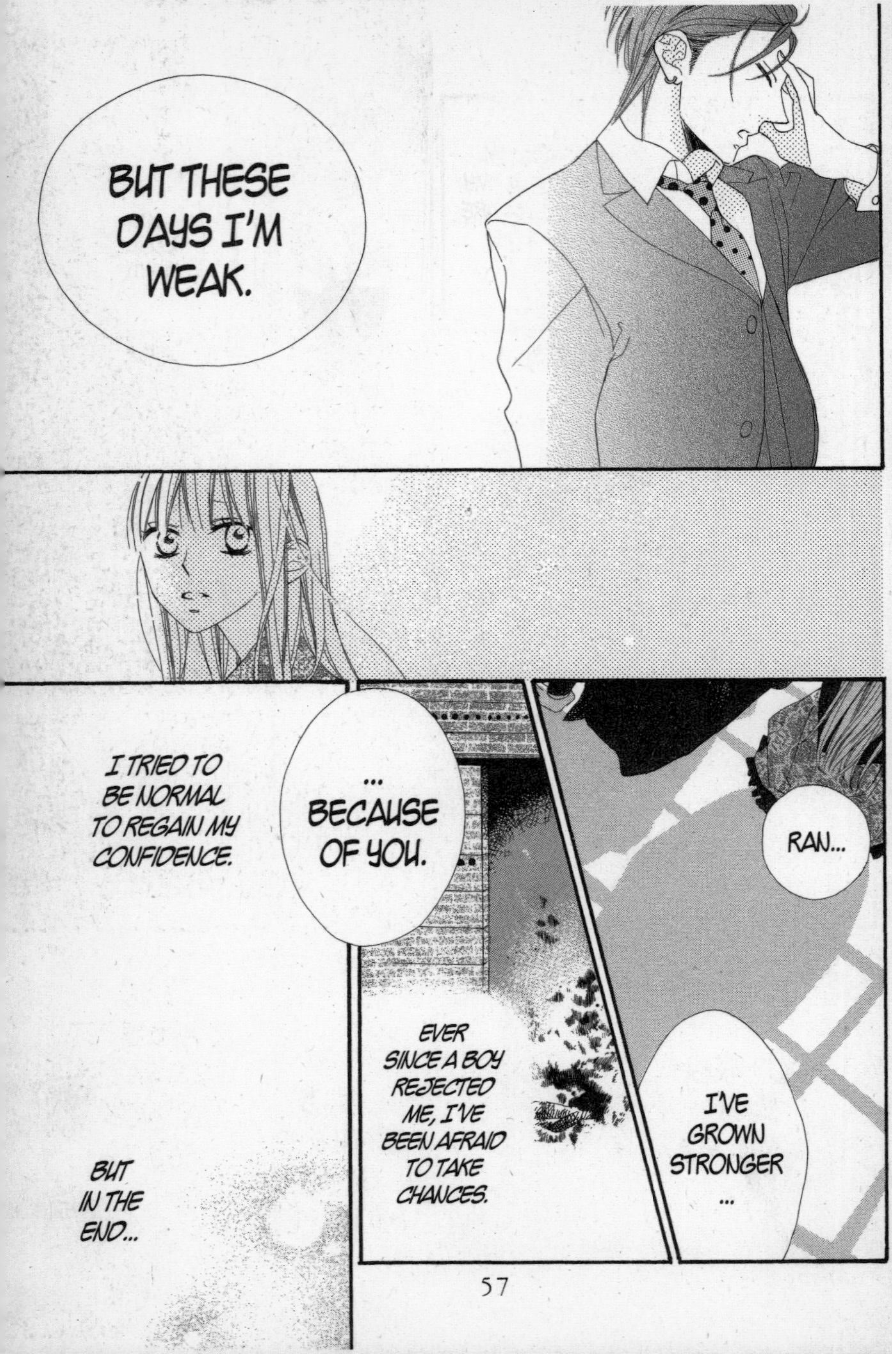
BUT THESE DAYS I'M WEAK.
RAN...
I'VE GROWN STRONGER ...
... BECAUSE OF YOU.
EVER SINCE A BOY REJECTED ME, I'VE BEEN AFRAID TO TAKE CHANCES.
I TRIED TO BE NORMAL TO REGAIN MY CONFIDENCE.
BUT IN THE END...

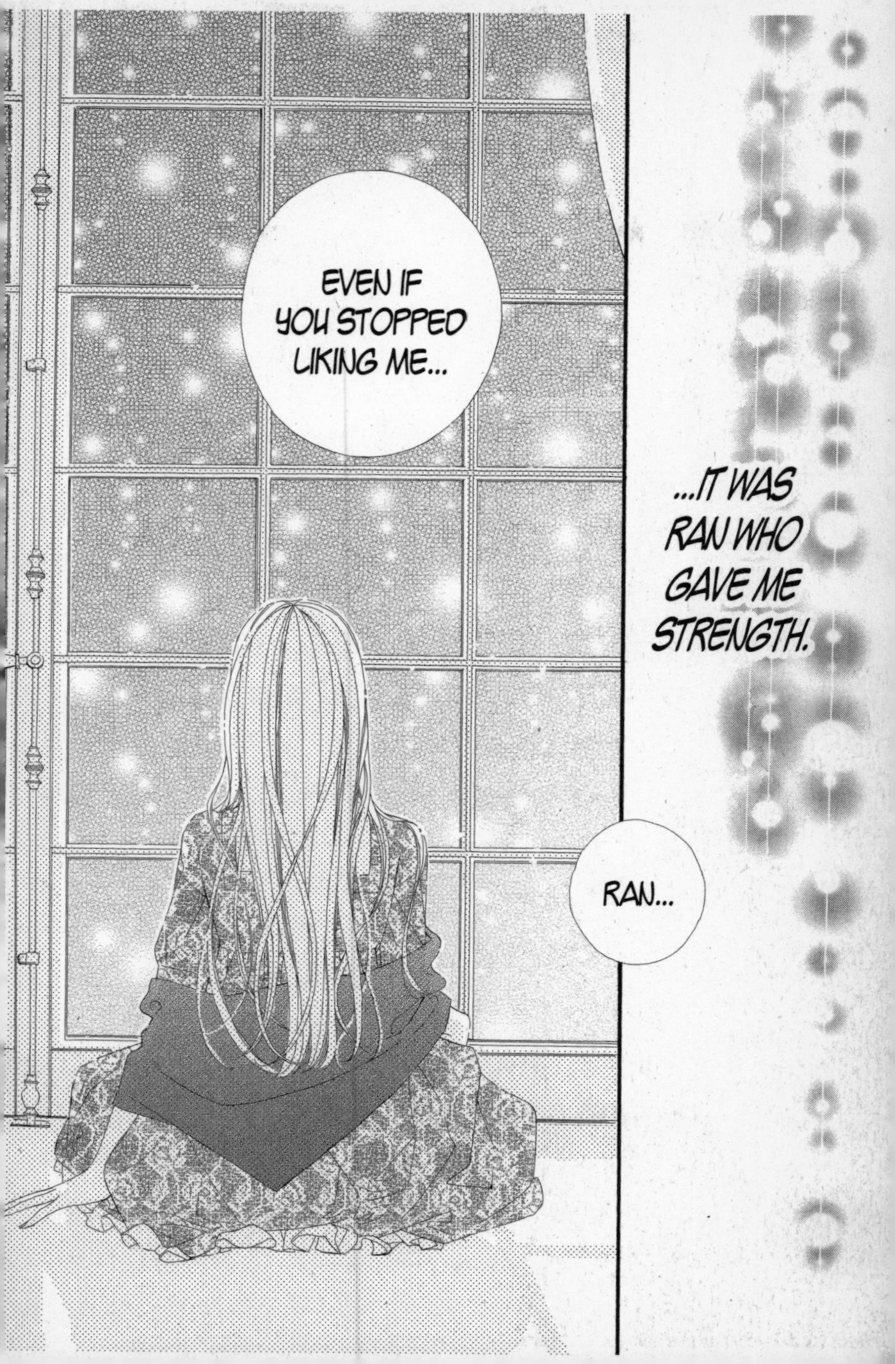
EVEN IF YOU STOPPED LIKING ME...
...IT WAS RAN WHO GAVE ME STRENGTH.
RAN...

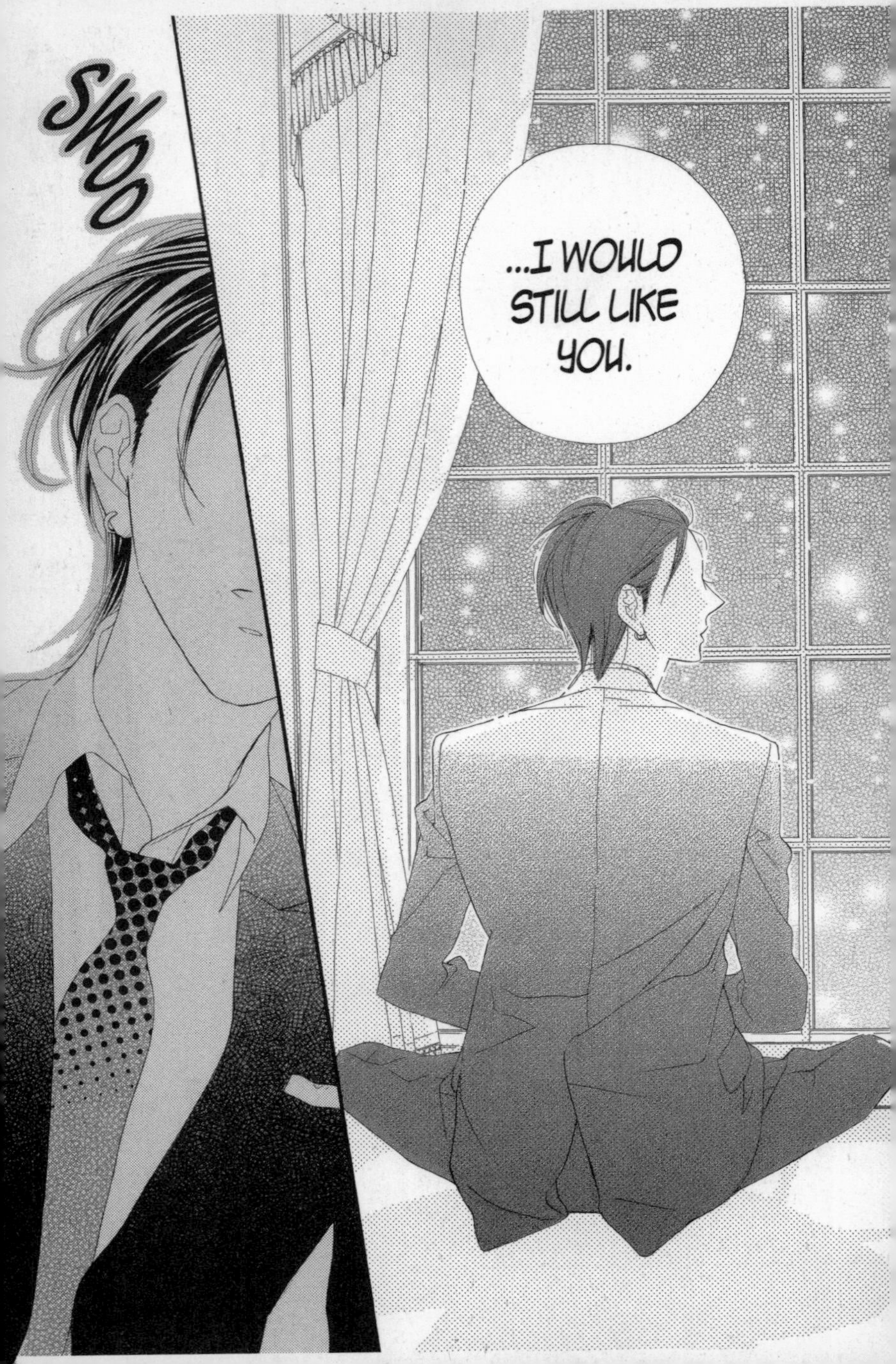
...I WOULD STILL LIKE YOU.
SNOO

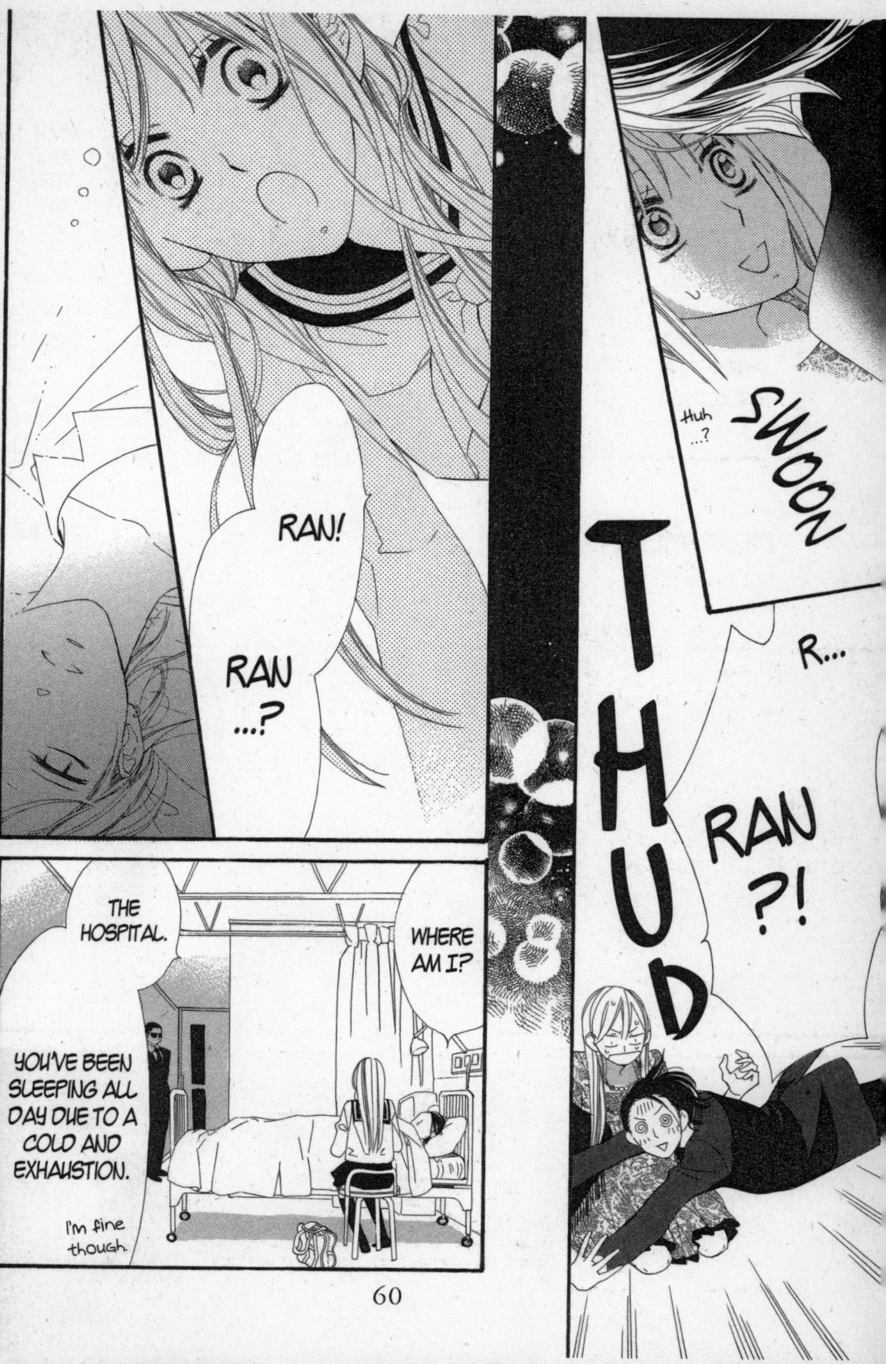
SWOON
Huh ...?
R...
RAN ?!
THUD
RAN!
RAN ...?
WHERE AM I?
THE HOSPITAL.
YOU'VE BEEN SLEEPING ALL DAY DUE TO A COLD AND EXHAUSTION.
I'm fine though.

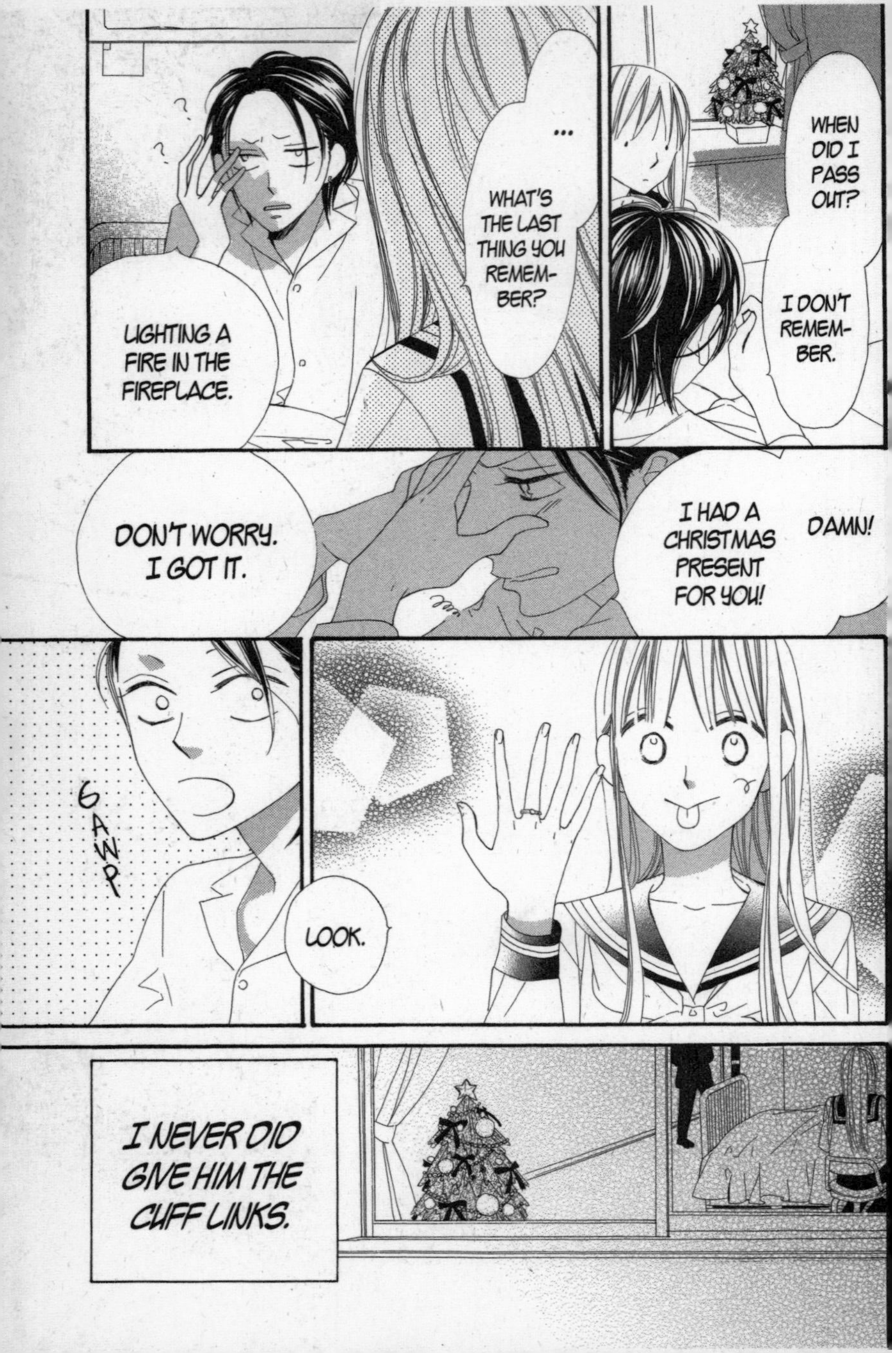
WHEN DID I PASS OUT?
I DON'T REMEMBER.
...
WHAT'S THE LAST THING YOU REMEMBER?
LIGHTING A FIRE IN THE FIREPLACE.
DAMN!
I HAD A CHRISTMAS PRESENT FOR YOU!
DON'T WORRY. I GOT IT.
LOOK.
GAWP
I NEVER DID GIVE HIM THE CUFF LINKS.

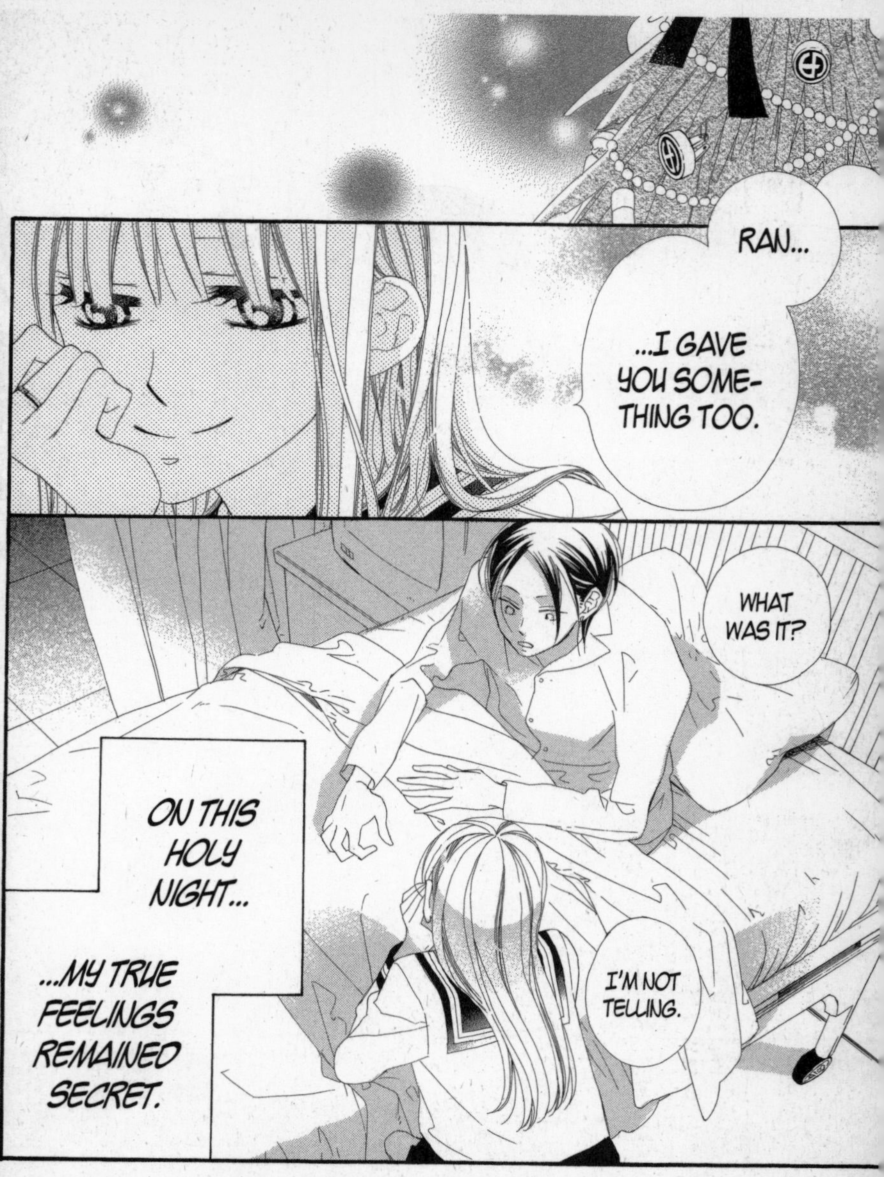
RAN...
...I GAVE YOU SOME-THING TOO.
WHAT WAS IT?
I'M NOT TELLING.
ON THIS HOLY NIGHT...
...MY TRUE FEELINGS REMAINED SECRET.

I WOULD TELL HIM AGAIN SOON.
OR SO I THOUGHT...

FLOWER IN A STORM CHAPTER 6 / END

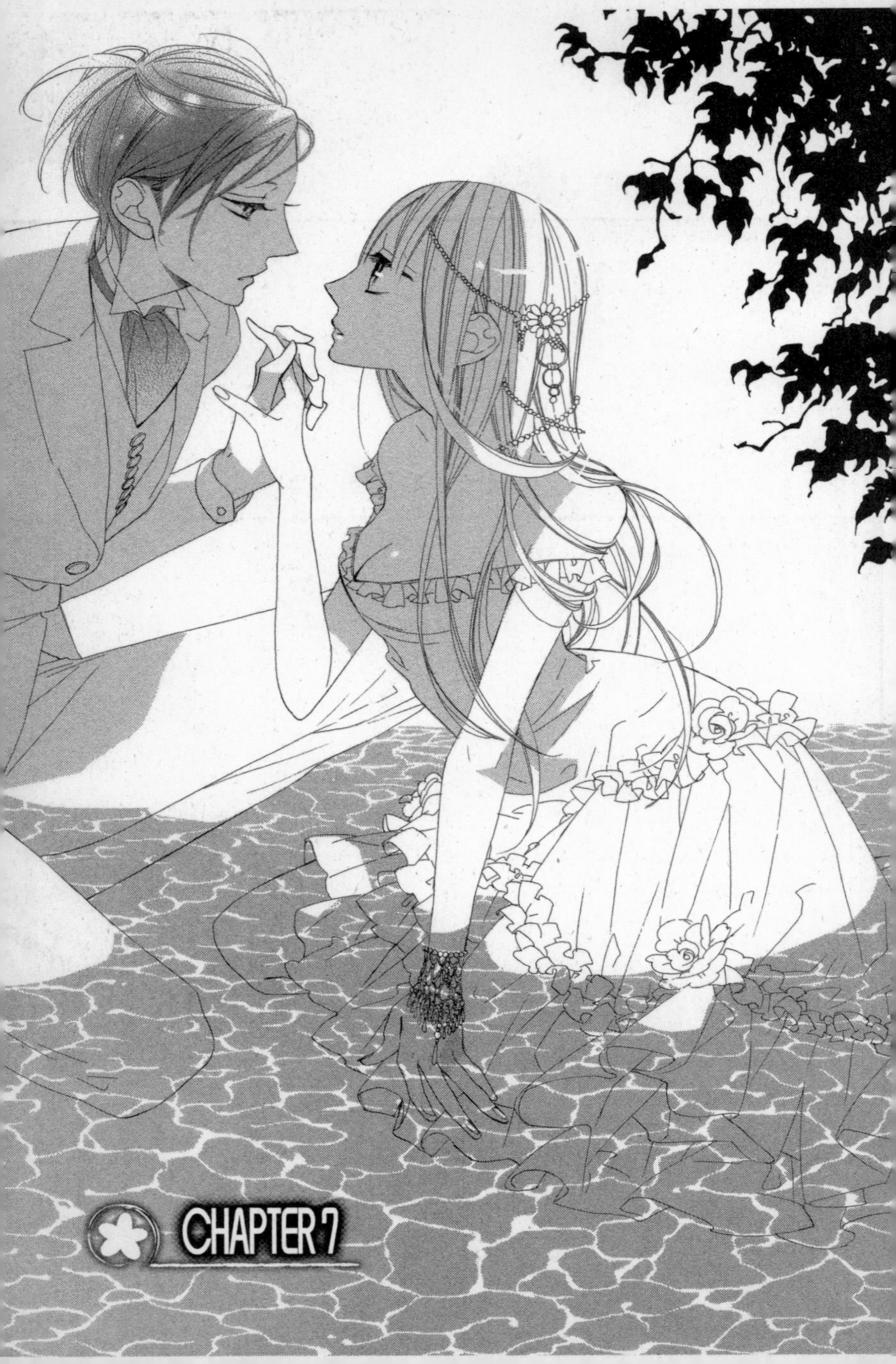
CHAPTER 7

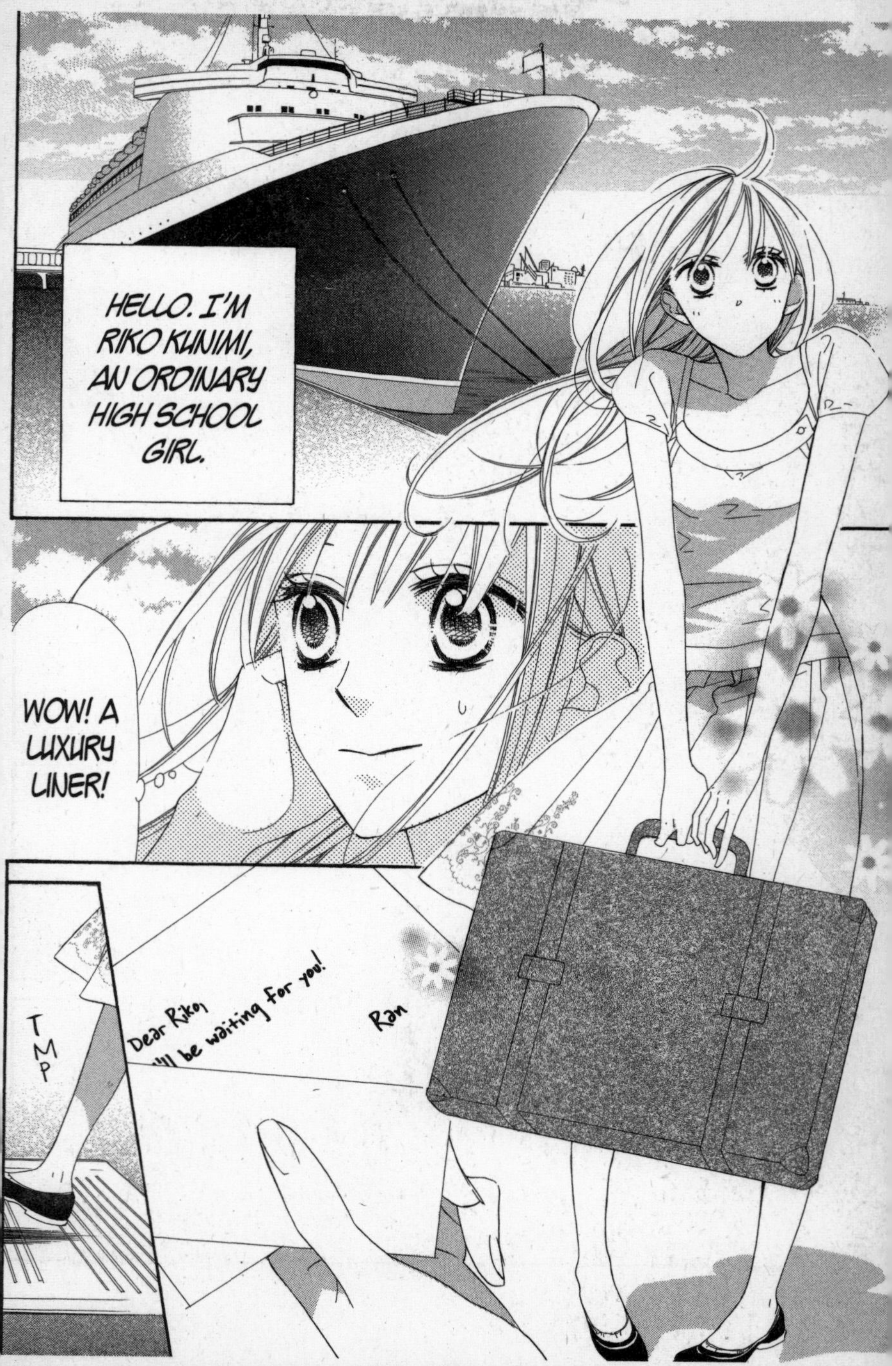
HELLO. I'M RIKO KUNIMI, AN ORDINARY HIGH SCHOOL GIRL.
WOW! A LUXURY LINER!
Dear Riko,
'll be waiting for you!
Ran
TMP

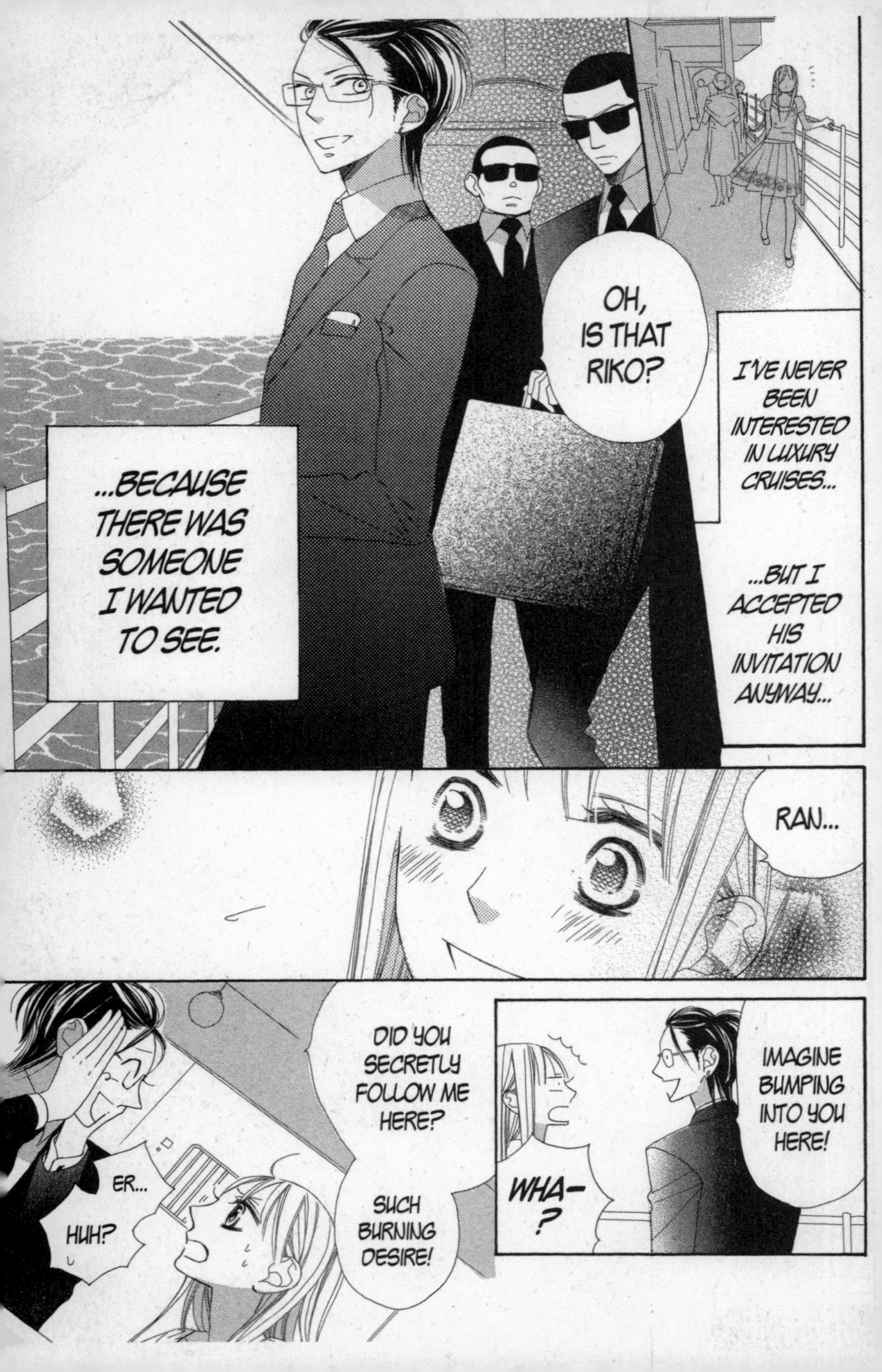
I'VE NEVER BEEN INTERESTED IN LUXURY CRUISES...
...BUT I ACCEPTED HIS INVITATION ANYWAY...
OH, IS THAT RIKO?
...BECAUSE THERE WAS SOMEONE I WANTED TO SEE.
RAN...
IMAGINE BUMPING INTO YOU HERE!
WHA-?
DID YOU SECRETLY FOLLOW ME HERE?
SUCH BURNING DESIRE!
ER...
HUH?

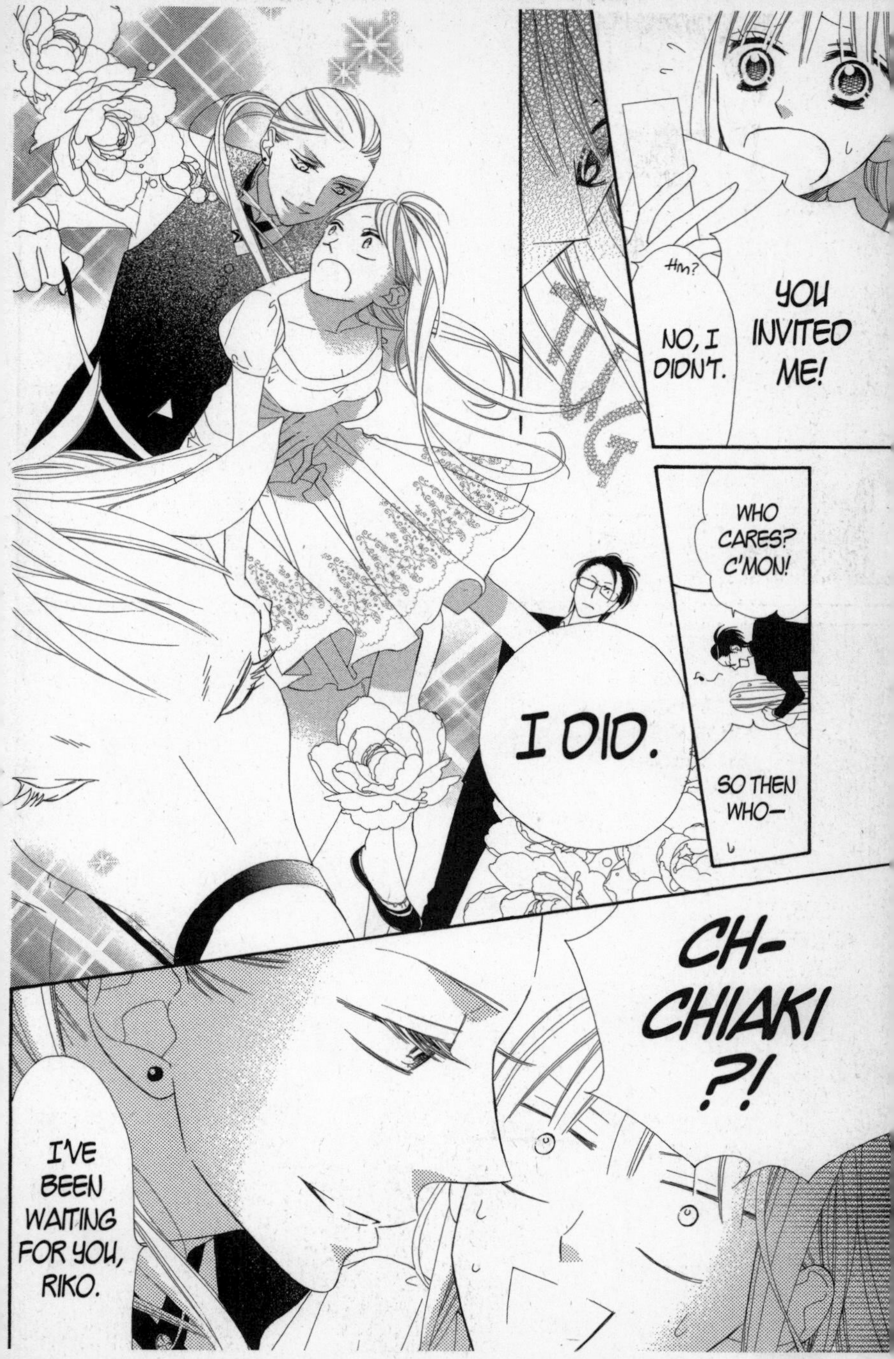
YOU INVITED ME!
Hm?
NO, I DIDN'T.
HUG
WHO CARES? C'MON!
SO THEN WHO—
I DID.
CH-CHIAKI?!
I'VE BEEN WAITING FOR YOU, RIKO.

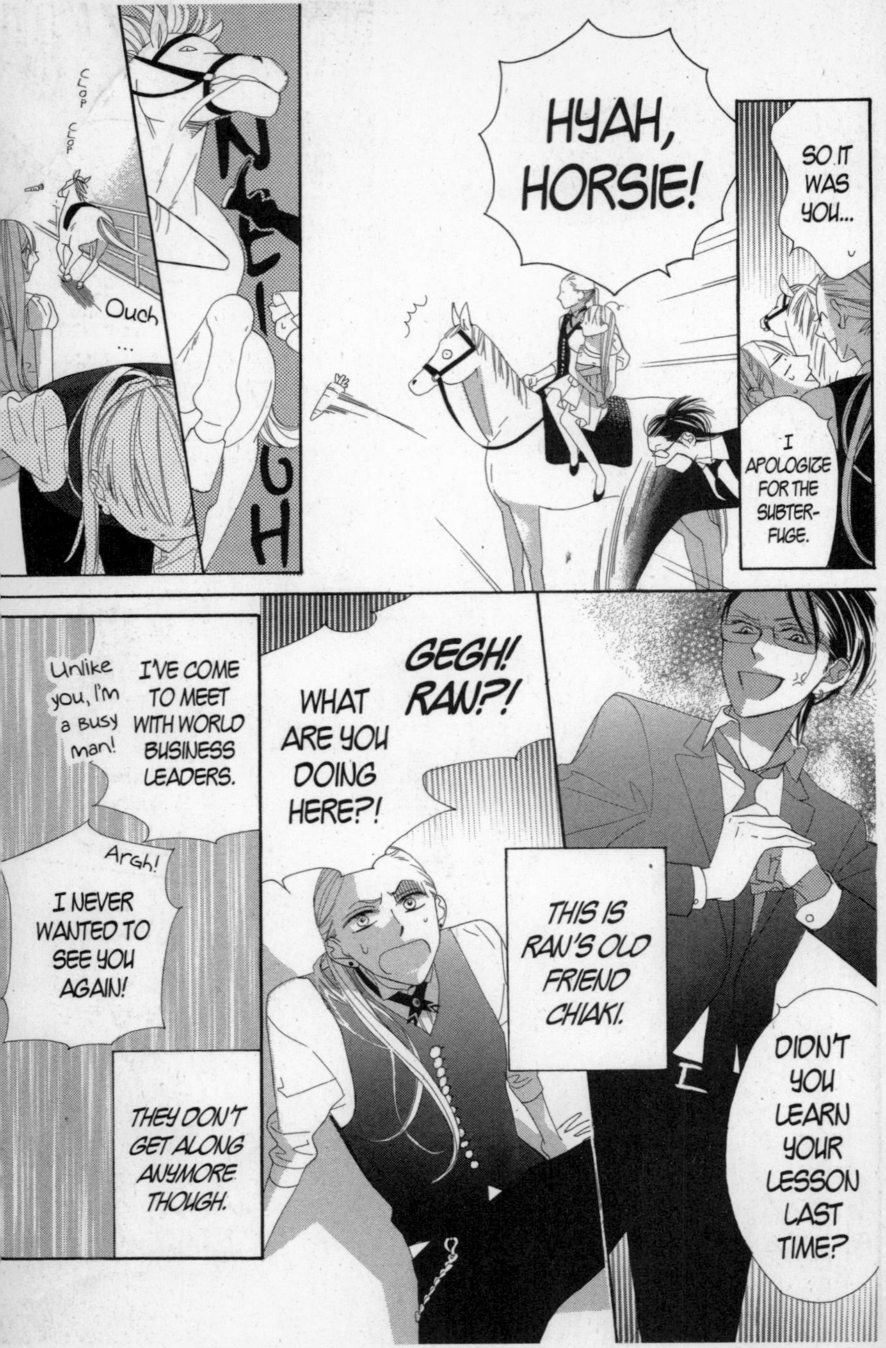
SO IT WAS YOU...
I APOLOGIZE FOR THE SUBTER-FUGE.
HYAH, HORSIE!
CLOP
CLOP
NEIGH
Ouch ...
DIDN'T YOU LEARN YOUR LESSON LAST TIME?
THIS IS RAN'S OLD FRIEND CHIAKI.
GEGH! RAN?!
WHAT ARE YOU DOING HERE?!
THEY DON'T GET ALONG ANYMORE THOUGH.
I'VE COME TO MEET WITH WORLD BUSINESS LEADERS.
Unlike you, I'm a busy man!
Argh!
I NEVER WANTED TO SEE YOU AGAIN!

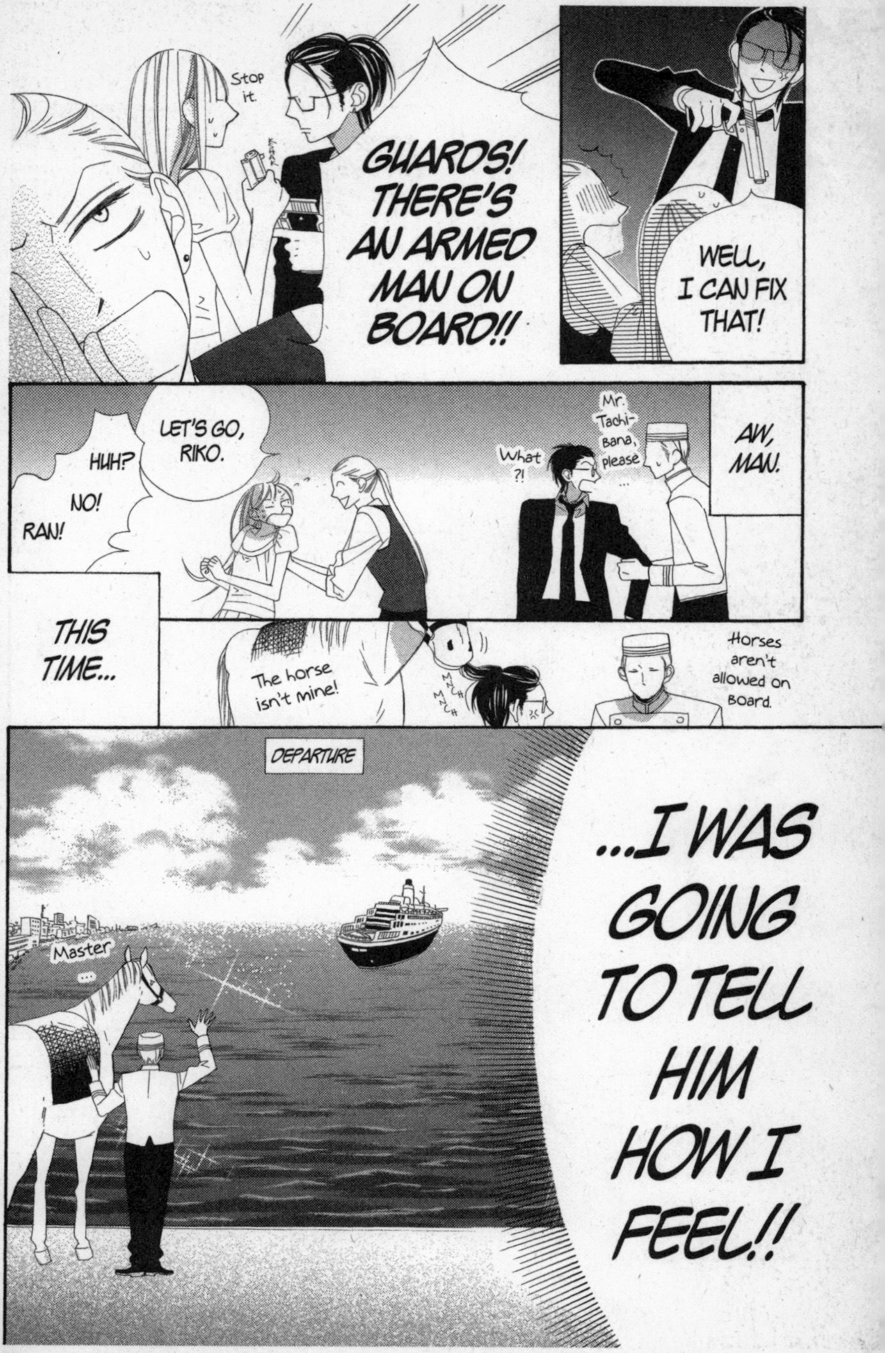
WELL, I CAN FIX THAT!
GUARDS! THERE'S AN ARMED MAN ON BOARD!!
Stop it.
KSHAK
AW, MAN.
Mr. Tachibana, please...
What?!
LET'S GO, RIKO.
HUH?
NO!
RAN!
Horses aren't allowed on board.
MNCH MNCH
The horse isn't mine!
THIS TIME...
...I WAS GOING TO TELL HIM HOW I FEEL!!
DEPARTURE
Master...

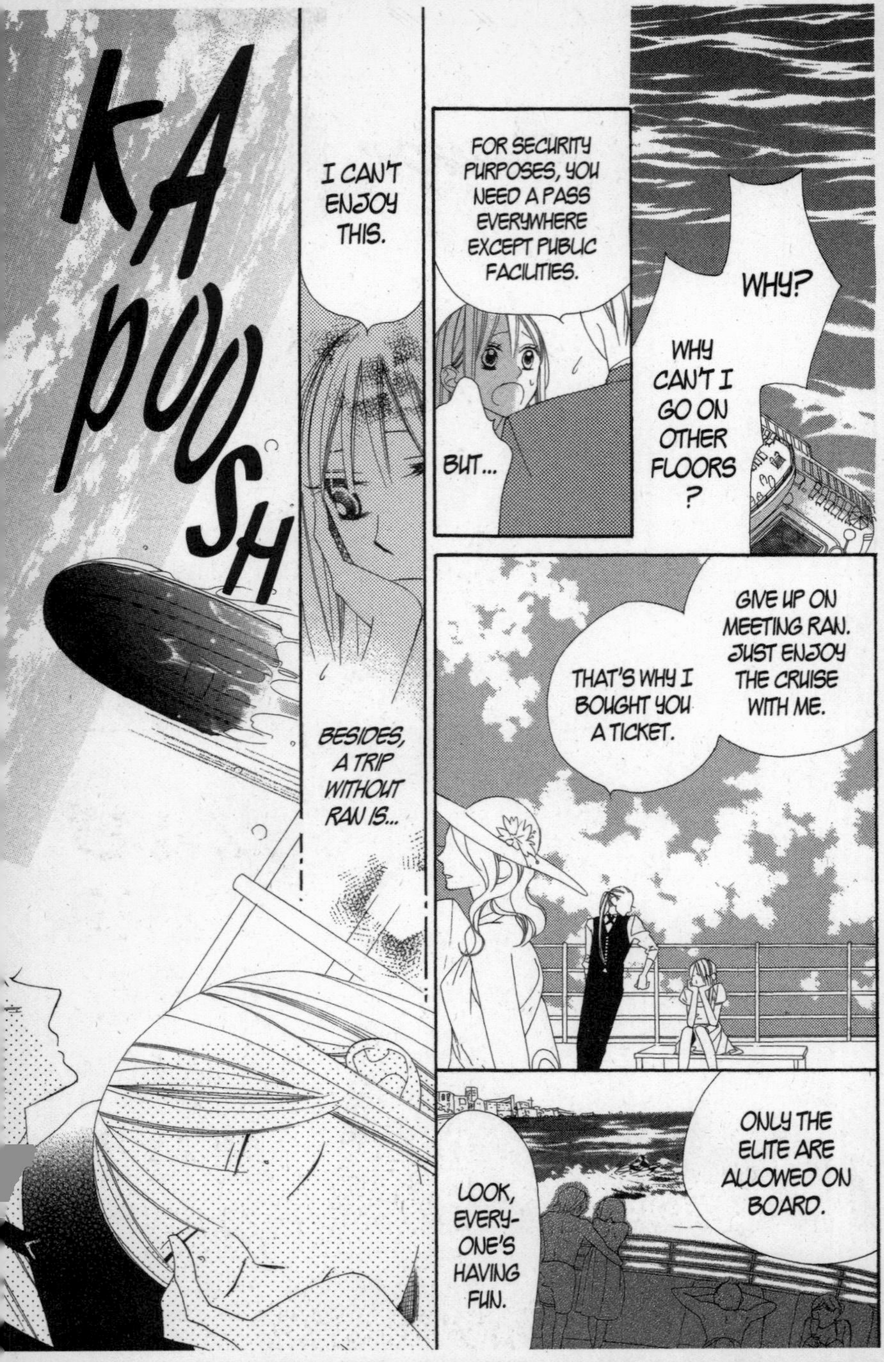
WHY?
WHY CAN'T I GO ON OTHER FLOORS?
FOR SECURITY PURPOSES, YOU NEED A PASS EVERYWHERE EXCEPT PUBLIC FACILITIES.
BUT...
GIVE UP ON MEETING RAN. JUST ENJOY THE CRUISE WITH ME.
THAT'S WHY I BOUGHT YOU A TICKET.
ONLY THE ELITE ARE ALLOWED ON BOARD.
LOOK, EVERY-ONE'S HAVING FUN.
I CAN'T ENJOY THIS.
BESIDES, A TRIP WITHOUT RAN IS...
KAPOOSH

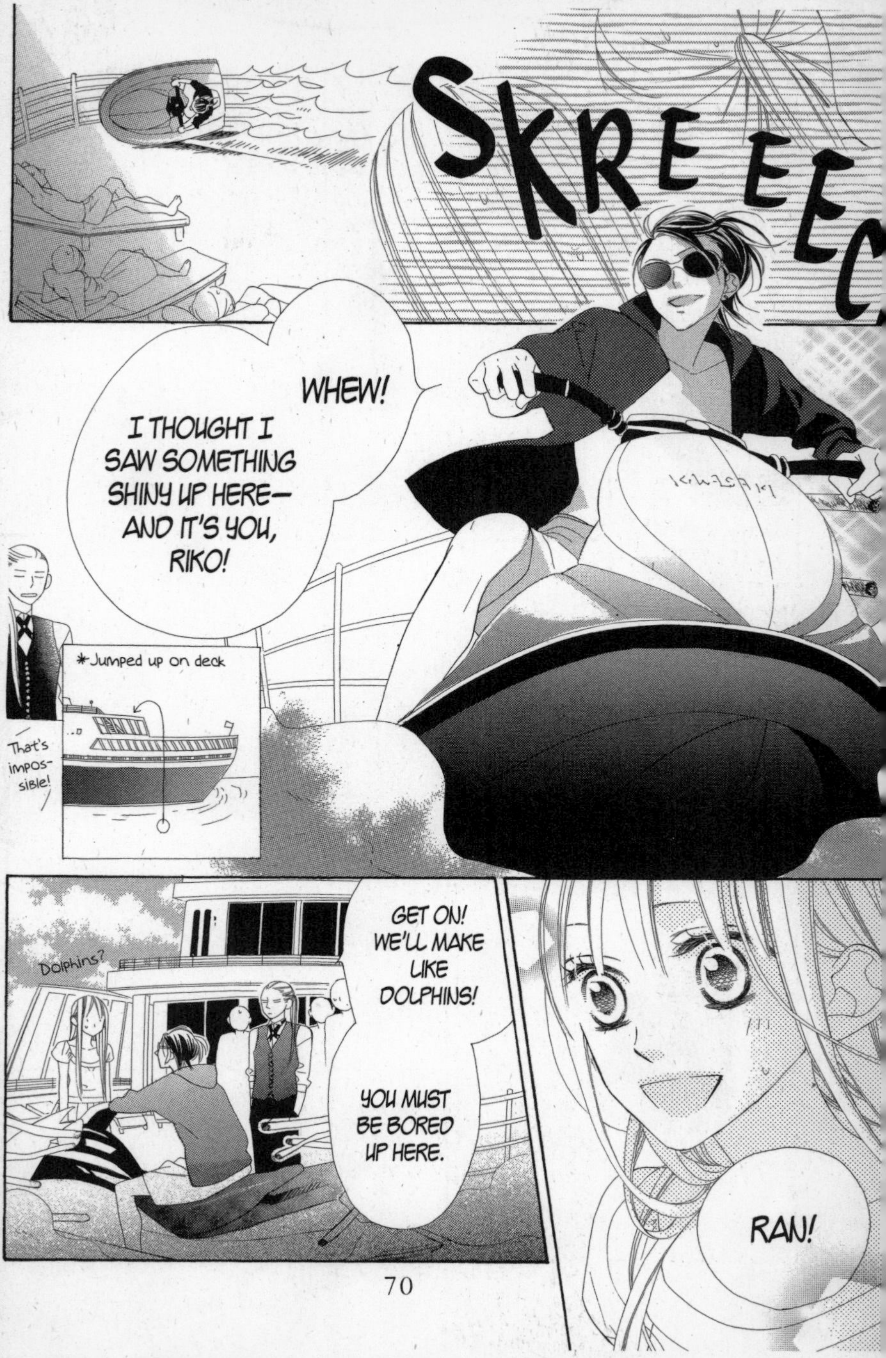
SKREEEC
WHEW!
I THOUGHT I SAW SOMETHING SHINY UP HERE— AND IT'S YOU, RIKO!
*Jumped up on deck
That's impossible!
RAN!
GET ON! WE'LL MAKE LIKE DOLPHINS!
YOU MUST BE BORED UP HERE.
Dolphins?

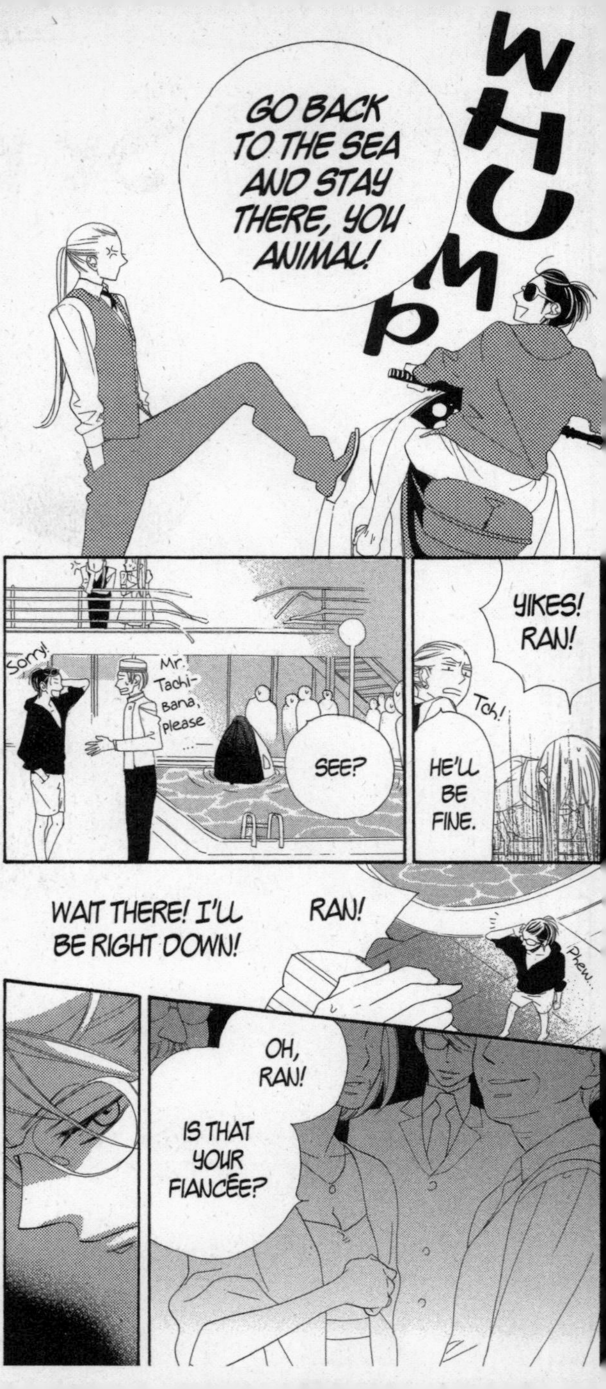

WHUMP
GO BACK TO THE SEA AND STAY THERE, YOU ANIMAL!
YIKES! RAN!
Tch!
HE'LL BE FINE.
SEE?
Mr. Tachi-bana, please ...
Sorry!
RAN!
Phew...
WAIT THERE! I'LL BE RIGHT DOWN!
OH, RAN!
IS THAT YOUR FIANCÉE?

A lot of people have mentioned Ran's hairstyle.

I like neat and tidy hairstyles, which is why so many characters in this manga don't have bangs. Nonetheless, in the latter half of the series I decided to try having more bangs. Did you notice?

I like suits, glasses and absurd hairstyles, but what I liked drawing the most was sideburns.

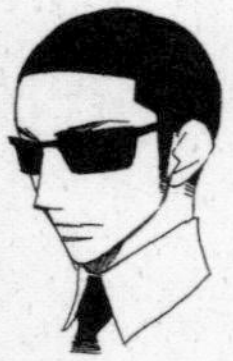

↑
The easiest character to draw

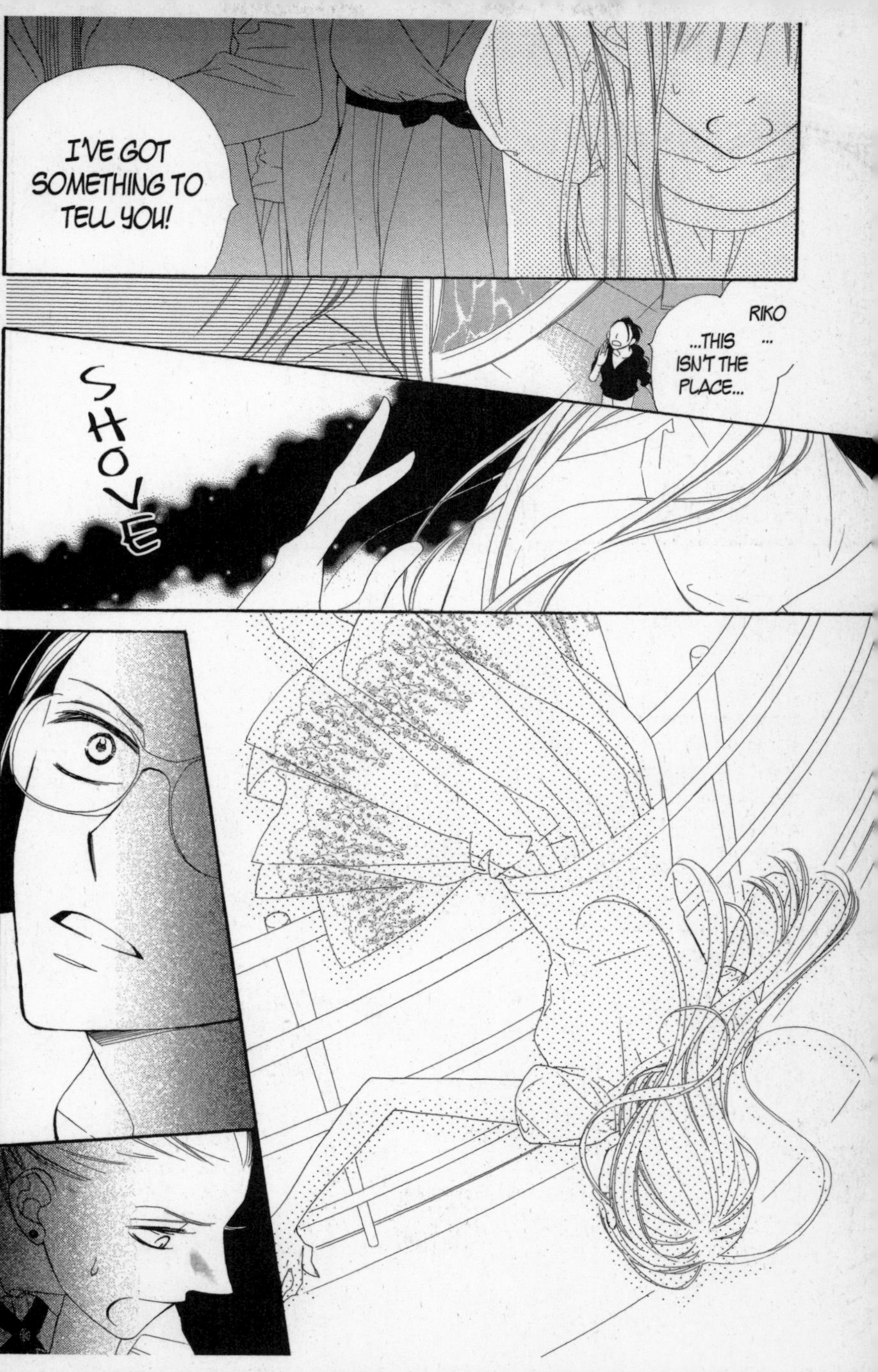
I'VE GOT SOMETHING TO TELL YOU!
RIKO ... ...THIS ISN'T THE PLACE...
SHOVE

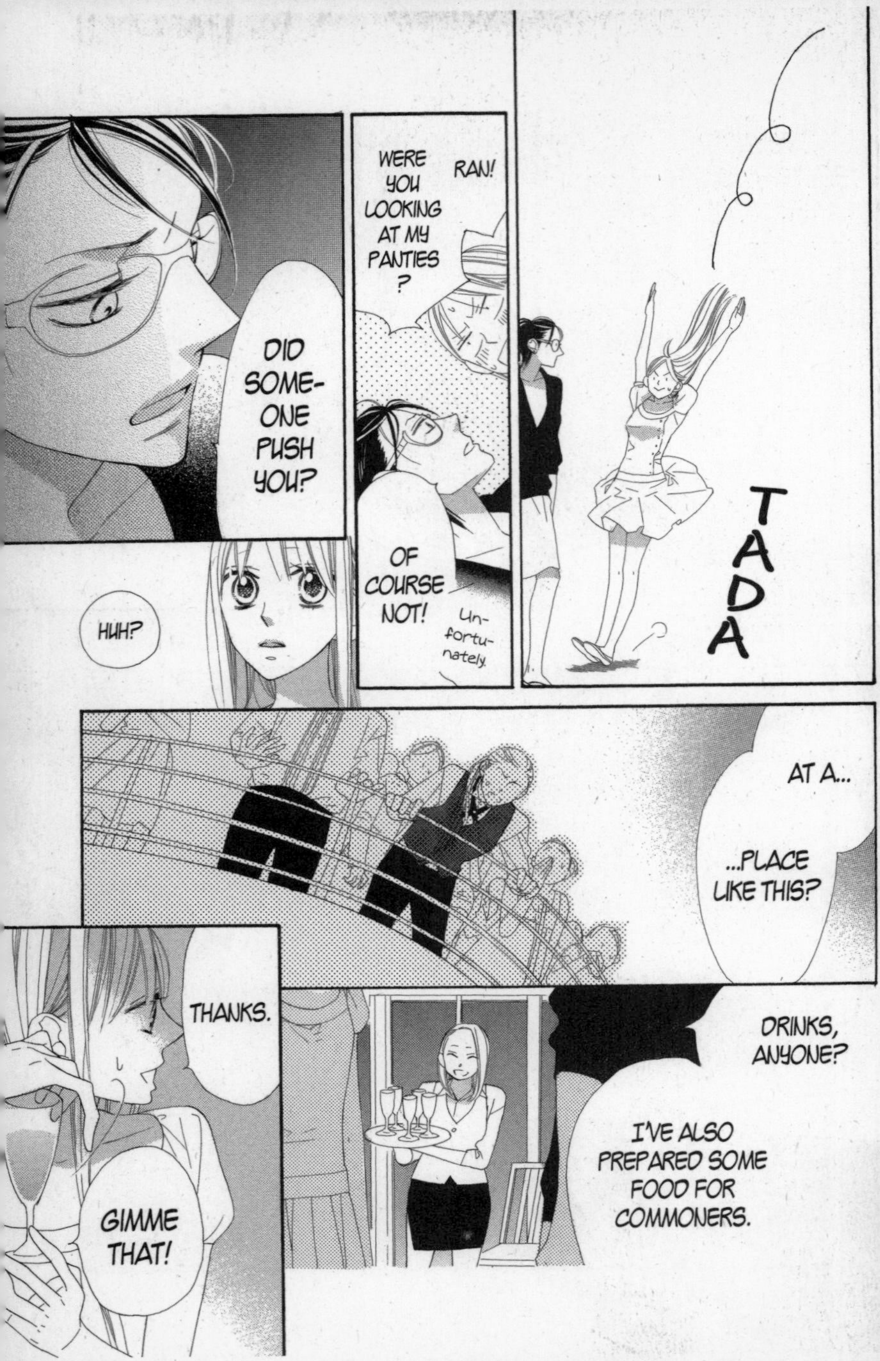
TADA
RAN!
WERE YOU LOOKING AT MY PANTIES?
OF COURSE NOT!
Unfortunately.
DID SOMEONE PUSH YOU?
HUH?
AT A...
...PLACE LIKE THIS?
DRINKS, ANYONE?
I'VE ALSO PREPARED SOME FOOD FOR COMMONERS.
THANKS.
GIMME THAT!

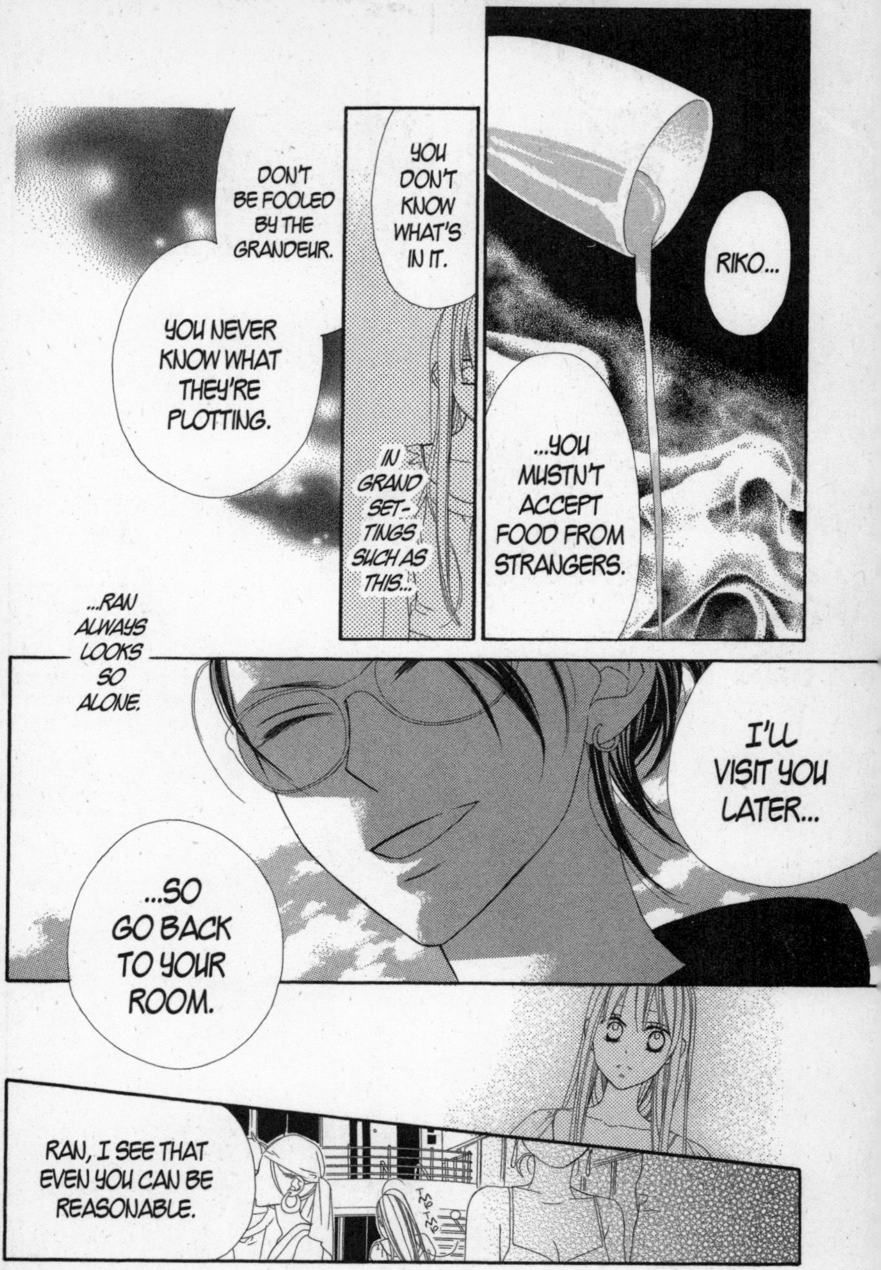
RIKO...
...YOU MUSTN'T ACCEPT FOOD FROM STRANGERS.
YOU DON'T KNOW WHAT'S IN IT.
IN GRAND SET-TINGS SUCH AS THIS...
DON'T BE FOOLED BY THE GRANDEUR.
YOU NEVER KNOW WHAT THEY'RE PLOTTING.
I'LL VISIT YOU LATER...
...SO GO BACK TO YOUR ROOM.
...RAN ALWAYS LOOKS SO ALONE.
RAN, I SEE THAT EVEN YOU CAN BE REASONABLE.

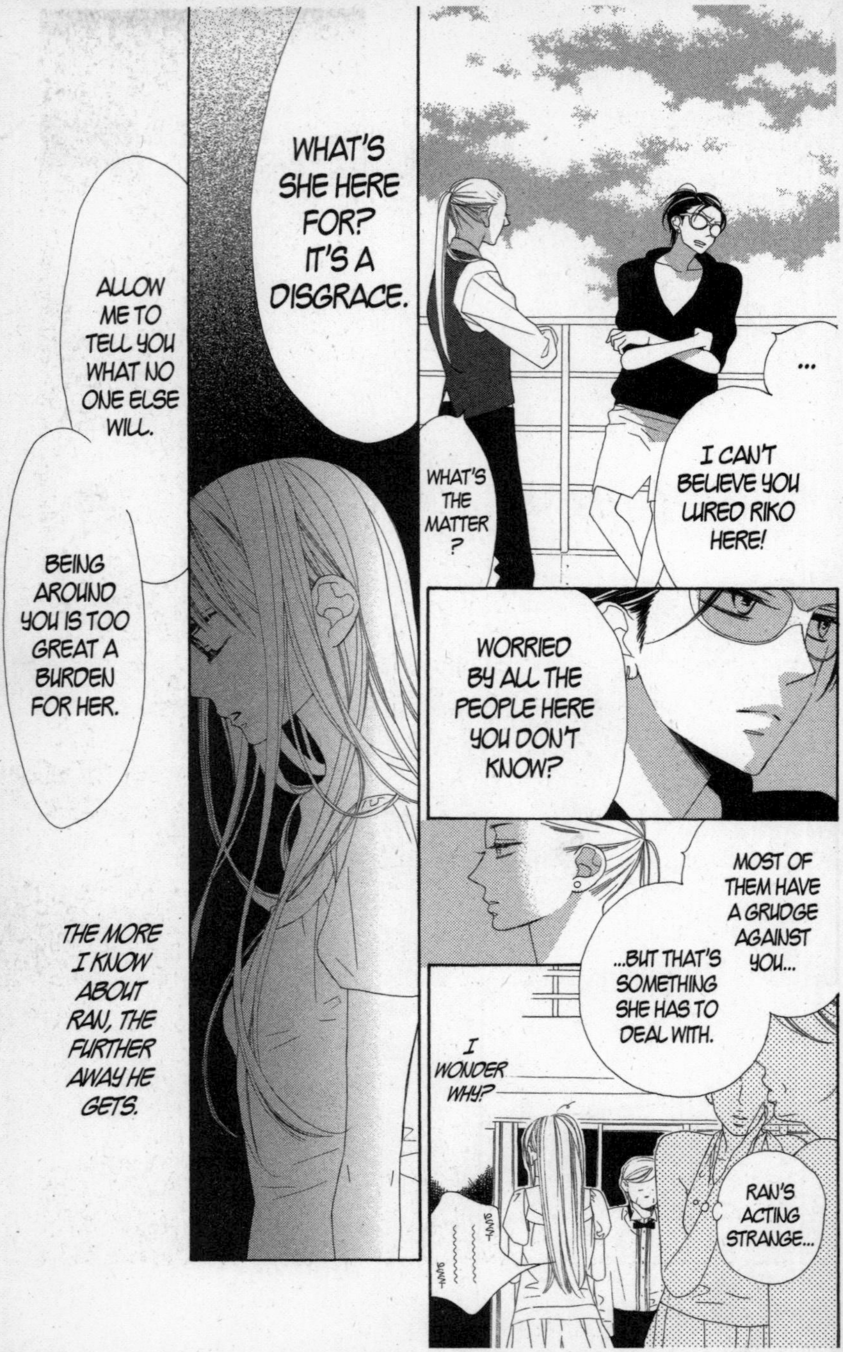
...
I CAN'T BELIEVE YOU LURED RIKO HERE!
WHAT'S THE MATTER?
WORRIED BY ALL THE PEOPLE HERE YOU DON'T KNOW?
MOST OF THEM HAVE A GRUDGE AGAINST YOU...
...BUT THAT'S SOMETHING SHE HAS TO DEAL WITH.
RAN'S ACTING STRANGE...
I WONDER WHY?
WHAT'S SHE HERE FOR? IT'S A DISGRACE.
ALLOW ME TO TELL YOU WHAT NO ONE ELSE WILL.
BEING AROUND YOU IS TOO GREAT A BURDEN FOR HER.
THE MORE I KNOW ABOUT RAN, THE FURTHER AWAY HE GETS.

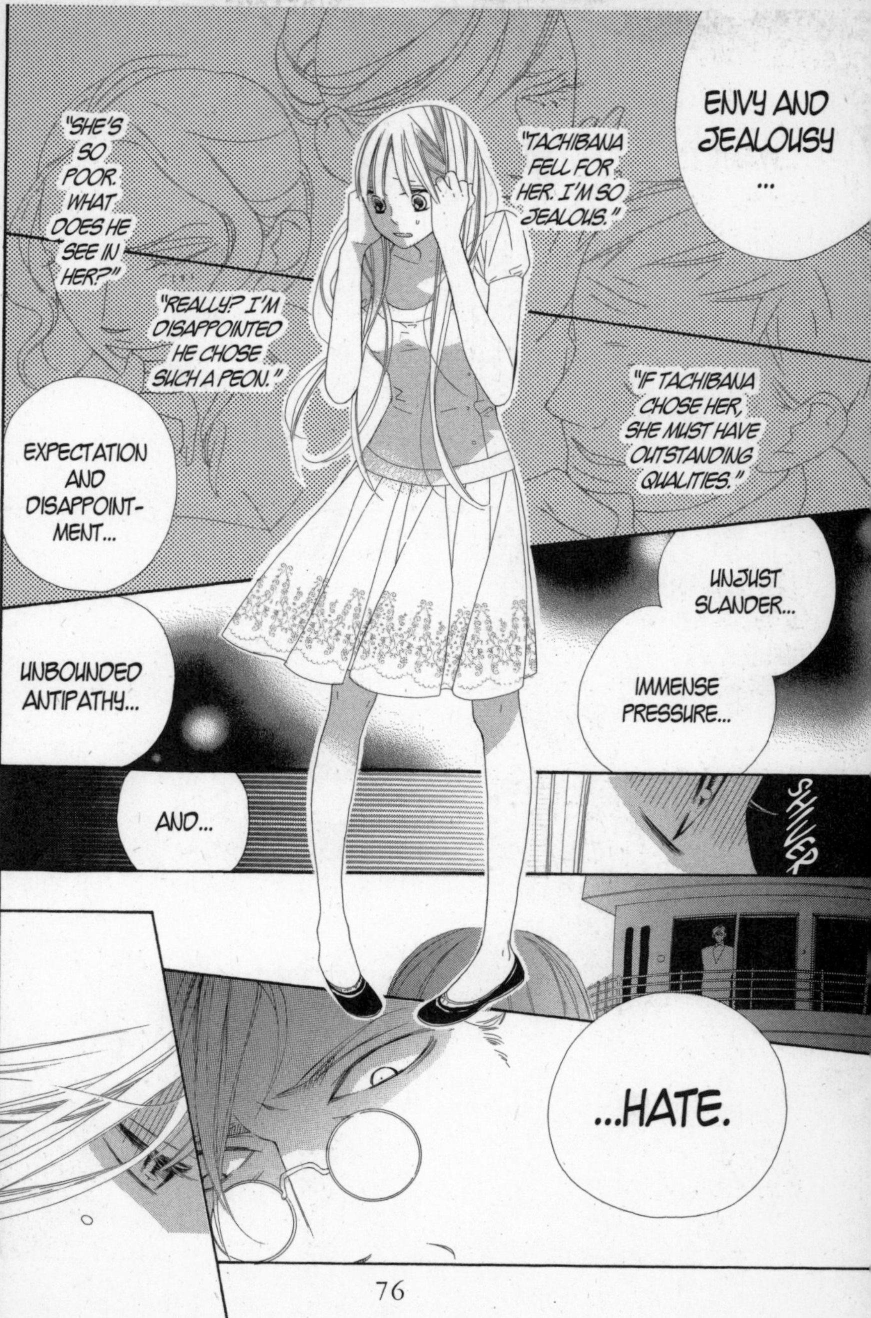
ENVY AND JEALOUSY ...
"TACHIBANA FELL FOR HER. I'M SO JEALOUS."
"SHE'S SO POOR. WHAT DOES HE SEE IN HER?"
"IF TACHIBANA CHOSE HER, SHE MUST HAVE OUTSTANDING QUALITIES."
"REALLY? I'M DISAPPOINTED HE CHOSE SUCH A PEON."
EXPECTATION AND DISAPPOINTMENT...
UNJUST SLANDER...
IMMENSE PRESSURE...
UNBOUNDED ANTIPATHY...
SHIVER
AND...
...HATE.

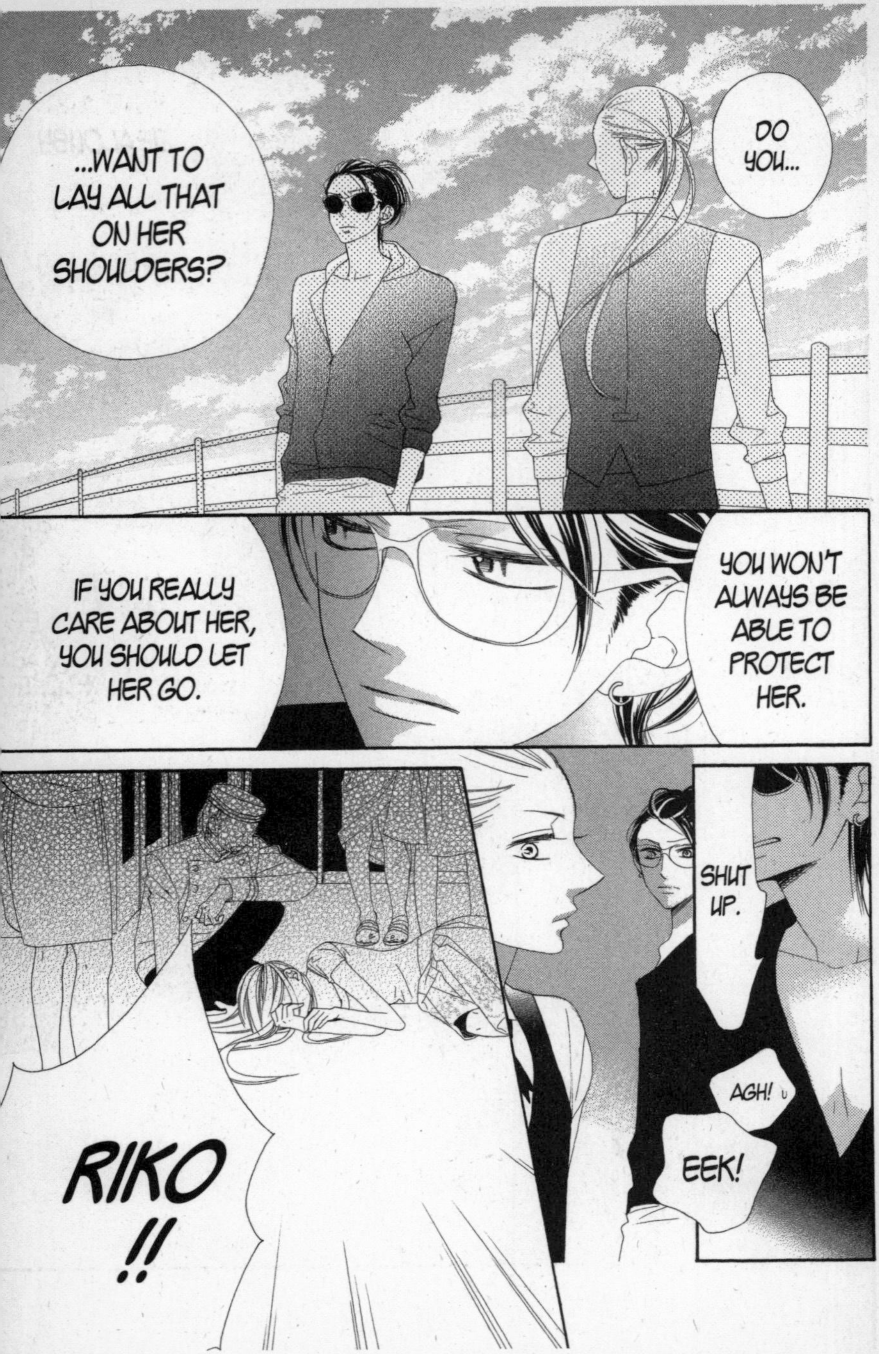
DO YOU...
...WANT TO LAY ALL THAT ON HER SHOULDERS?
YOU WON'T ALWAYS BE ABLE TO PROTECT HER.
IF YOU REALLY CARE ABOUT HER, YOU SHOULD LET HER GO.
SHUT UP.
AGH!
EEK!
RIKO!!

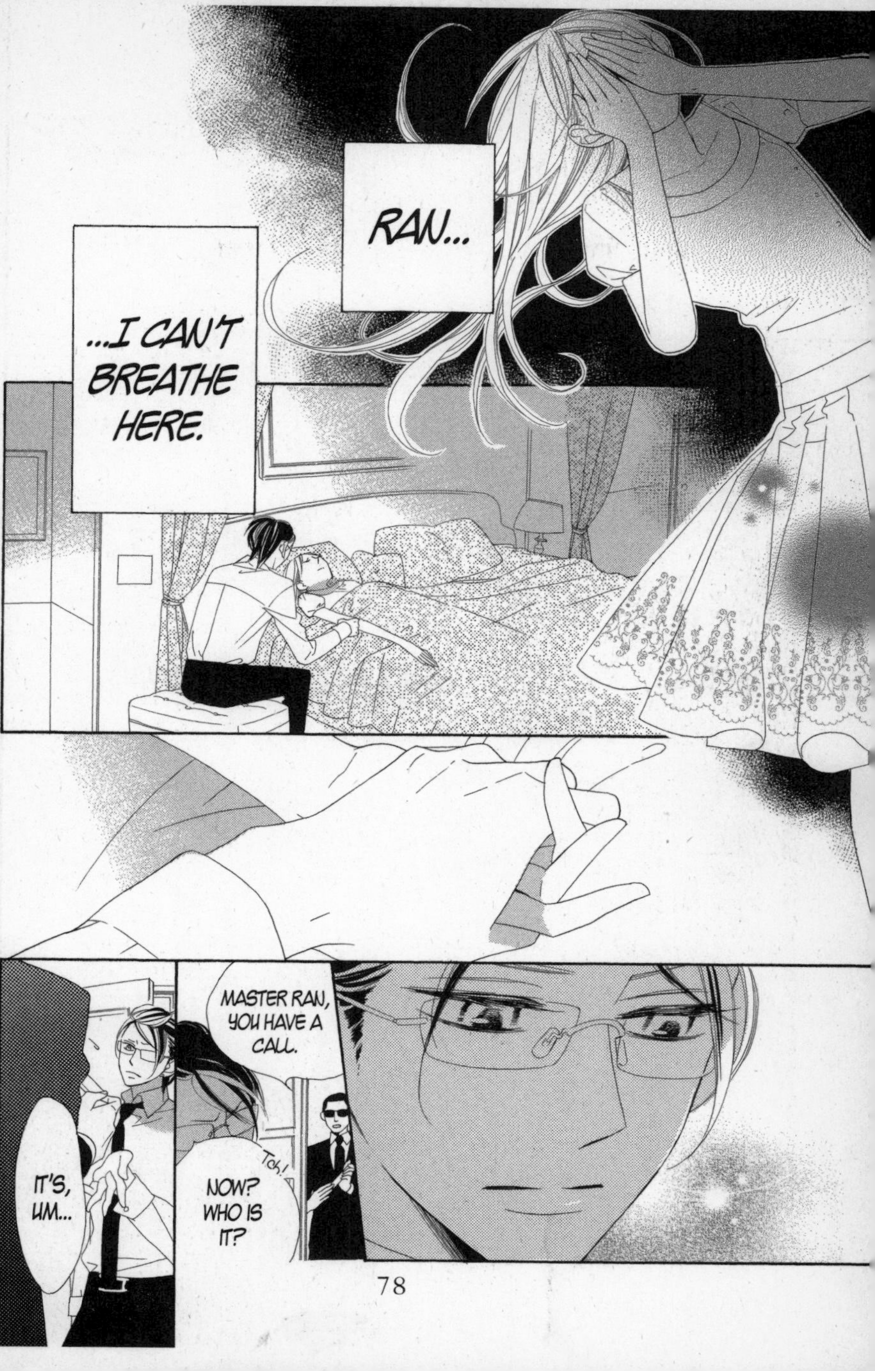
RAN...
...I CAN'T BREATHE HERE.
MASTER RAN, YOU HAVE A CALL.
Tch!
NOW? WHO IS IT?
IT'S, UM...

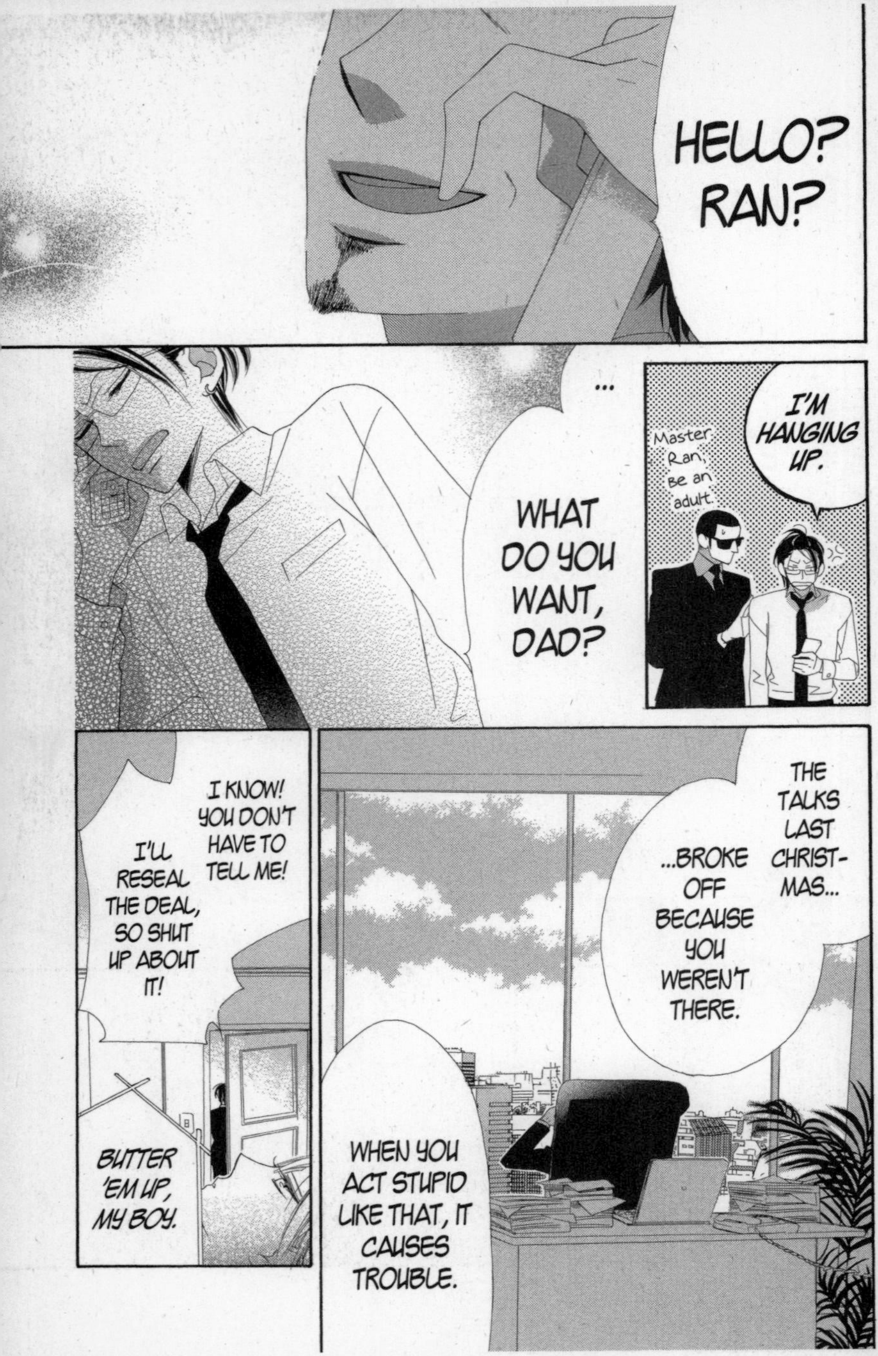
HELLO? RAN?
I'M HANGING UP.
Master Ran, Be an adult.
...
WHAT DO YOU WANT, DAD?
THE TALKS LAST CHRISTMAS...
...BROKE OFF BECAUSE YOU WEREN'T THERE.
WHEN YOU ACT STUPID LIKE THAT, IT CAUSES TROUBLE.
I KNOW! YOU DON'T HAVE TO TELL ME!
I'LL RESEAL THE DEAL, SO SHUT UP ABOUT IT!
BUTTER 'EM UP, MY BOY.

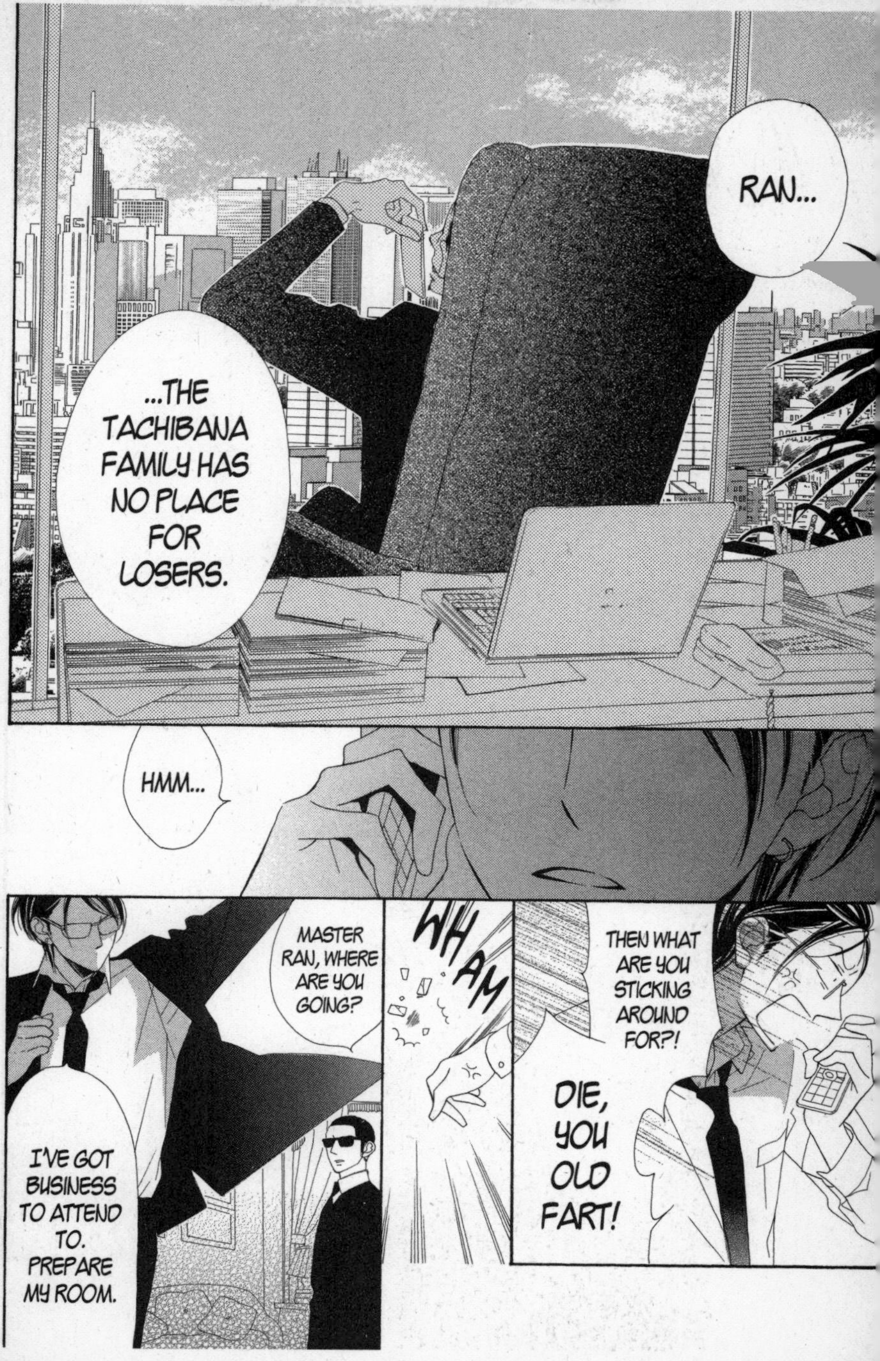
RAN...
...THE TACHIBANA FAMILY HAS NO PLACE FOR LOSERS.
HMM...
THEN WHAT ARE YOU STICKING AROUND FOR?!
DIE, YOU OLD FART!
WHAM
MASTER RAN, WHERE ARE YOU GOING?
I'VE GOT BUSINESS TO ATTEND TO. PREPARE MY ROOM.

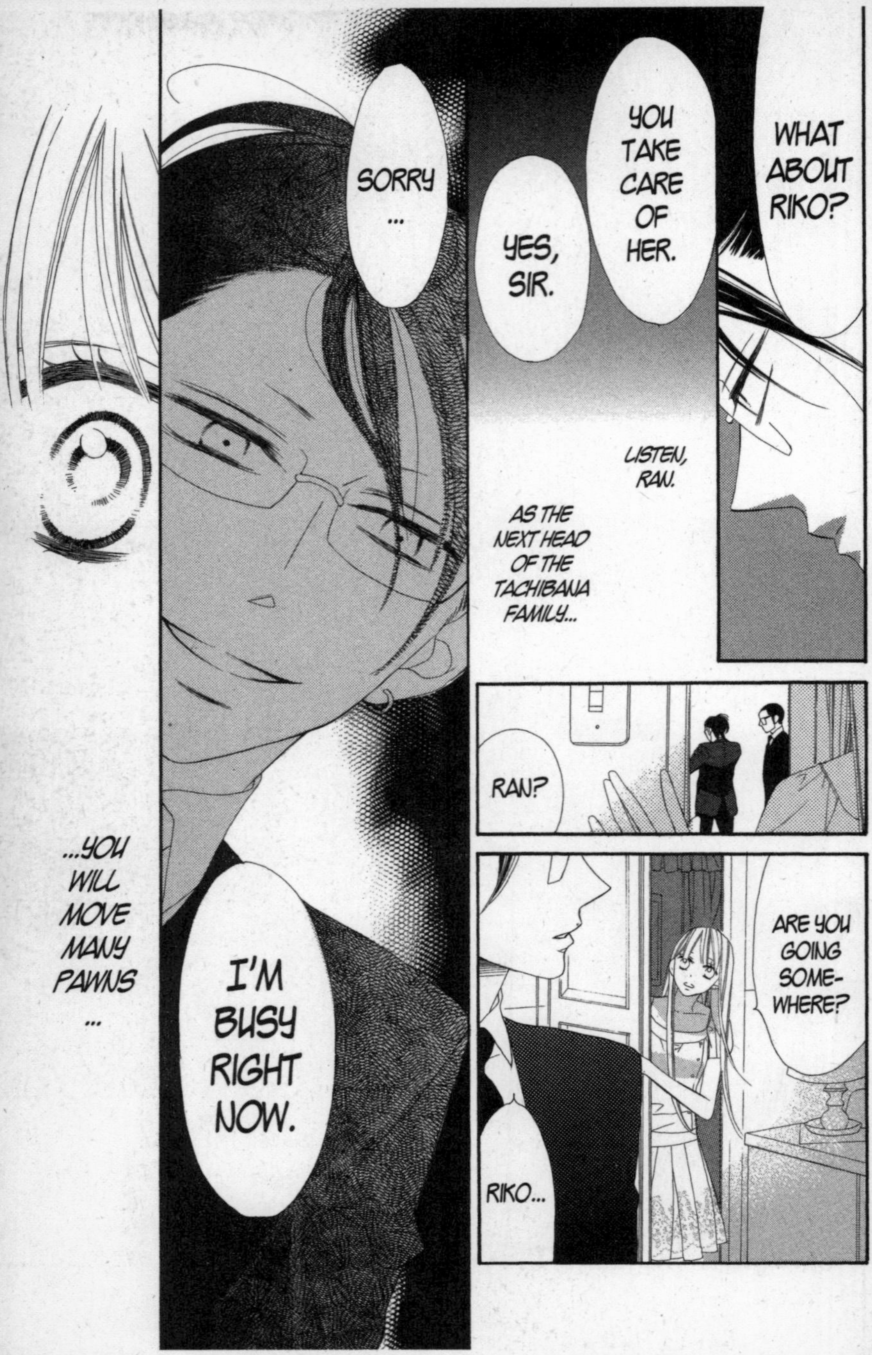
WHAT ABOUT RIKO?
YOU TAKE CARE OF HER.
YES, SIR.
LISTEN, RAN.
AS THE NEXT HEAD OF THE TACHIBANA FAMILY...
RAN?
ARE YOU GOING SOME-WHERE?
RIKO...
SORRY...
I'M BUSY RIGHT NOW.
...YOU WILL MOVE MANY PAWNS...

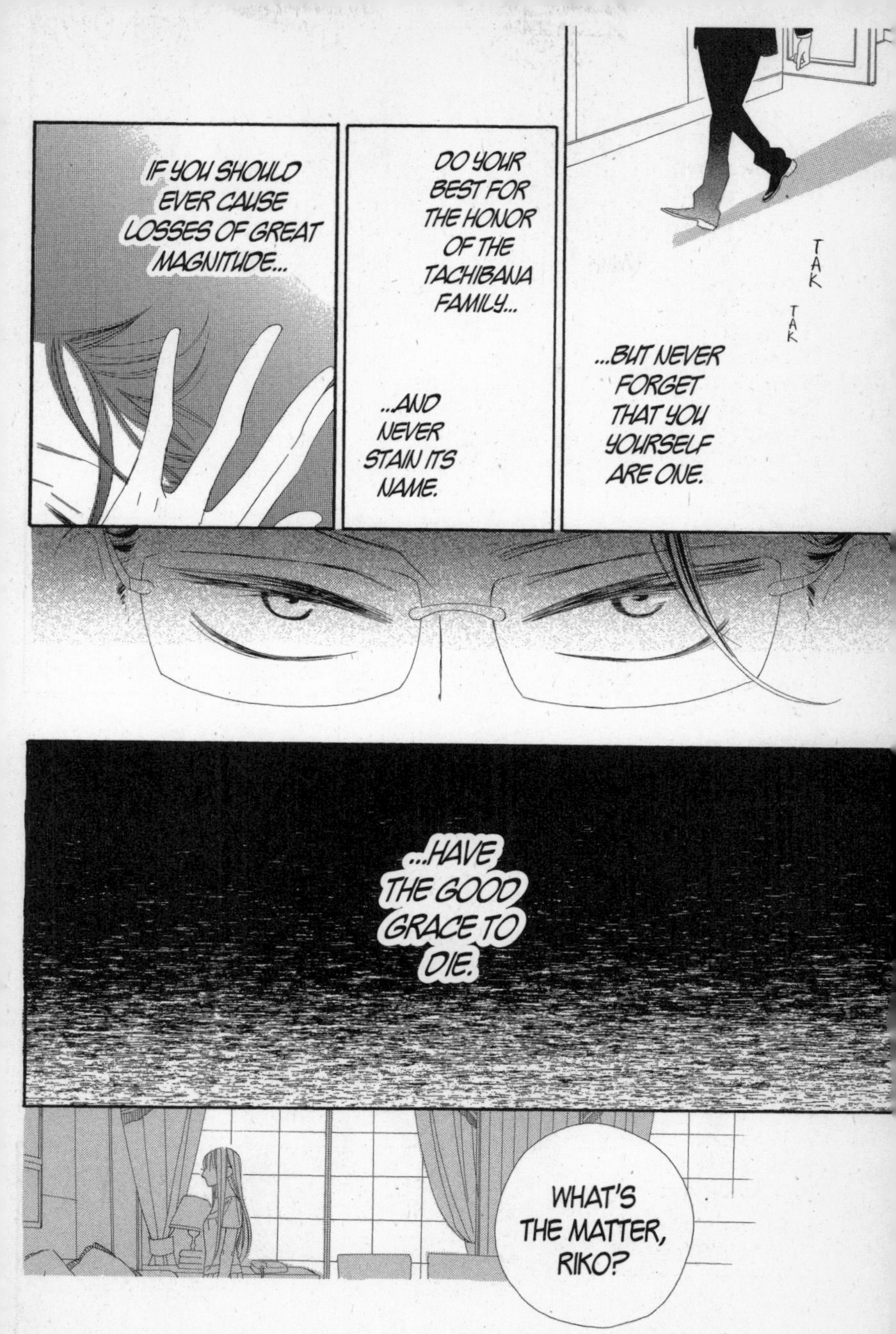
TAK
TAK
...BUT NEVER FORGET THAT YOU YOURSELF ARE ONE.
DO YOUR BEST FOR THE HONOR OF THE TACHIBANA FAMILY...
...AND NEVER STAIN ITS NAME.
IF YOU SHOULD EVER CAUSE LOSSES OF GREAT MAGNITUDE...
...HAVE THE GOOD GRACE TO DIE.
WHAT'S THE MATTER, RIKO?

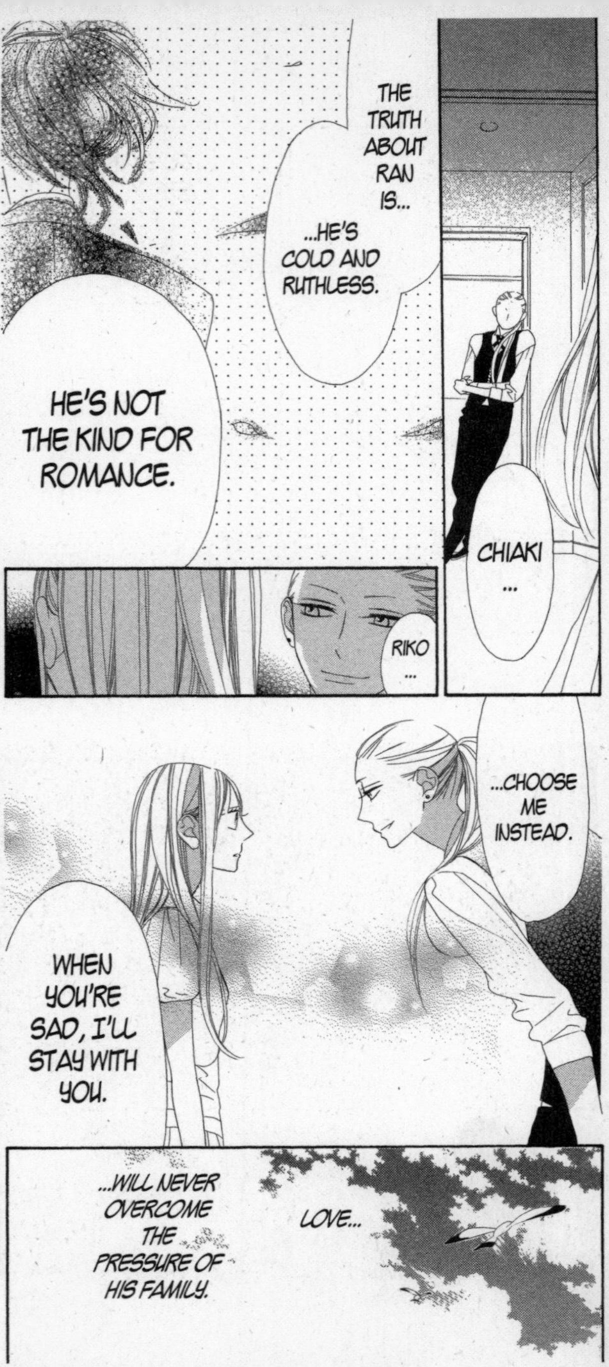
CHIAKI ...
THE TRUTH ABOUT RAN IS...
...HE'S COLD AND RUTHLESS.
HE'S NOT THE KIND FOR ROMANCE.
RIKO ...
...CHOOSE ME INSTEAD.
WHEN YOU'RE SAD, I'LL STAY WITH YOU.
LOVE...
...WILL NEVER OVERCOME THE PRESSURE OF HIS FAMILY.

Flower in a Storm
About Volume 1

When I saw the final book, I was impressed. I handed the graphic novel editor a mess of illustrations, but it turned out great. That impressed me. The table of contents and logo-thingies on the chapter title pages were so cute! If you've got volume 1, check 'em out!

As I was working, it was a solitary struggle, but when the graphic novel came out, I realized lots of people were rooting for me. I'm truly a lucky person.

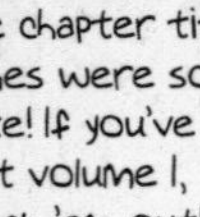
Flower in a Storm

Flower in a Storm 1
Check it out!

(What is this? An advertisement?)

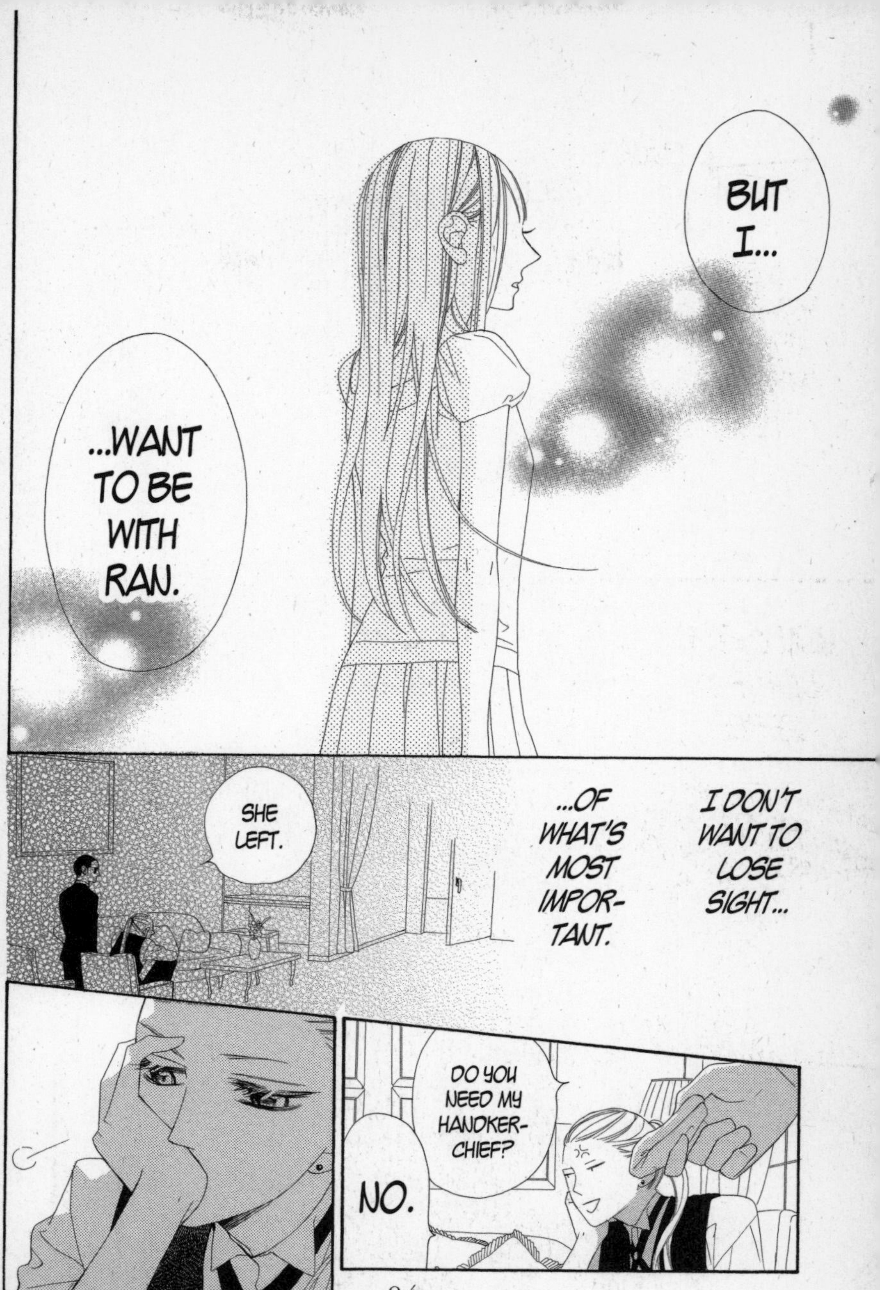
BUT I...
...WANT TO BE WITH RAN.
I DON'T WANT TO LOSE SIGHT...
...OF WHAT'S MOST IMPOR-TANT.
SHE LEFT.
DO YOU NEED MY HANDKER-CHIEF?
NO.

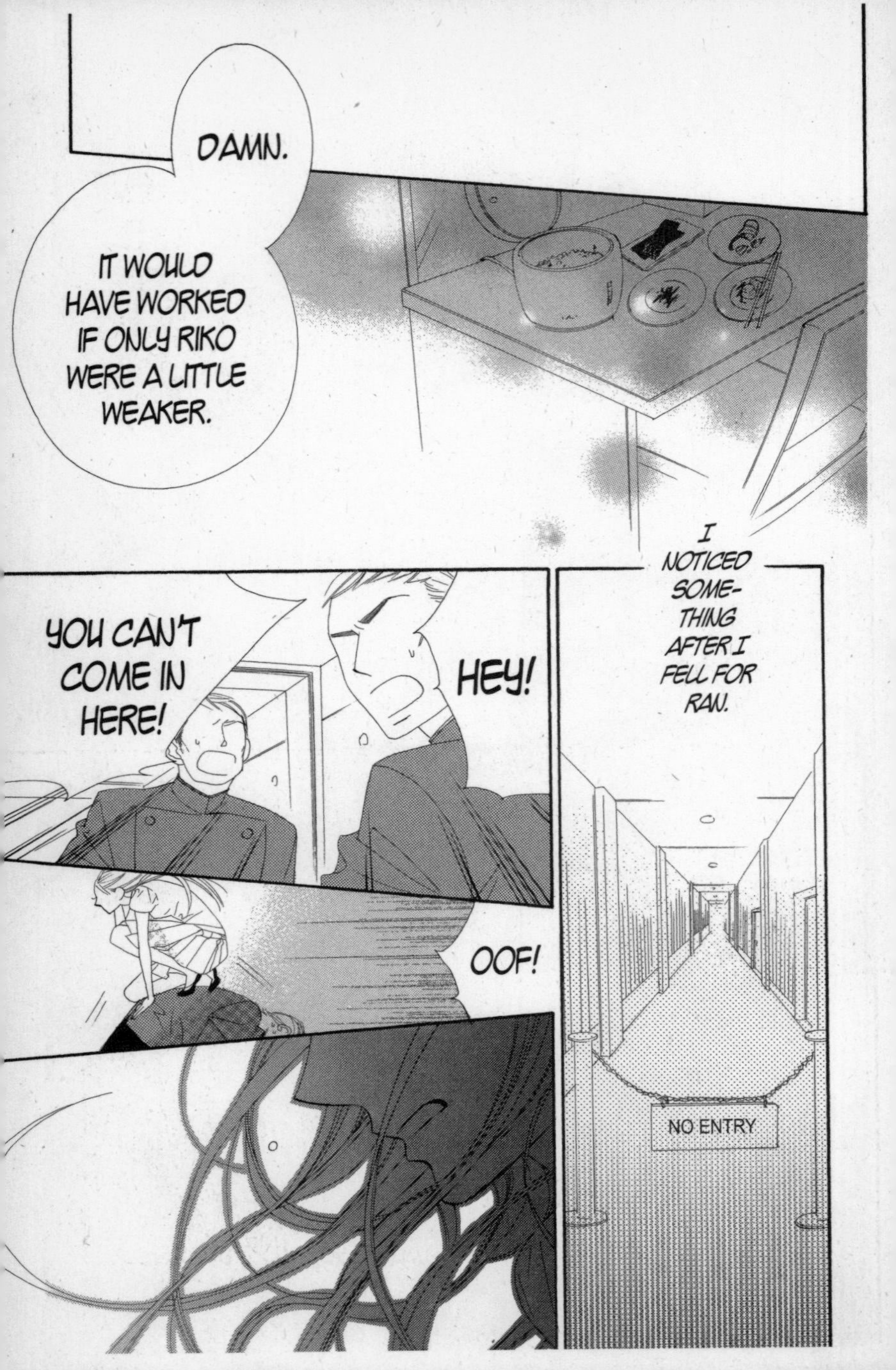
DAMN.
IT WOULD HAVE WORKED IF ONLY RIKO WERE A LITTLE WEAKER.
I NOTICED SOME-THING AFTER I FELL FOR RAN.
NO ENTRY
HEY!
YOU CAN'T COME IN HERE!
OOF!

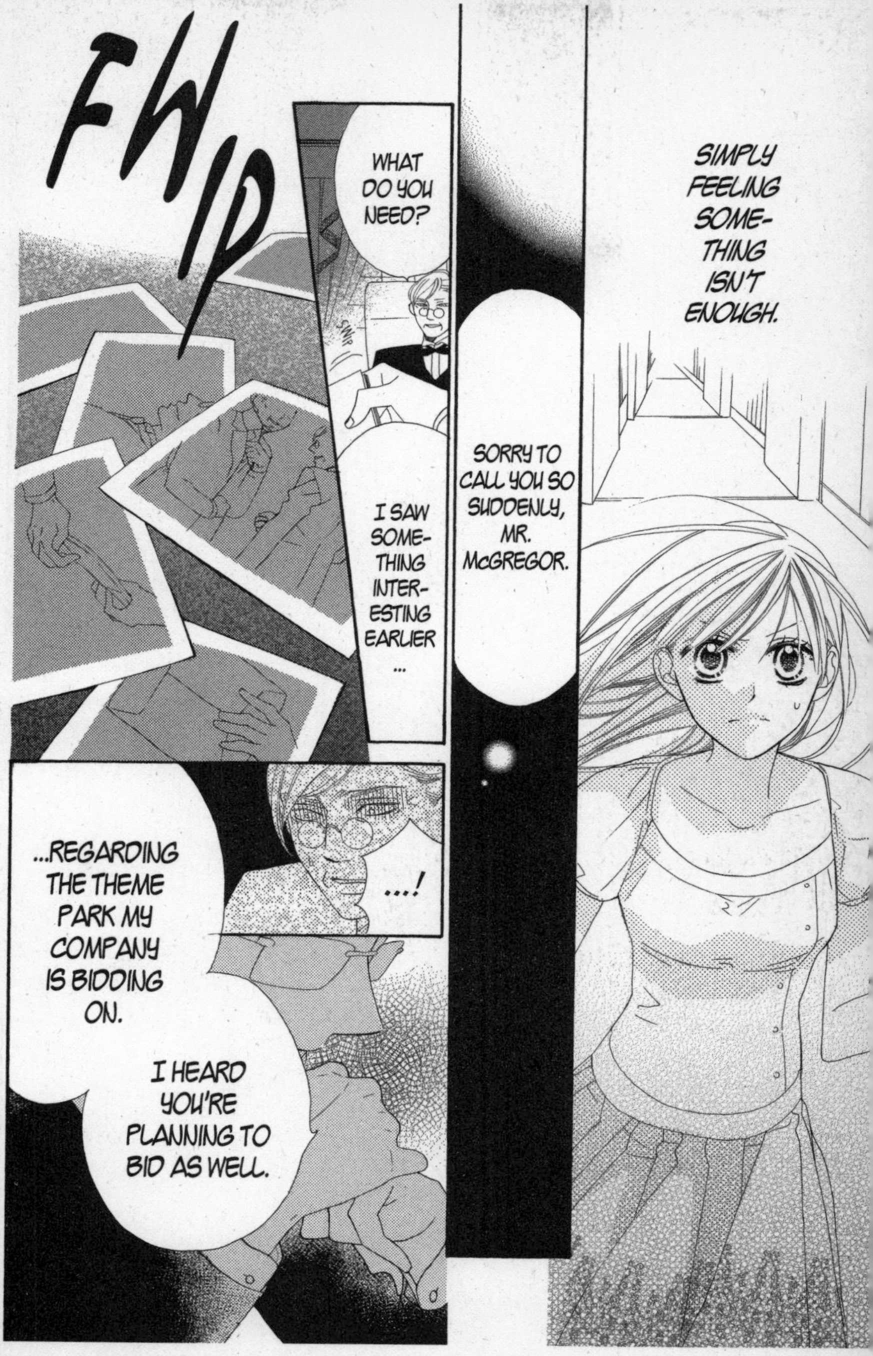
SIMPLY FEELING SOME-THING ISN'T ENOUGH.
SORRY TO CALL YOU SO SUDDENLY, MR. McGREGOR.
WHAT DO YOU NEED?
I SAW SOME-THING INTER-ESTING EARLIER ...
FWIP
...!
...REGARDING THE THEME PARK MY COMPANY IS BIDDING ON.
I HEARD YOU'RE PLANNING TO BID AS WELL.

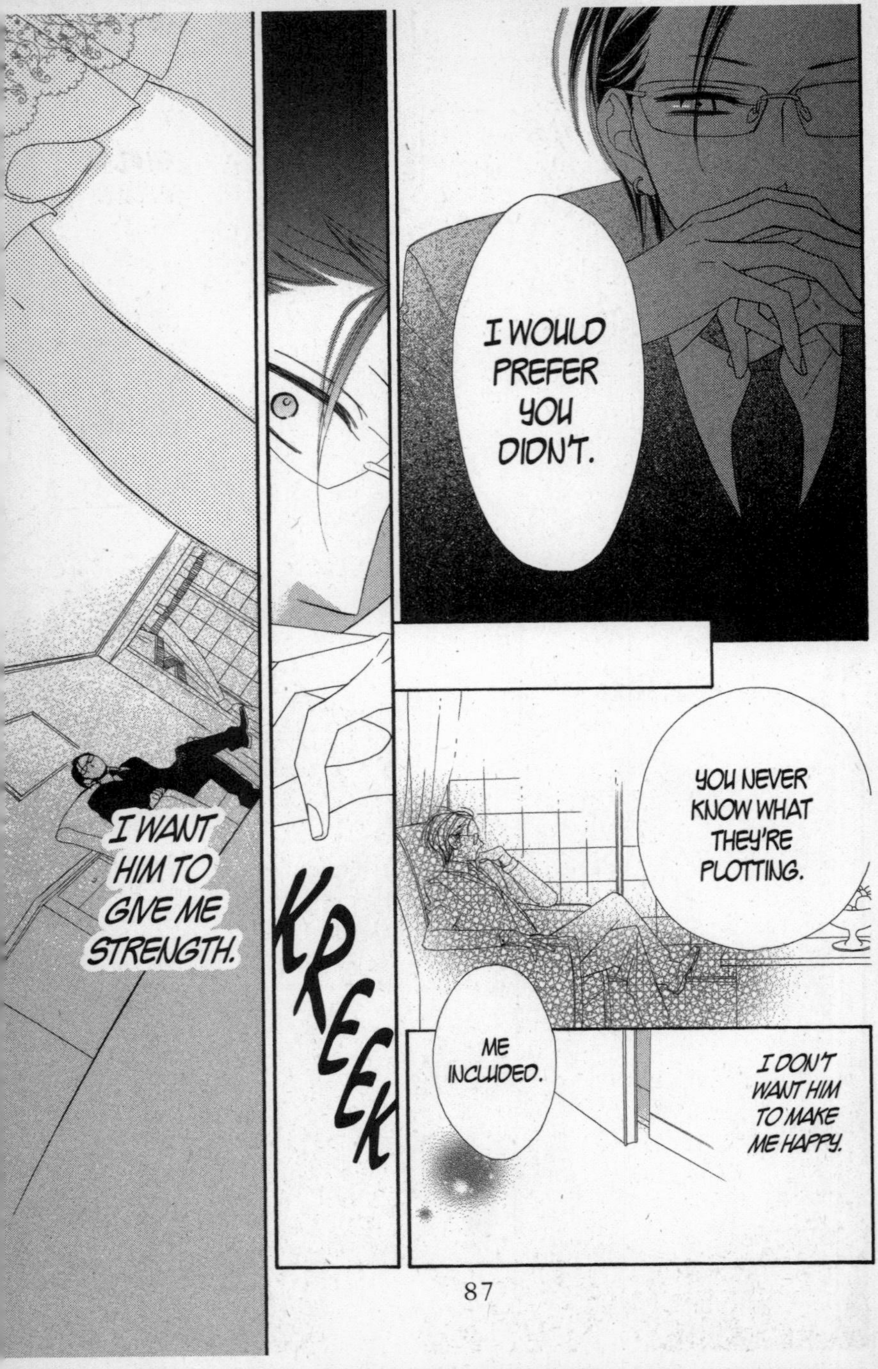
I WOULD PREFER YOU DIDN'T.
YOU NEVER KNOW WHAT THEY'RE PLOTTING.
ME INCLUDED.
I DON'T WANT HIM TO MAKE ME HAPPY.
KREEEK
I WANT HIM TO GIVE ME STRENGTH.

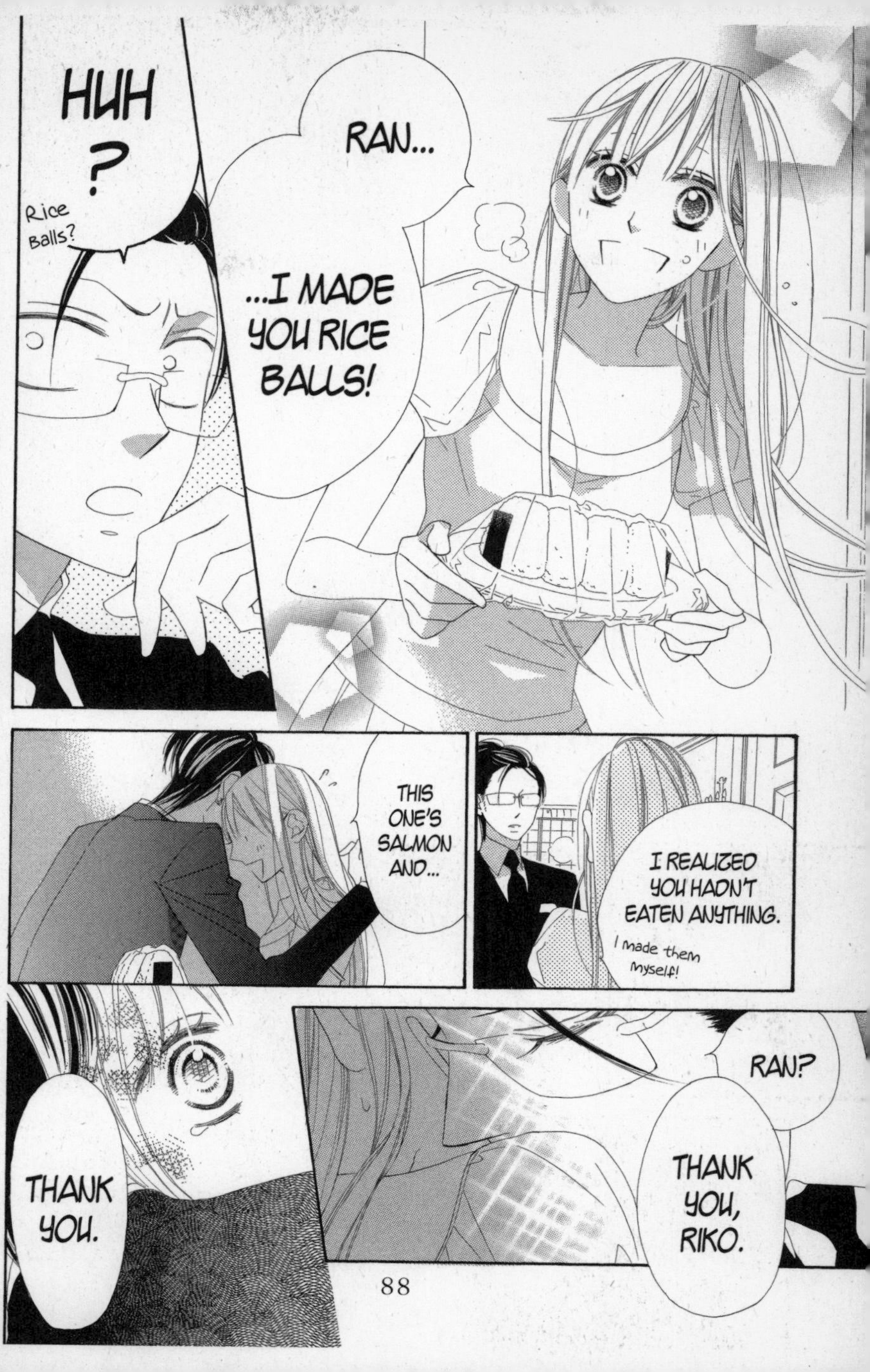
RAN...
...I MADE YOU RICE BALLS!
HUH ?
Rice Balls?
I REALIZED YOU HADN'T EATEN ANYTHING.
I made them Myself!
THIS ONE'S SALMON AND...
RAN?
THANK YOU, RIKO.
THANK YOU.

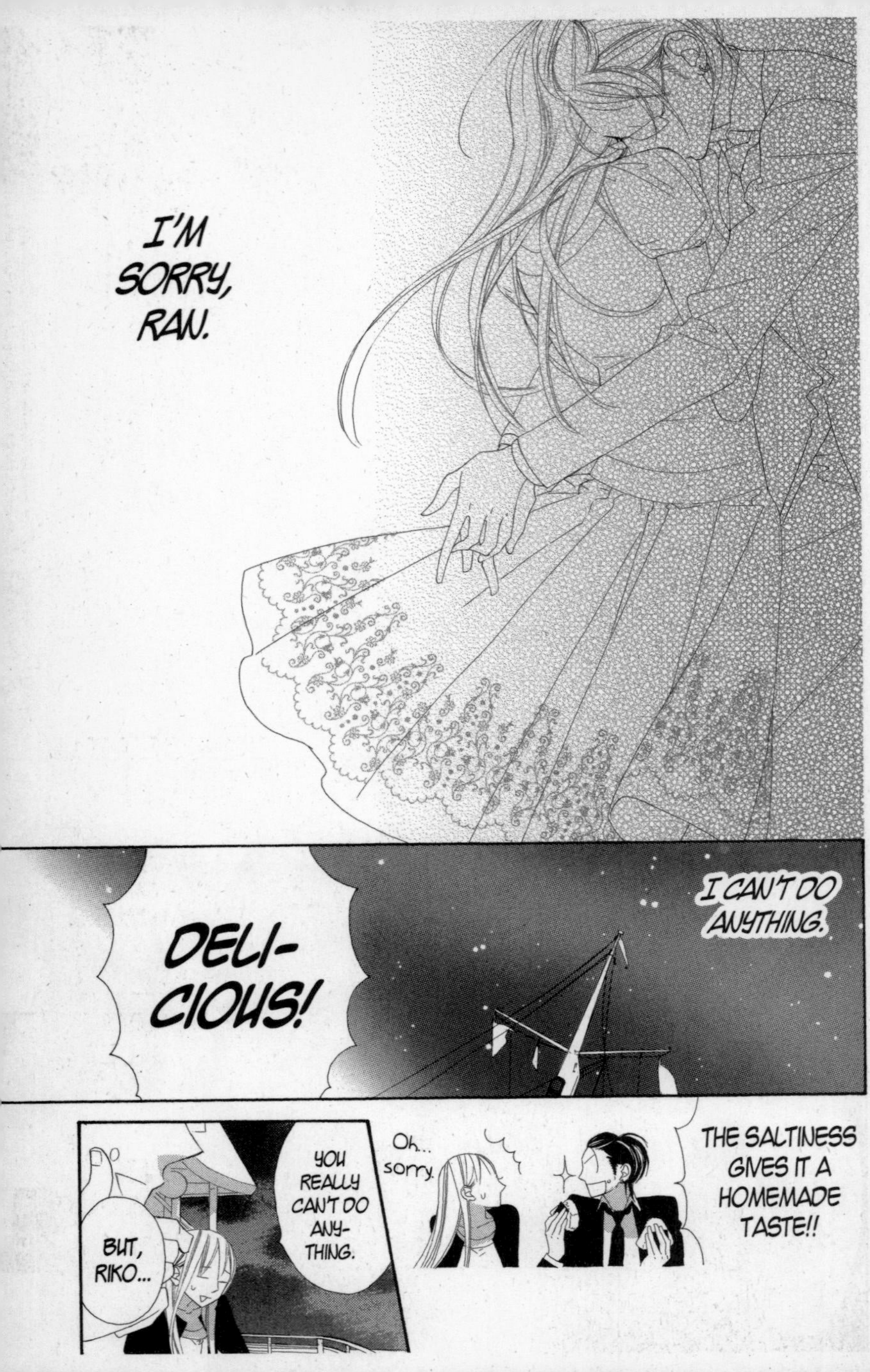
I'M SORRY, RAN.
I CAN'T DO ANYTHING.
DELI-CIOUS!
THE SALTINESS GIVES IT A HOMEMADE TASTE!!
Oh... sorry.
YOU REALLY CAN'T DO ANY-THING.
BUT, RIKO...

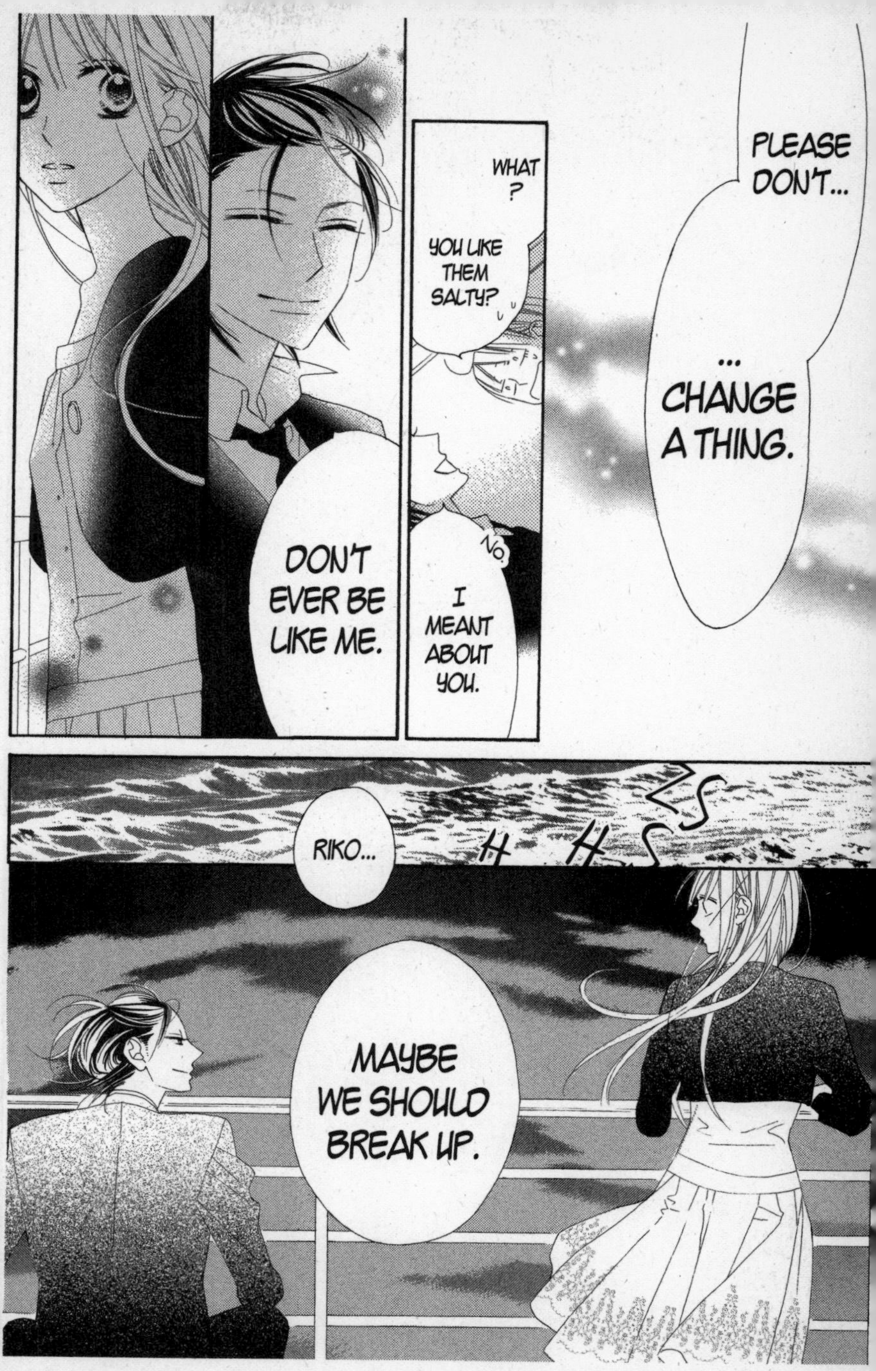
PLEASE DON'T...
...CHANGE A THING.
WHAT?
YOU LIKE THEM SALTY?
NO.
I MEANT ABOUT YOU.
DON'T EVER BE LIKE ME.
RIKO...
MAYBE WE SHOULD BREAK UP.

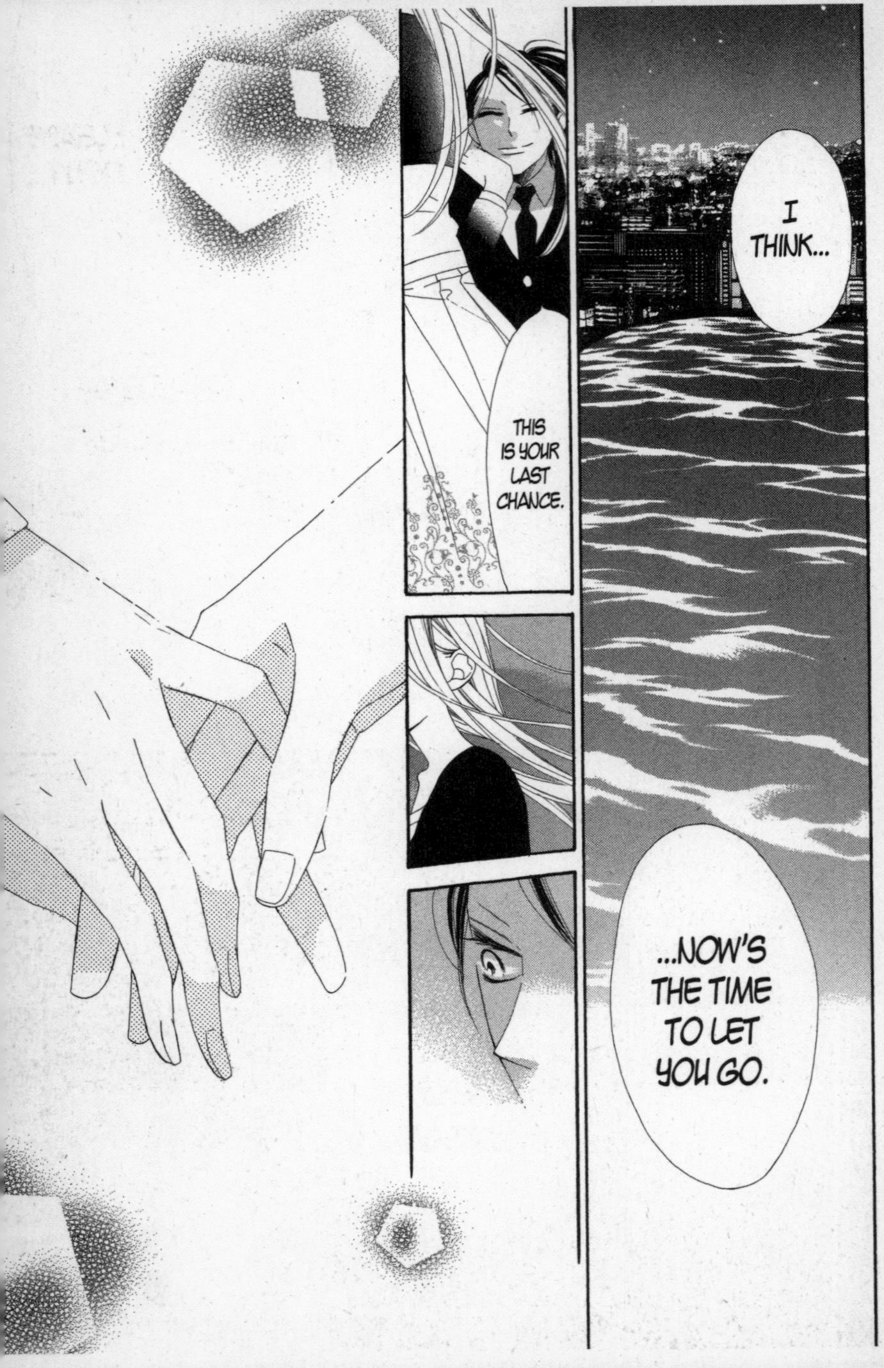
I THINK...
...NOW'S THE TIME TO LET YOU GO.
THIS IS YOUR LAST CHANCE.

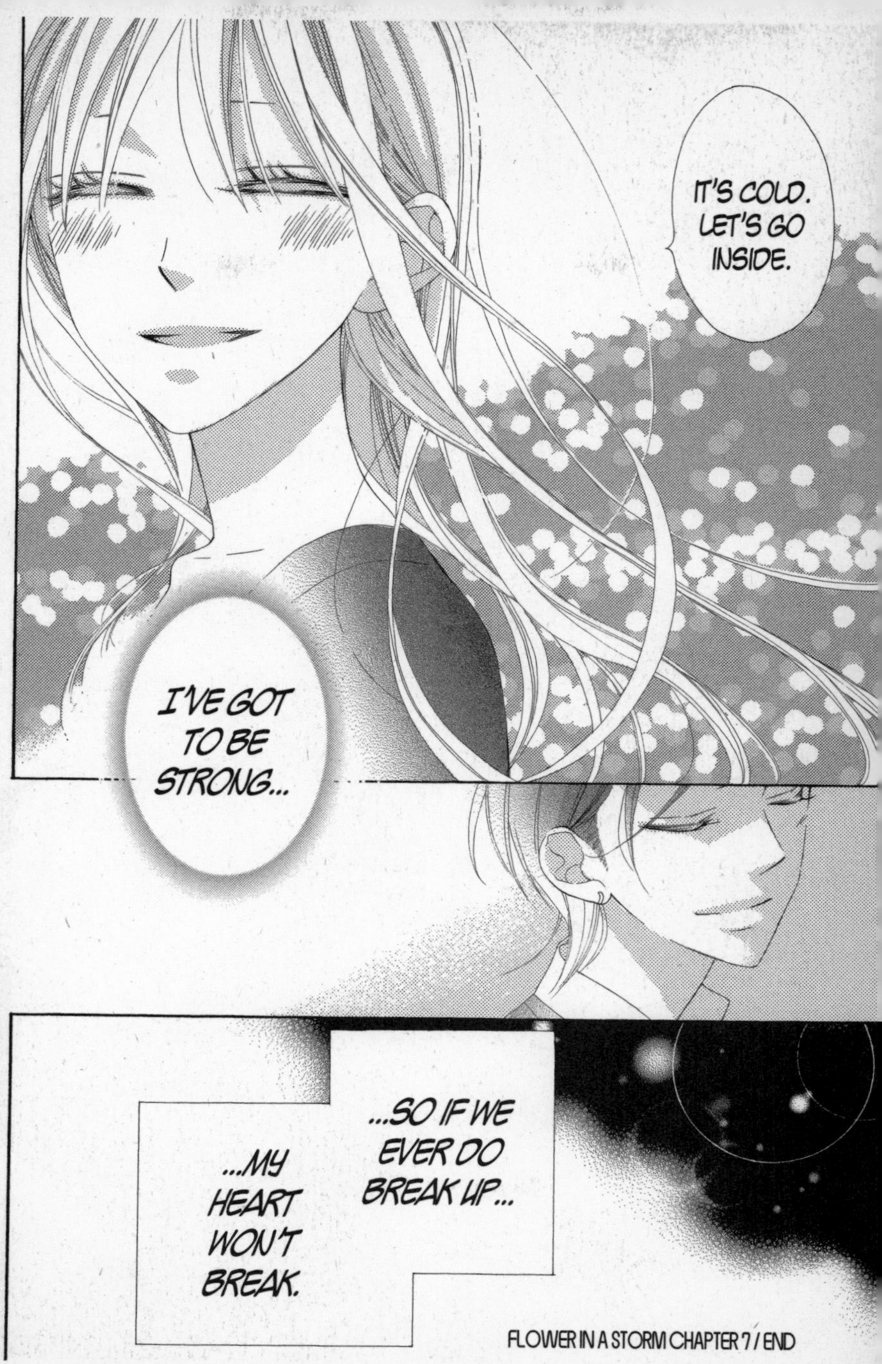
IT'S COLD. LET'S GO INSIDE.
I'VE GOT TO BE STRONG...
...SO IF WE EVER DO BREAK UP...
...MY HEART WON'T BREAK.
FLOWER IN A STORM CHAPTER 7 / END

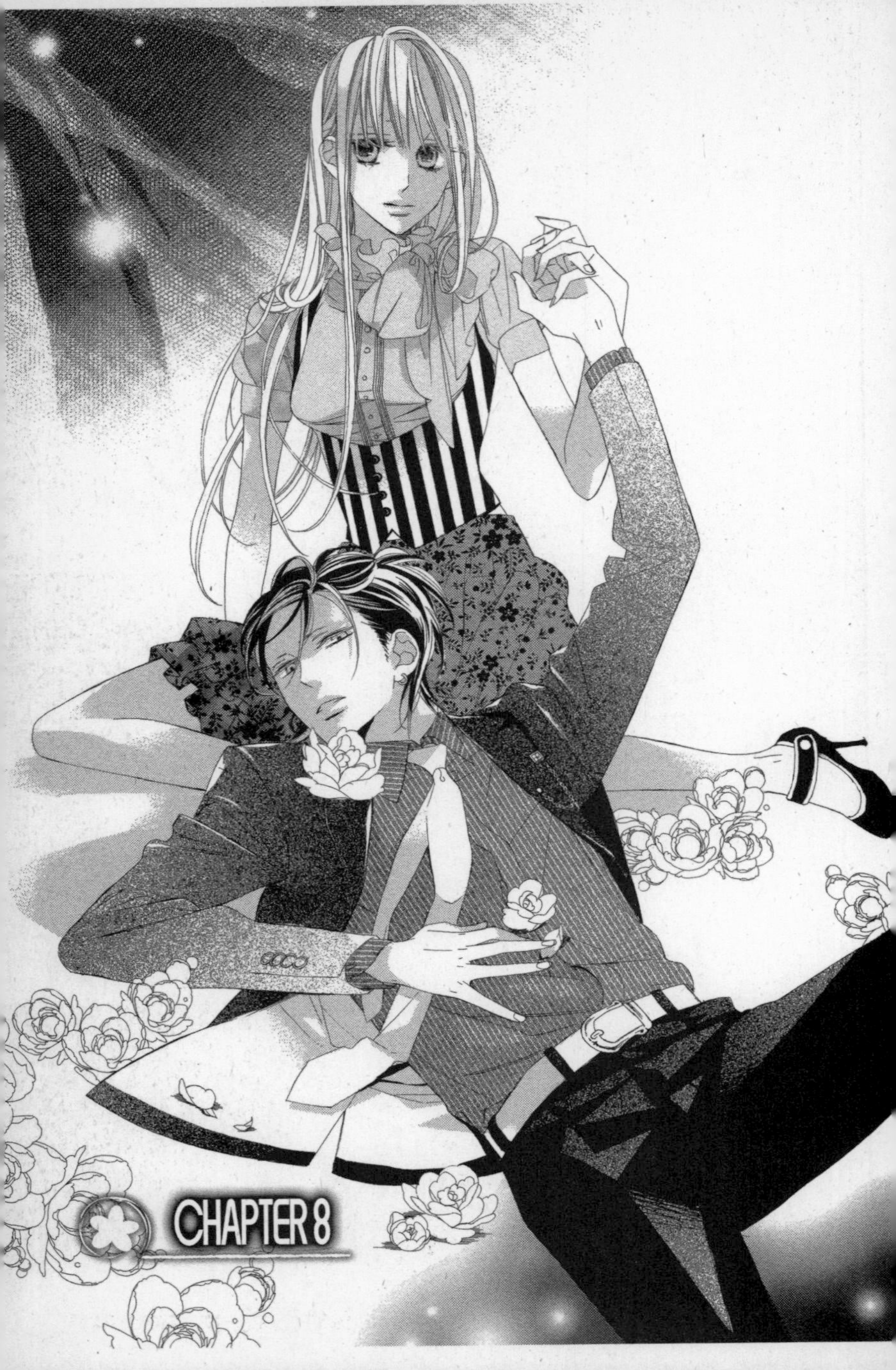
CHAPTER 8

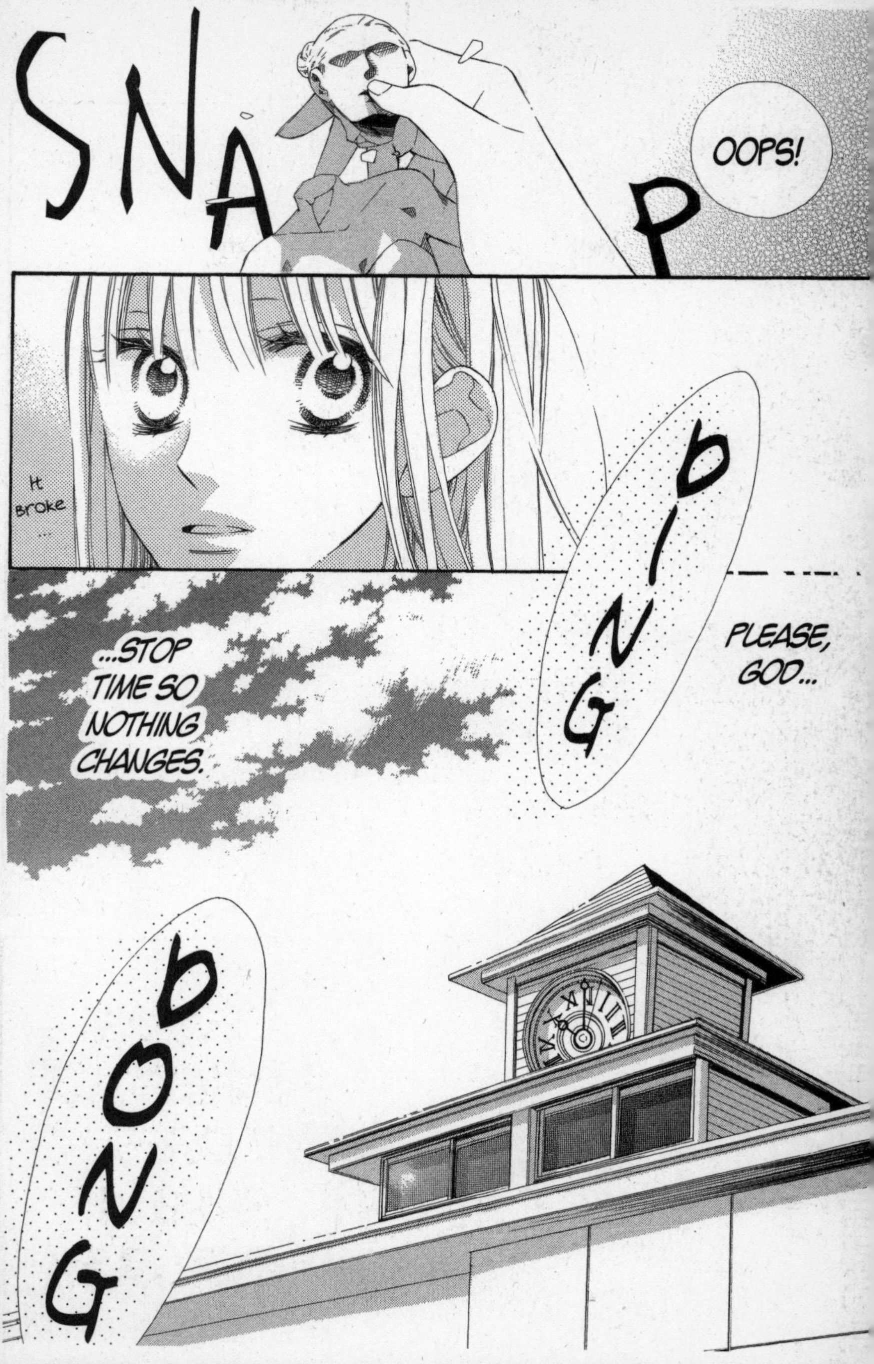
OOPS!
SNAP
It broke...
PLEASE, GOD...
DING
...STOP TIME SO NOTHING CHANGES.
DONG

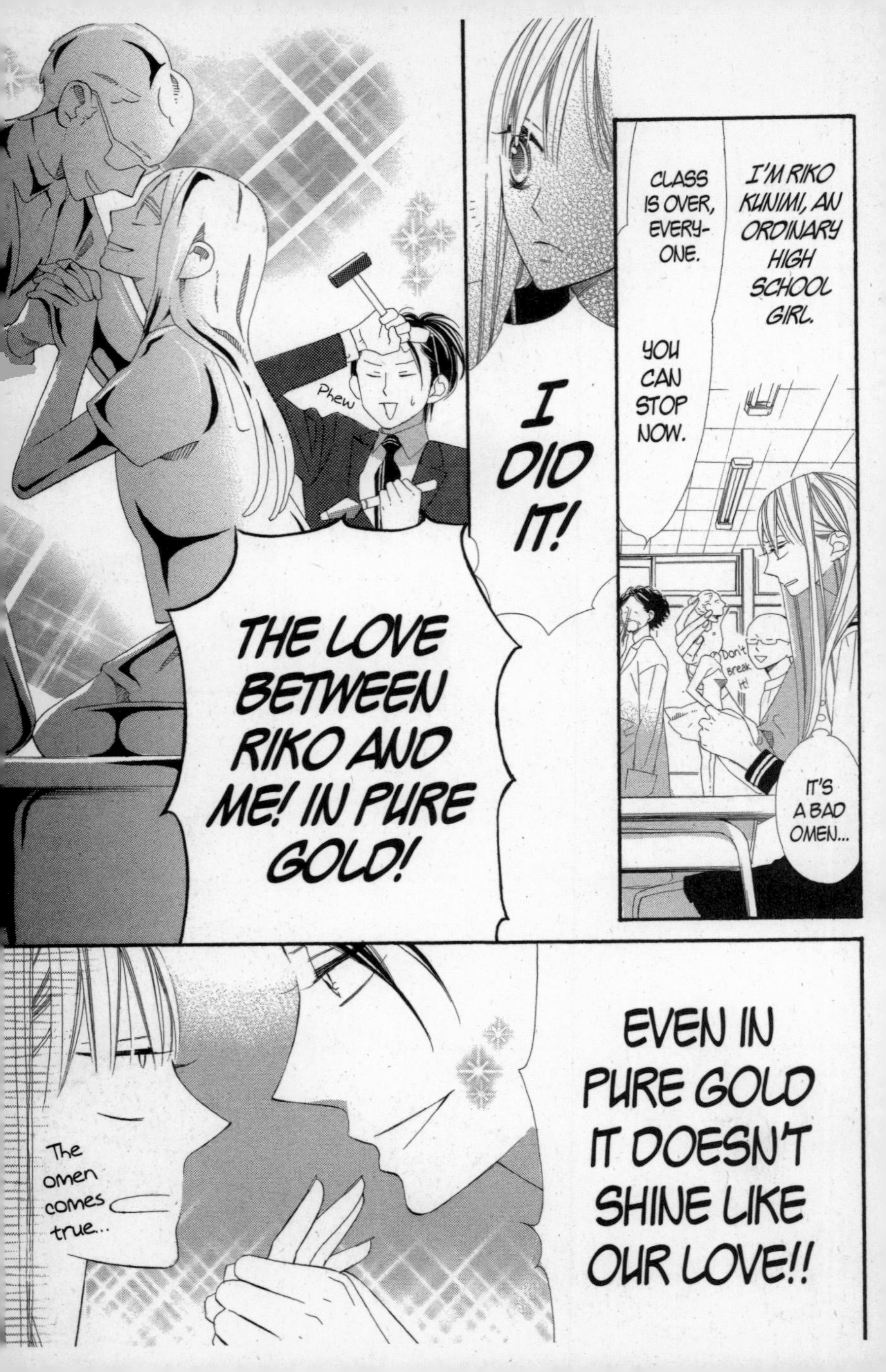
I'M RIKO KUNIMI, AN ORDINARY HIGH SCHOOL GIRL.
CLASS IS OVER, EVERY-ONE.
YOU CAN STOP NOW.
Don't break it!
IT'S A BAD OMEN...
I DID IT!
Phew
THE LOVE BETWEEN RIKO AND ME! IN PURE GOLD!
EVEN IN PURE GOLD IT DOESN'T SHINE LIKE OUR LOVE!!
The omen comes true...

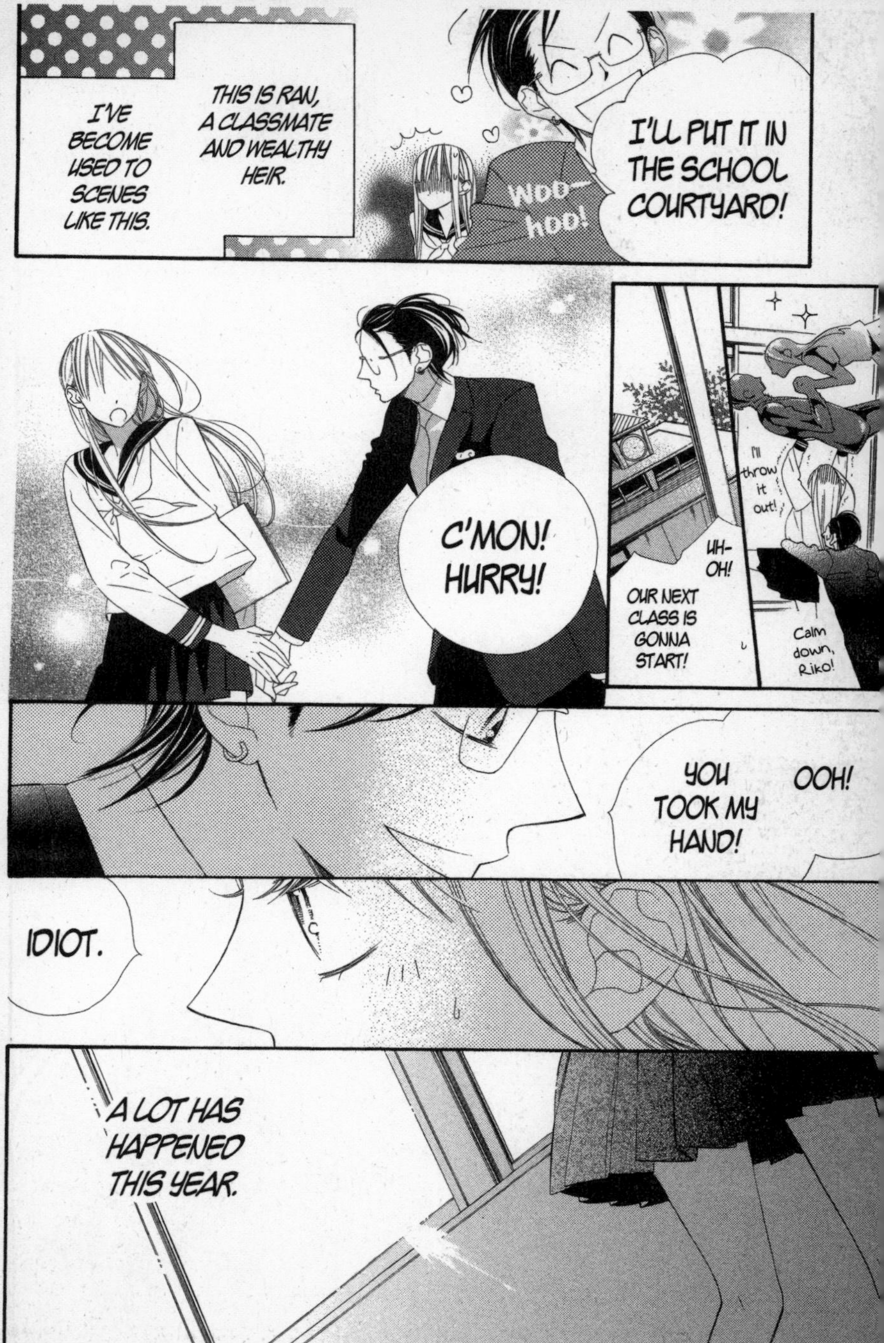
I'LL PUT IT IN THE SCHOOL COURTYARD!
WOO-hoo!
THIS IS RAN, A CLASSMATE AND WEALTHY HEIR.
I'VE BECOME USED TO SCENES LIKE THIS.
I'll throw it out!
Calm down, Riko!
UH-OH!
OUR NEXT CLASS IS GONNA START!
C'MON! HURRY!
OOH!
YOU TOOK MY HAND!
IDIOT.
A LOT HAS HAPPENED THIS YEAR.

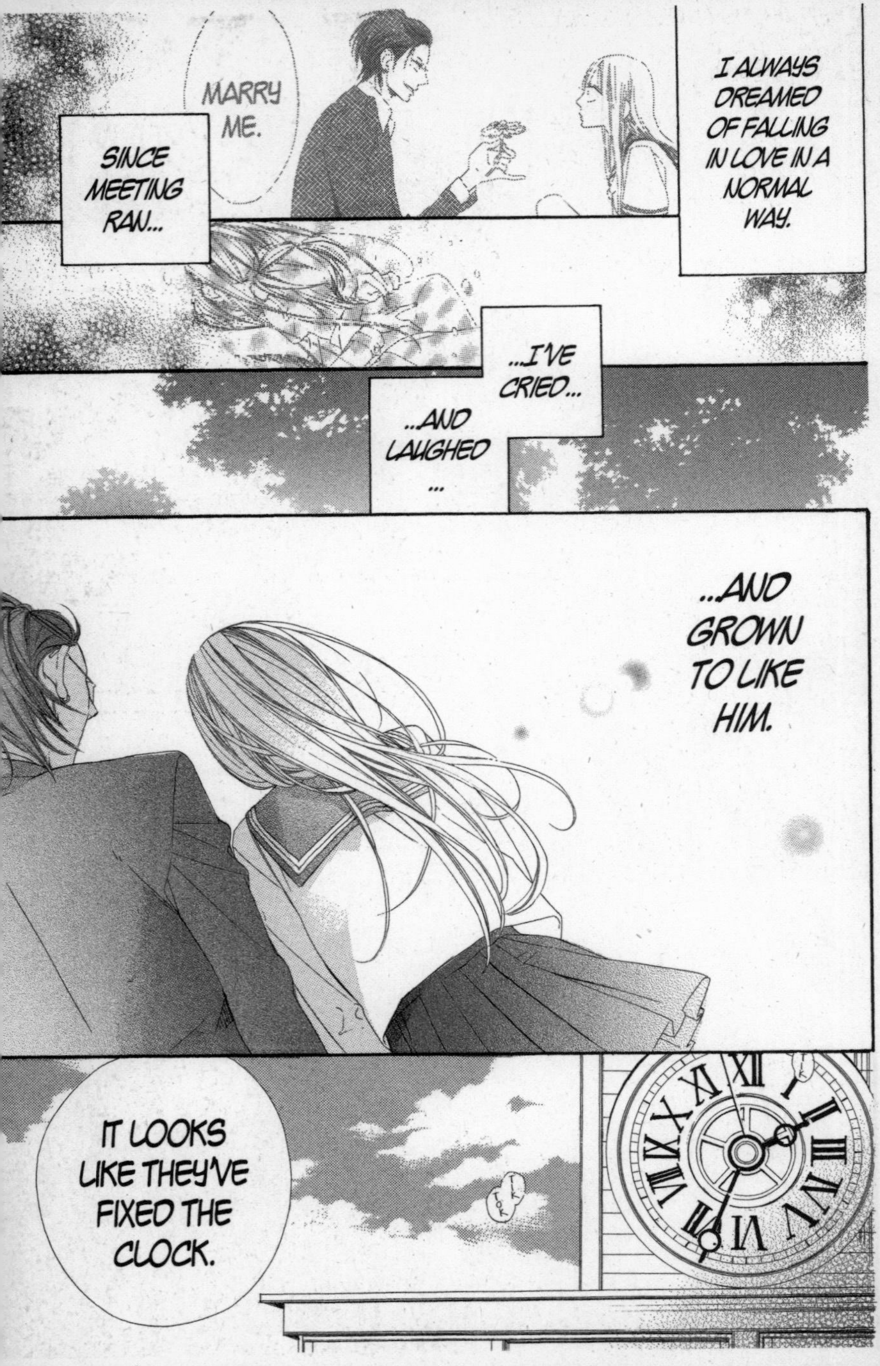

I ALWAYS DREAMED OF FALLING IN LOVE IN A NORMAL WAY.
MARRY ME.
SINCE MEETING RAN...
...I'VE CRIED...
...AND LAUGHED ...
...AND GROWN TO LIKE HIM.
TIK
TIK TOK
IT LOOKS LIKE THEY'VE FIXED THE CLOCK.

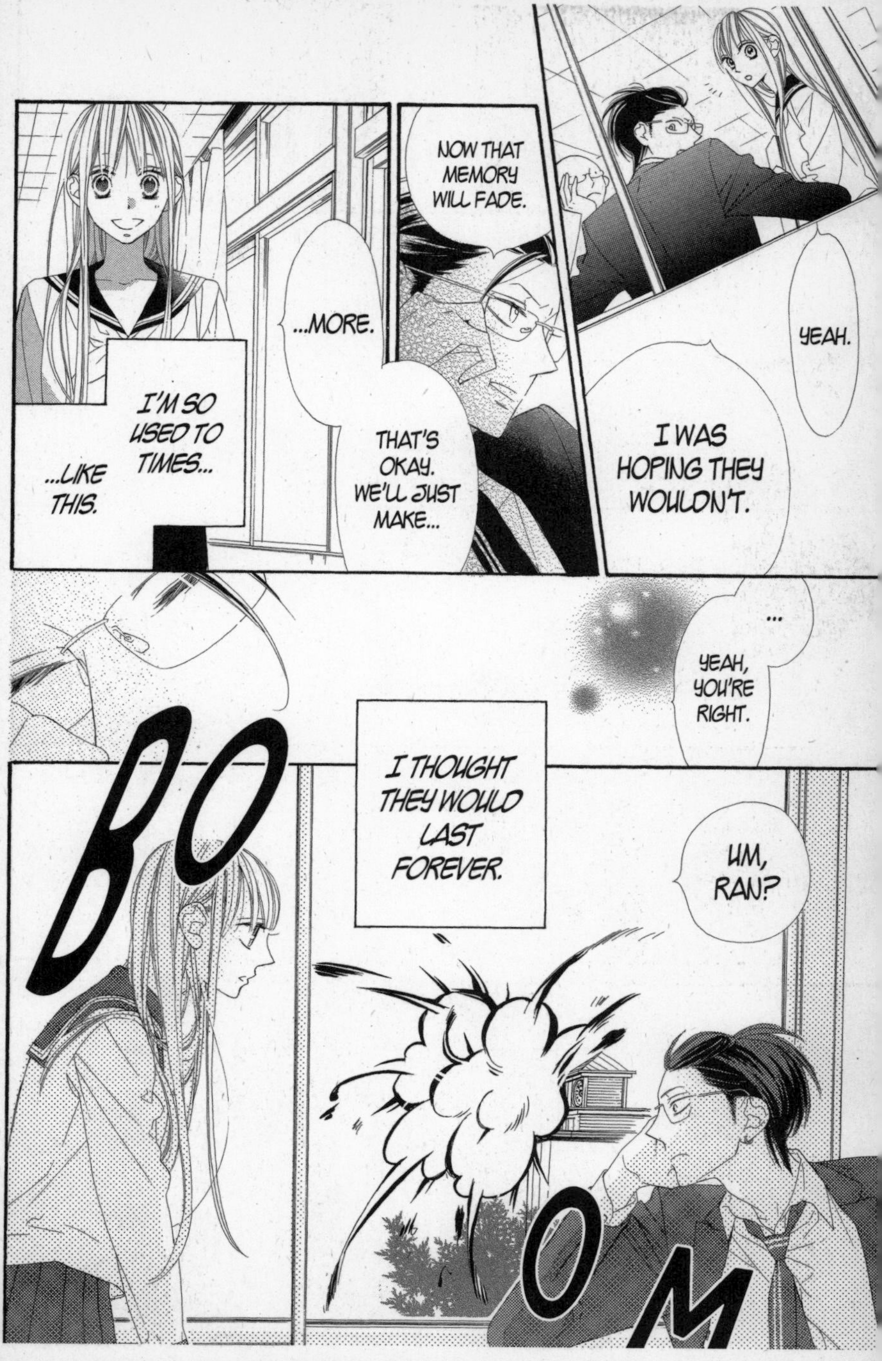

YEAH.
I WAS HOPING THEY WOULDN'T.
NOW THAT MEMORY WILL FADE.
THAT'S OKAY. WE'LL JUST MAKE...
...MORE.
I'M SO USED TO TIMES...
...LIKE THIS.
...
YEAH, YOU'RE RIGHT.
UM, RAN?
I THOUGHT THEY WOULD LAST FOREVER.
BOOM

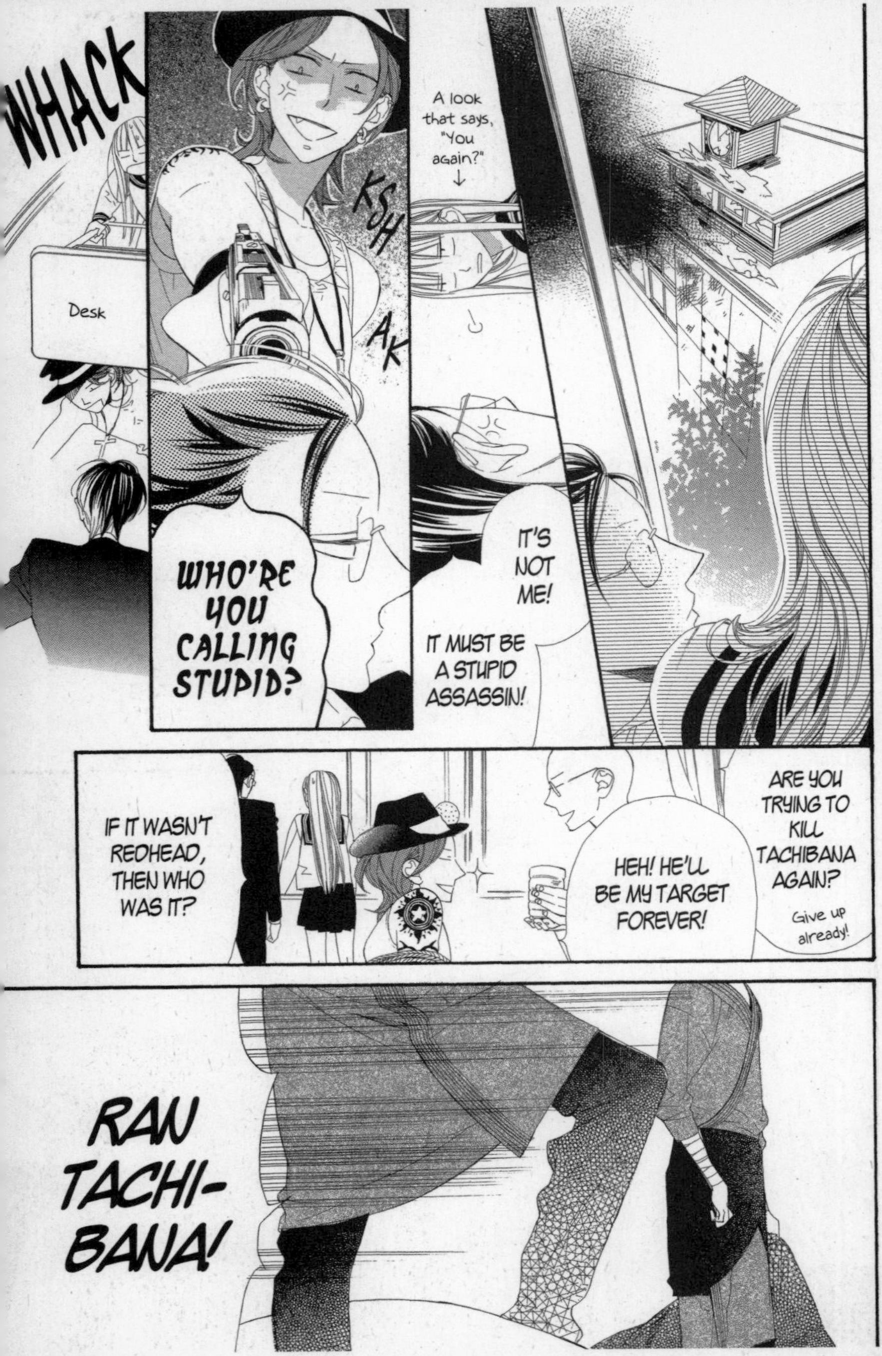
A look that says, "You again?"
IT'S NOT ME!
IT MUST BE A STUPID ASSASSIN!
KSH
AK
WHO'RE YOU CALLING STUPID?
WHACK
Desk
ARE YOU TRYING TO KILL TACHIBANA AGAIN?
Give up already!
HEH! HE'LL BE MY TARGET FOREVER!
IF IT WASN'T REDHEAD, THEN WHO WAS IT?
RAN TACHI-BANA!

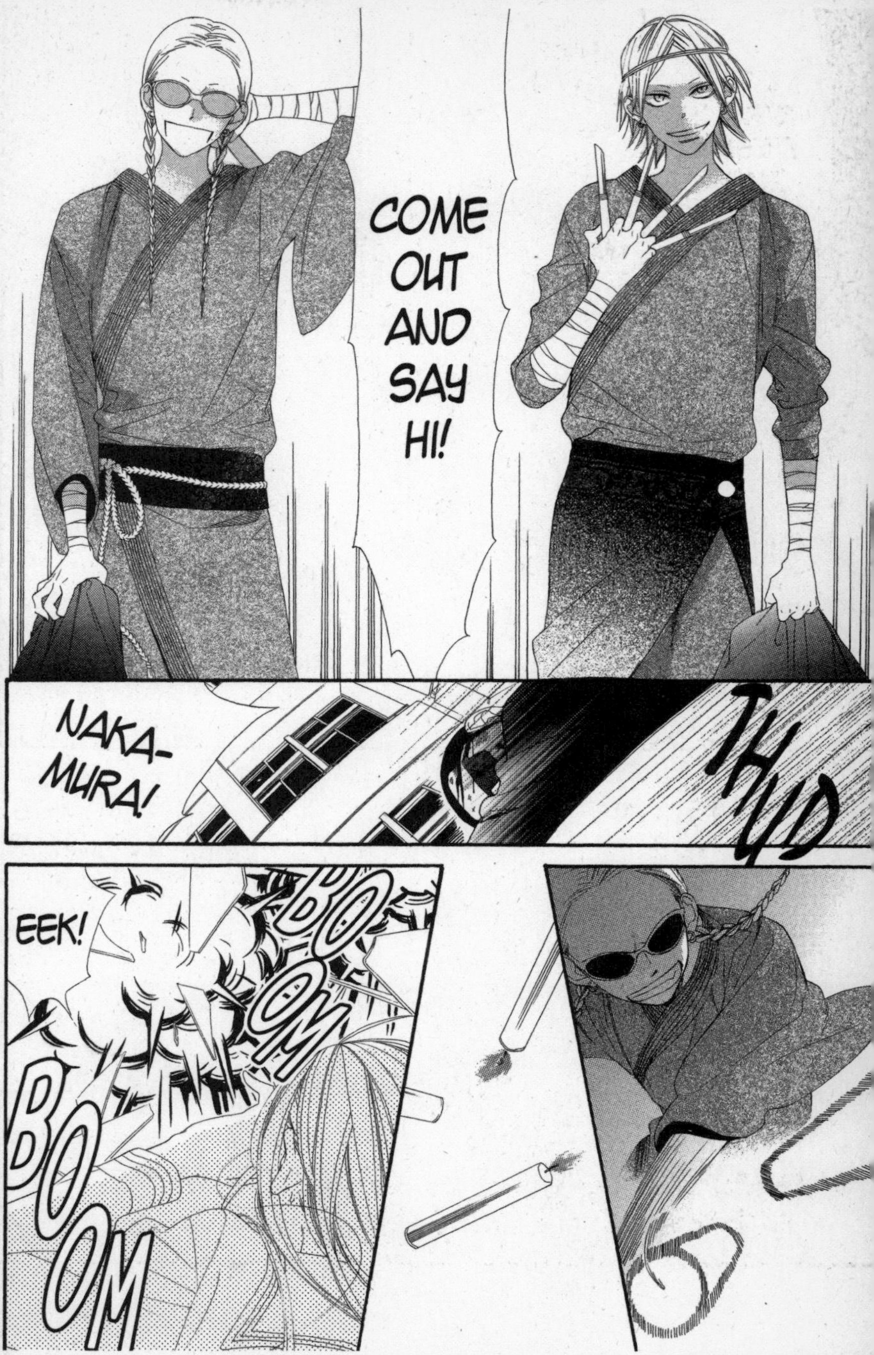
COME OUT AND SAY HI!
THUD
NAKA-MURA!
BOOM
EEK!
BOOM

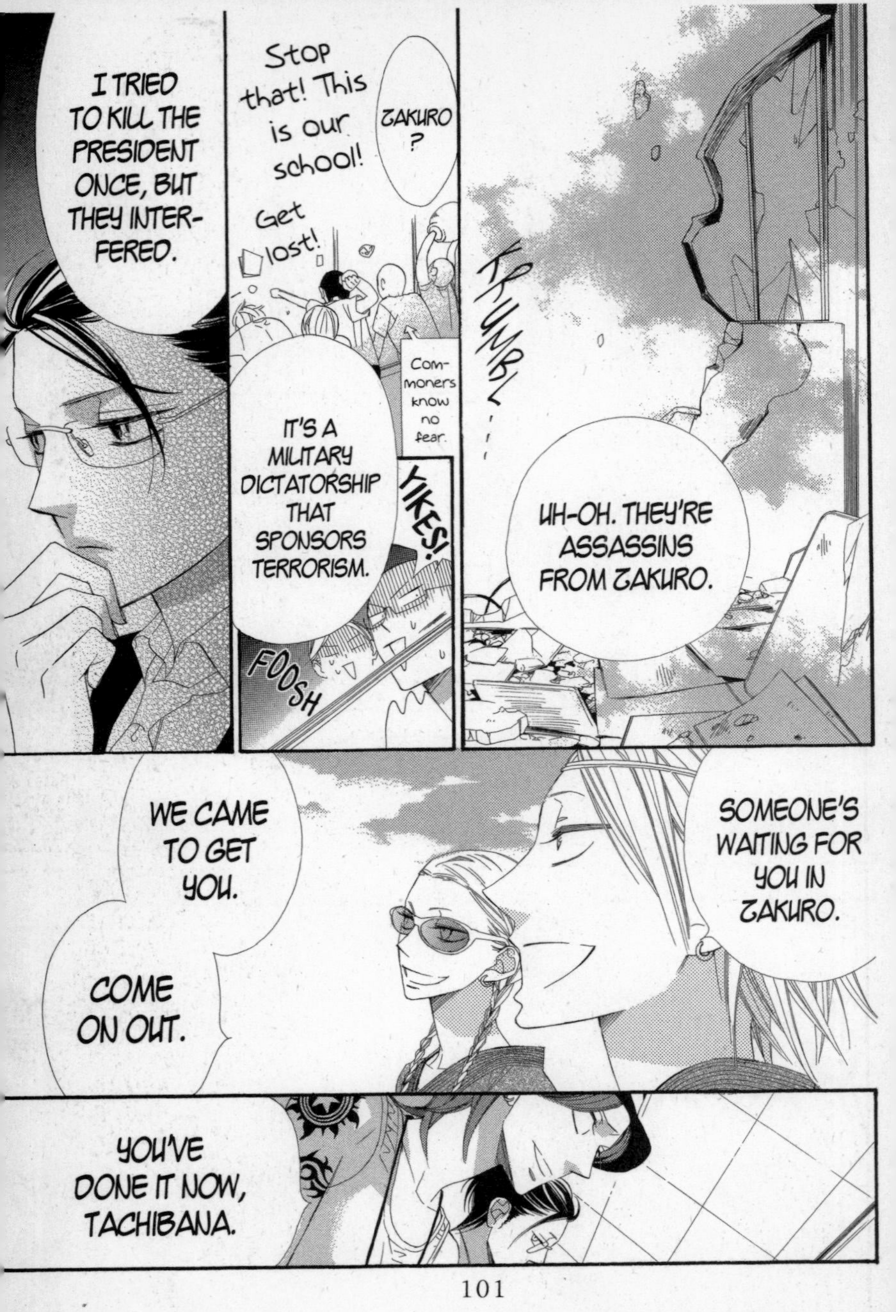
KRUMBL...
UH-OH. THEY'RE ASSASSINS FROM ZAKURO.
ZAKURO?
Stop that! This is our school!
Get lost!
Commoners know no fear.
IT'S A MILITARY DICTATORSHIP THAT SPONSORS TERRORISM.
YIKES!
FOOSH
I TRIED TO KILL THE PRESIDENT ONCE, BUT THEY INTERFERED.
SOMEONE'S WAITING FOR YOU IN ZAKURO.
WE CAME TO GET YOU.
COME ON OUT.
YOU'VE DONE IT NOW, TACHIBANA.

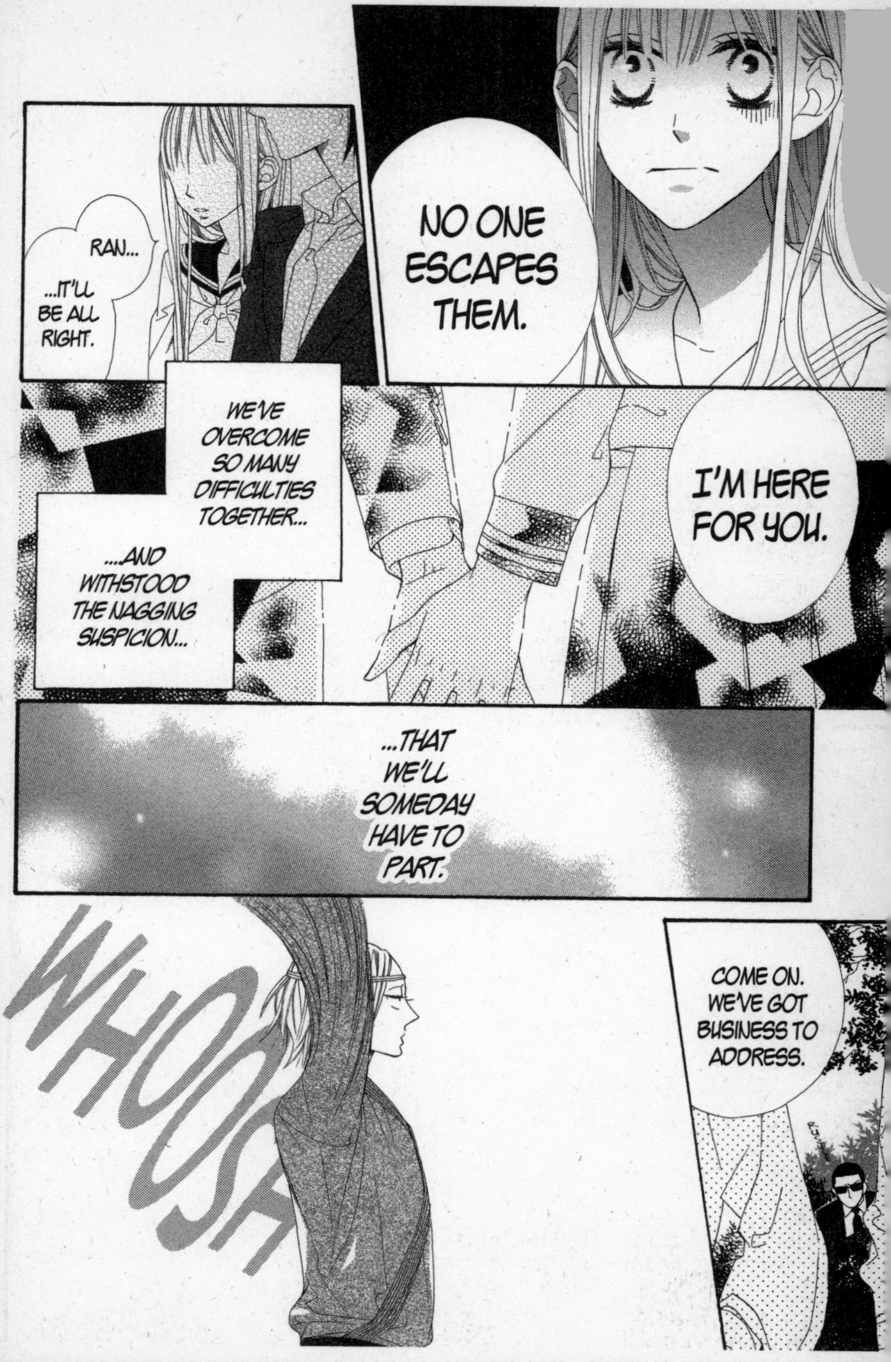

NO ONE ESCAPES THEM.
RAN...
...IT'LL BE ALL RIGHT.
I'M HERE FOR YOU.
WE'VE OVERCOME SO MANY DIFFICULTIES TOGETHER...
...AND WITHSTOOD THE NAGGING SUSPICION...
...THAT WE'LL SOMEDAY HAVE TO PART.
COME ON. WE'VE GOT BUSINESS TO ADDRESS.
WHOSH

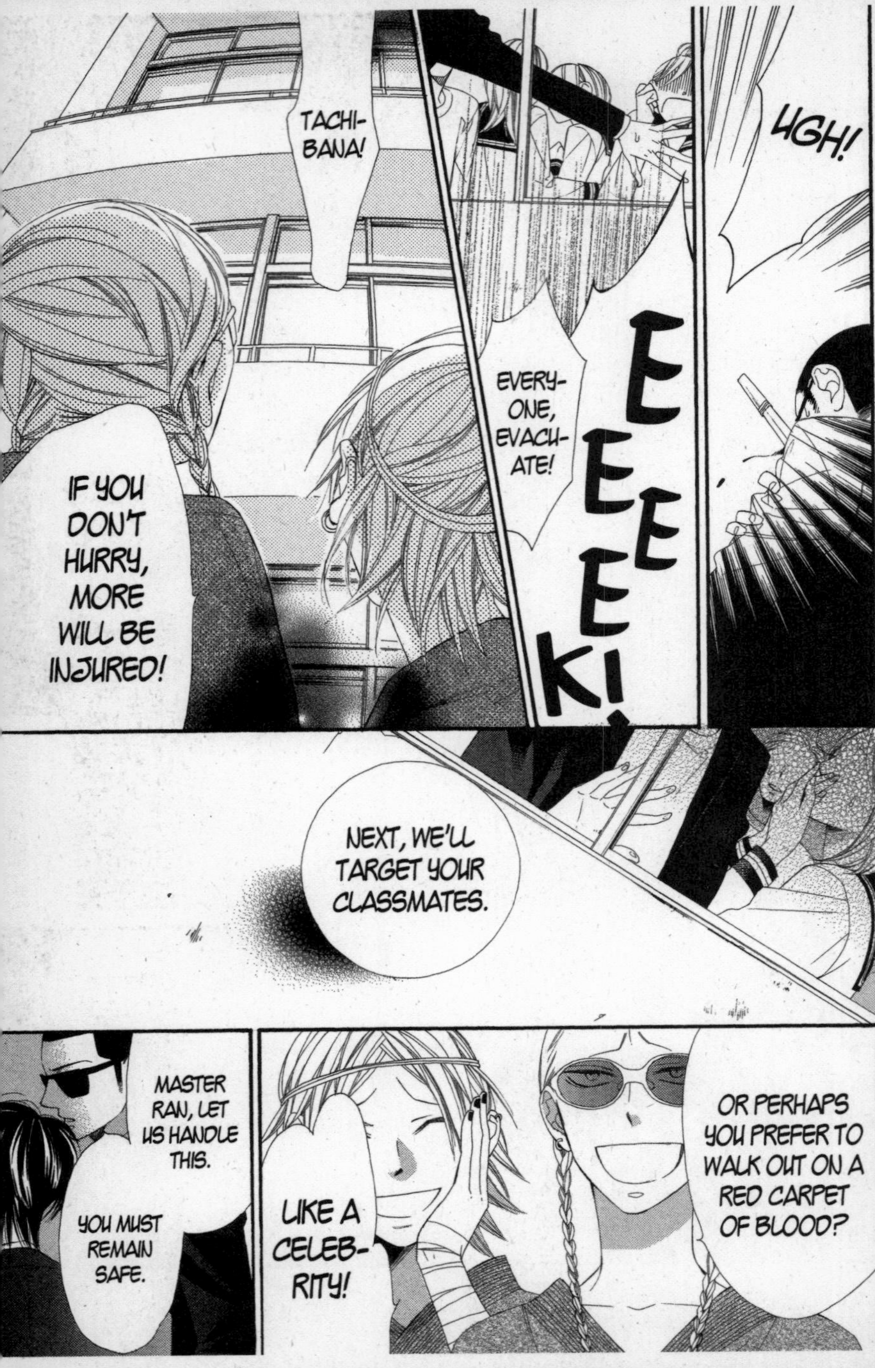
UGH!
EEEEK!
EVERY-ONE, EVACU-ATE!
TACHI-BANA!
IF YOU DON'T HURRY, MORE WILL BE INJURED!
NEXT, WE'LL TARGET YOUR CLASSMATES.
OR PERHAPS YOU PREFER TO WALK OUT ON A RED CARPET OF BLOOD?
LIKE A CELEB-RITY!
MASTER RAN, LET US HANDLE THIS.
YOU MUST REMAIN SAFE.

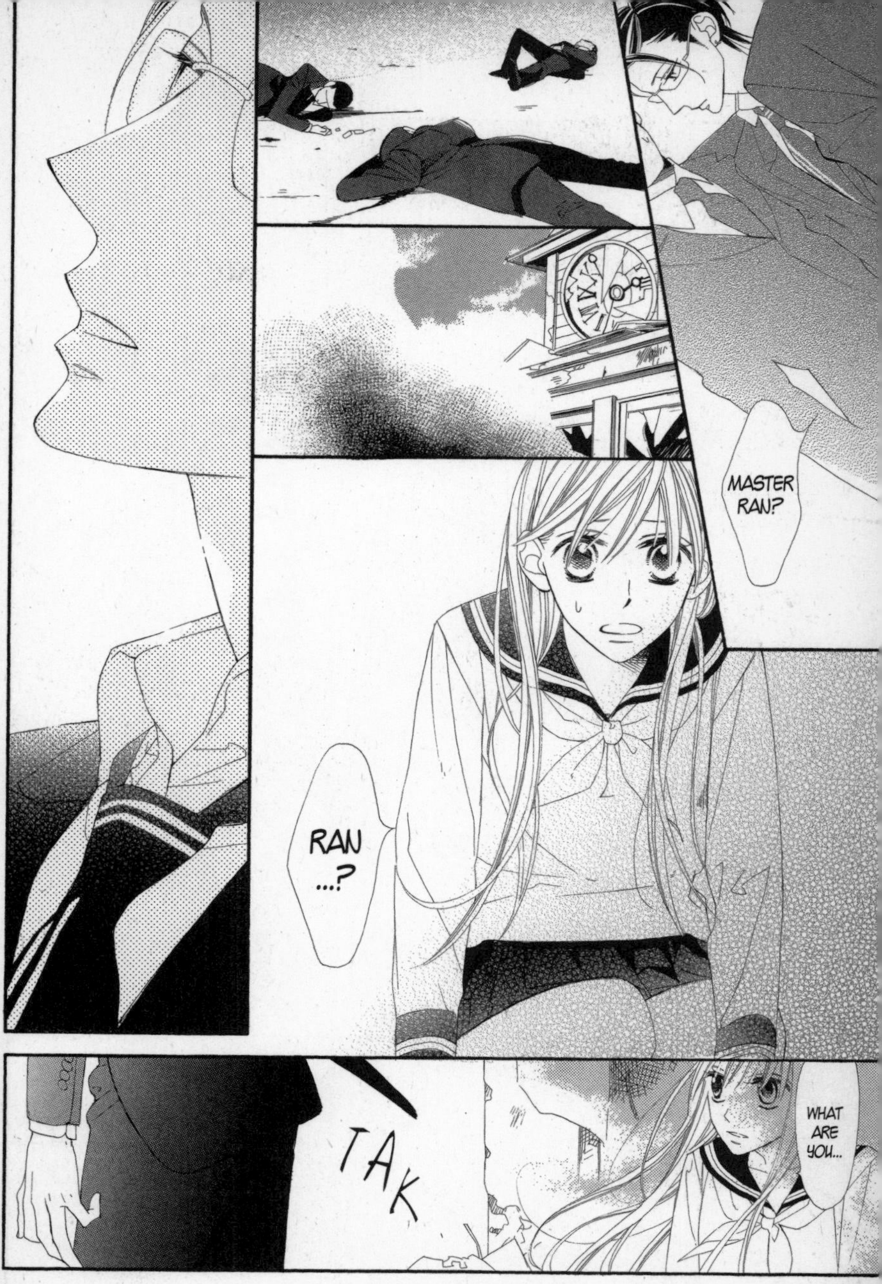
MASTER RAN?
RAN ...?
WHAT ARE YOU...
TAK

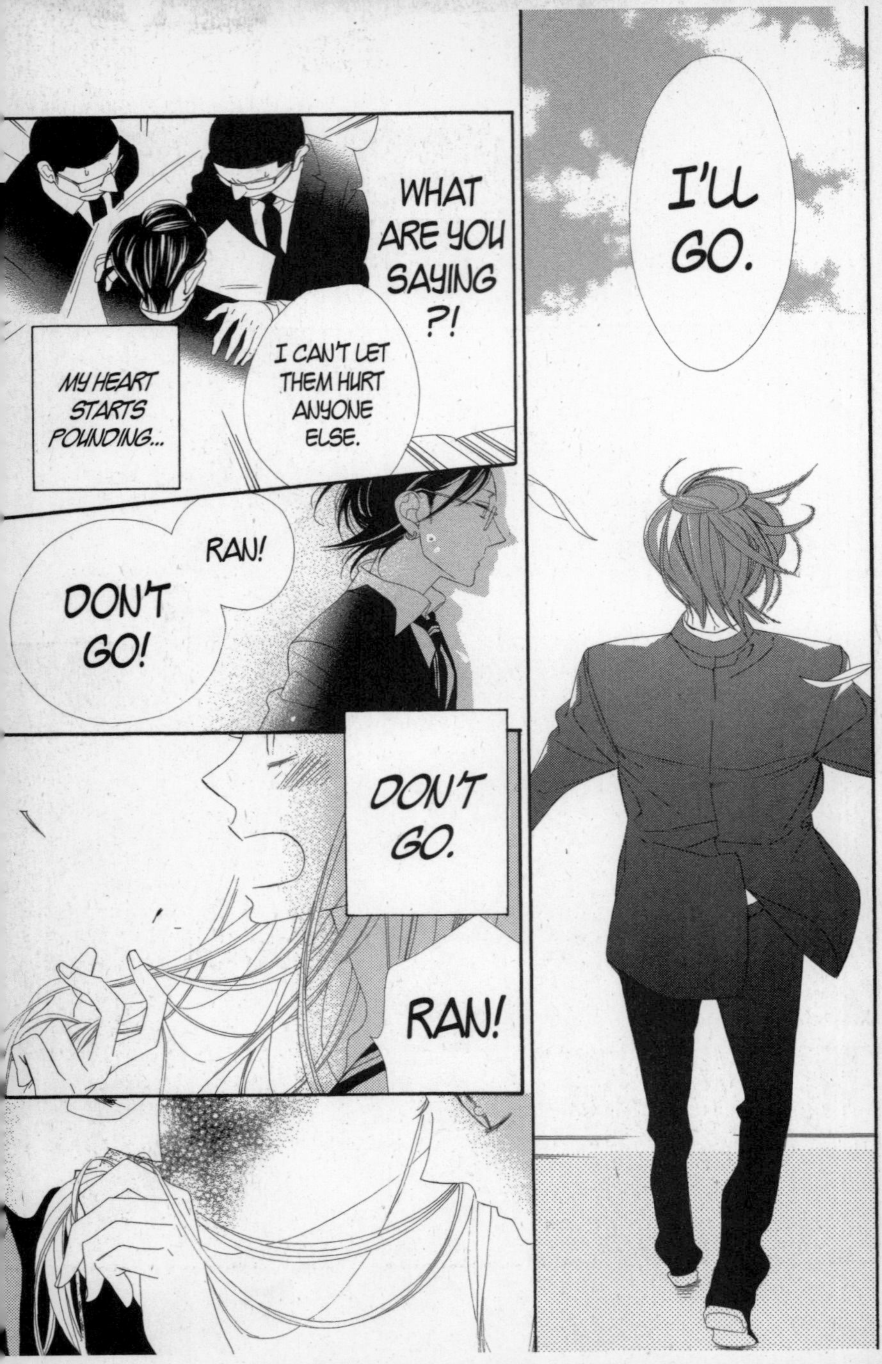
I'LL GO.
WHAT ARE YOU SAYING?!
I CAN'T LET THEM HURT ANYONE ELSE.
MY HEART STARTS POUNDING...
RAN!
DON'T GO!
DON'T GO.
RAN!

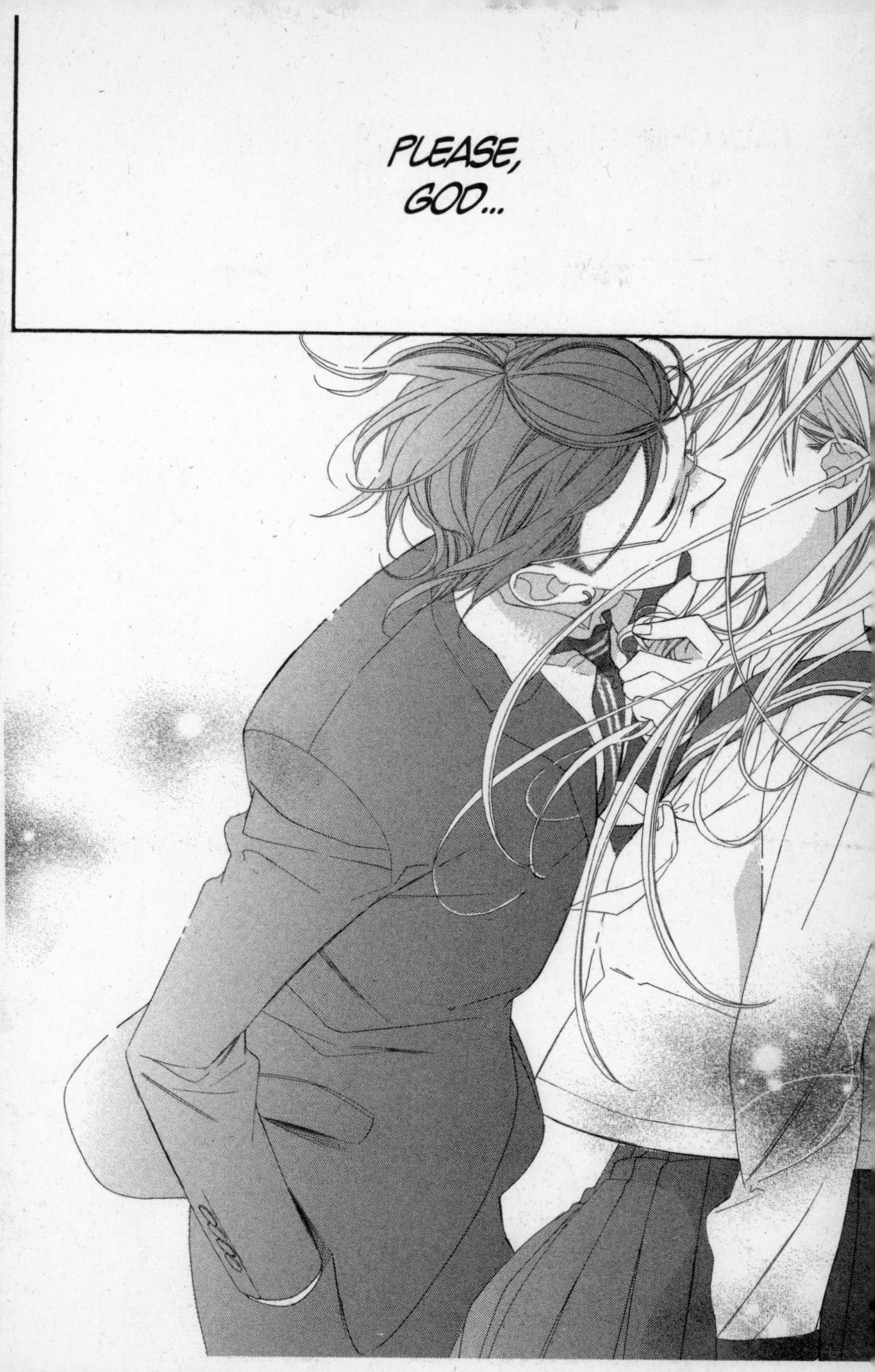
PLEASE, GOD...

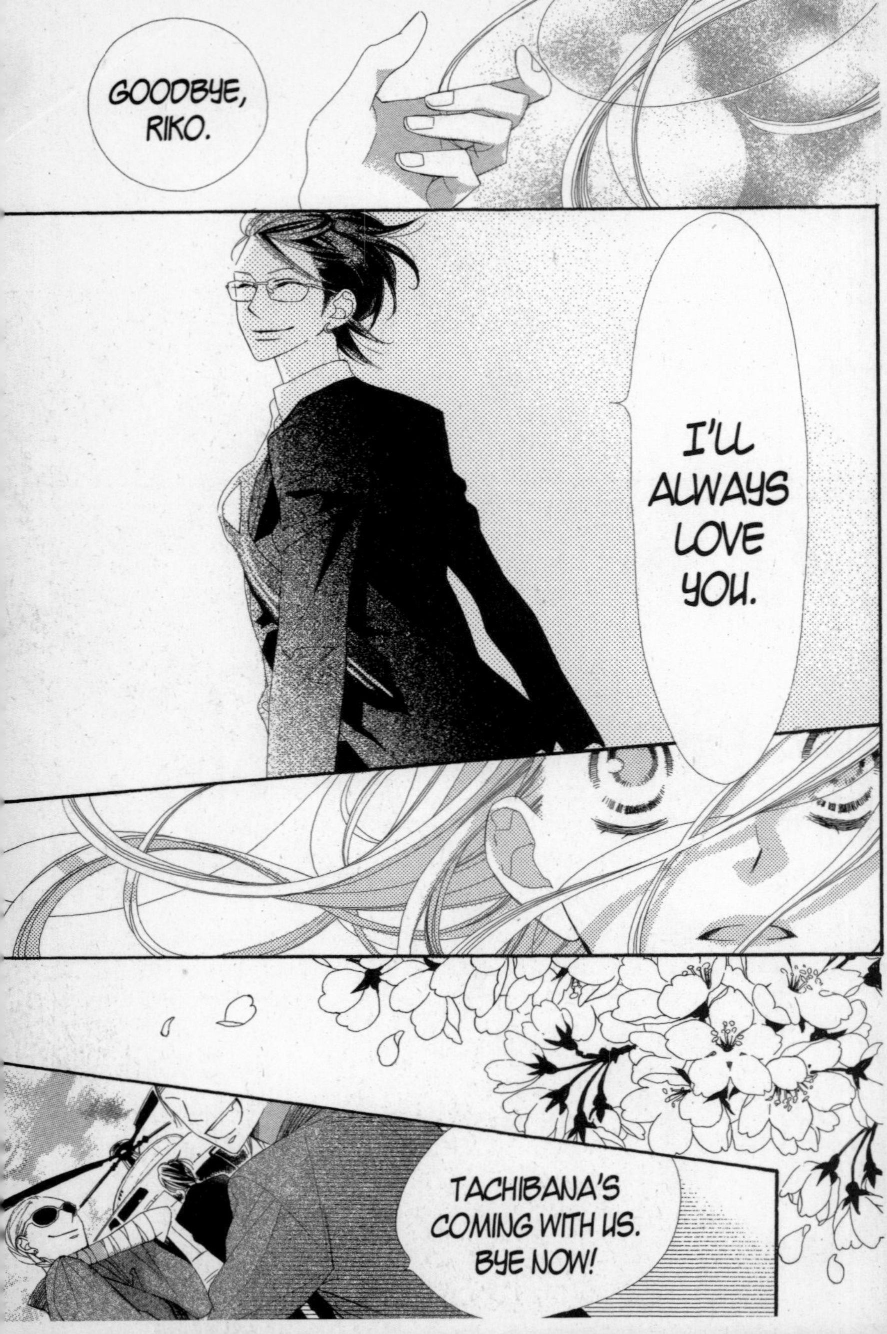
GOODBYE, RIKO.
I'LL ALWAYS LOVE YOU.
TACHIBANA'S COMING WITH US. BYE NOW!

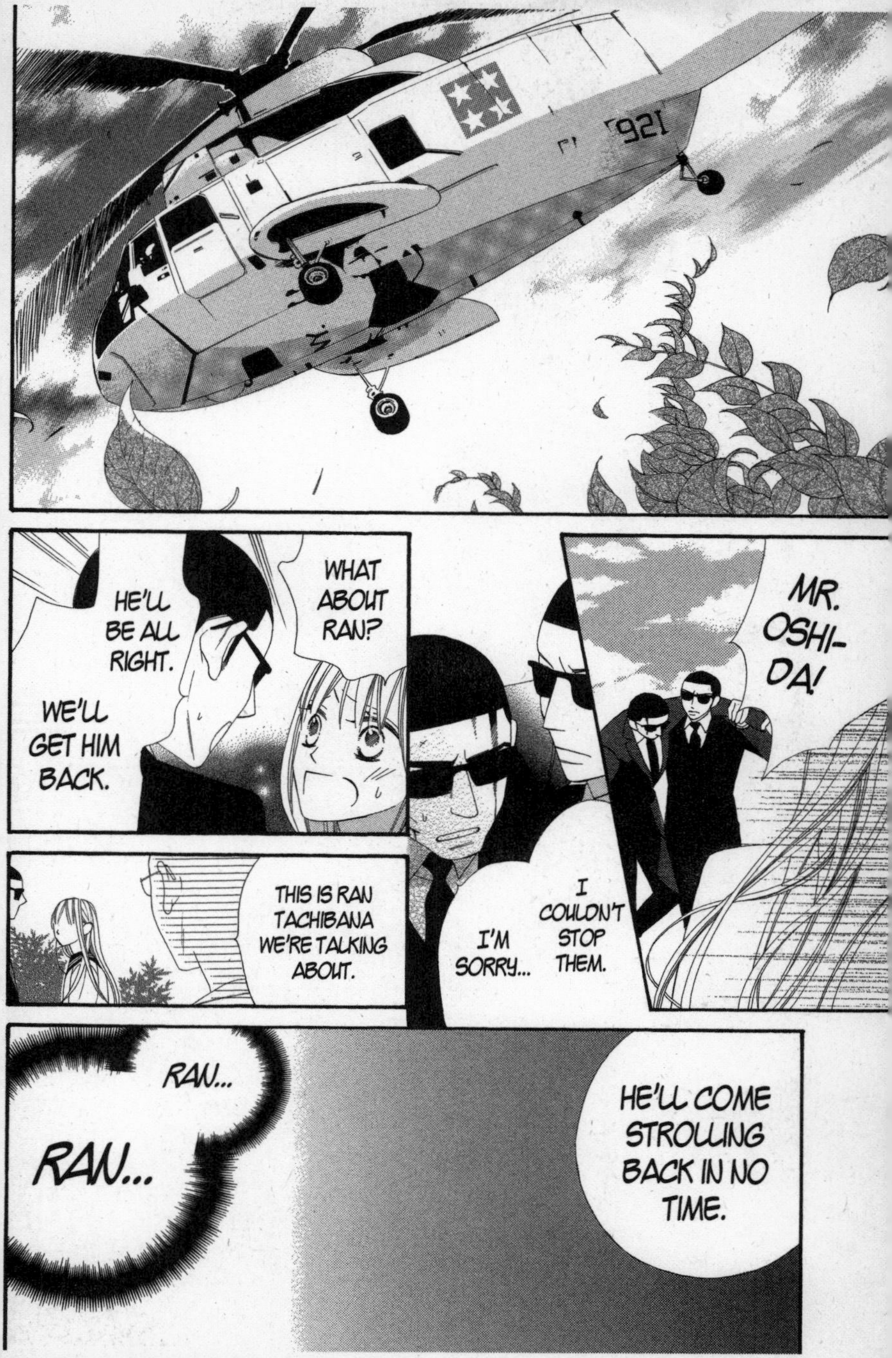
MR. OSHI-DA!
I COULDN'T STOP THEM.
I'M SORRY...
WHAT ABOUT RAN?
HE'LL BE ALL RIGHT.
WE'LL GET HIM BACK.
THIS IS RAN TACHIBANA WE'RE TALKING ABOUT.
HE'LL COME STROLLING BACK IN NO TIME.
RAN...
RAN...

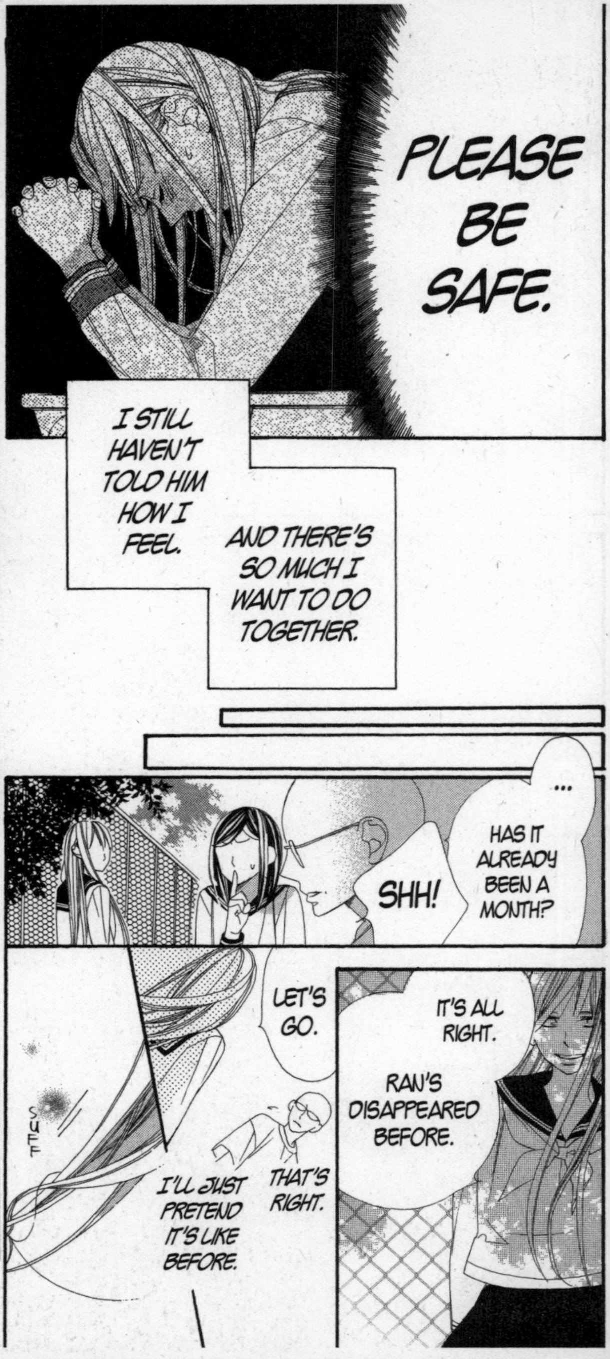
PLEASE BE SAFE.
I STILL HAVEN'T TOLD HIM HOW I FEEL.
AND THERE'S SO MUCH I WANT TO DO TOGETHER.
...
HAS IT ALREADY BEEN A MONTH?
SHH!
IT'S ALL RIGHT.
RAN'S DISAPPEARED BEFORE.
LET'S GO.
THAT'S RIGHT.
I'LL JUST PRETEND IT'S LIKE BEFORE.

· Character · Profile

McGregor and His Minions

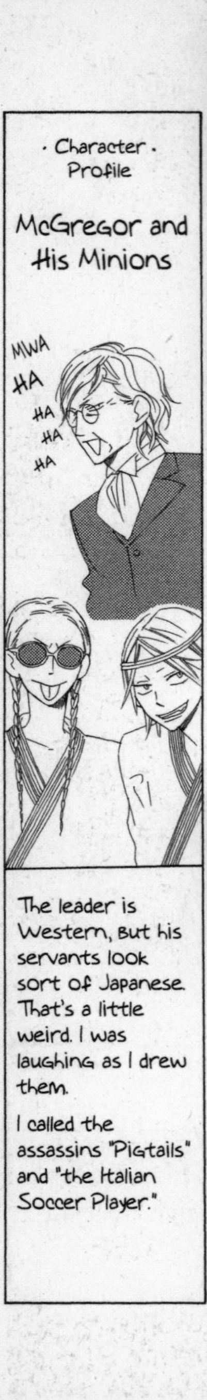
MWA
HA
HA
HA
HA

The leader is Western, but his servants look sort of Japanese. That's a little weird. I was laughing as I drew them.

I called the assassins "Pigtails" and "the Italian Soccer Player."

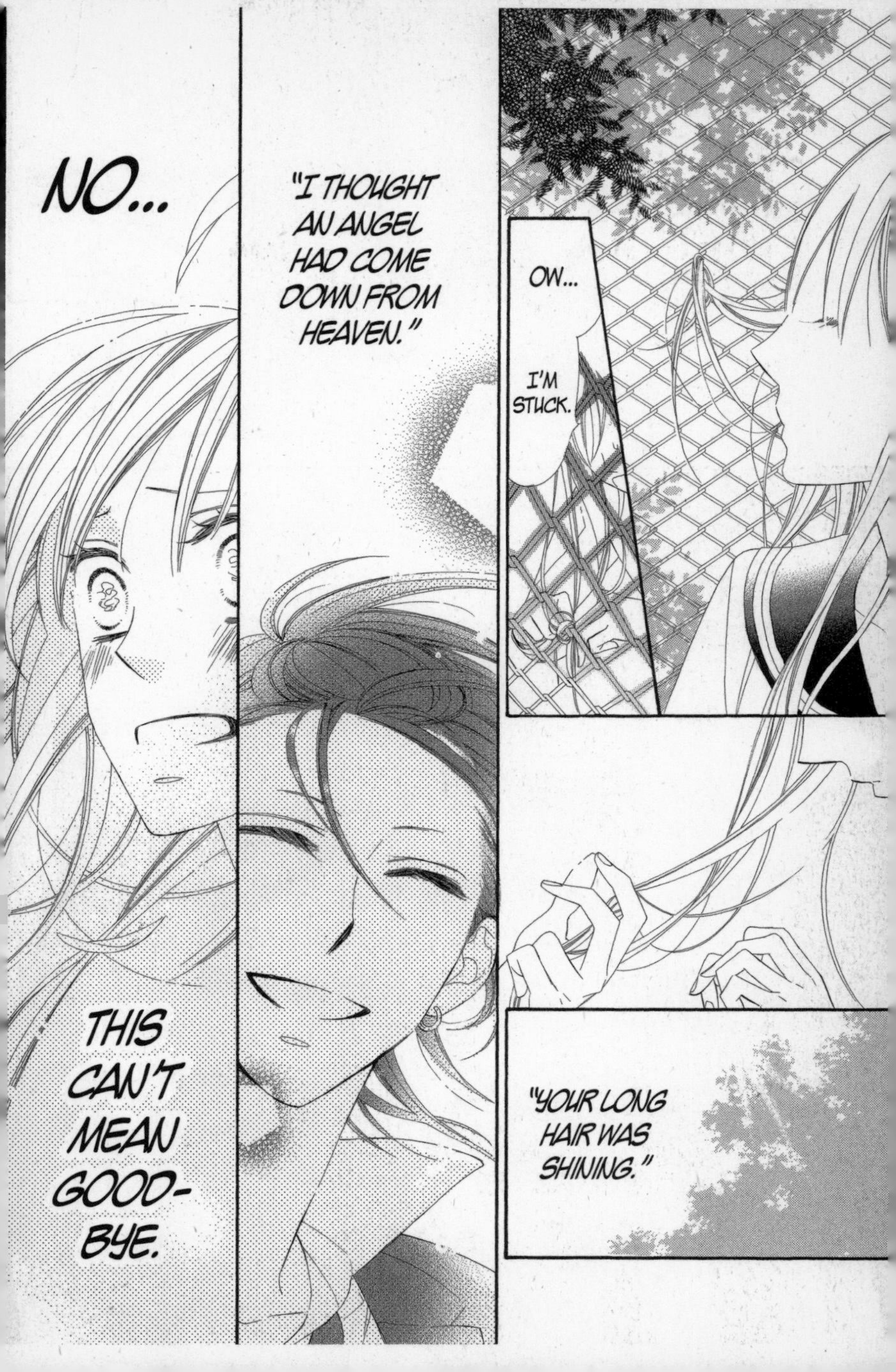
OW...
I'M STUCK.
"YOUR LONG HAIR WAS SHINING."
"I THOUGHT AN ANGEL HAD COME DOWN FROM HEAVEN."
NO...
THIS CAN'T MEAN GOOD-BYE.

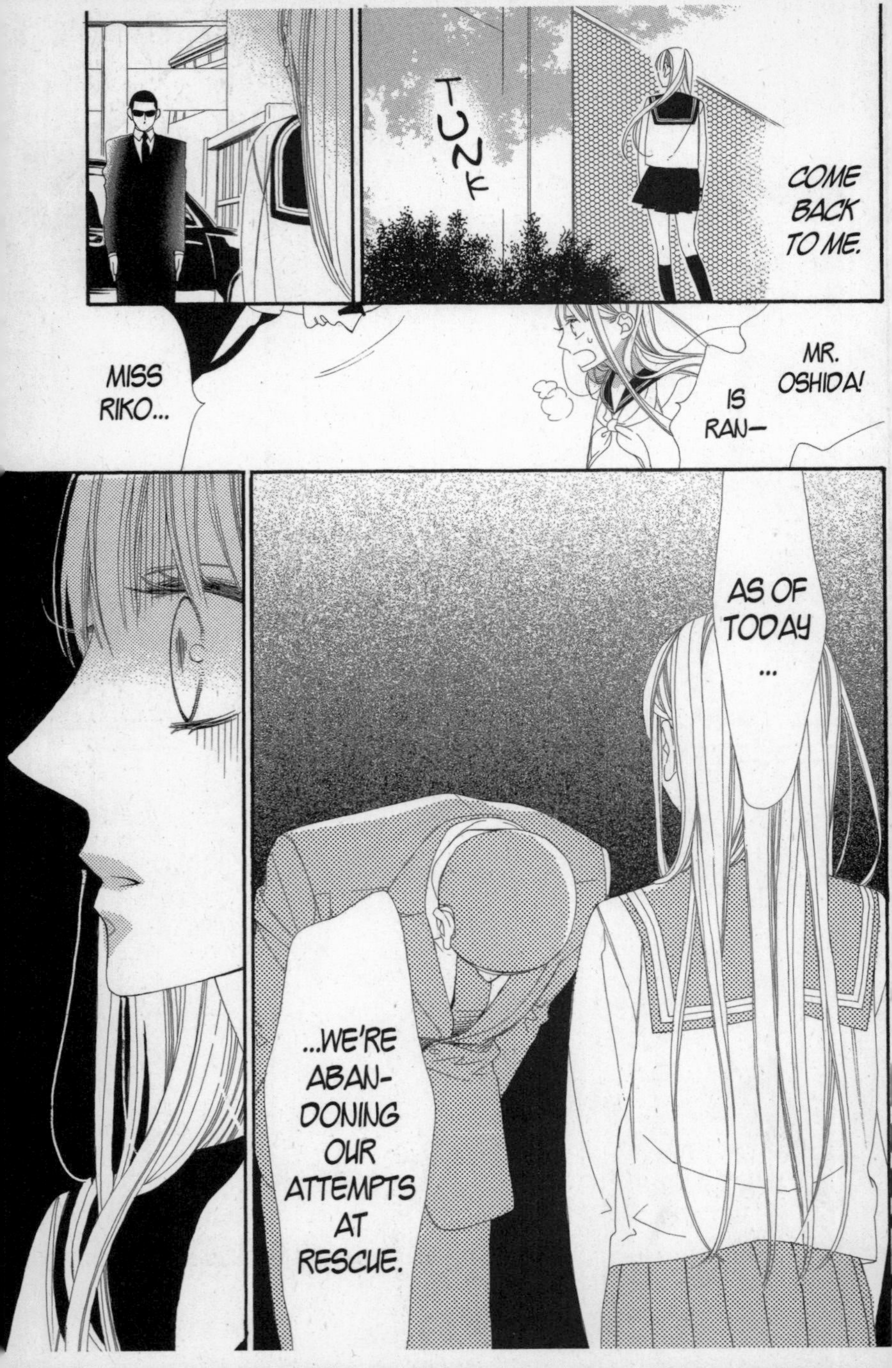
COME BACK TO ME.
TUNK
MR. OSHIDA!
IS RAN—
MISS RIKO...
AS OF TODAY ...
...WE'RE ABAN-DONING OUR ATTEMPTS AT RESCUE.

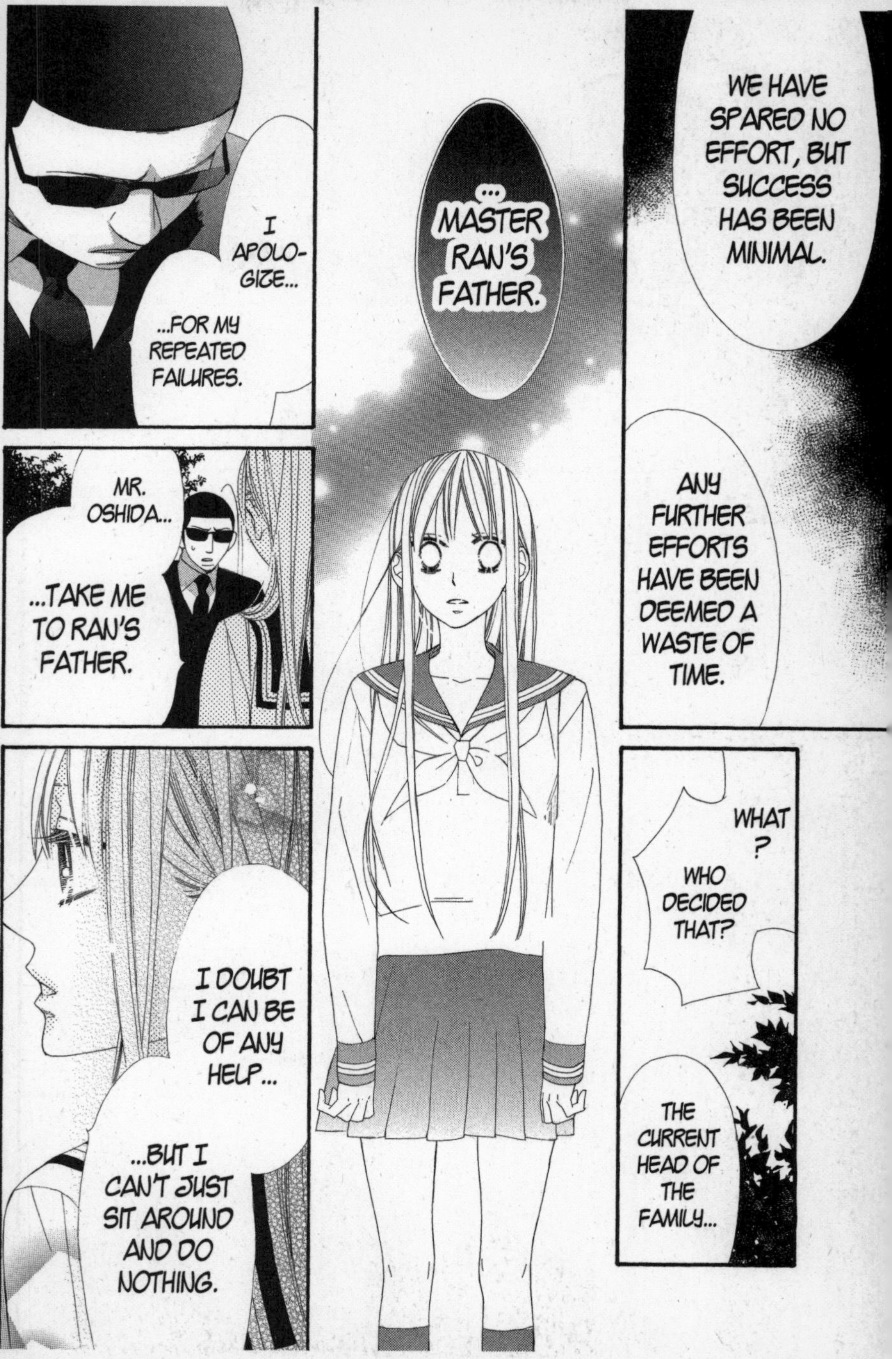
WE HAVE SPARED NO EFFORT, BUT SUCCESS HAS BEEN MINIMAL.
ANY FURTHER EFFORTS HAVE BEEN DEEMED A WASTE OF TIME.
WHAT? WHO DECIDED THAT?
THE CURRENT HEAD OF THE FAMILY...
...MASTER RAN'S FATHER.
I APOLOGIZE...
...FOR MY REPEATED FAILURES.
MR. OSHIDA...
...TAKE ME TO RAN'S FATHER.
I DOUBT I CAN BE OF ANY HELP...
...BUT I CAN'T JUST SIT AROUND AND DO NOTHING.

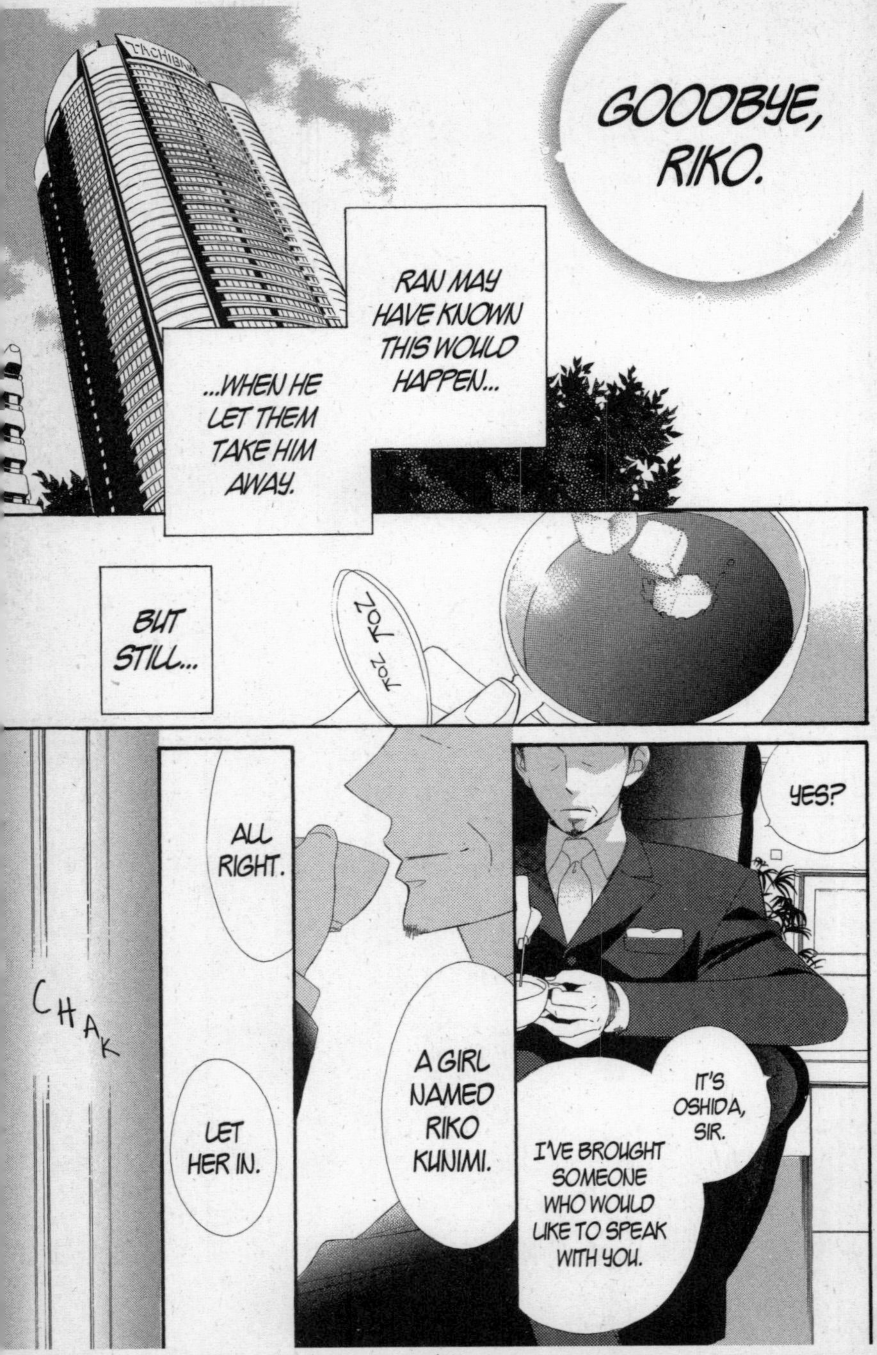
GOODBYE, RIKO.
RAN MAY HAVE KNOWN THIS WOULD HAPPEN...
...WHEN HE LET THEM TAKE HIM AWAY.
TOZ TOZ
BUT STILL...
YES?
IT'S OSHIDA, SIR.
I'VE BROUGHT SOMEONE WHO WOULD LIKE TO SPEAK WITH YOU.
A GIRL NAMED RIKO KUNIMI.
ALL RIGHT.
LET HER IN.
CHAK

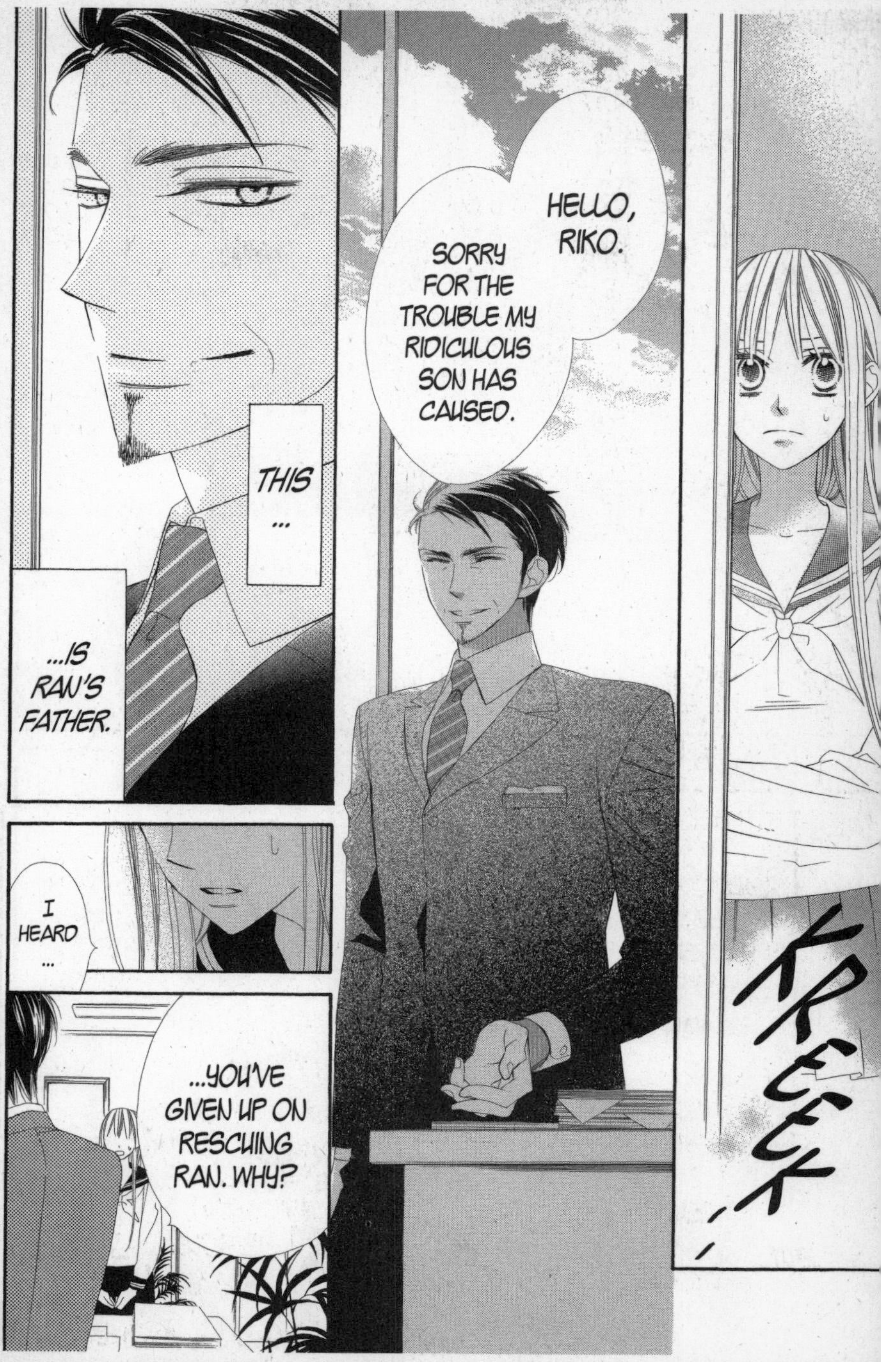
KREEEK!!
HELLO, RIKO.
SORRY FOR THE TROUBLE MY RIDICULOUS SON HAS CAUSED.
THIS ...
...IS RAN'S FATHER.
I HEARD ...
...YOU'VE GIVEN UP ON RESCUING RAN. WHY?

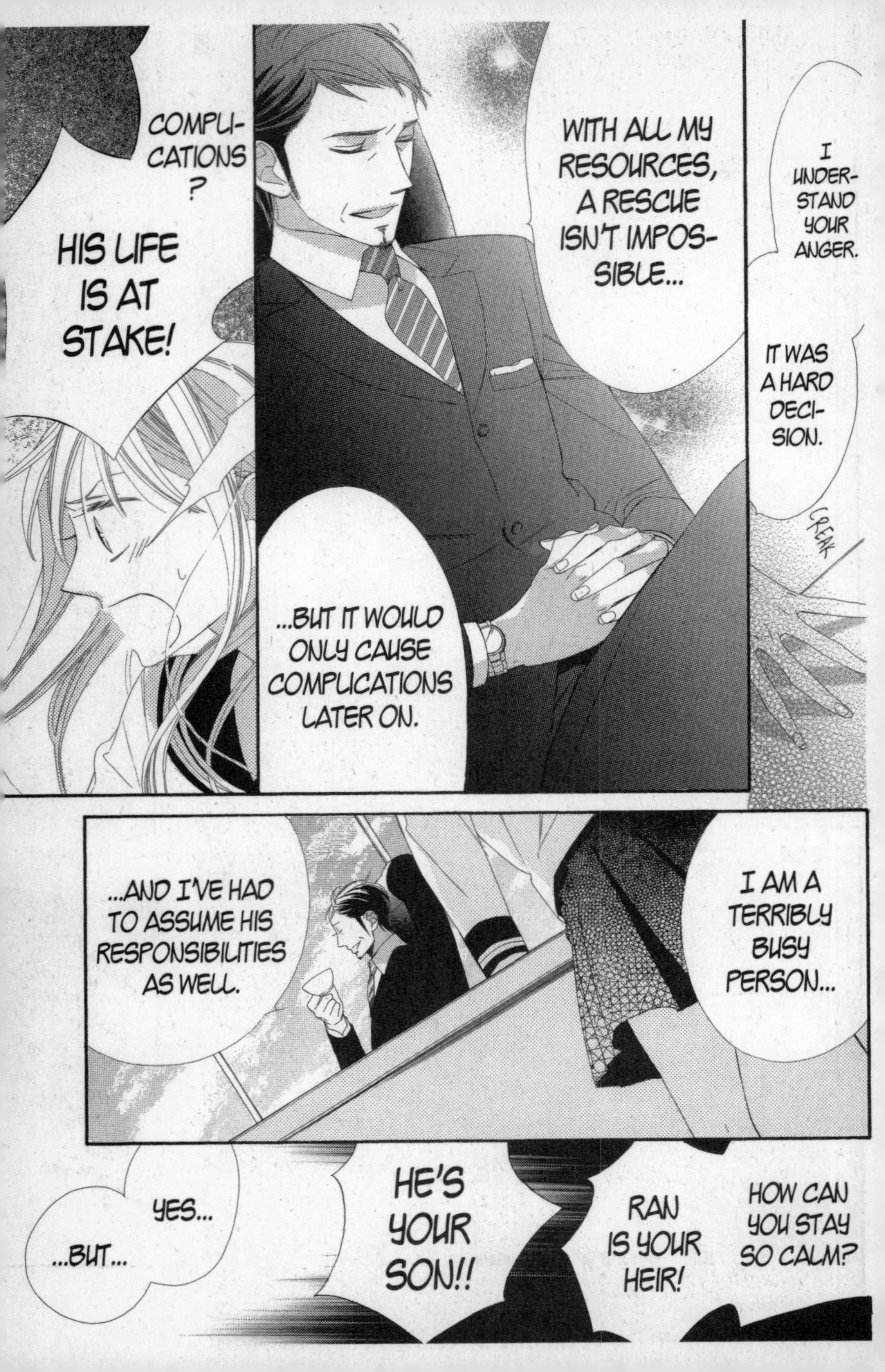

I UNDERSTAND YOUR ANGER.
IT WAS A HARD DECISION.
CREAK
WITH ALL MY RESOURCES, A RESCUE ISN'T IMPOSSIBLE...
...BUT IT WOULD ONLY CAUSE COMPLICATIONS LATER ON.
COMPLICATIONS?
HIS LIFE IS AT STAKE!
I AM A TERRIBLY BUSY PERSON...
...AND I'VE HAD TO ASSUME HIS RESPONSIBILITIES AS WELL.
HOW CAN YOU STAY SO CALM?
RAN IS YOUR HEIR!
HE'S YOUR SON!!
YES...
...BUT...

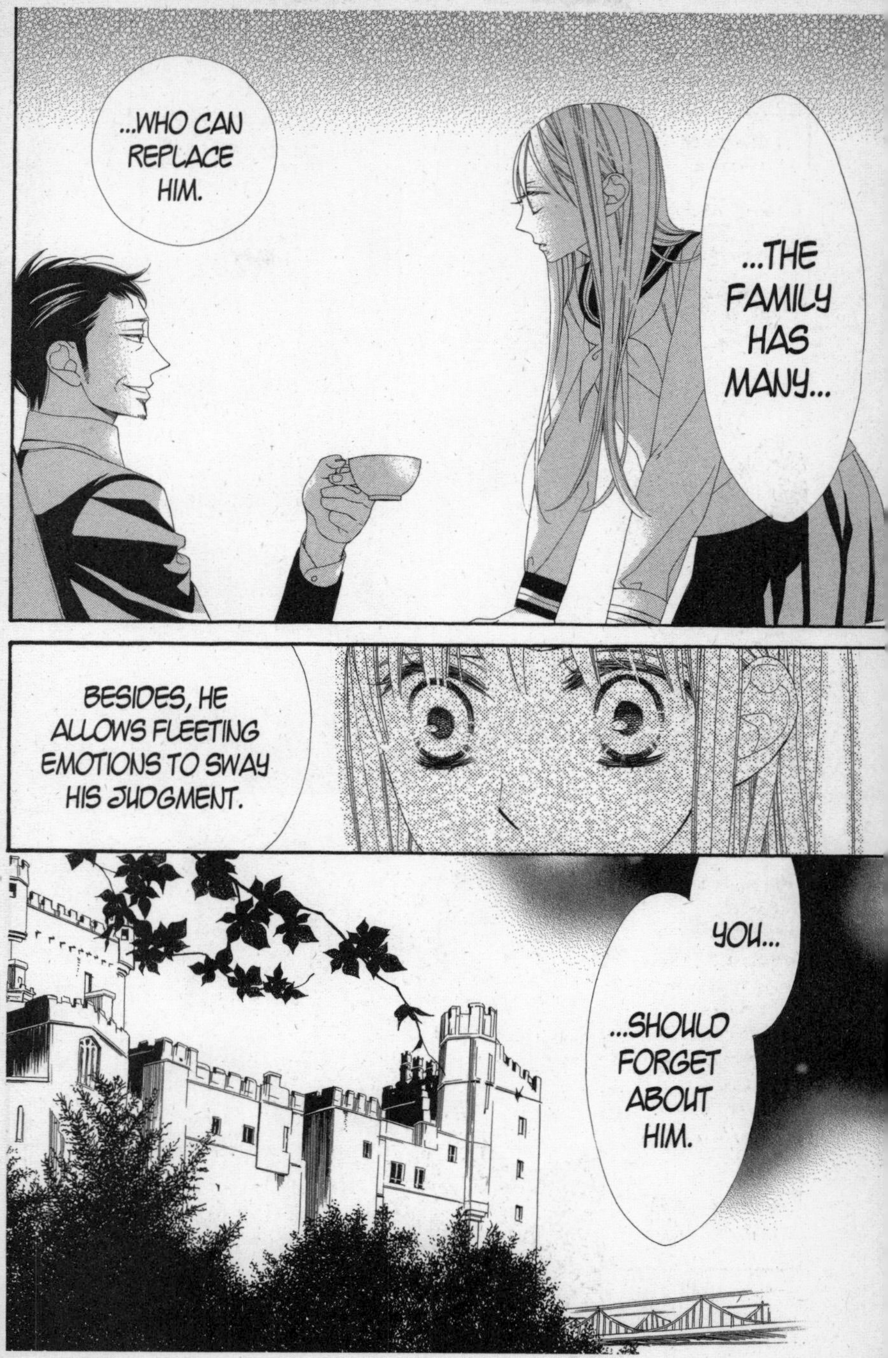
...THE FAMILY HAS MANY...
...WHO CAN REPLACE HIM.
BESIDES, HE ALLOWS FLEETING EMOTIONS TO SWAY HIS JUDGMENT.
YOU...
...SHOULD FORGET ABOUT HIM.

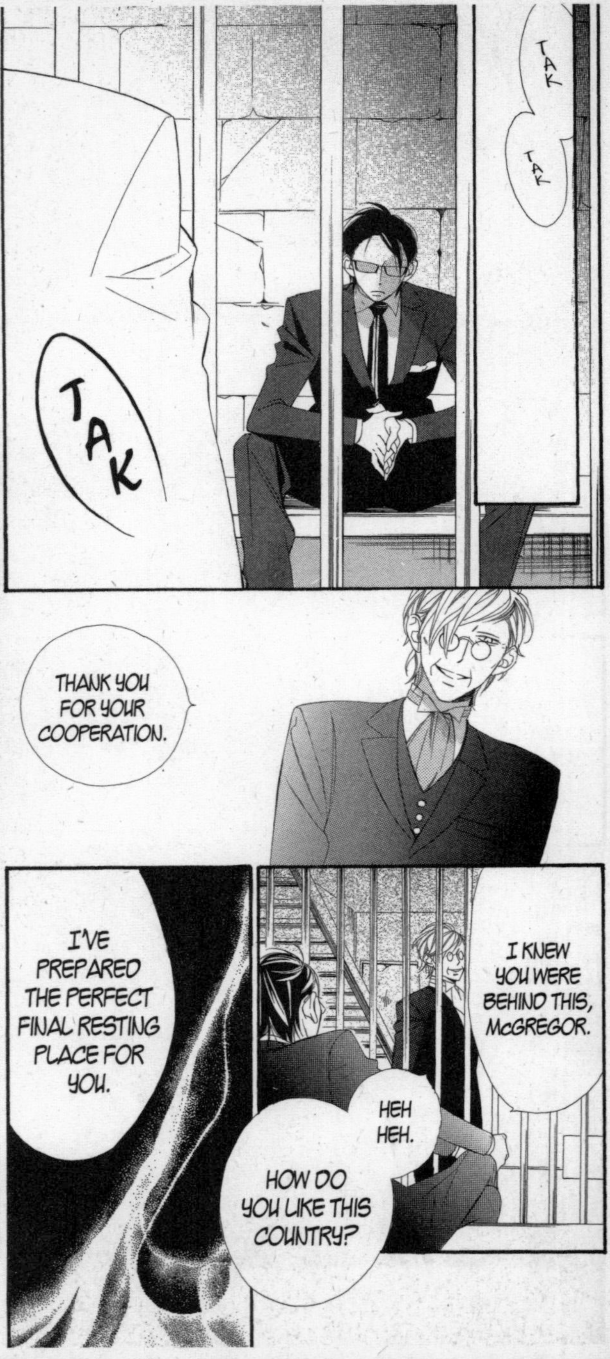
TAK
TAK
TAK
THANK YOU FOR YOUR COOPERATION.
I KNEW YOU WERE BEHIND THIS, McGREGOR.
HEH HEH.
HOW DO YOU LIKE THIS COUNTRY?
I'VE PREPARED THE PERFECT FINAL RESTING PLACE FOR YOU.

· Character ·
Profile

Father Tachibana
(not his name)
37 years old, 5' 11 1/2"

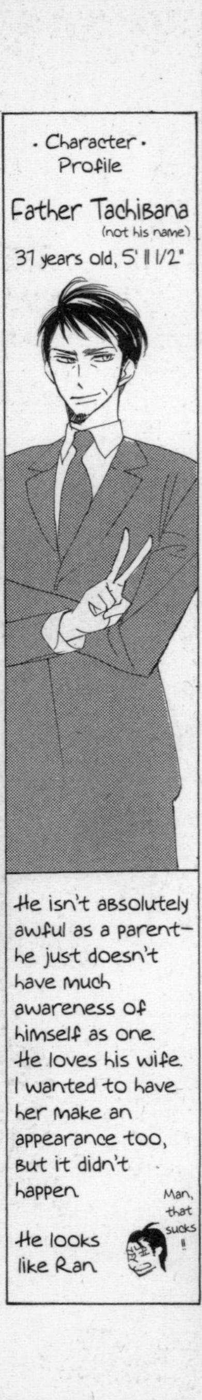

He isn't absolutely awful as a parent—he just doesn't have much awareness of himself as one. He loves his wife. I wanted to have her make an appearance too, but it didn't happen.

He looks like Ran.

Man, that sucks!!

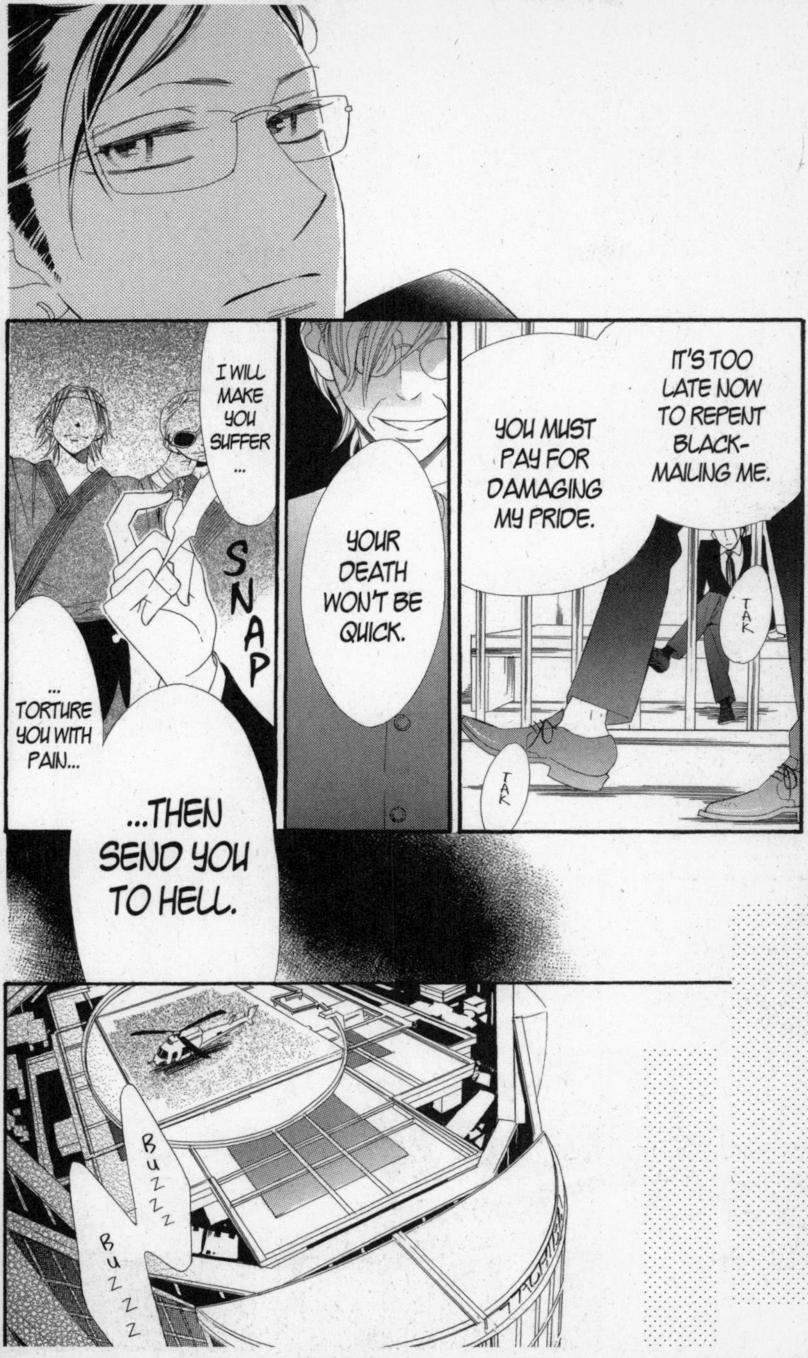
IT'S TOO LATE NOW TO REPENT BLACK-MAILING ME.
YOU MUST PAY FOR DAMAGING MY PRIDE.
TAK
TAK
YOUR DEATH WON'T BE QUICK.
I WILL MAKE YOU SUFFER ...
SNAP
... TORTURE YOU WITH PAIN...
...THEN SEND YOU TO HELL.
BUZZZ
BUZZZ

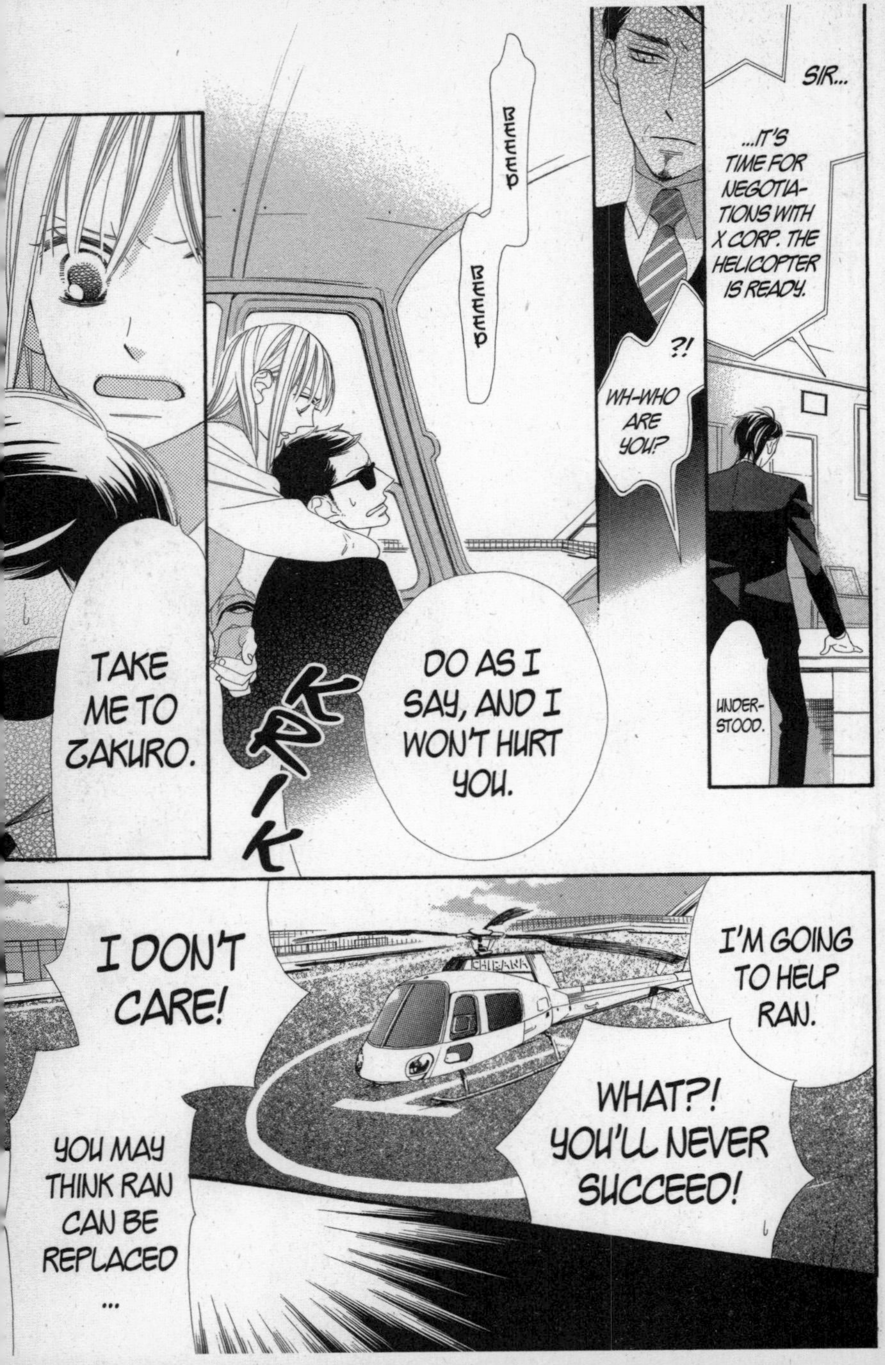
SIR...
...IT'S TIME FOR NEGOTIATIONS WITH X CORP. THE HELICOPTER IS READY.
?!
WH-WHO ARE YOU?
UNDERSTOOD.
BEEEP
BEEEP
DO AS I SAY, AND I WON'T HURT YOU.
KRIK
TAKE ME TO ZAKURO.
I'M GOING TO HELP RAN.
WHAT?! YOU'LL NEVER SUCCEED!
I DON'T CARE!
YOU MAY THINK RAN CAN BE REPLACED
...

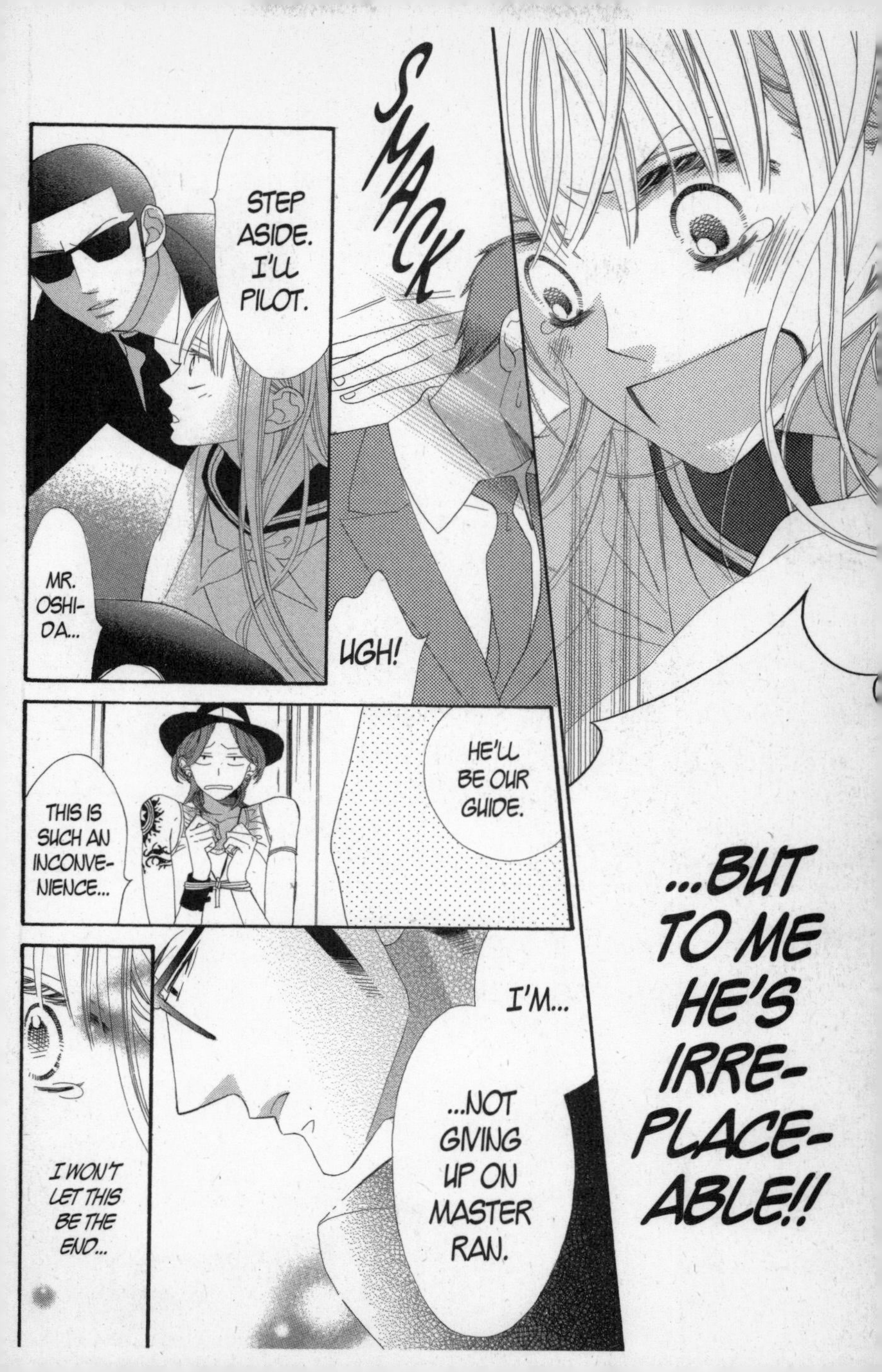
SMACK
...BUT TO ME HE'S IRRE-PLACE-ABLE!!
STEP ASIDE. I'LL PILOT.
MR. OSHI-DA...
UGH!
HE'LL BE OUR GUIDE.
THIS IS SUCH AN INCONVE-NIENCE...
I'M...
...NOT GIVING UP ON MASTER RAN.
I WON'T LET THIS BE THE END...

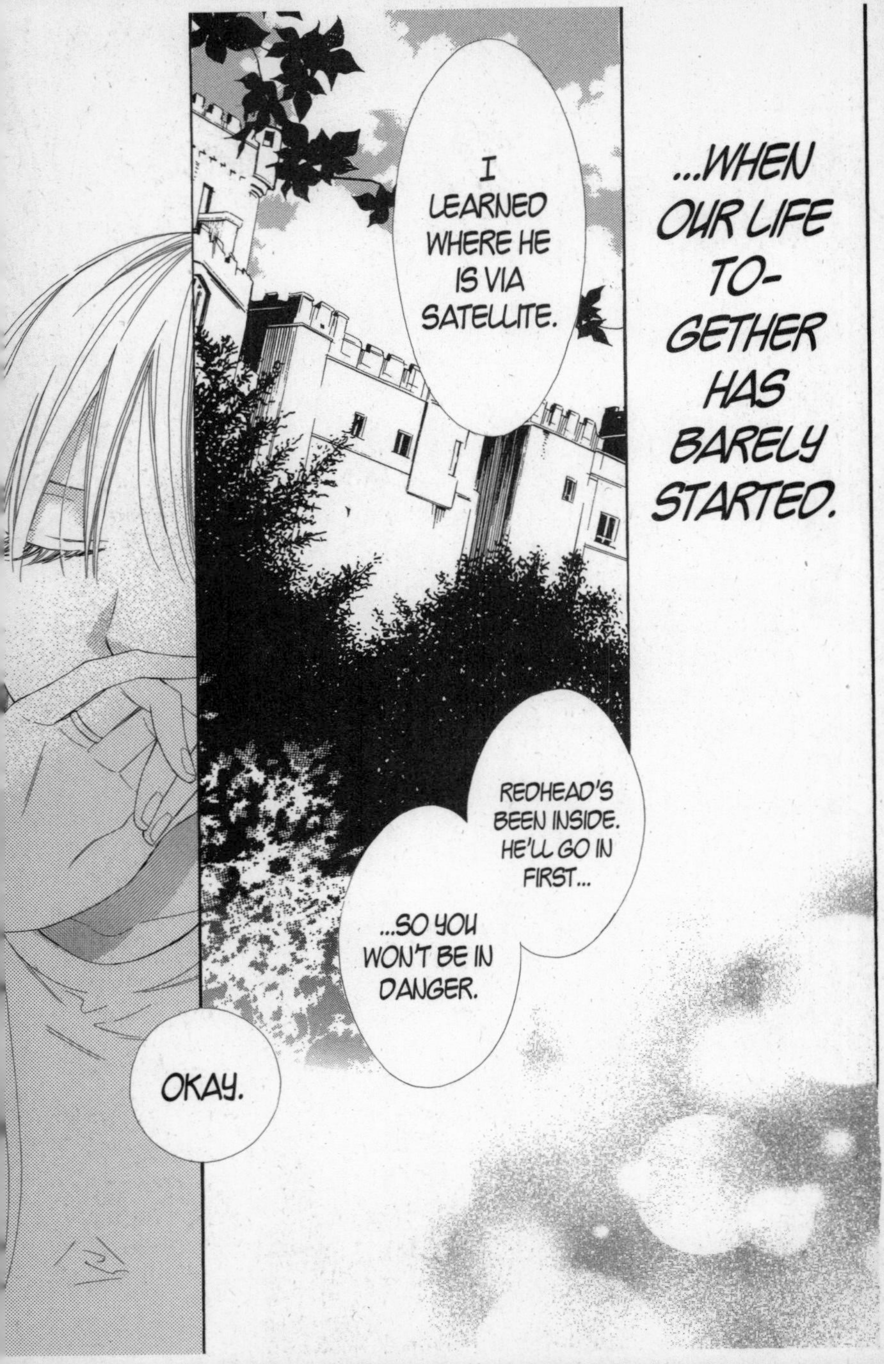
...WHEN OUR LIFE TO-GETHER HAS BARELY STARTED.
I LEARNED WHERE HE IS VIA SATELLITE.
REDHEAD'S BEEN INSIDE. HE'LL GO IN FIRST...
...SO YOU WON'T BE IN DANGER.
OKAY.

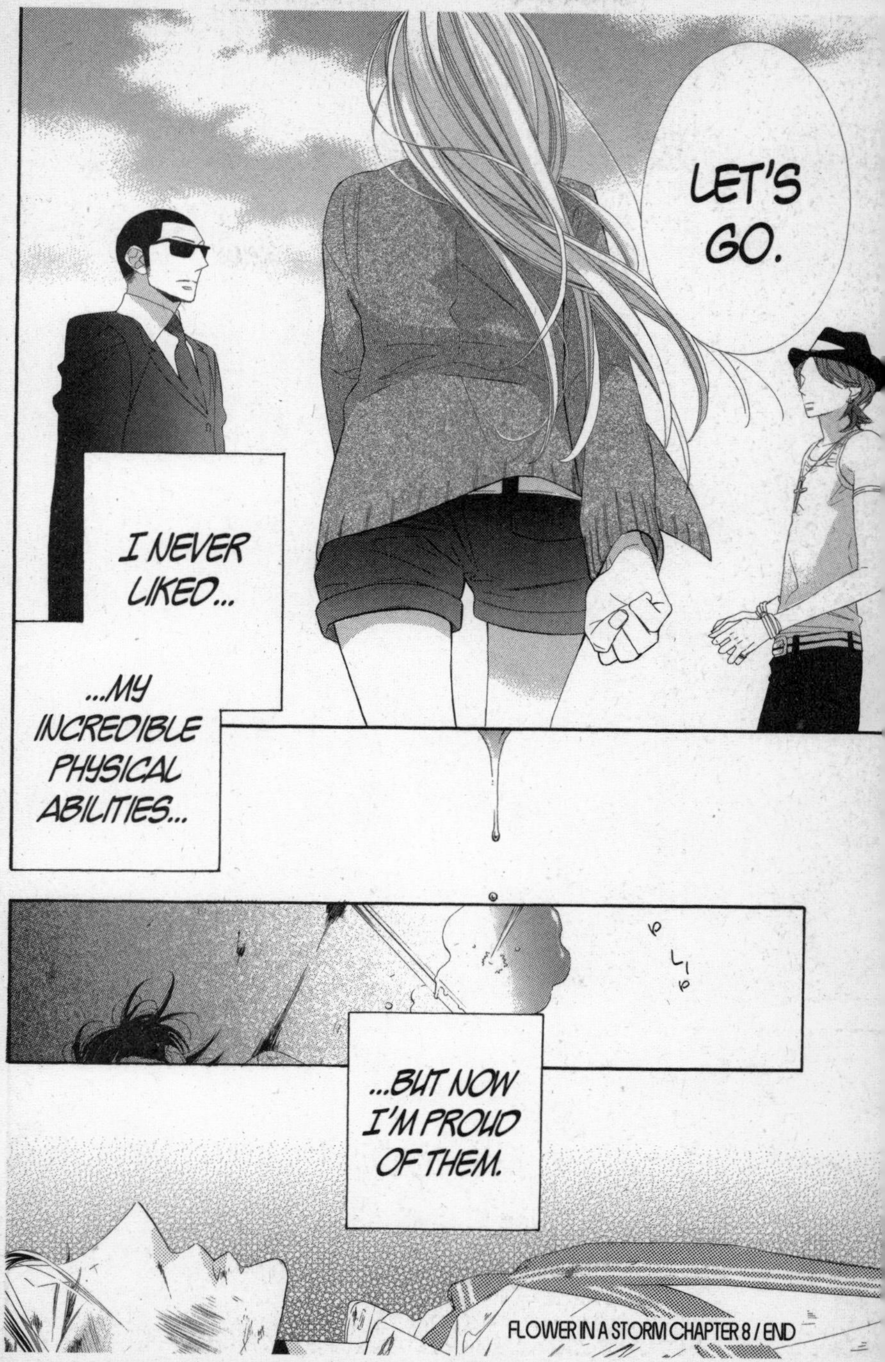
LET'S GO.
I NEVER LIKED...
...MY INCREDIBLE PHYSICAL ABILITIES...
...BUT NOW I'M PROUD OF THEM.
FLOWER IN A STORM CHAPTER 8 / END

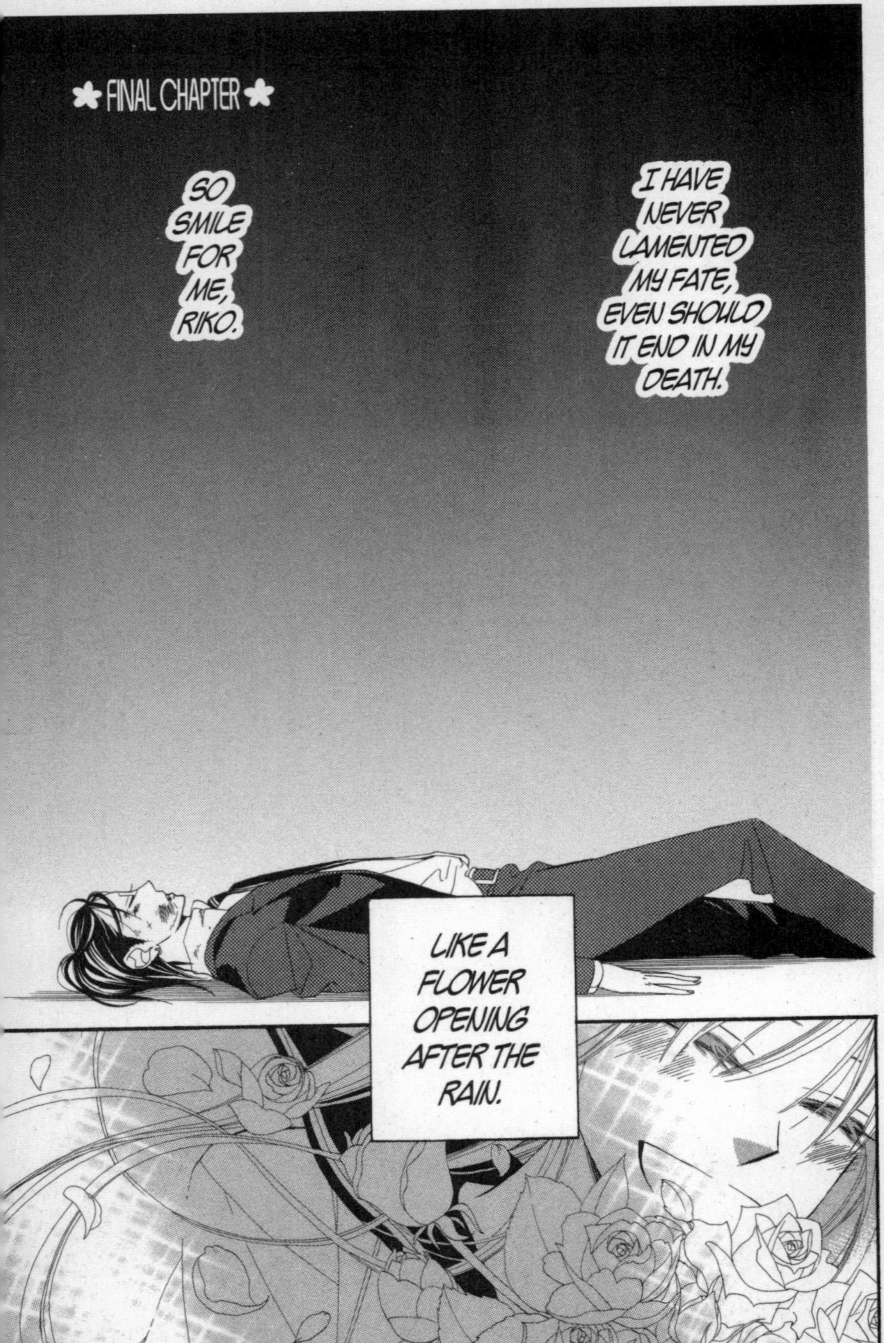
FINAL CHAPTER
I HAVE NEVER LAMENTED MY FATE, EVEN SHOULD IT END IN MY DEATH.
SO SMILE FOR ME, RIKO.
LIKE A FLOWER OPENING AFTER THE RAIN.

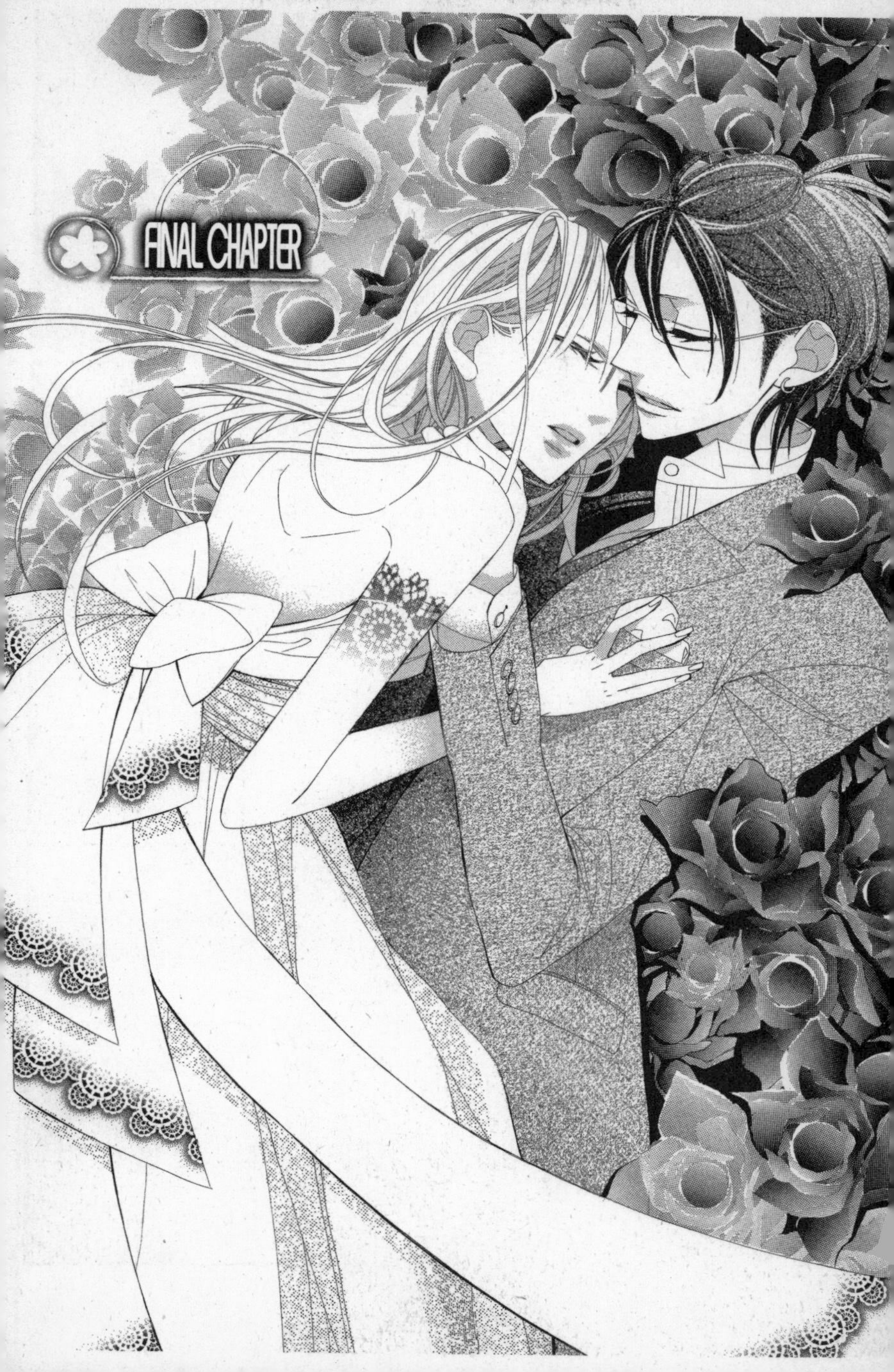
FINAL CHAPTER

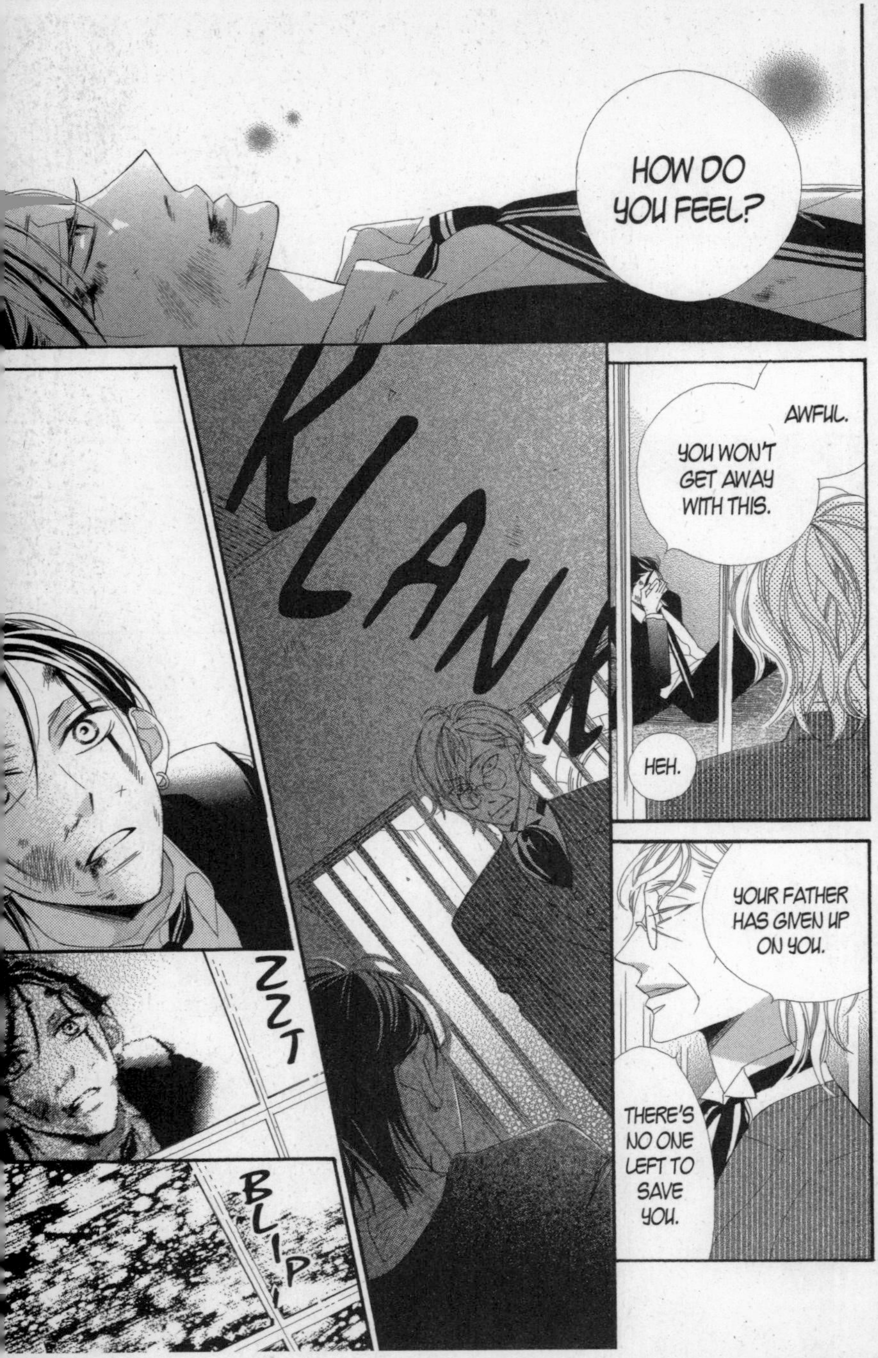
HOW DO YOU FEEL?
AWFUL.
YOU WON'T GET AWAY WITH THIS.
HEH.
YOUR FATHER HAS GIVEN UP ON YOU.
THERE'S NO ONE LEFT TO SAVE YOU.
KLANK
ZZZT
BLIP

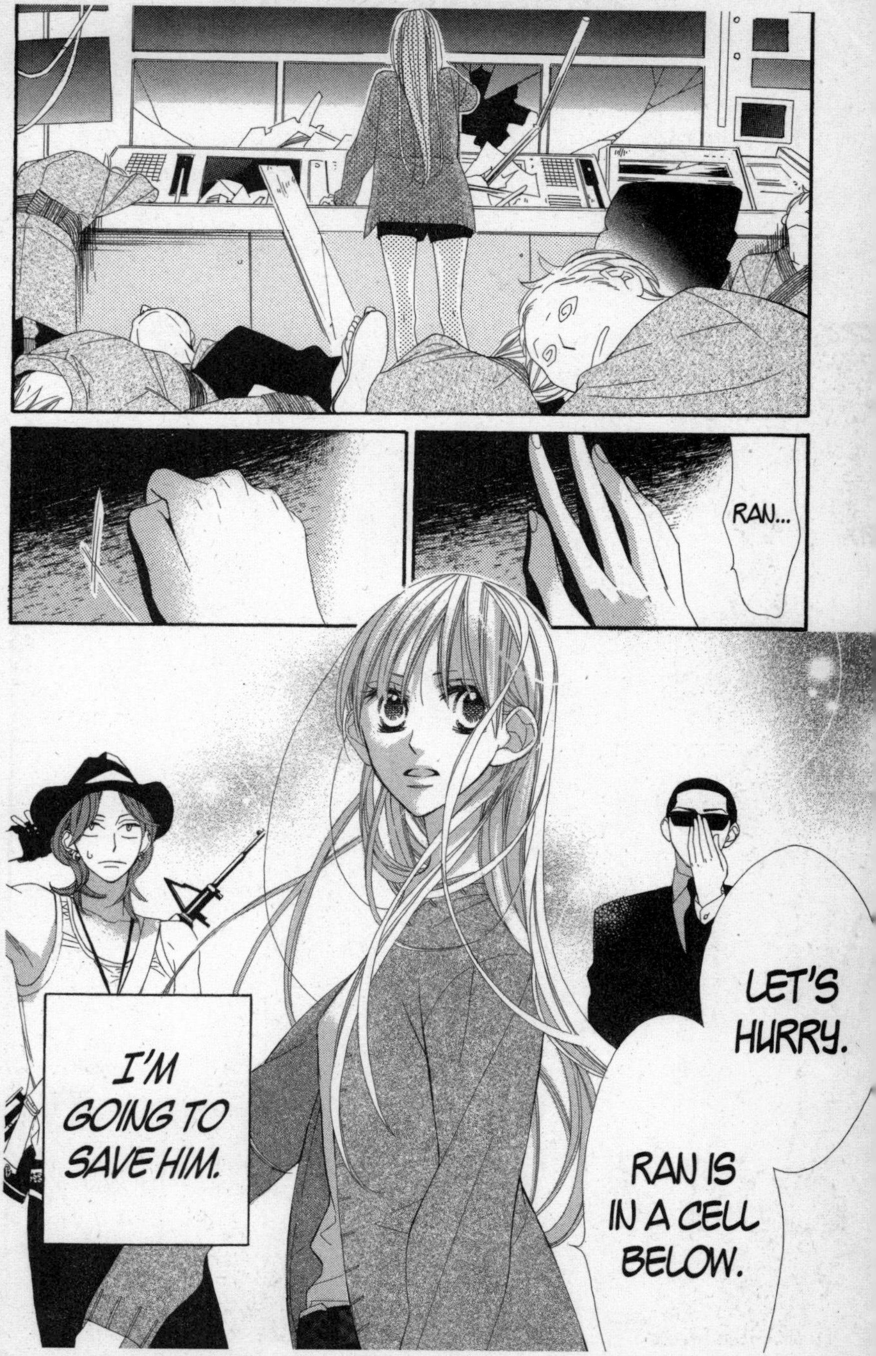
RAN...
LET'S HURRY.
RAN IS IN A CELL BELOW.
I'M GOING TO SAVE HIM.

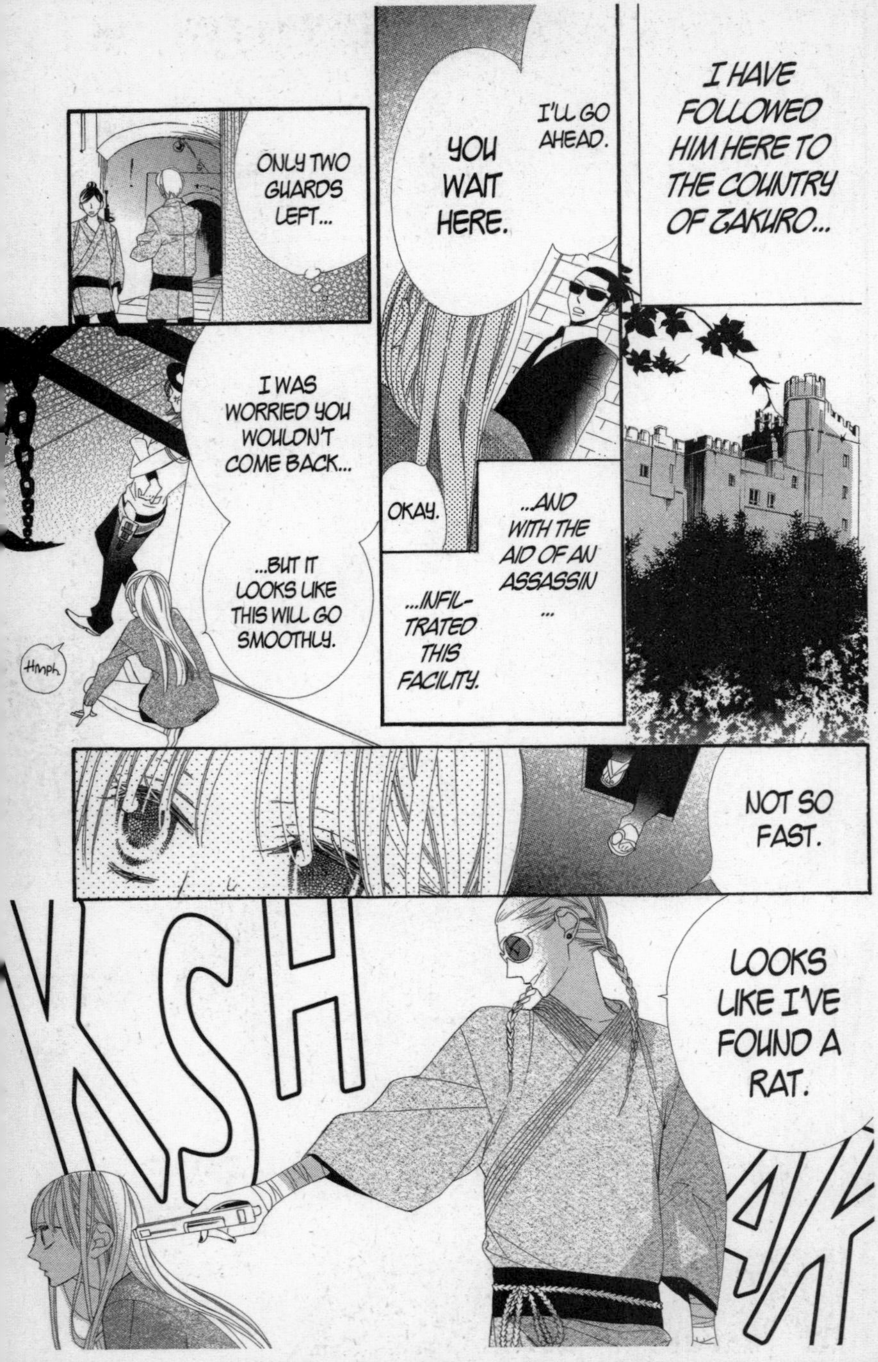
I HAVE FOLLOWED HIM HERE TO THE COUNTRY OF ZAKURO...
I'LL GO AHEAD.
YOU WAIT HERE.
OKAY.
...AND WITH THE AID OF AN ASSASSIN...
...INFIL-TRATED THIS FACILITY.
ONLY TWO GUARDS LEFT...
I WAS WORRIED YOU WOULDN'T COME BACK...
...BUT IT LOOKS LIKE THIS WILL GO SMOOTHLY.
Hmph.
NOT SO FAST.
LOOKS LIKE I'VE FOUND A RAT.
KSH

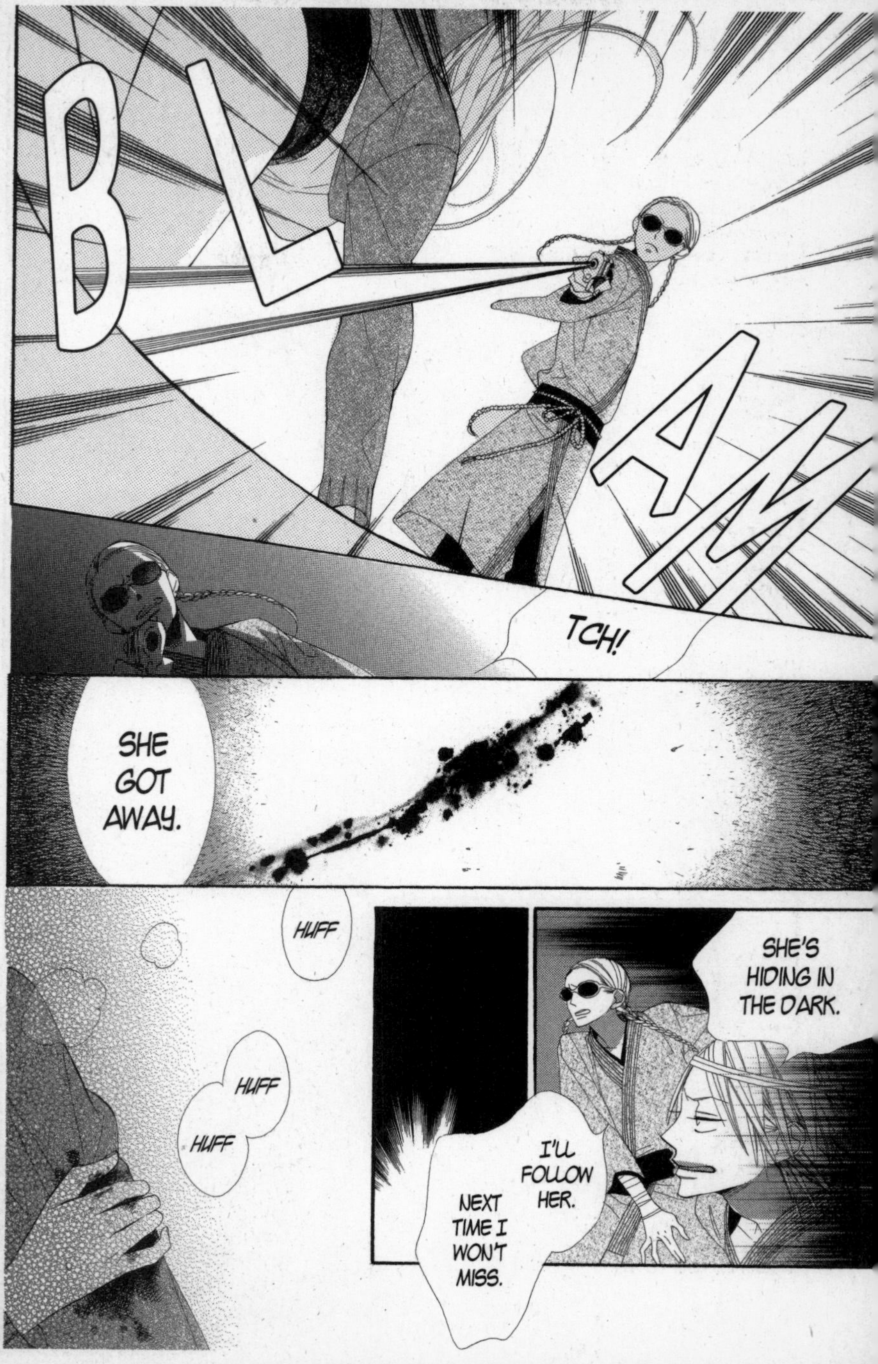
BLAM
TCH!
SHE GOT AWAY.
SHE'S HIDING IN THE DARK.
I'LL FOLLOW HER.
NEXT TIME I WON'T MISS.
HUFF
HUFF
HUFF

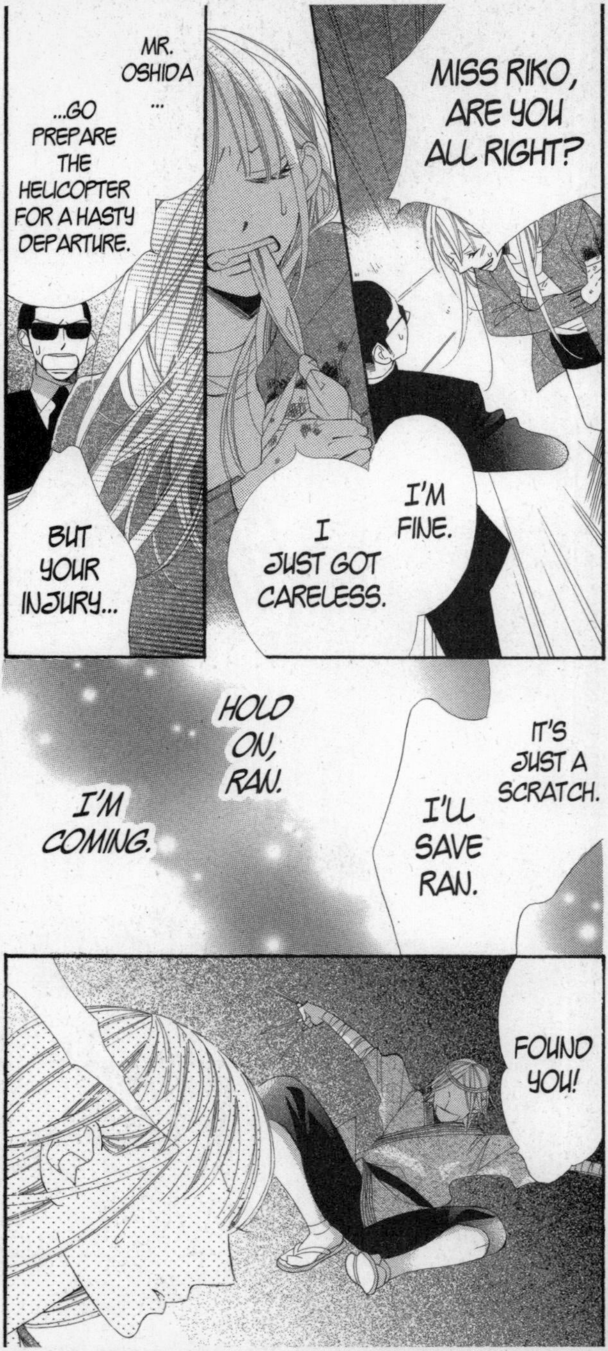
MISS RIKO, ARE YOU ALL RIGHT?
I'M FINE.
I JUST GOT CARELESS.
MR. OSHIDA...
...GO PREPARE THE HELICOPTER FOR A HASTY DEPARTURE.
BUT YOUR INJURY...
IT'S JUST A SCRATCH.
I'LL SAVE RAN.
HOLD ON, RAN.
I'M COMING.
FOUND YOU!

From chapter 5 on, it was extremely difficult to complete one story in a mere 30 pages.

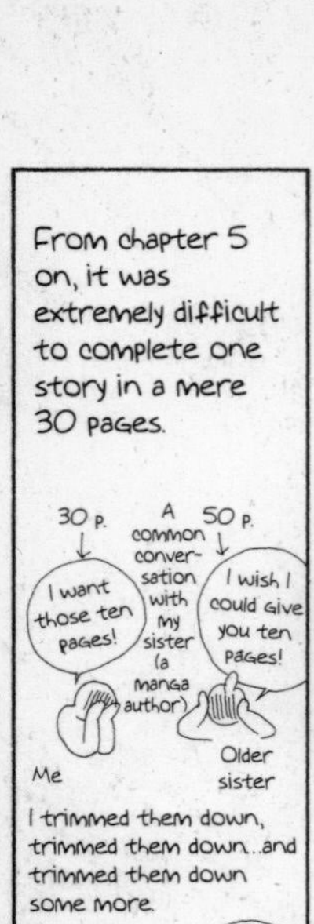
30 p.
A common conversation with my sister (a manga author)
50 p.
I wish I could give you ten pages!
I want those ten pages!
Me
Older sister

I trimmed them down, trimmed them down...and trimmed them down some more.

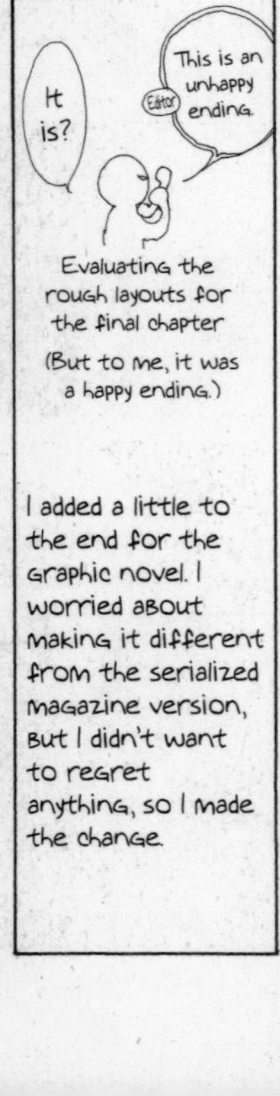
This is an unhappy ending.
Editor
It is?

Evaluating the rough layouts for the final chapter

(But to me, it was a happy ending.)

I added a little to the end for the graphic novel. I worried about making it different from the serialized magazine version, but I didn't want to regret anything, so I made the change.

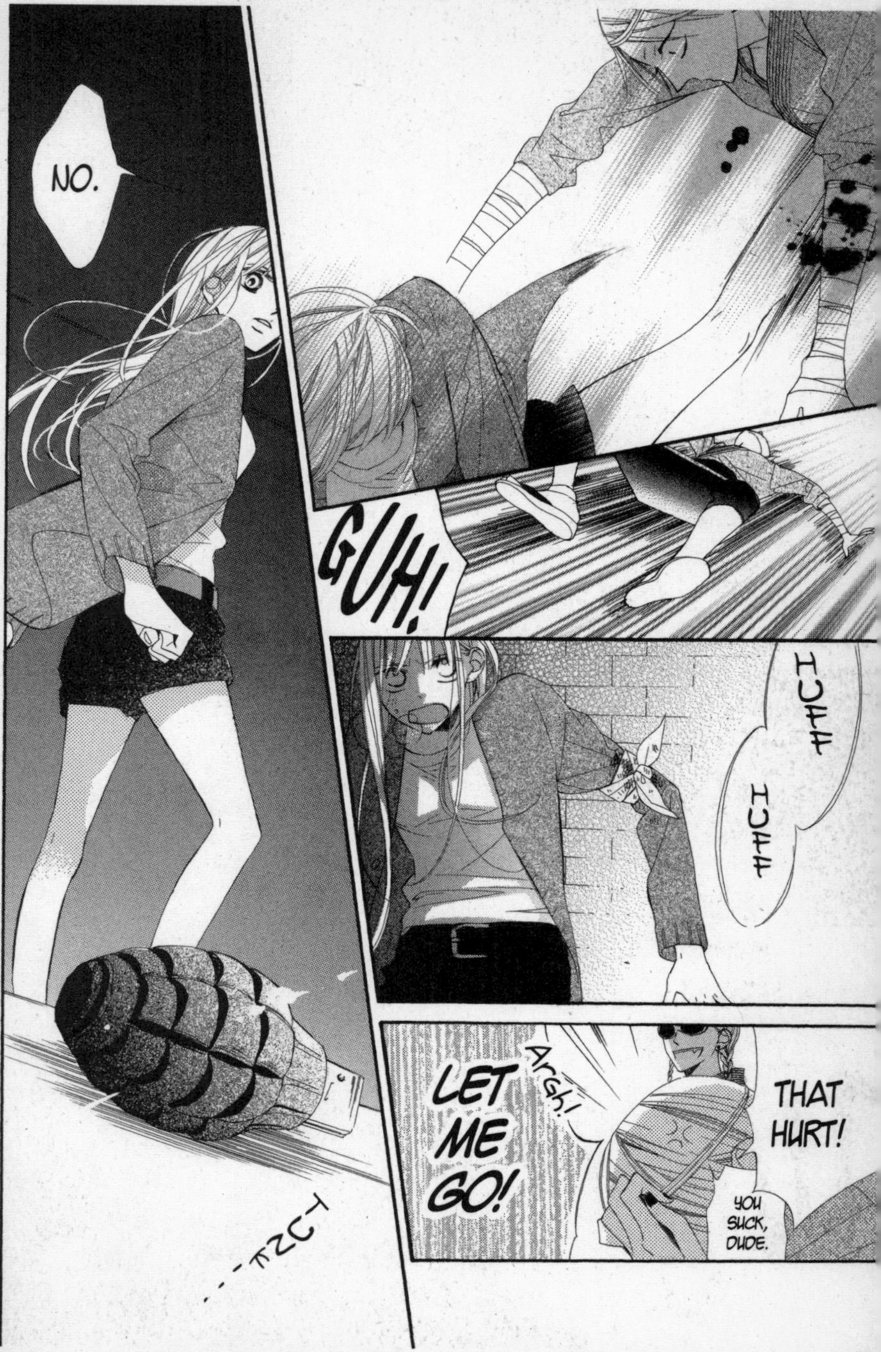
GUH!
HUFF
HUFF
THAT HURT!
YOU SUCK, DUDE.
Argh!
LET ME GO!
NO.
...TZZT

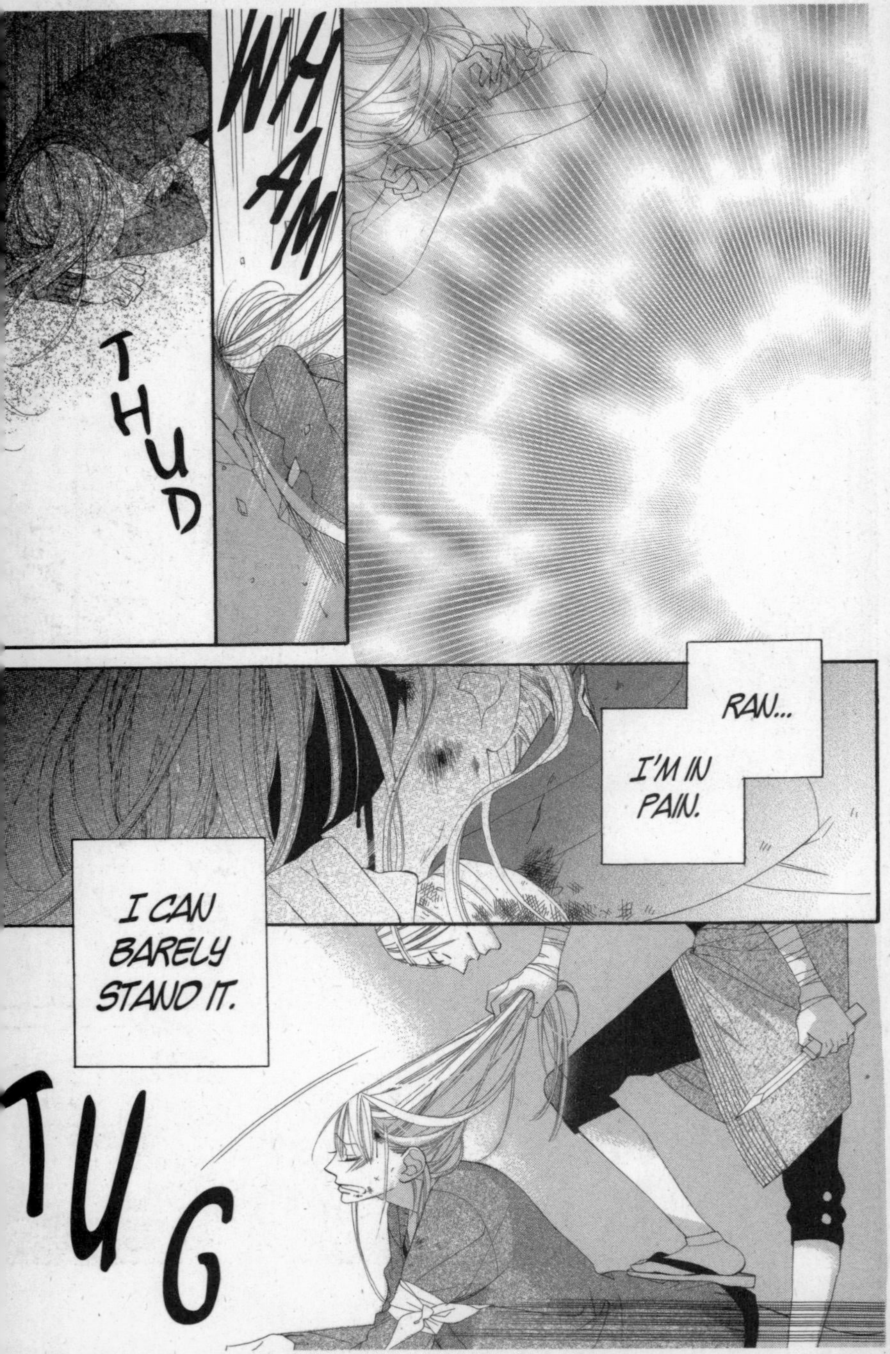
WHAM
THUD
RAN...
I'M IN PAIN.
I CAN BARELY STAND IT.
TUG

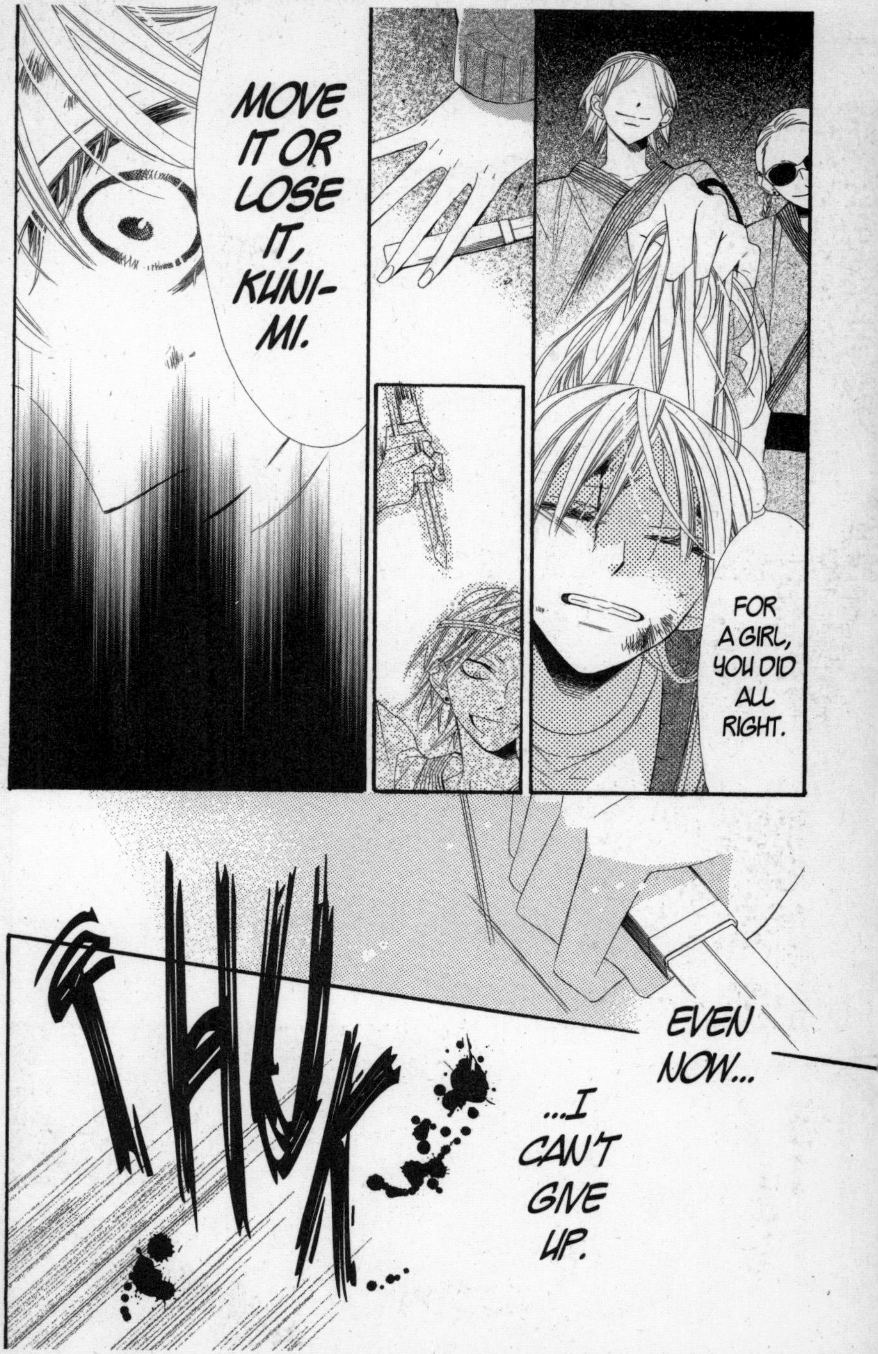
FOR A GIRL, YOU DID ALL RIGHT.
MOVE IT OR LOSE IT, KUNI-MI.
EVEN NOW...
...I CAN'T GIVE UP.
THUK

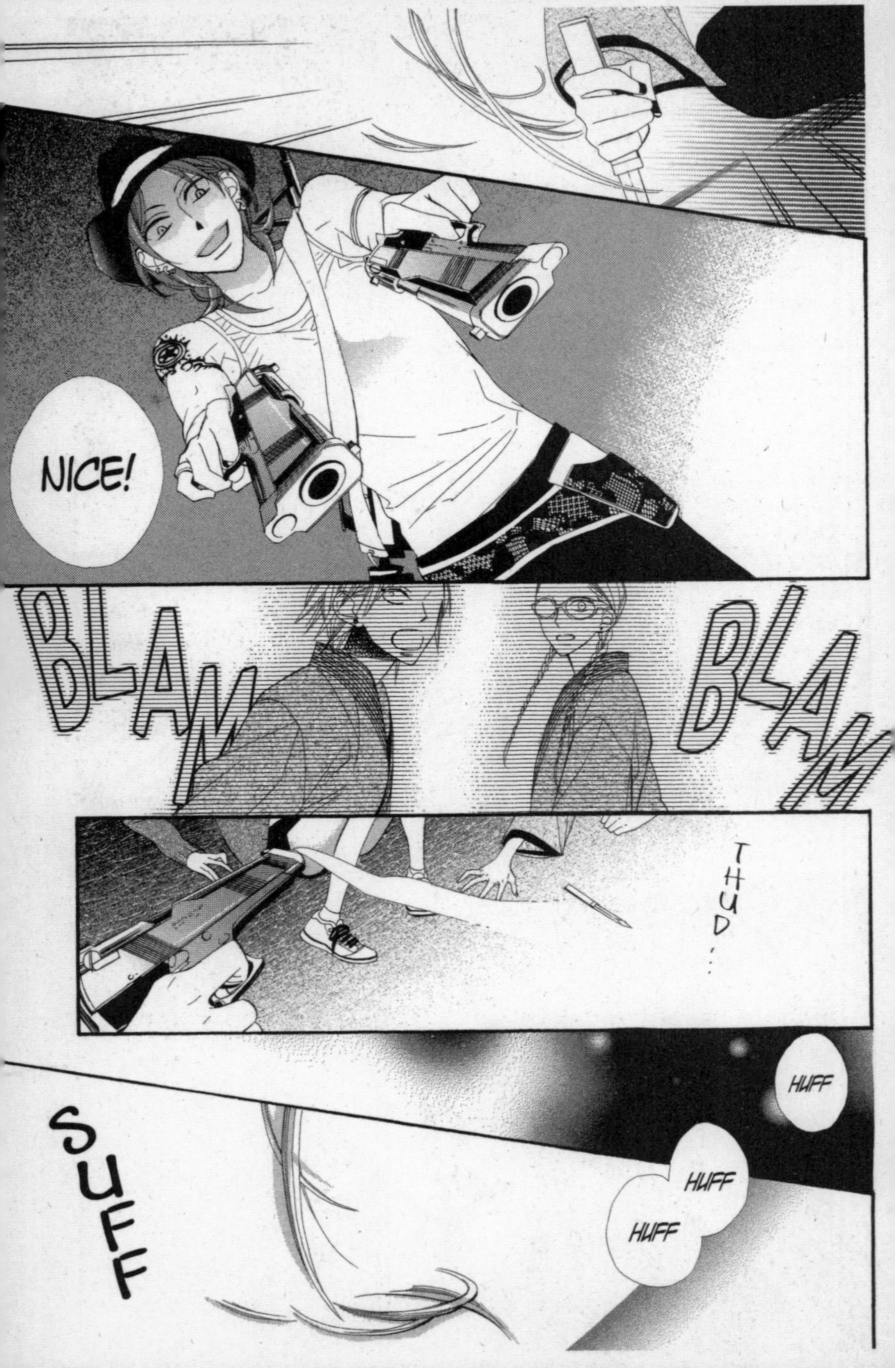
NICE!
BLAM
BLAM
THUD...
HUFF
HUFF
HUFF
SUFF

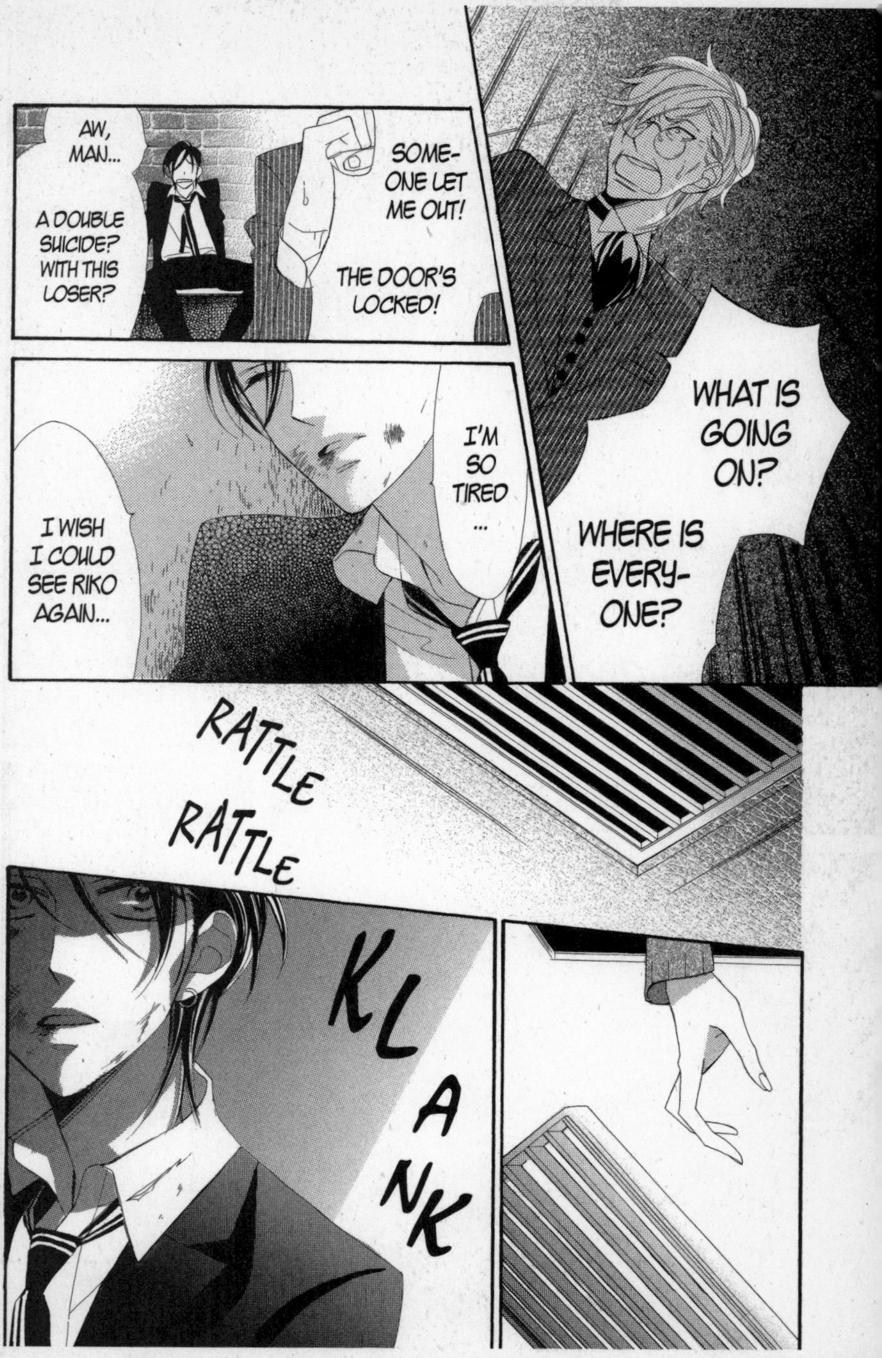
WHAT IS GOING ON?
WHERE IS EVERY-ONE?
SOME-ONE LET ME OUT!
THE DOOR'S LOCKED!
AW, MAN...
A DOUBLE SUICIDE? WITH THIS LOSER?
I'M SO TIRED ...
I WISH I COULD SEE RIKO AGAIN...
RATTLE RATTLE
KLANK

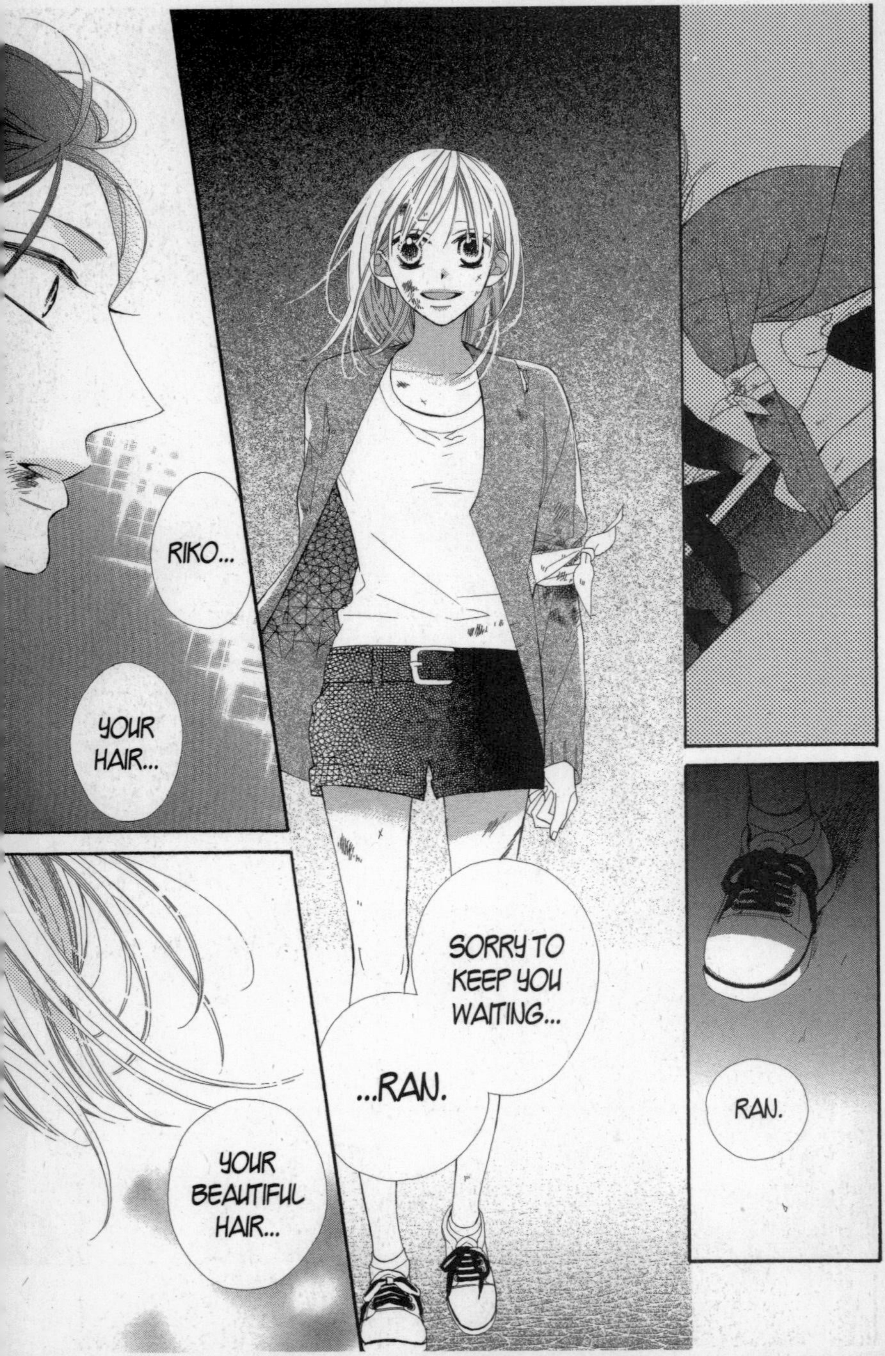
RAN.
SORRY TO KEEP YOU WAITING...
...RAN.
RIKO...
YOUR HAIR...
YOUR BEAUTIFUL HAIR...

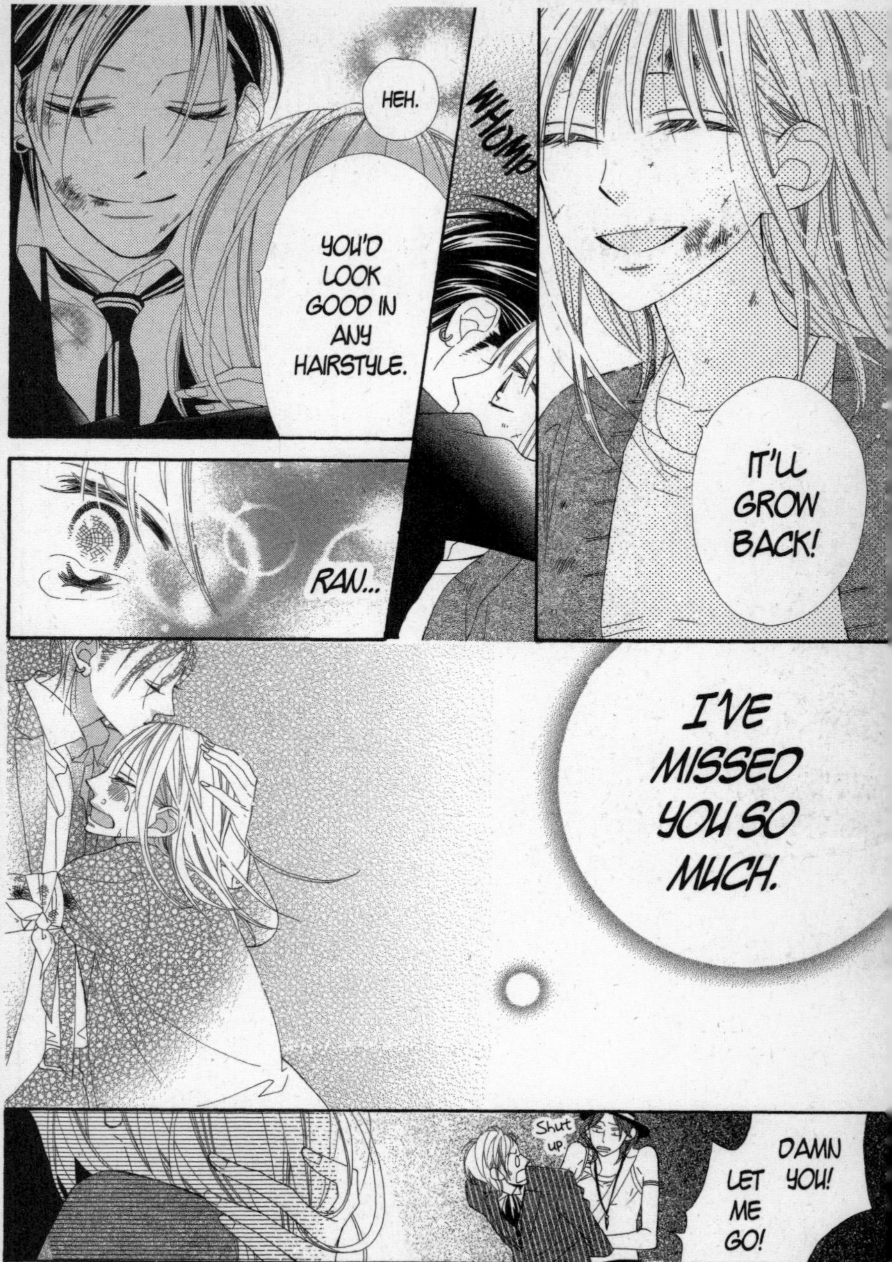
IT'LL GROW BACK!
WHOMP
HEH.
YOU'D LOOK GOOD IN ANY HAIRSTYLE.
RAN...
I'VE MISSED YOU SO MUCH.
DAMN YOU!
LET ME GO!
Shut up.

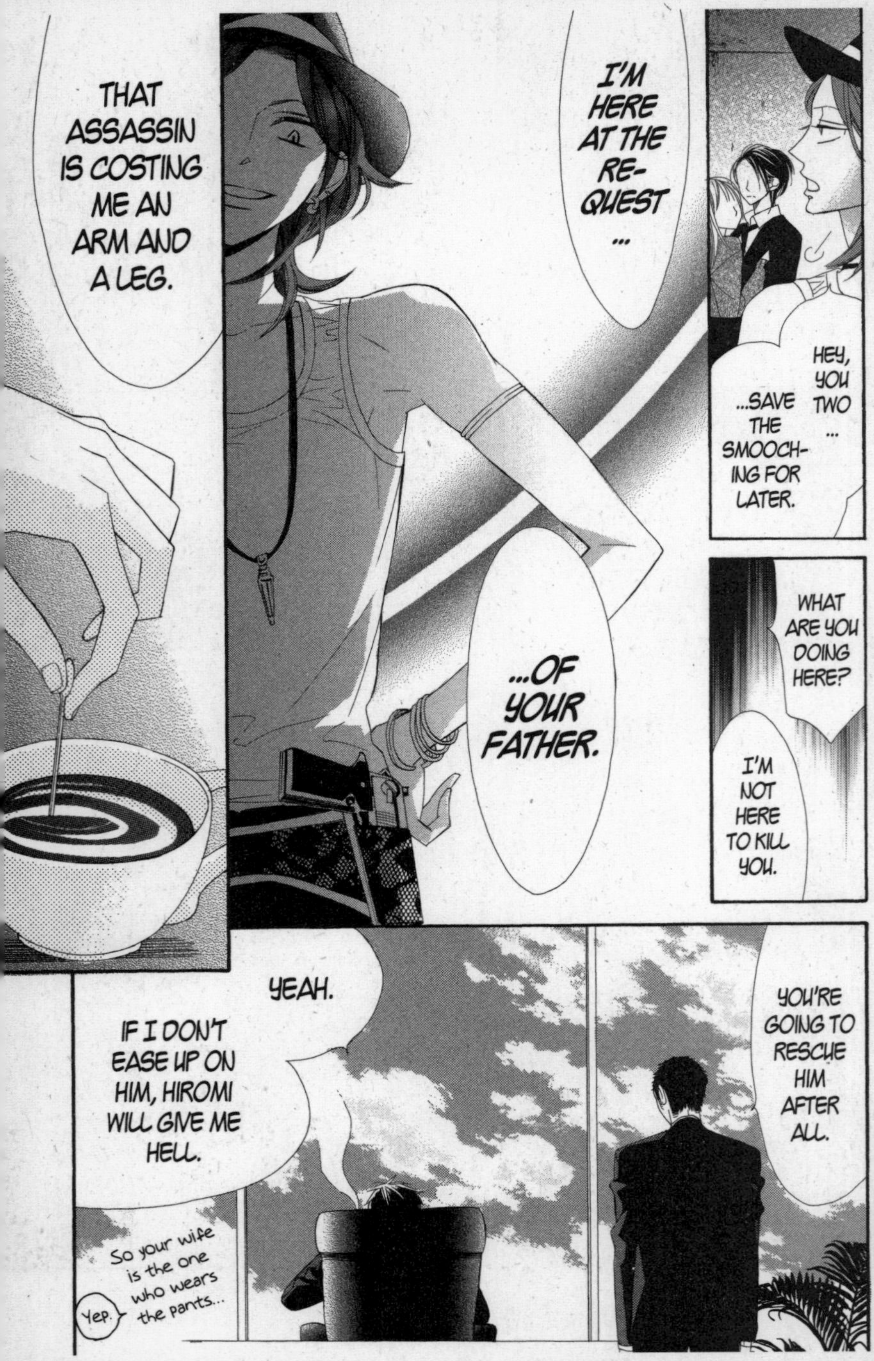
HEY, YOU TWO...
...SAVE THE SMOOCHING FOR LATER.
WHAT ARE YOU DOING HERE?
I'M NOT HERE TO KILL YOU.
I'M HERE AT THE REQUEST...
...OF YOUR FATHER.
THAT ASSASSIN IS COSTING ME AN ARM AND A LEG.
YOU'RE GOING TO RESCUE HIM AFTER ALL.
YEAH.
IF I DON'T EASE UP ON HIM, HIROMI WILL GIVE ME HELL.
So your wife is the one who wears the pants...
Yep.

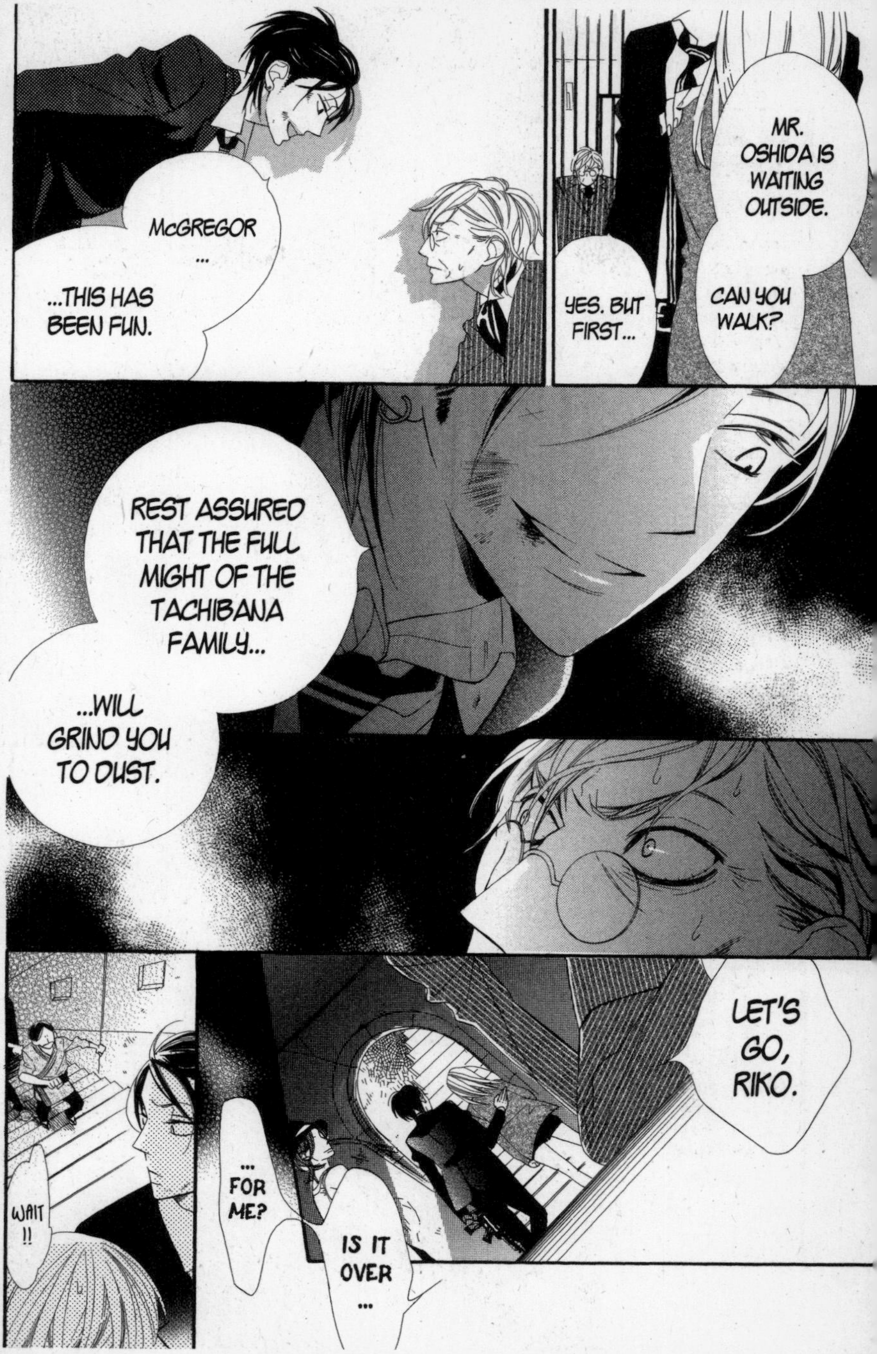
MR. OSHIDA IS WAITING OUTSIDE.
CAN YOU WALK?
YES. BUT FIRST...
McGREGOR...
...THIS HAS BEEN FUN.
REST ASSURED THAT THE FULL MIGHT OF THE TACHIBANA FAMILY...
...WILL GRIND YOU TO DUST.
LET'S GO, RIKO.
IS IT OVER...
...FOR ME?
WAIT!!

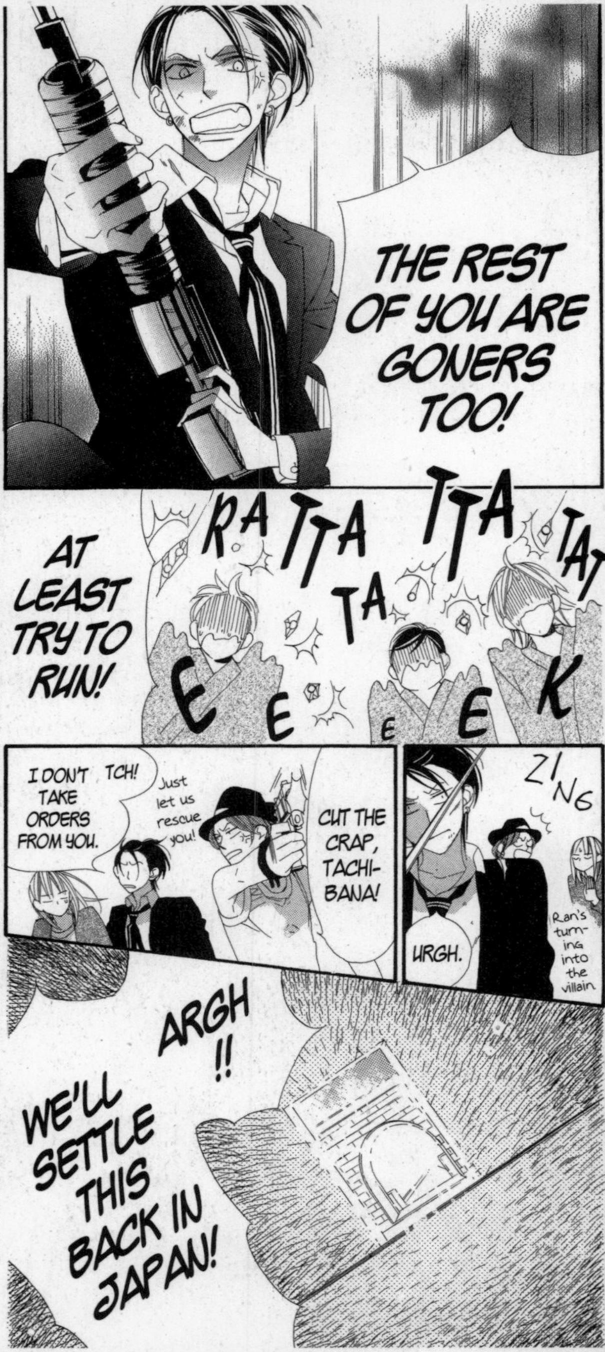
THE REST OF YOU ARE GONERS TOO!
RA TTA TA TTA TAT
EEEEK
AT LEAST TRY TO RUN!
ZING
URGH.
Ran's turning into the villain.
CUT THE CRAP, TACHIBANA!
Just let us rescue you!
TCH!
I DON'T TAKE ORDERS FROM YOU.
ARGH!!
WE'LL SETTLE THIS BACK IN JAPAN!

A few last comments...

I spent two whole years writing Flower in a Storm for publication in the magazine LaLa DX.

Time after time I thought I was going to collapse, but thanks to everyone who propped me up, I was able to pull through.

There was a lot I wanted to write but couldn't. Nonetheless, I think I gave it my all and wrote the best manga I could.

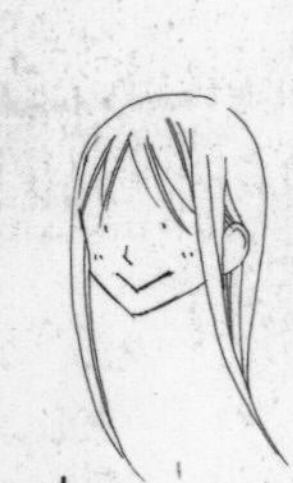

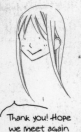

Thank you! Hope we meet again sometime! ♡♡♡

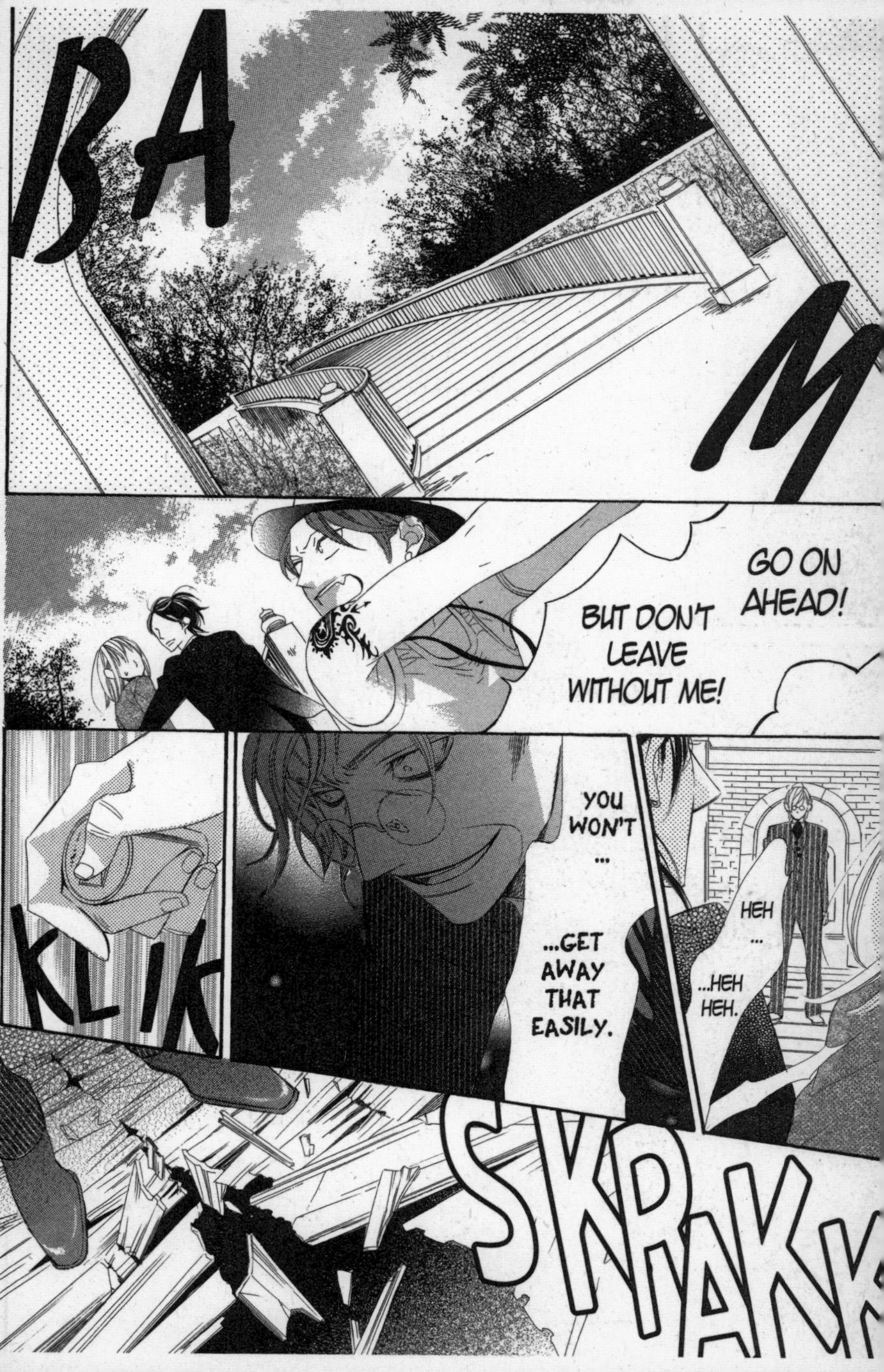
BAM
GO ON AHEAD!
BUT DON'T LEAVE WITHOUT ME!
HEH ...
...HEH HEH.
YOU WON'T ...
...GET AWAY THAT EASILY.
KLIK
SKRAKK

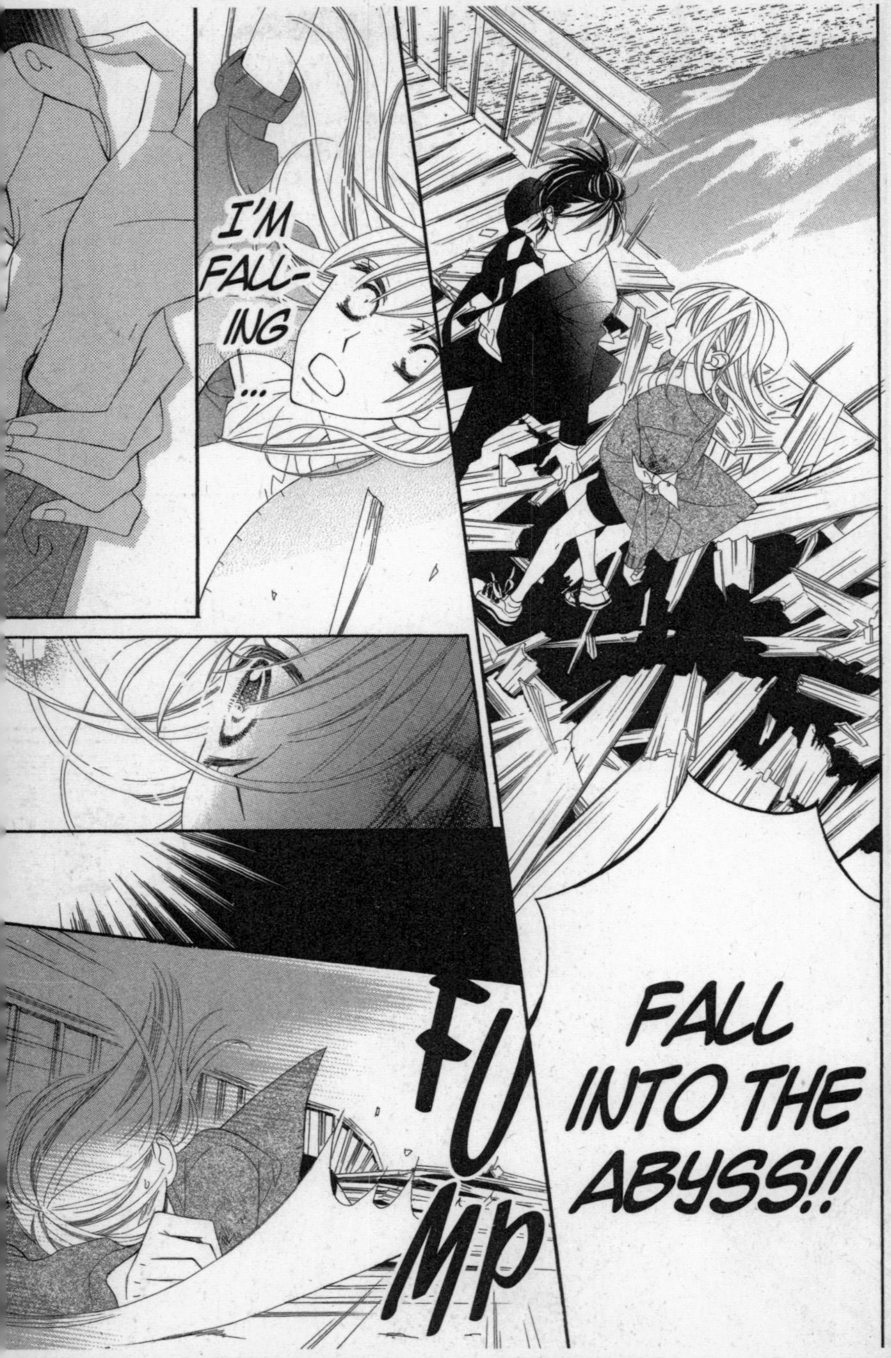
FALL INTO THE ABYSS!!
I'M FALLING ...
FUMP

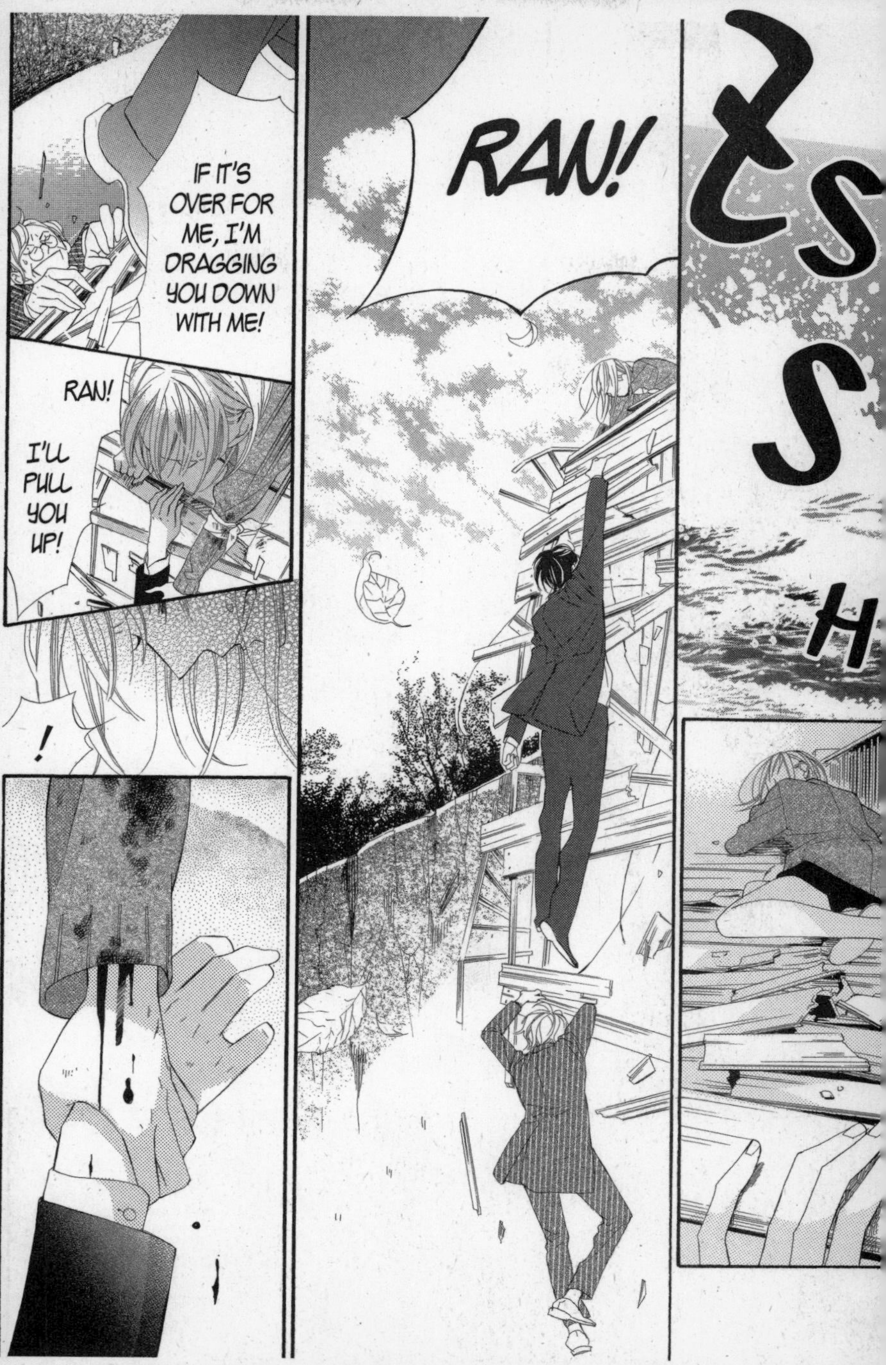
RAN!
IF IT'S OVER FOR ME, I'M DRAGGING YOU DOWN WITH ME!
RAN!
I'LL PULL YOU UP!
!

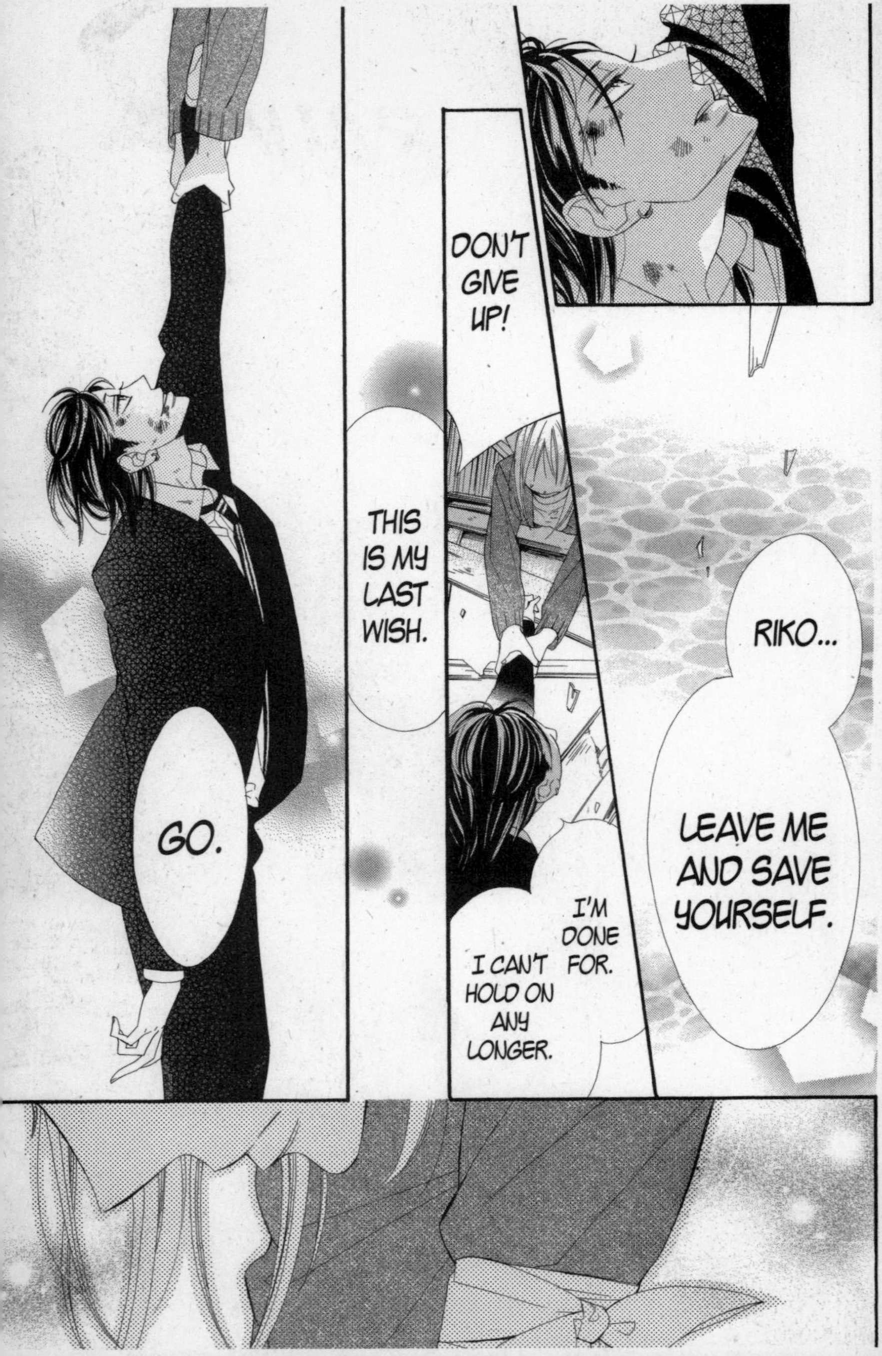
RIKO...
LEAVE ME AND SAVE YOURSELF.
DON'T GIVE UP!
I'M DONE FOR.
I CAN'T HOLD ON ANY LONGER.
THIS IS MY LAST WISH.
GO.

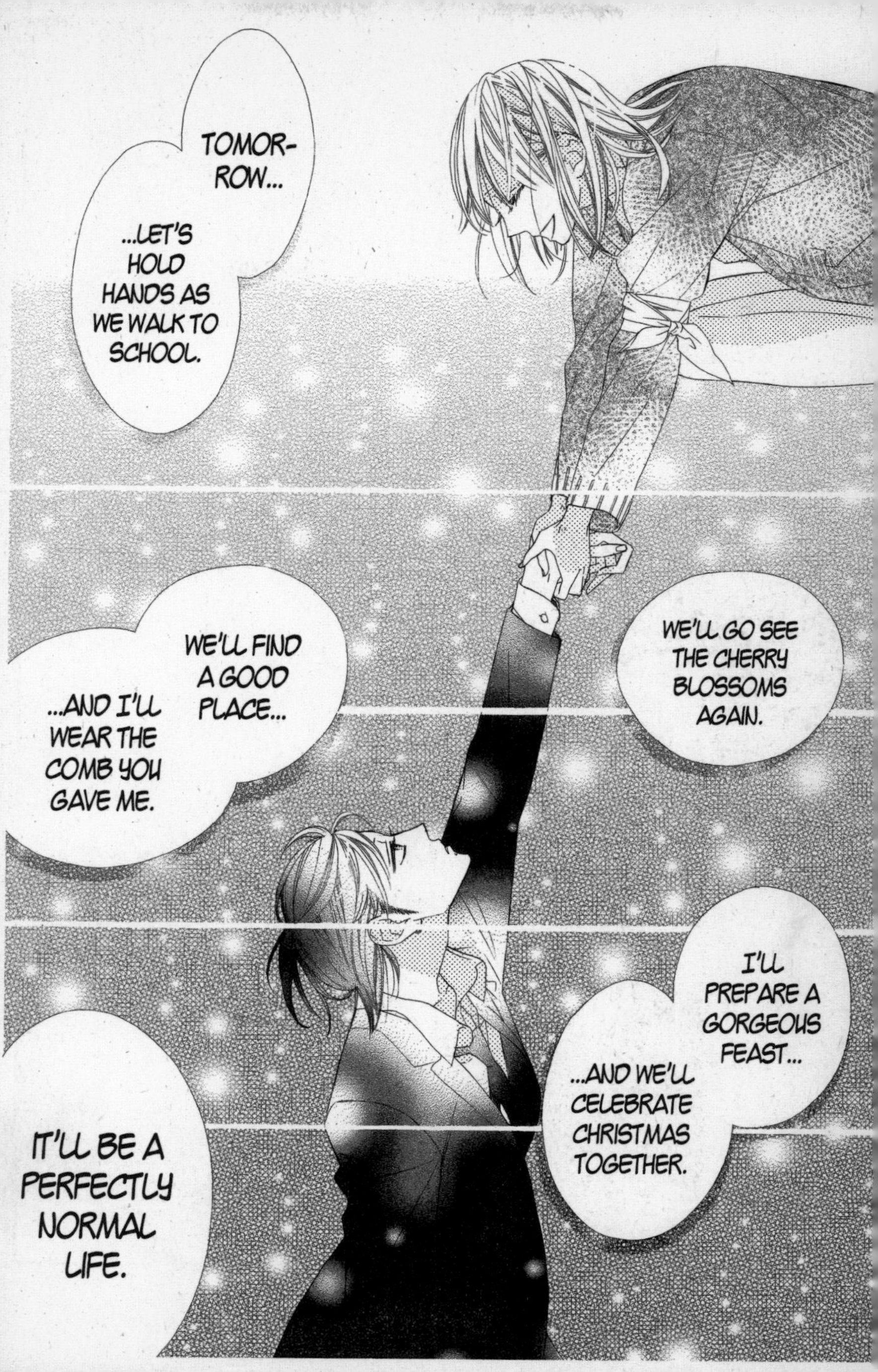
TOMORROW...
...LET'S HOLD HANDS AS WE WALK TO SCHOOL.
WE'LL GO SEE THE CHERRY BLOSSOMS AGAIN.
WE'LL FIND A GOOD PLACE...
...AND I'LL WEAR THE COMB YOU GAVE ME.
I'LL PREPARE A GORGEOUS FEAST...
...AND WE'LL CELEBRATE CHRISTMAS TOGETHER.
IT'LL BE A PERFECTLY NORMAL LIFE.

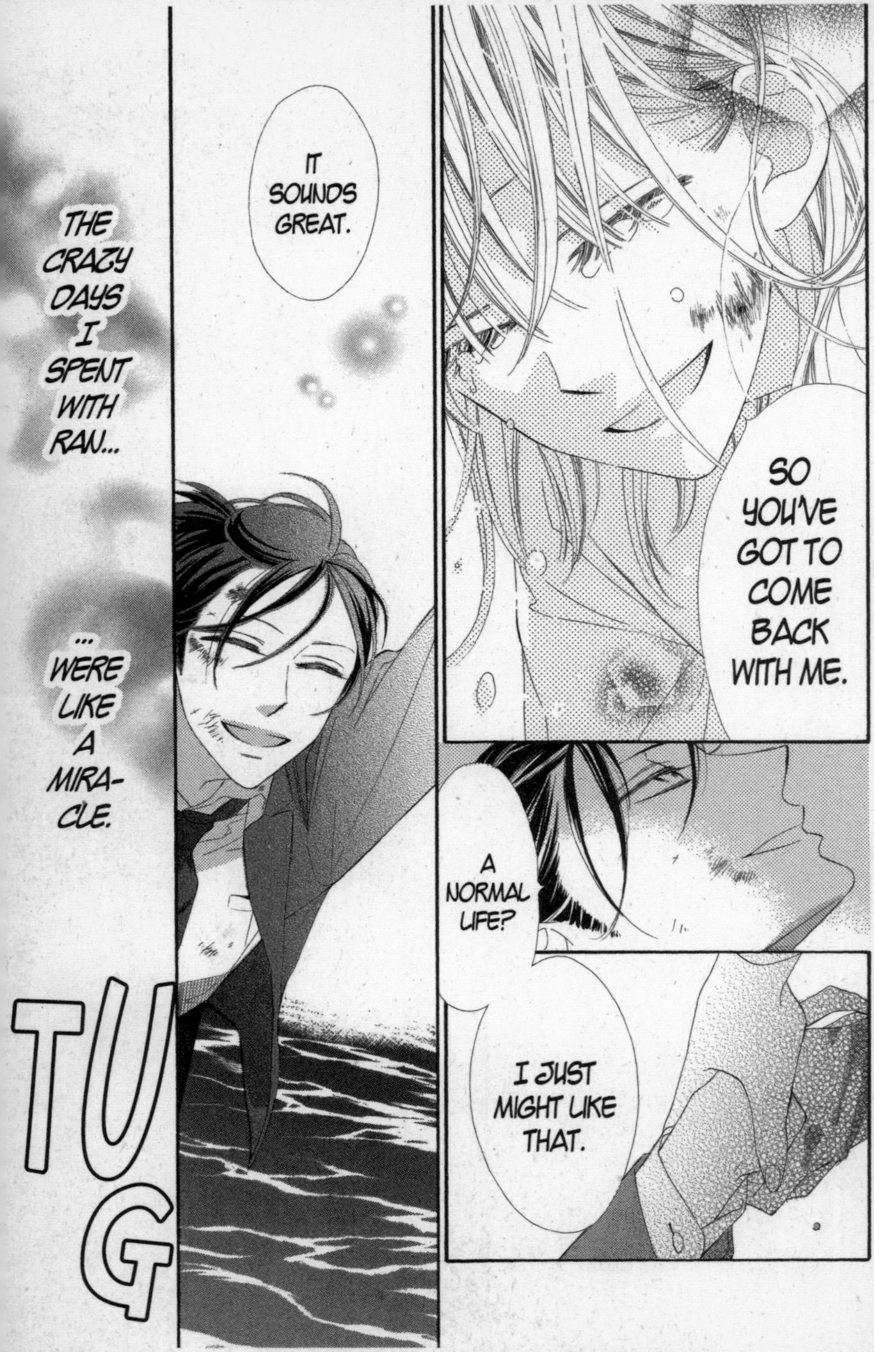
SO YOU'VE GOT TO COME BACK WITH ME.
A NORMAL LIFE?
I JUST MIGHT LIKE THAT.
IT SOUNDS GREAT.
THE CRAZY DAYS I SPENT WITH RAN...
...WERE LIKE A MIRA-CLE.
TUG

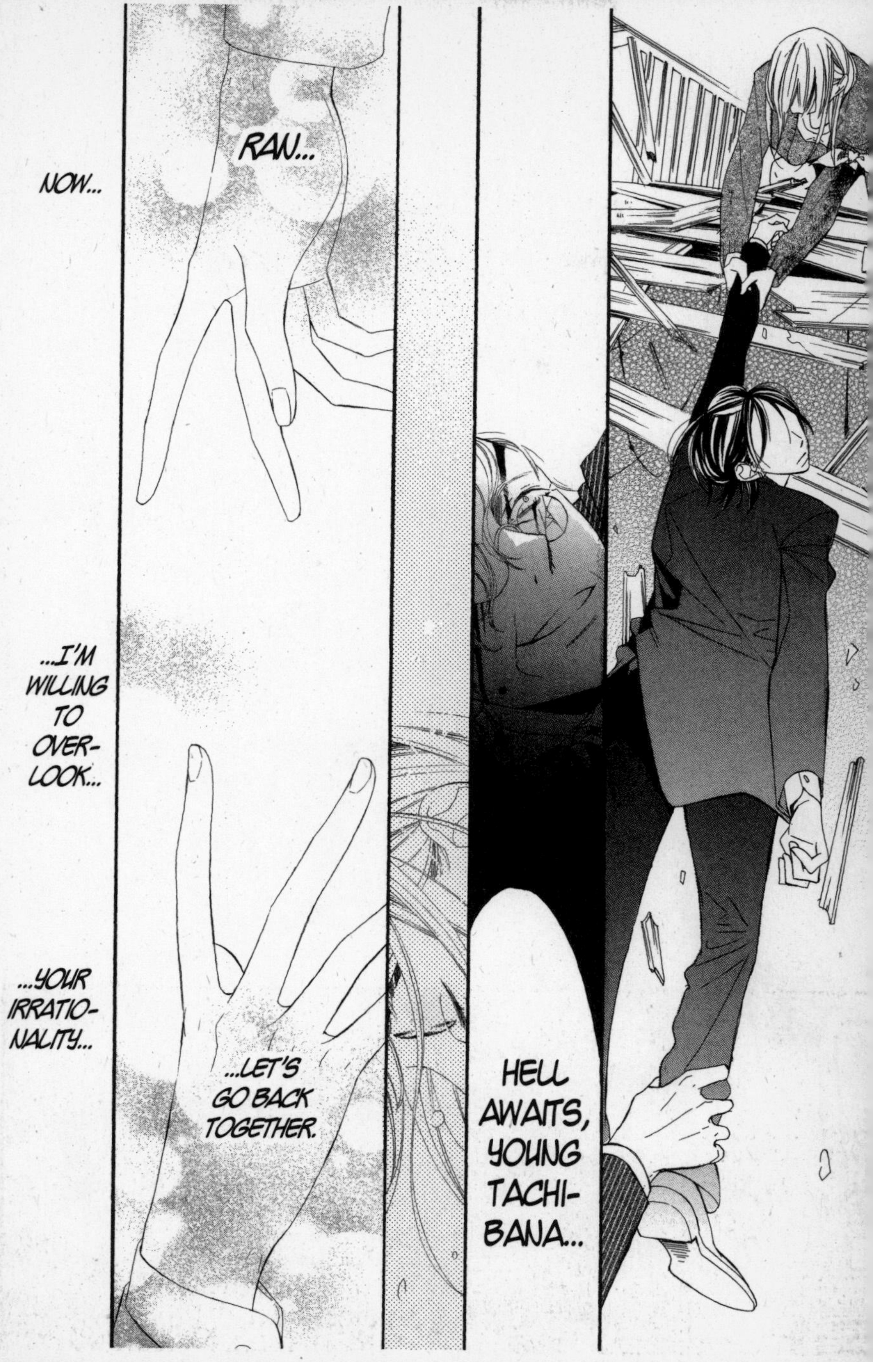

HELL AWAITS, YOUNG TACHI-BANA...
RAN...
NOW...
...I'M WILLING TO OVER-LOOK...
...YOUR IRRATIO-NALITY...
...LET'S GO BACK TOGETHER.

...SO LET'S
GO HOME
TOGETHER.

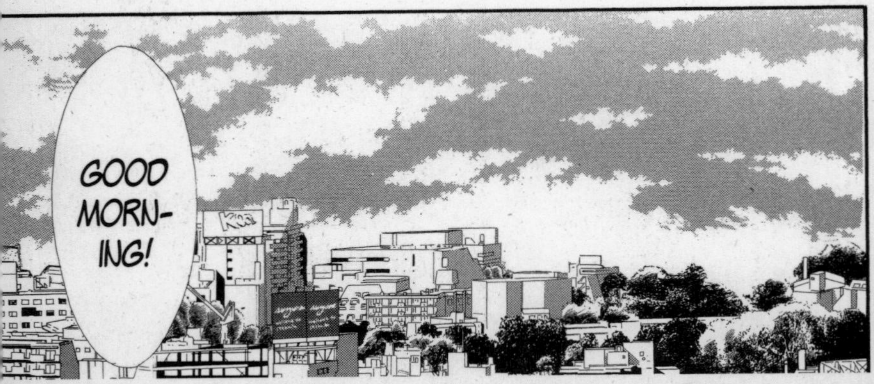
GOOD MORN-ING!

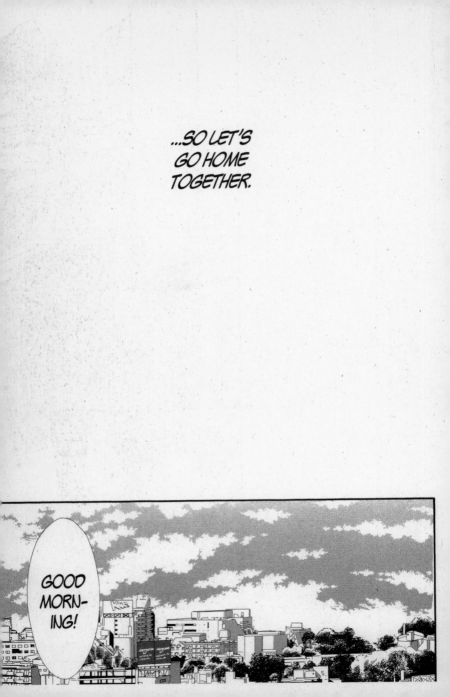

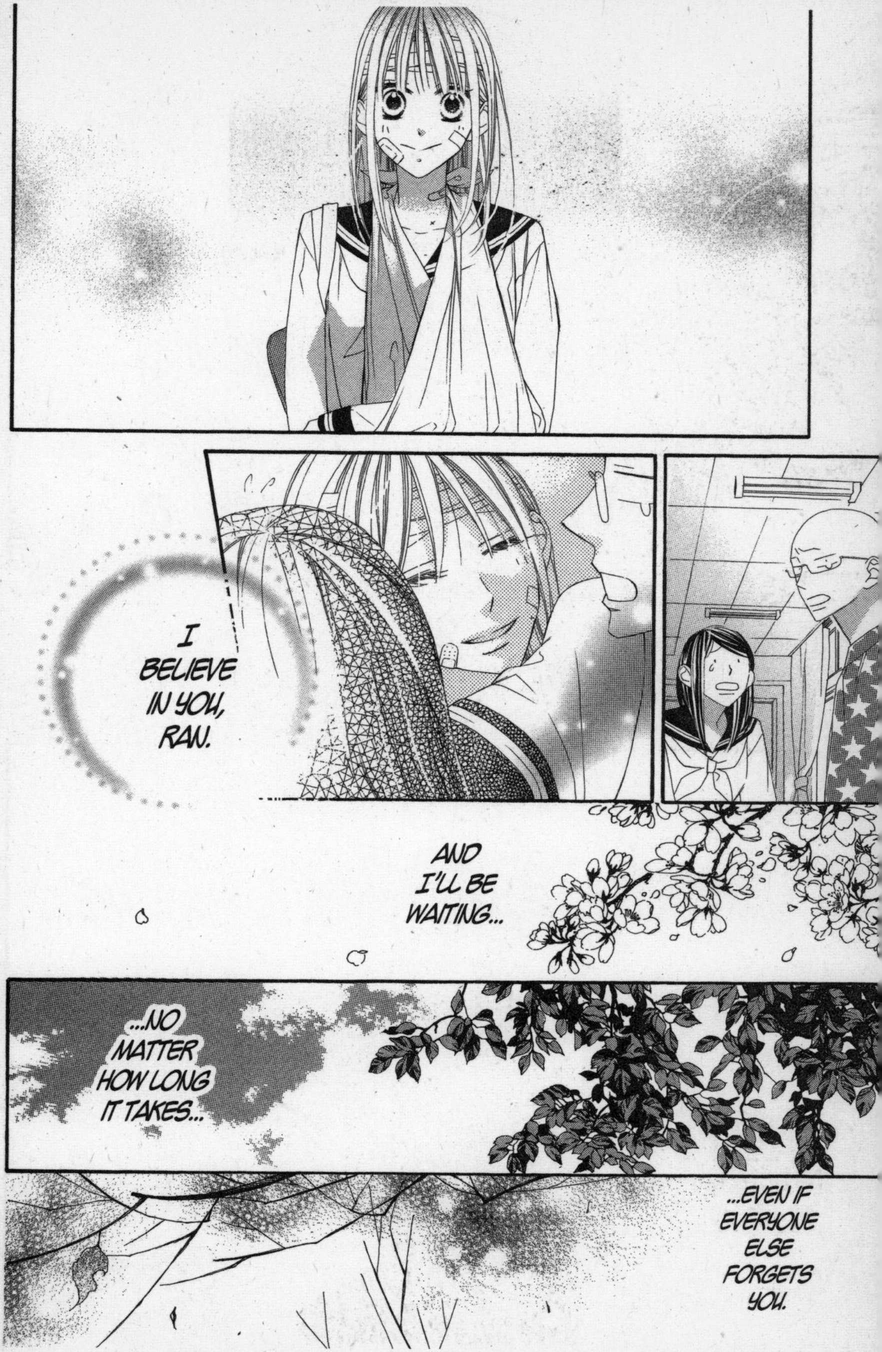
I BELIEVE IN YOU, RAN.
AND I'LL BE WAITING...
...NO MATTER HOW LONG IT TAKES...
...EVEN IF EVERYONE ELSE FORGETS YOU.

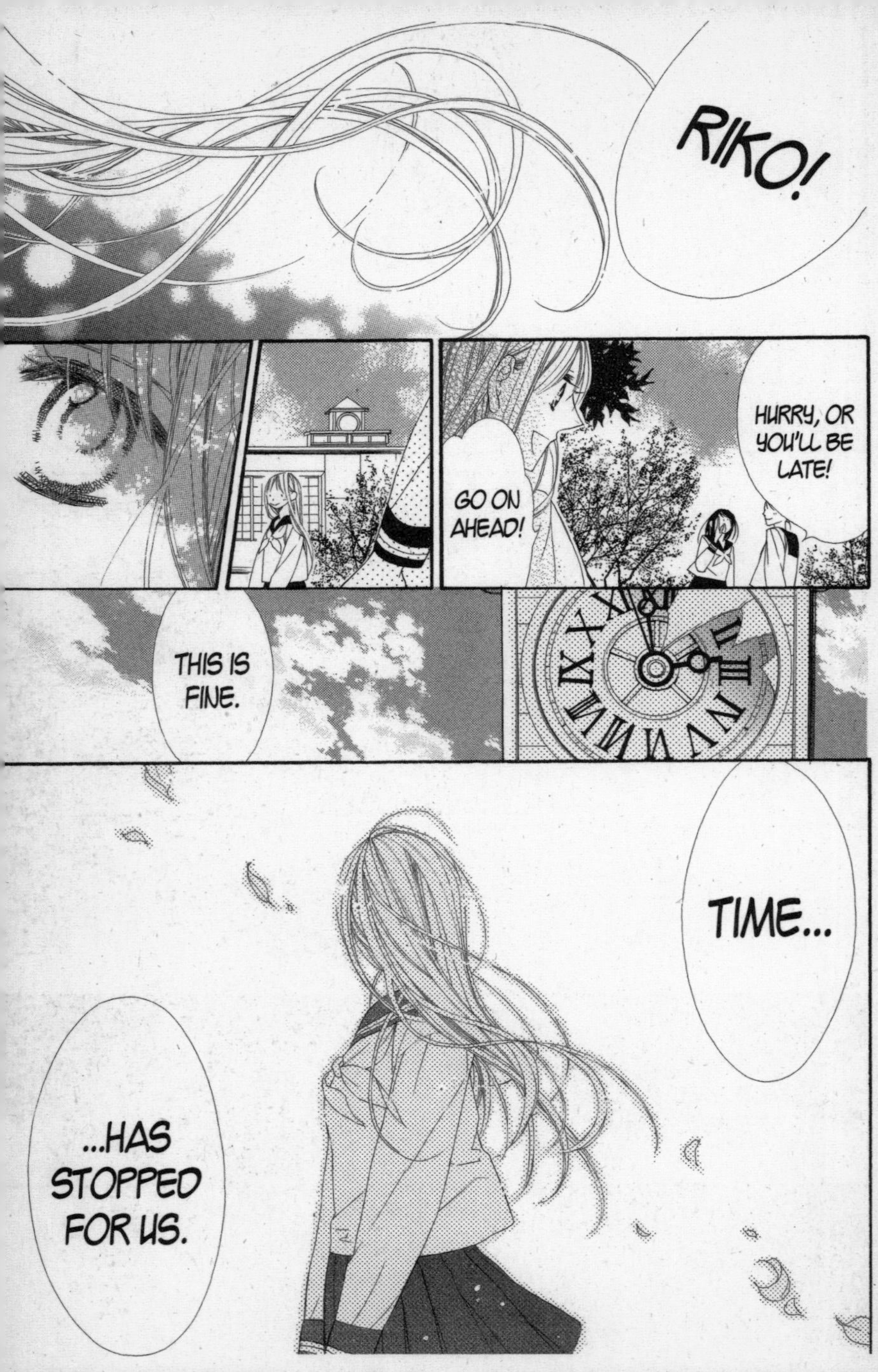
RIKO!
HURRY, OR YOU'LL BE LATE!
GO ON AHEAD!
THIS IS FINE.
TIME...
...HAS STOPPED FOR US.

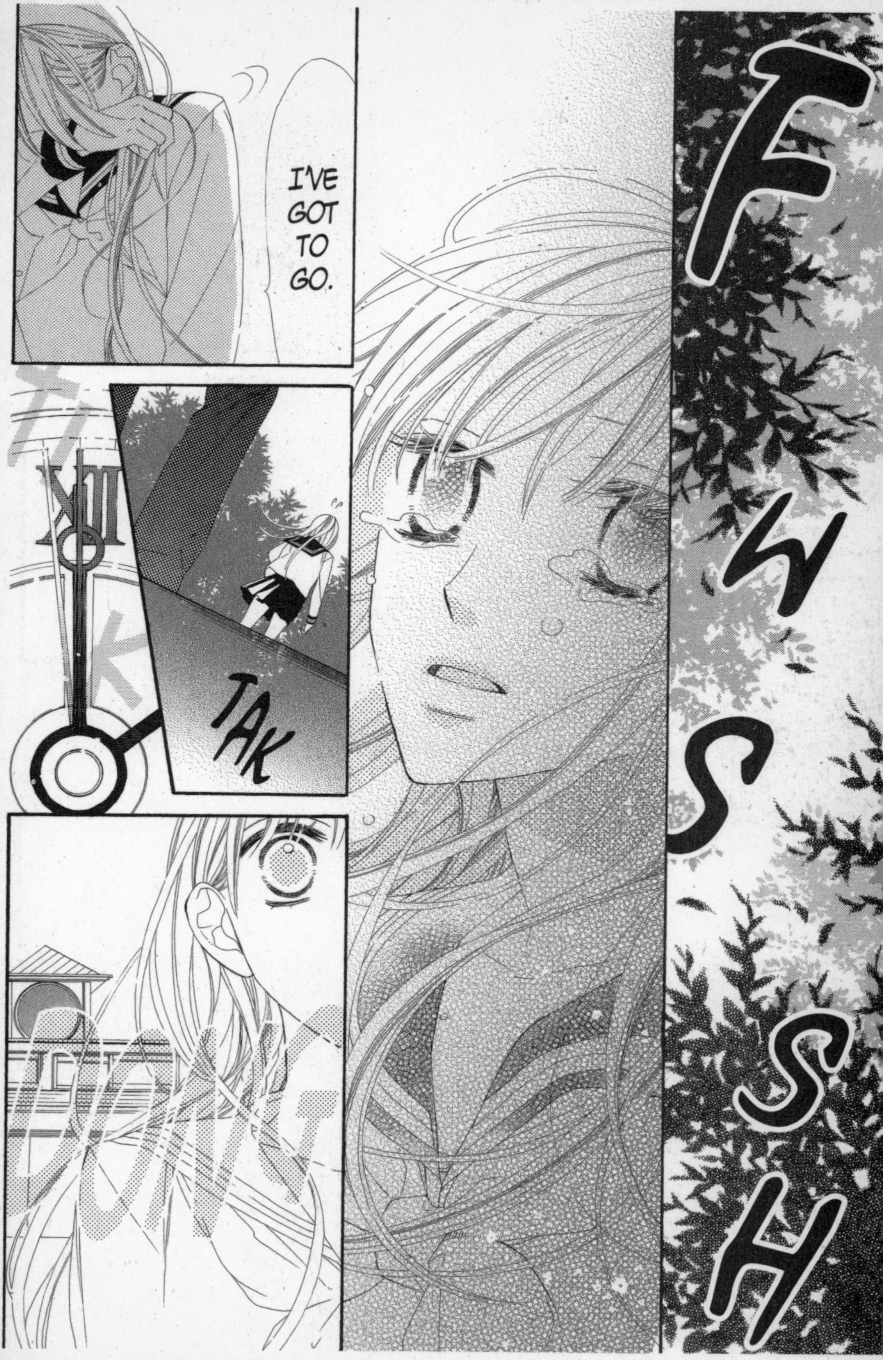
FWSSH
I'VE GOT TO GO.
TAK

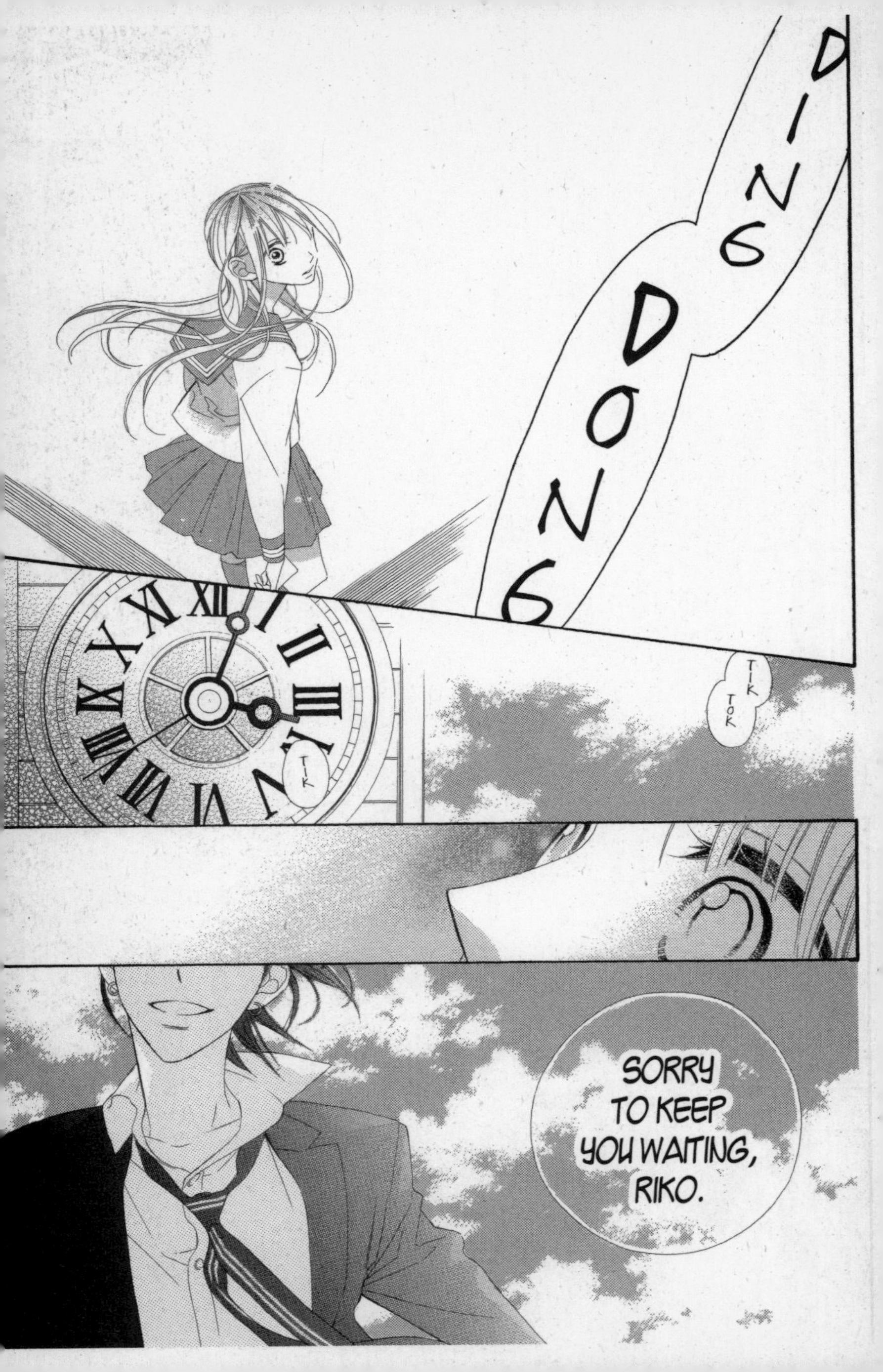
DING DONG
TIK TOK
TIK
SORRY TO KEEP YOU WAITING, RIKO.

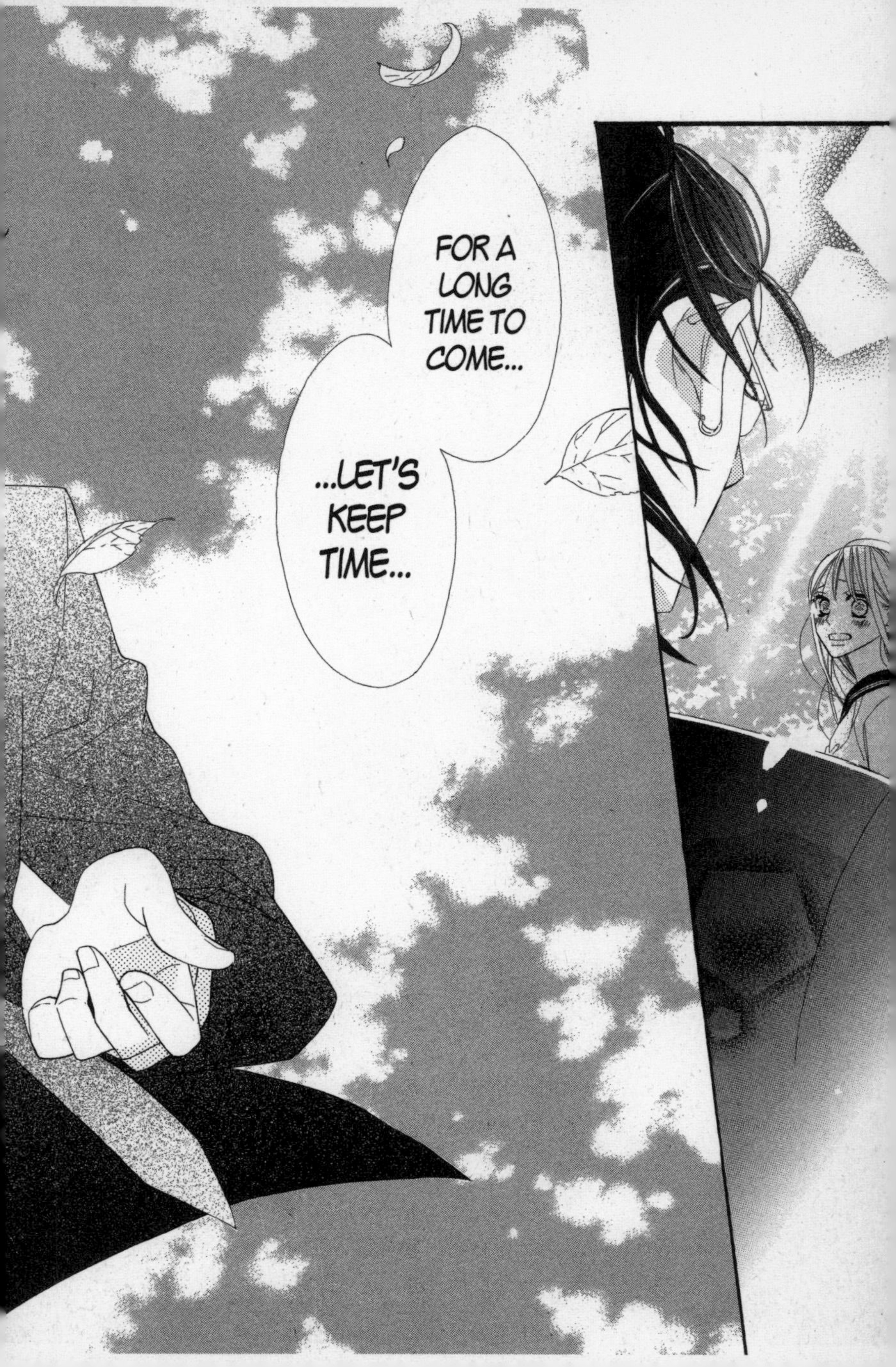
FOR A LONG TIME TO COME...
...LET'S KEEP TIME...

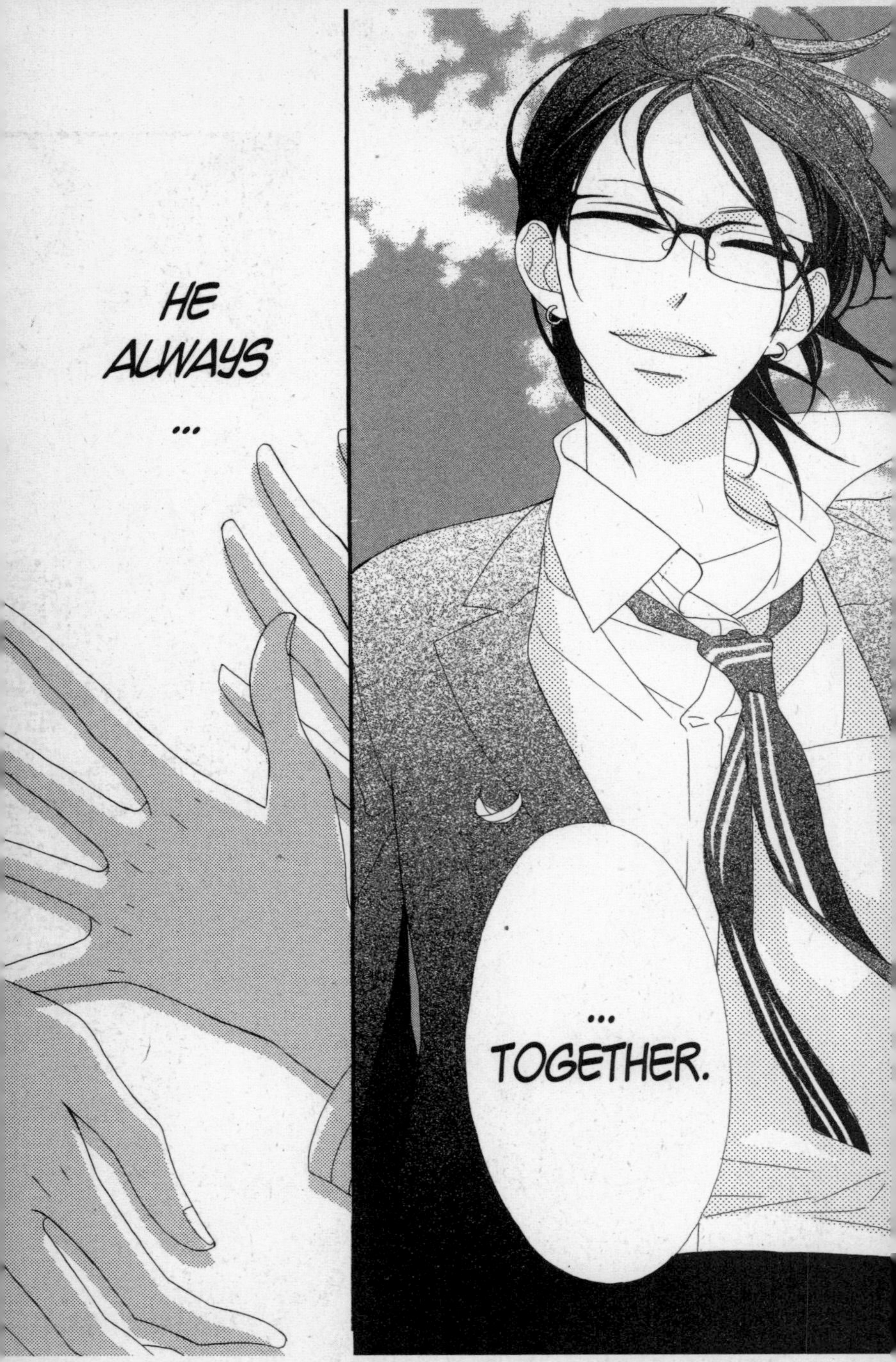

... TOGETHER.
HE ALWAYS ...

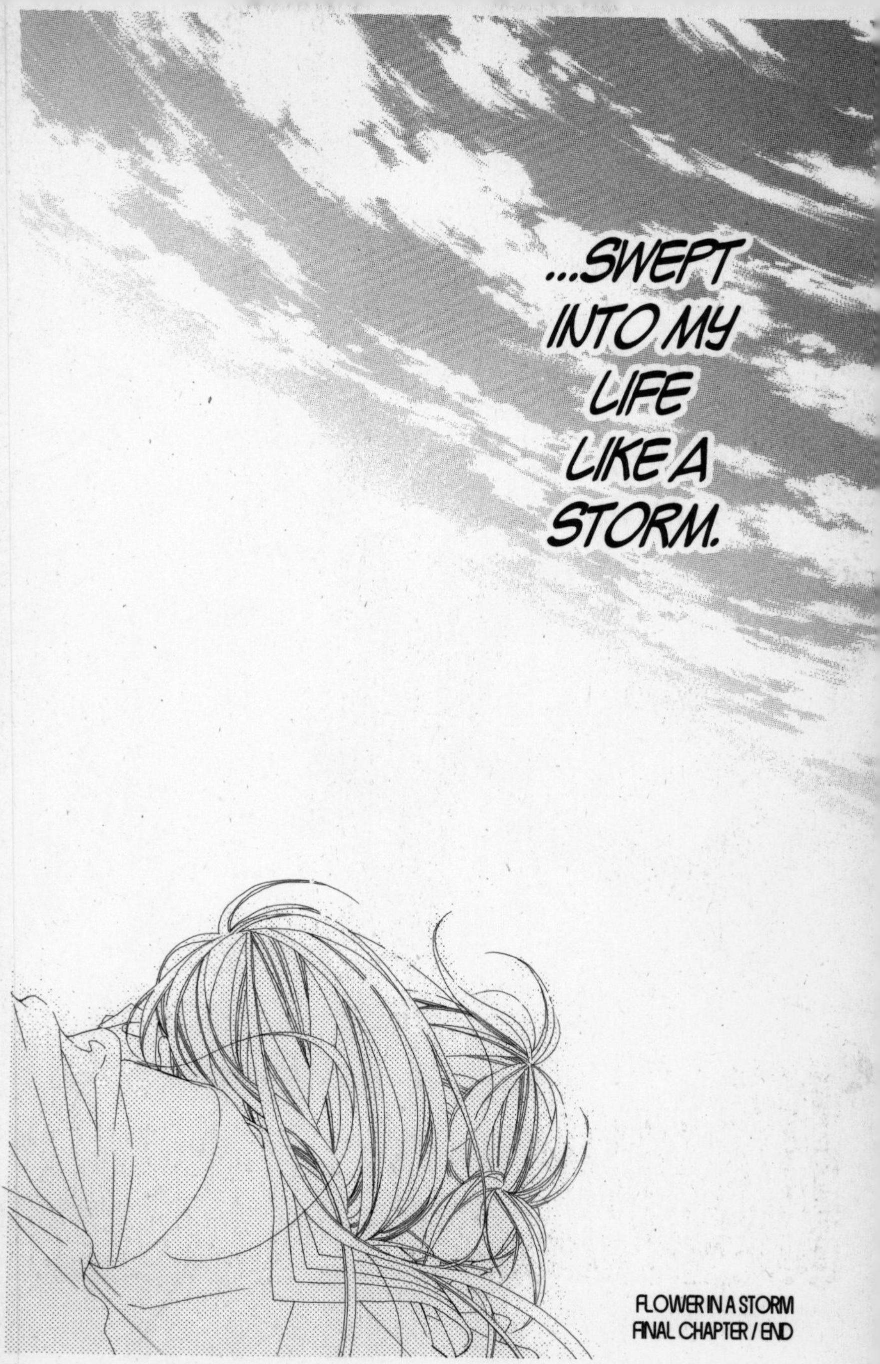
...SWEPT INTO MY LIFE LIKE A STORM.
FLOWER IN A STORM
FINAL CHAPTER / END

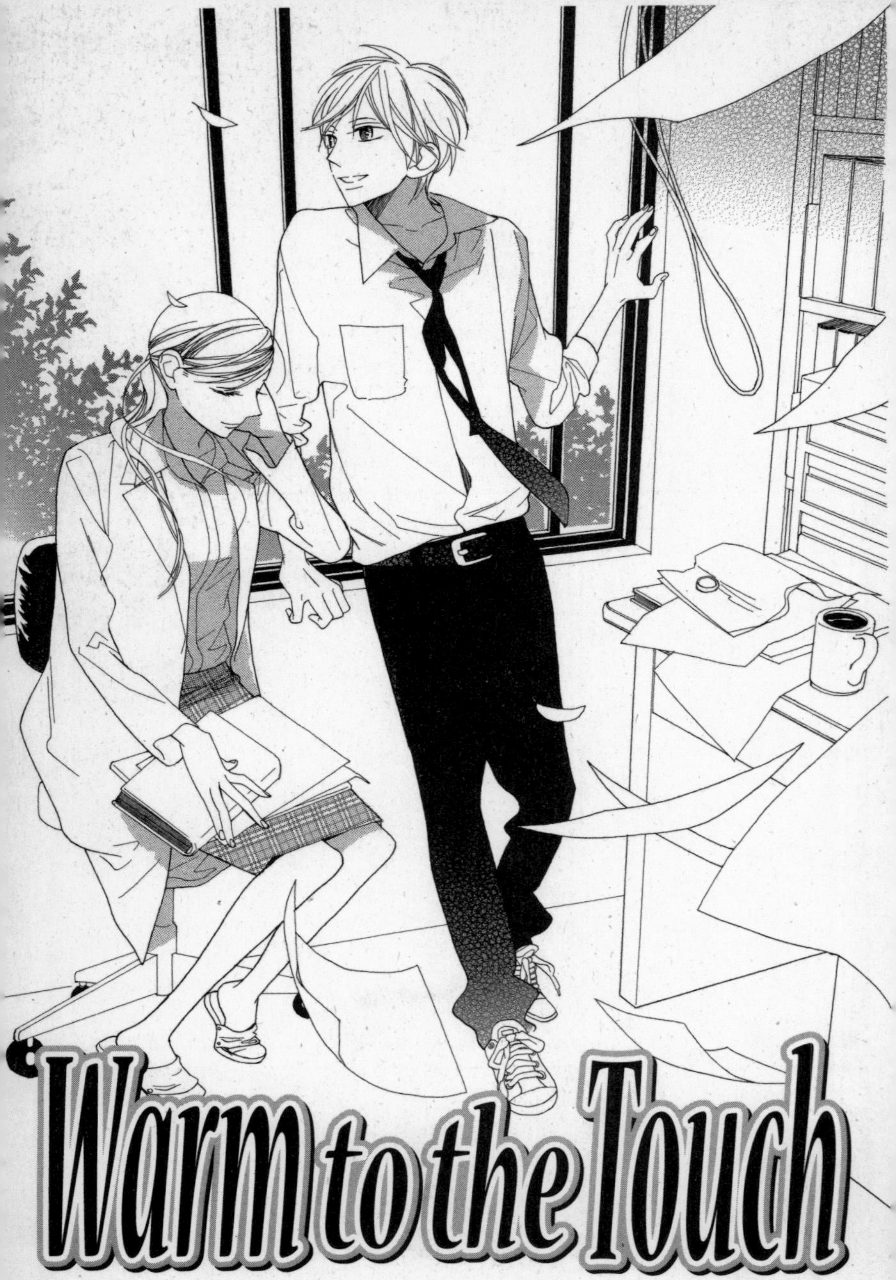
Warm to the Touch

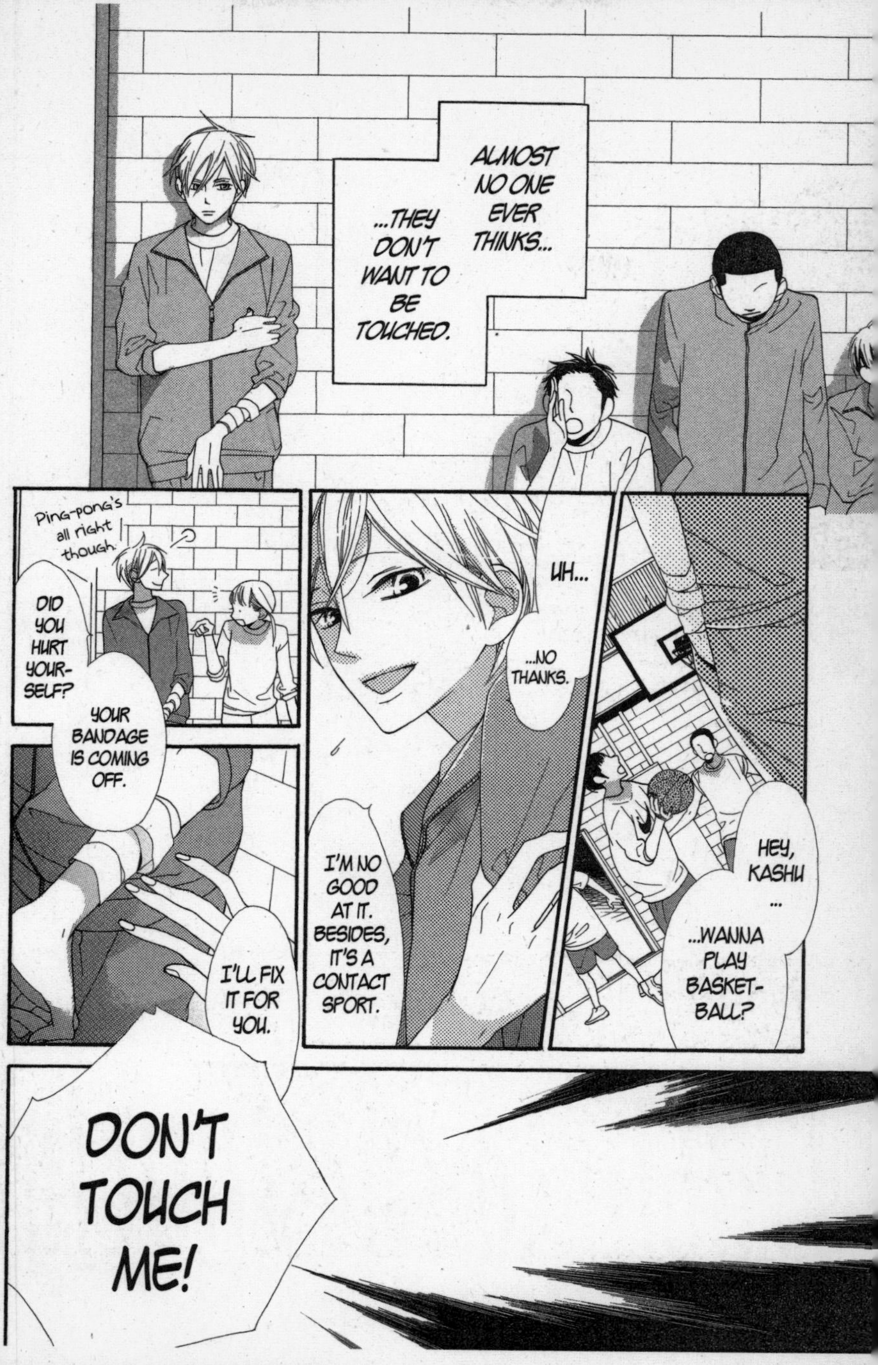
ALMOST NO ONE EVER THINKS...
...THEY DON'T WANT TO BE TOUCHED.
HEY, KASHU ...
...WANNA PLAY BASKET-BALL?
UH...
...NO THANKS.
I'M NO GOOD AT IT. BESIDES, IT'S A CONTACT SPORT.
Ping-pong's all right though.
DID YOU HURT YOURSELF?
YOUR BANDAGE IS COMING OFF.
I'LL FIX IT FOR YOU.
DON'T TOUCH ME!

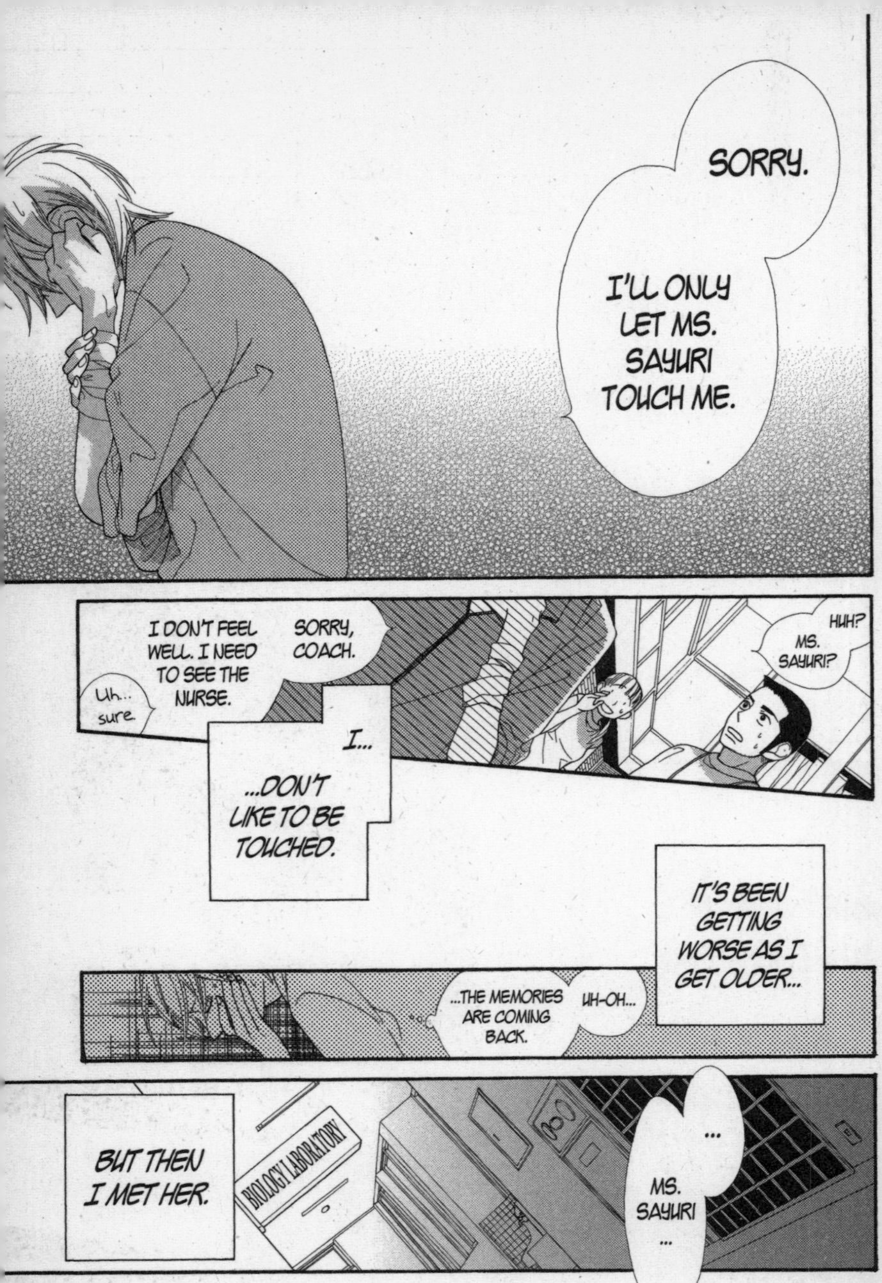
SORRY.
I'LL ONLY LET MS. SAYURI TOUCH ME.
HUH? MS. SAYURI?
SORRY, COACH.
I DON'T FEEL WELL. I NEED TO SEE THE NURSE.
Uh... sure.
I... ...DON'T LIKE TO BE TOUCHED.
IT'S BEEN GETTING WORSE AS I GET OLDER...
UH-OH...
...THE MEMORIES ARE COMING BACK.
... MS. SAYURI ...
BIOLOGY LABORATORY
BUT THEN I MET HER.

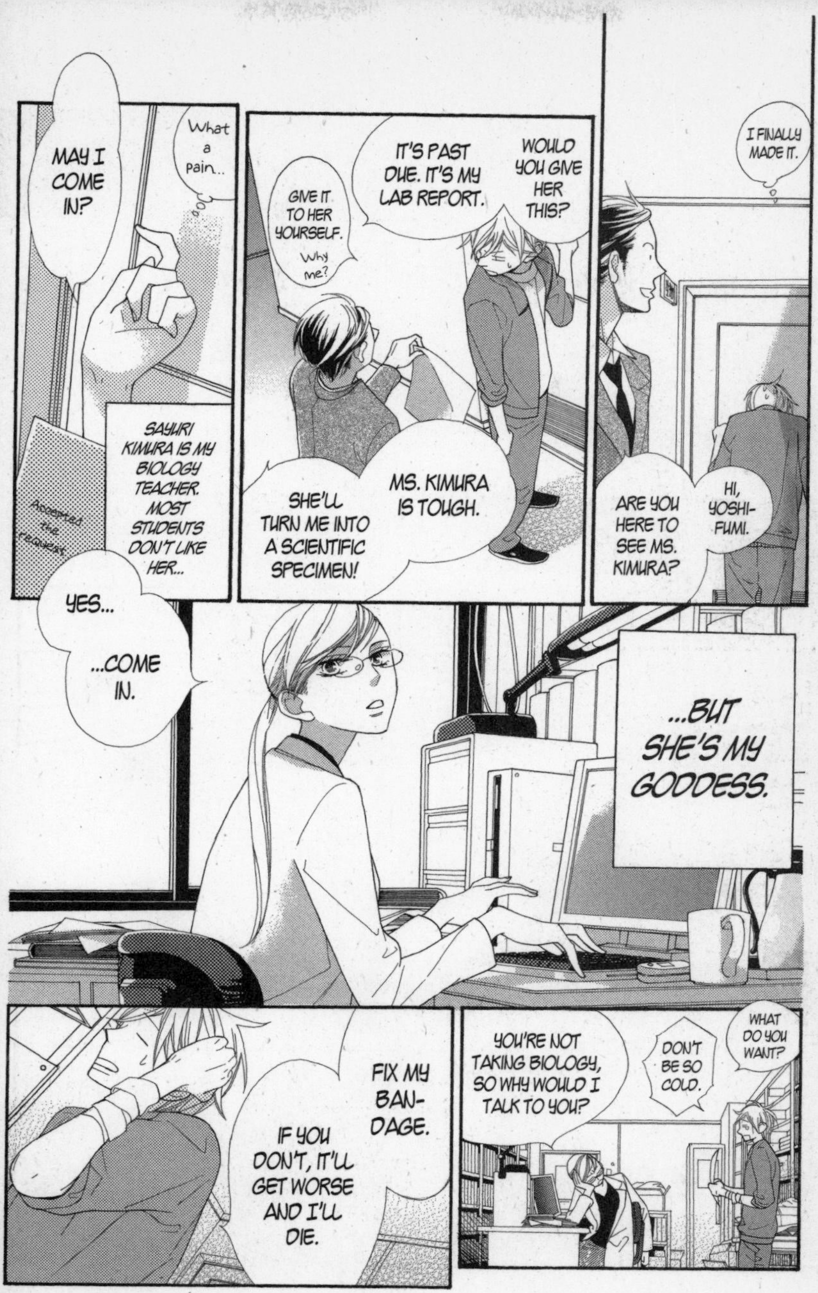
I FINALLY MADE IT.
HI, YOSHI-FUMI.
ARE YOU HERE TO SEE MS. KIMURA?
WOULD YOU GIVE HER THIS?
IT'S PAST DUE. IT'S MY LAB REPORT.
GIVE IT TO HER YOURSELF.
Why me?
MS. KIMURA IS TOUGH.
SHE'LL TURN ME INTO A SCIENTIFIC SPECIMEN!
What a pain...
MAY I COME IN?
SAYURI KIMURA IS MY BIOLOGY TEACHER. MOST STUDENTS DON'T LIKE HER...
Accepted the request.
...BUT SHE'S MY GODDESS.
YES...
...COME IN.
WHAT DO YOU WANT?
DON'T BE SO COLD.
YOU'RE NOT TAKING BIOLOGY, SO WHY WOULD I TALK TO YOU?
FIX MY BAN-DAGE.
IF YOU DON'T, IT'LL GET WORSE AND I'LL DIE.

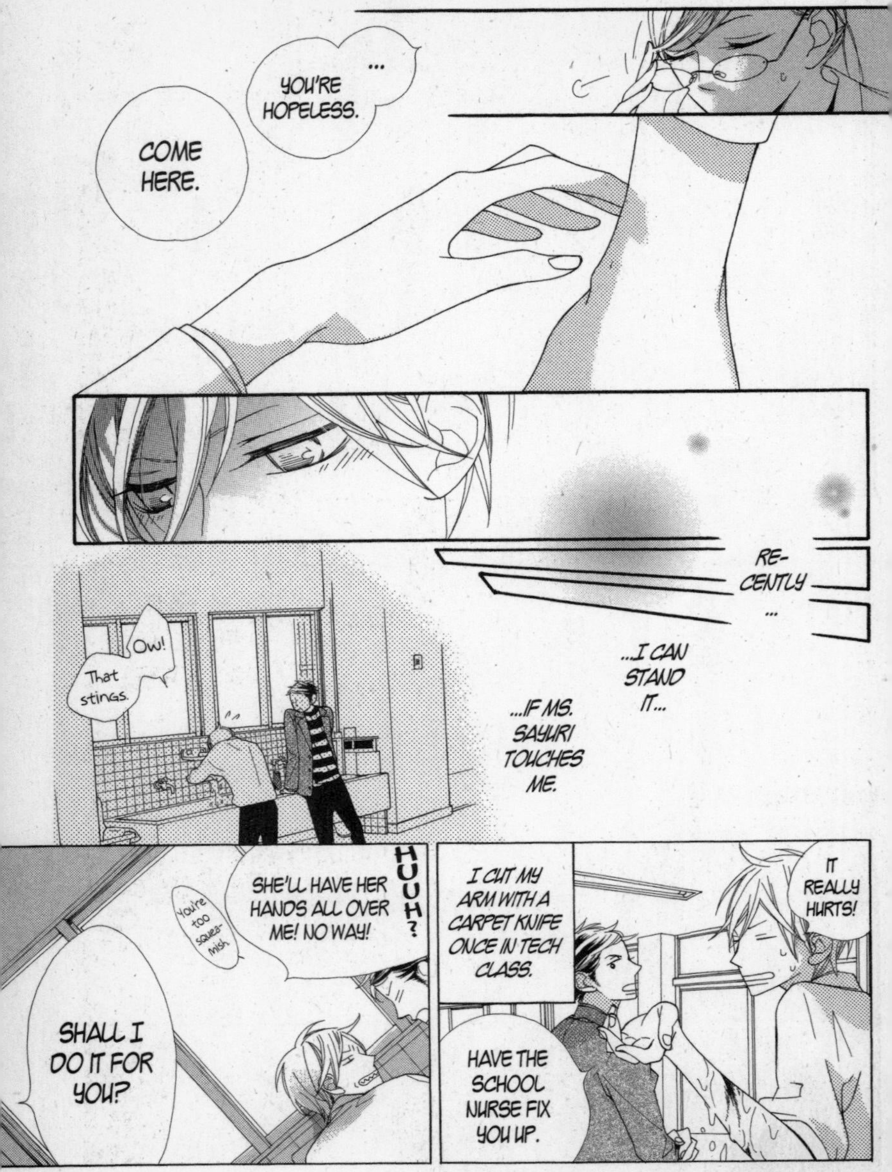

... YOU'RE HOPELESS.
COME HERE.
RE-CENTLY ...
...I CAN STAND IT...
...IF MS. SAYURI TOUCHES ME.
Ow!
That stings.
IT REALLY HURTS!
I CUT MY ARM WITH A CARPET KNIFE ONCE IN TECH CLASS.
HAVE THE SCHOOL NURSE FIX YOU UP.
HUUH?
SHE'LL HAVE HER HANDS ALL OVER ME! NO WAY!
You're too squea-mish.
SHALL I DO IT FOR YOU?

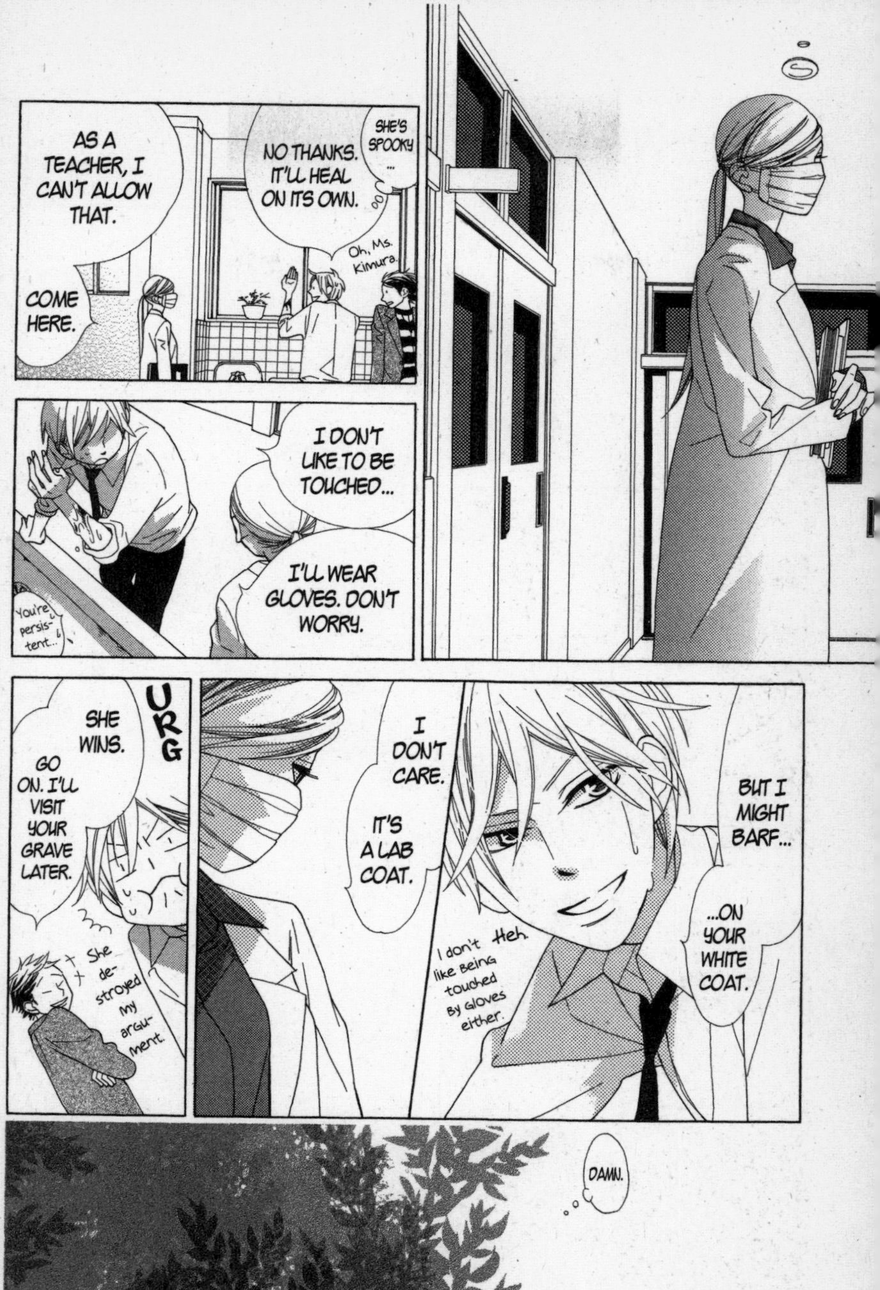
SHE'S SPOOKY...
NO THANKS. IT'LL HEAL ON ITS OWN.
Oh, Ms. Kimura.
AS A TEACHER, I CAN'T ALLOW THAT.
COME HERE.
I DON'T LIKE TO BE TOUCHED...
I'LL WEAR GLOVES. DON'T WORRY.
You're persistent...
BUT I MIGHT BARF...
...ON YOUR WHITE COAT.
Heh.
I don't like being touched by gloves either.
I DON'T CARE.
IT'S A LAB COAT.
URG
SHE WINS.
GO ON. I'LL VISIT YOUR GRAVE LATER.
She destroyed my argument.
DAMN.

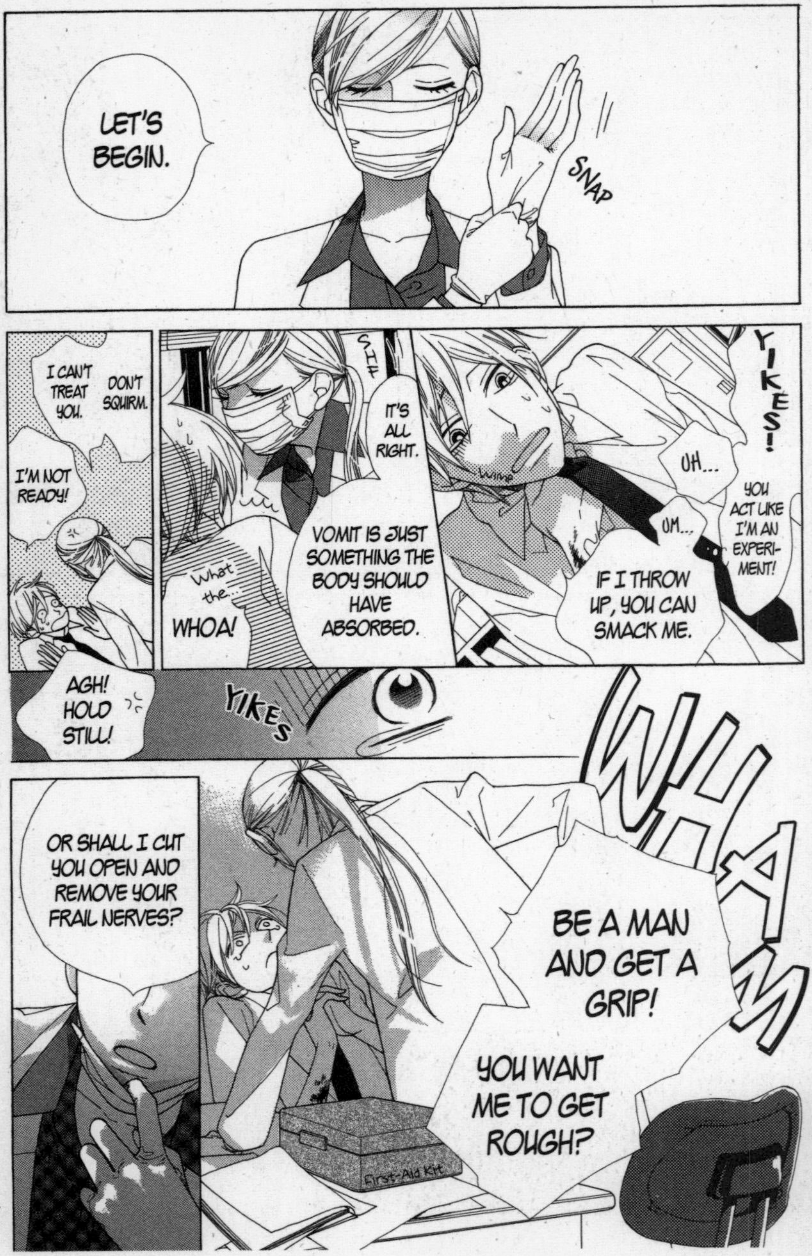
LET'S BEGIN.
SNAP
YIKES!
UH...
UM...
YOU ACT LIKE I'M AN EXPERIMENT!
IF I THROW UP, YOU CAN SMACK ME.
SHF
IT'S ALL RIGHT.
VOMIT IS JUST SOMETHING THE BODY SHOULD HAVE ABSORBED.
What the...
WHOA!
DON'T SQUIRM.
I CAN'T TREAT YOU.
I'M NOT READY!
WHAM
YIKES
AGH! HOLD STILL!
BE A MAN AND GET A GRIP!
YOU WANT ME TO GET ROUGH?
OR SHALL I CUT YOU OPEN AND REMOVE YOUR FRAIL NERVES?
First-Aid Kit

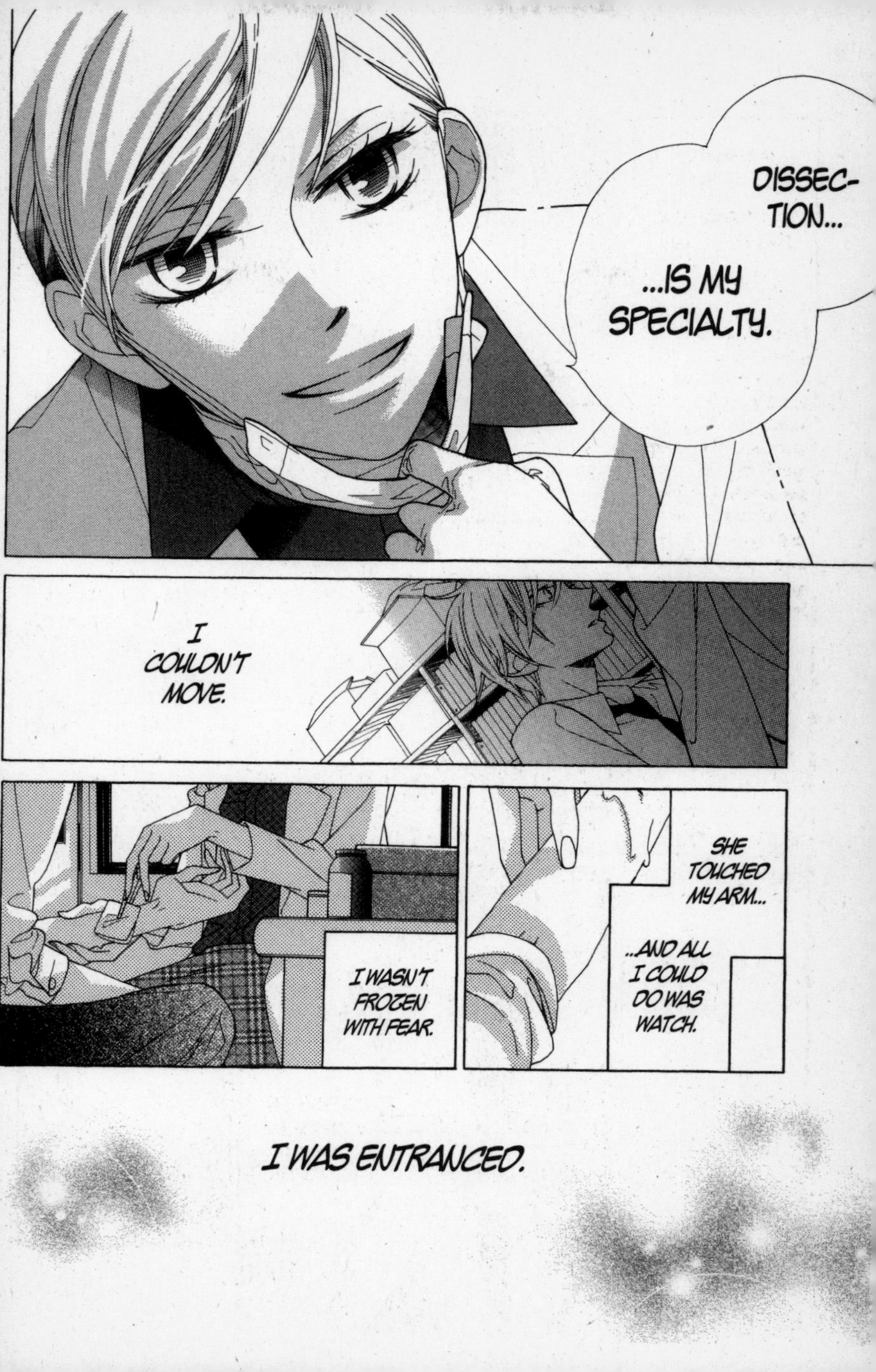
DISSECTION...
...IS MY SPECIALTY.
I COULDN'T MOVE.
SHE TOUCHED MY ARM...
...AND ALL I COULD DO WAS WATCH.
I WASN'T FROZEN WITH FEAR.
I WAS ENTRANCED.

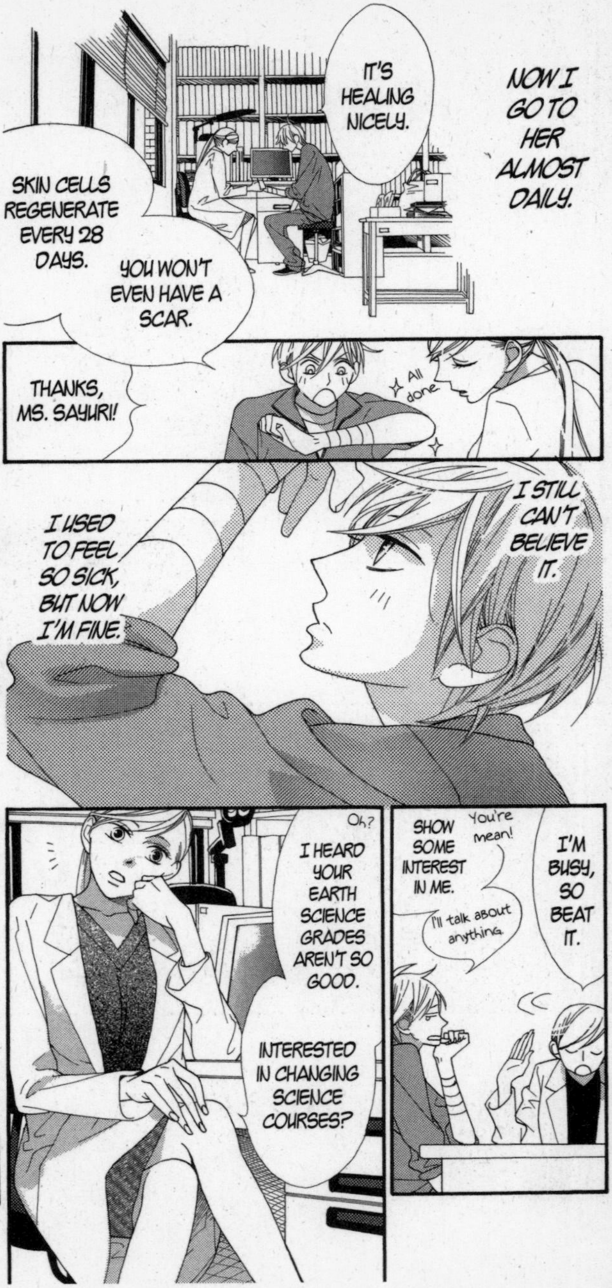
NOW I GO TO HER ALMOST DAILY.
IT'S HEALING NICELY.
SKIN CELLS REGENERATE EVERY 28 DAYS.
YOU WON'T EVEN HAVE A SCAR.
All done
THANKS, MS. SAYURI!
I STILL CAN'T BELIEVE IT.
I USED TO FEEL SO SICK, BUT NOW I'M FINE.
I'M BUSY, SO BEAT IT.
SHOW SOME INTEREST IN ME.
You're mean!
I'll talk about anything.
Oh?
I HEARD YOUR EARTH SCIENCE GRADES AREN'T SO GOOD.
INTERESTED IN CHANGING SCIENCE COURSES?

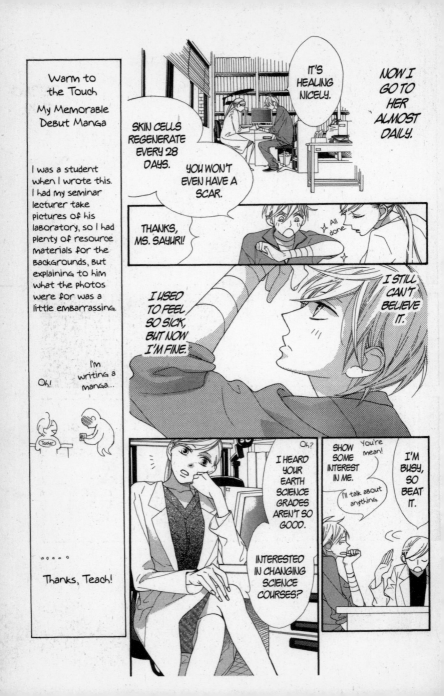

Warm to the Touch

My Memorable Debut Manga

I was a student when I wrote this. I had my seminar lecturer take pictures of his laboratory, so I had plenty of resource materials for the backgrounds, but explaining to him what the photos were for was a little embarrassing.

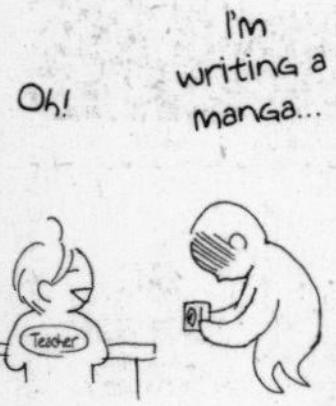
I'm writing a manga...
Oh!
Teacher

.....

Thanks, Teach!

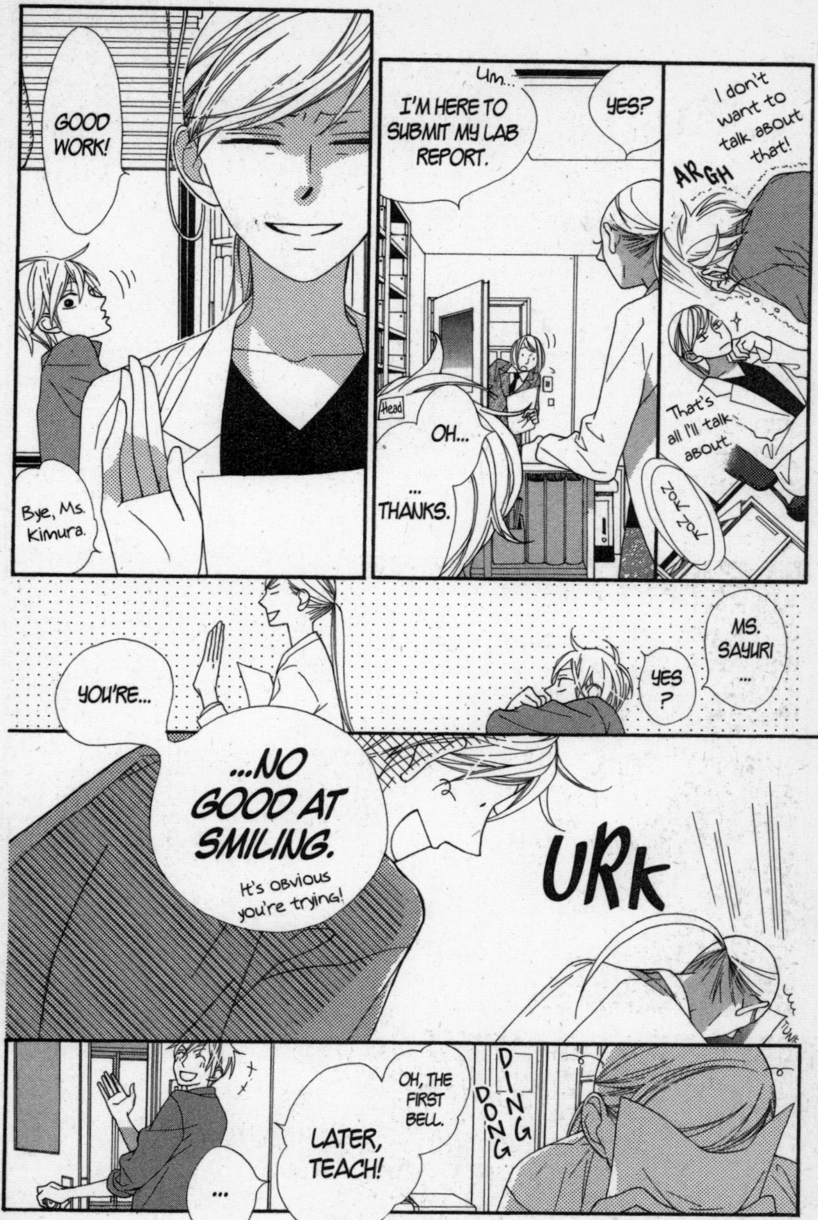
I don't want to talk about that!
ARGH
That's all I'll talk about.
ZOK ZOK
YES?
Um...
I'M HERE TO SUBMIT MY LAB REPORT.
Head
OH...
... THANKS.
GOOD WORK!
Bye, Ms. Kimura.
MS. SAYURI ...
YES?
YOU'RE...
URK
...NO GOOD AT SMILING.
It's obvious you're trying!
DING DONG
OH, THE FIRST BELL.
LATER, TEACH!
...

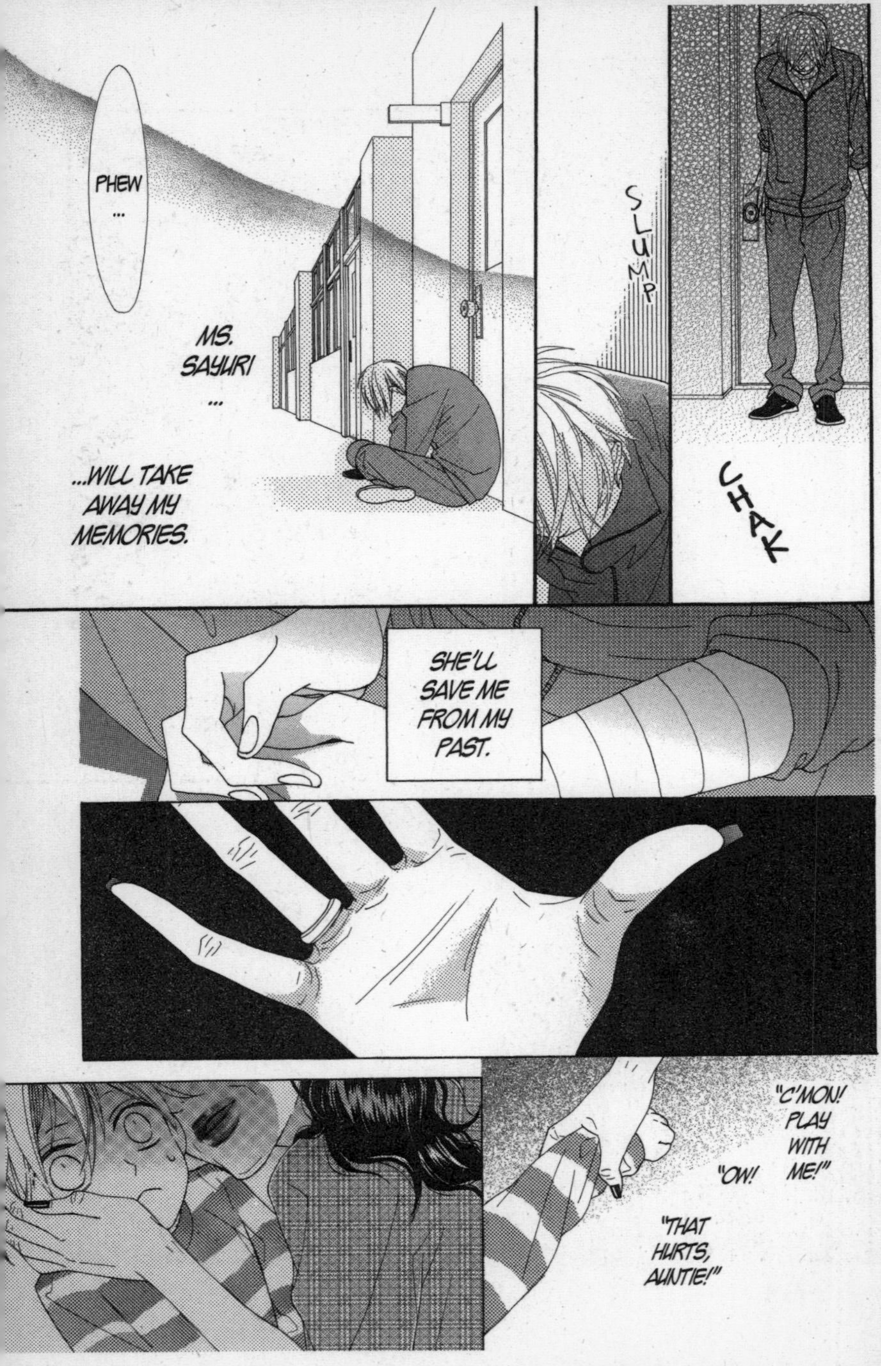
CHAK
SLUMP
PHEW ...
MS. SAYURI ...
...WILL TAKE AWAY MY MEMORIES.
SHE'LL SAVE ME FROM MY PAST.
"C'MON! PLAY WITH ME!"
"OW!
"THAT HURTS, AUNTIE!"

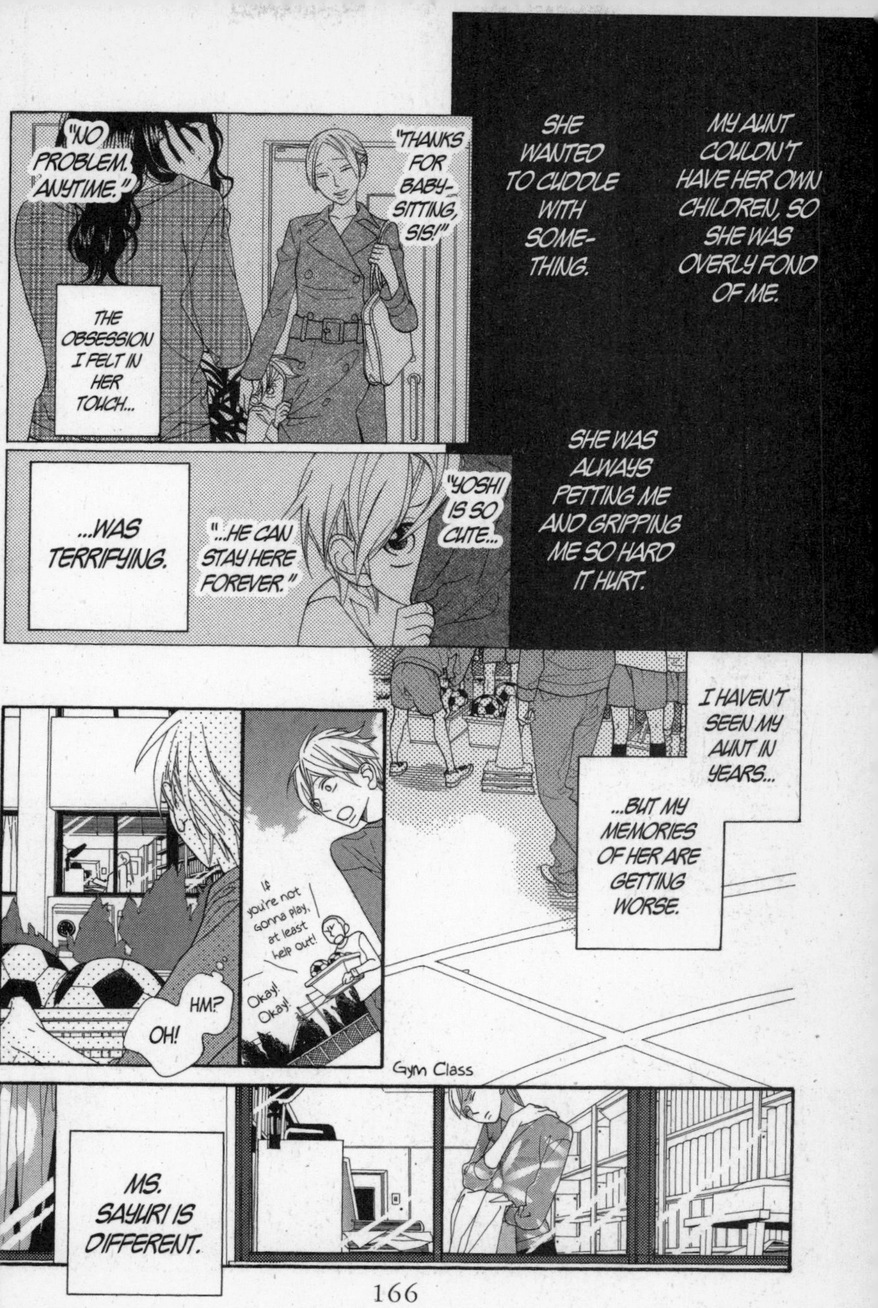
MY AUNT COULDN'T HAVE HER OWN CHILDREN, SO SHE WAS OVERLY FOND OF ME.
SHE WANTED TO CUDDLE WITH SOME-THING.
"THANKS FOR BABY-SITTING, SIS!"
"NO PROBLEM. ANYTIME."
THE OBSESSION I FELT IN HER TOUCH...
SHE WAS ALWAYS PETTING ME AND GRIPPING ME SO HARD IT HURT.
"YOSHI IS SO CUTE...
"...HE CAN STAY HERE FOREVER."
...WAS TERRIFYING.
I HAVEN'T SEEN MY AUNT IN YEARS...
...BUT MY MEMORIES OF HER ARE GETTING WORSE.
Gym Class
If you're not gonna play, at least help out!
Okay! Okay!
HM?
OH!
MS. SAYURI IS DIFFERENT.

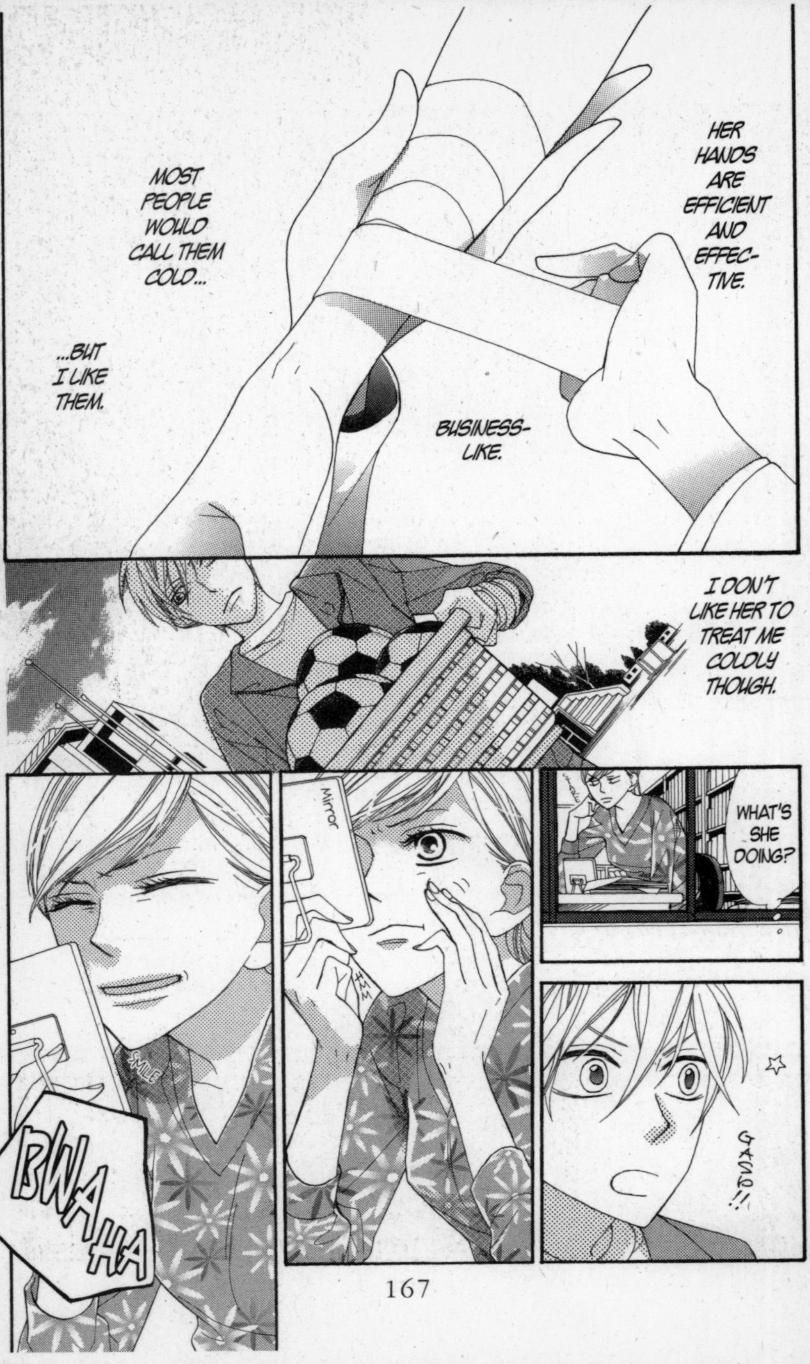
HER HANDS ARE EFFICIENT AND EFFEC-TIVE.
BUSINESS-LIKE.
MOST PEOPLE WOULD CALL THEM COLD...
...BUT I LIKE THEM.
I DON'T LIKE HER TO TREAT ME COLDLY THOUGH.
WHAT'S SHE DOING?
GASP!!
Mirror
HMM
SMILE
BWAHAHA

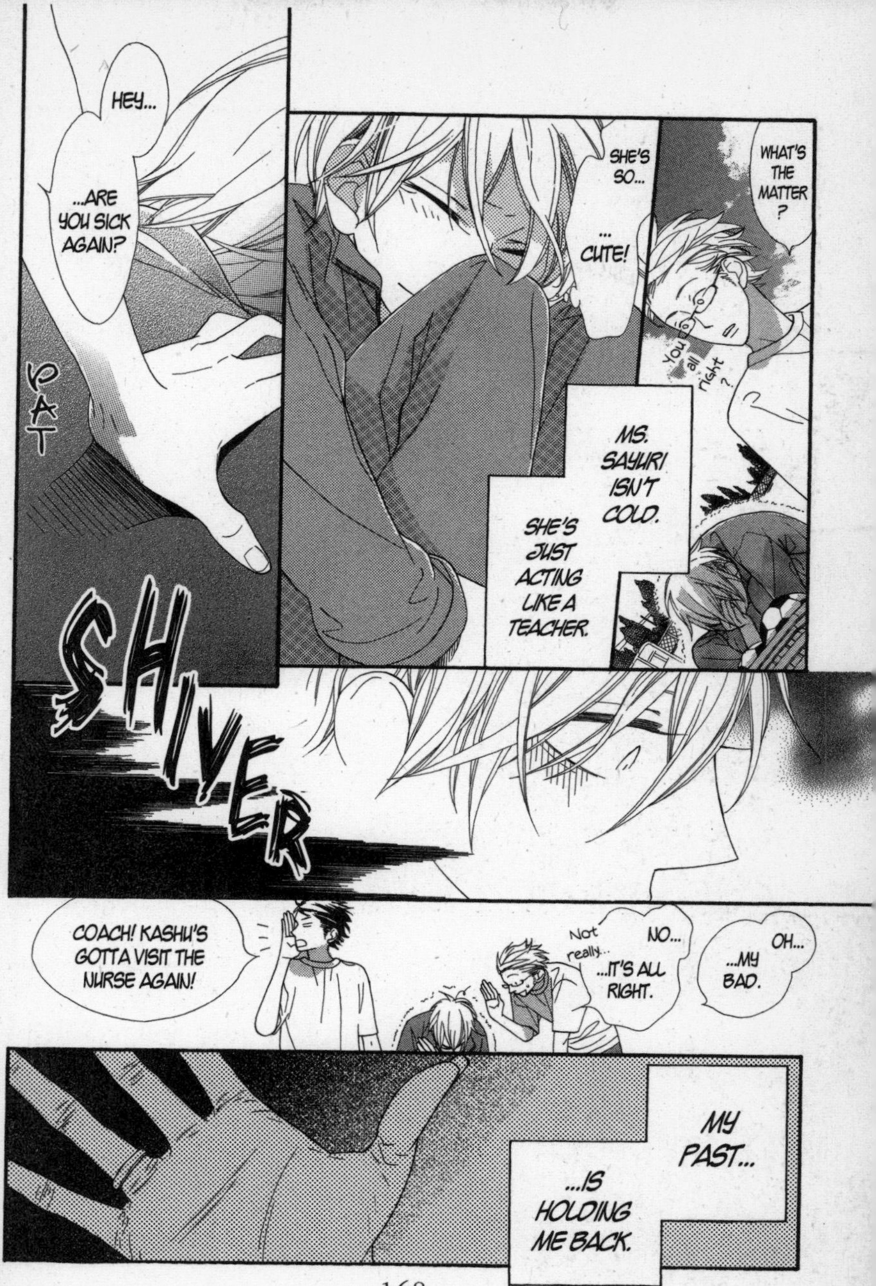
WHAT'S THE MATTER?
You all right?
SHE'S SO... ...CUTE!
MS. SAYURI ISN'T COLD.
SHE'S JUST ACTING LIKE A TEACHER.
HEY...
...ARE YOU SICK AGAIN?
PAT
SHIVER
OH... ...MY BAD.
NO... ...IT'S ALL RIGHT.
Not really...
COACH! KASHU'S GOTTA VISIT THE NURSE AGAIN!
MY PAST...
...IS HOLDING ME BACK.

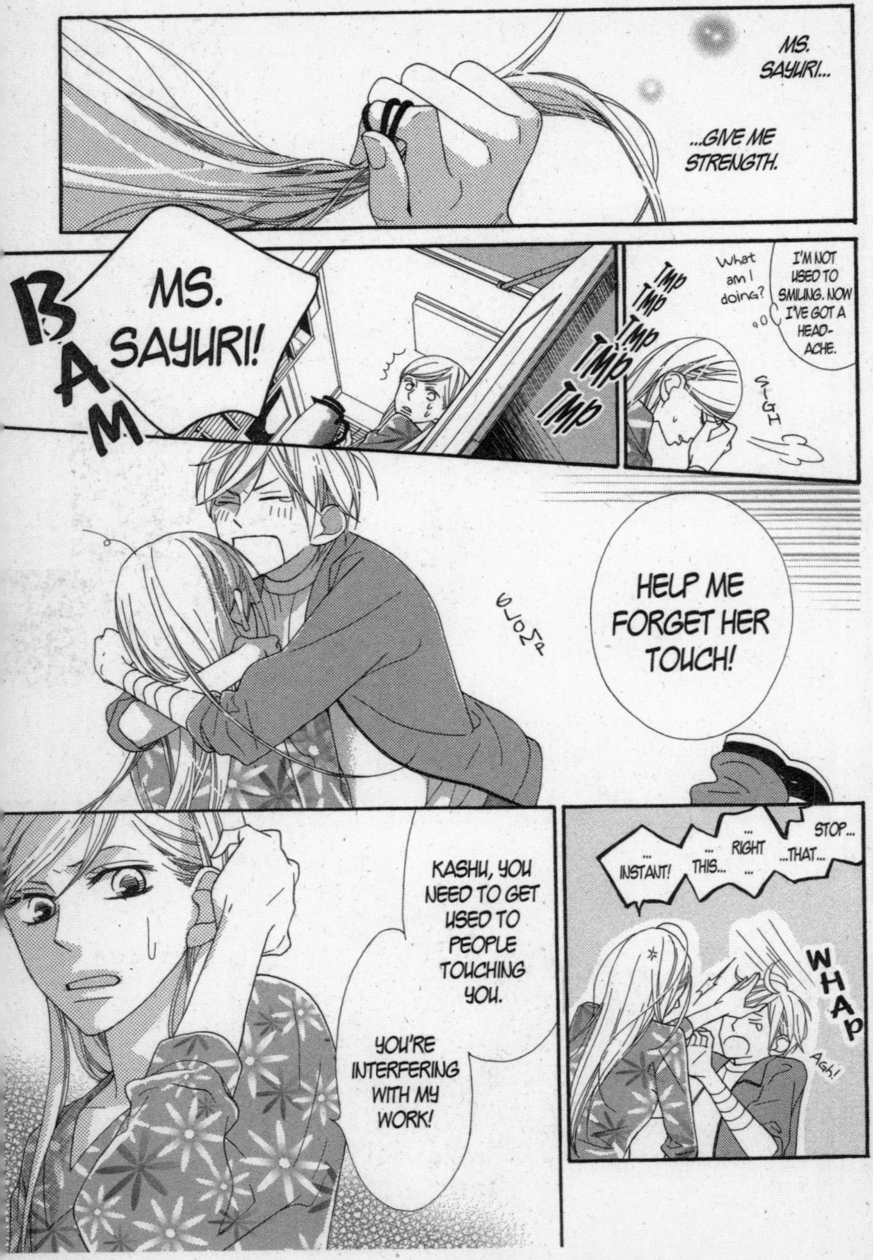
MS. SAYURI...
...GIVE ME STRENGTH.
I'M NOT USED TO SMILING. NOW I'VE GOT A HEAD-ACHE.
What am I doing?
SIGH
TMP TMP TMP TMP TMP
BAM
MS. SAYURI!
HELP ME FORGET HER TOUCH!
GLOMP
STOP... ...THAT... ...RIGHT... ...THIS... ...INSTANT!
WHAP
Agh!
KASHU, YOU NEED TO GET USED TO PEOPLE TOUCHING YOU.
YOU'RE INTERFERING WITH MY WORK!

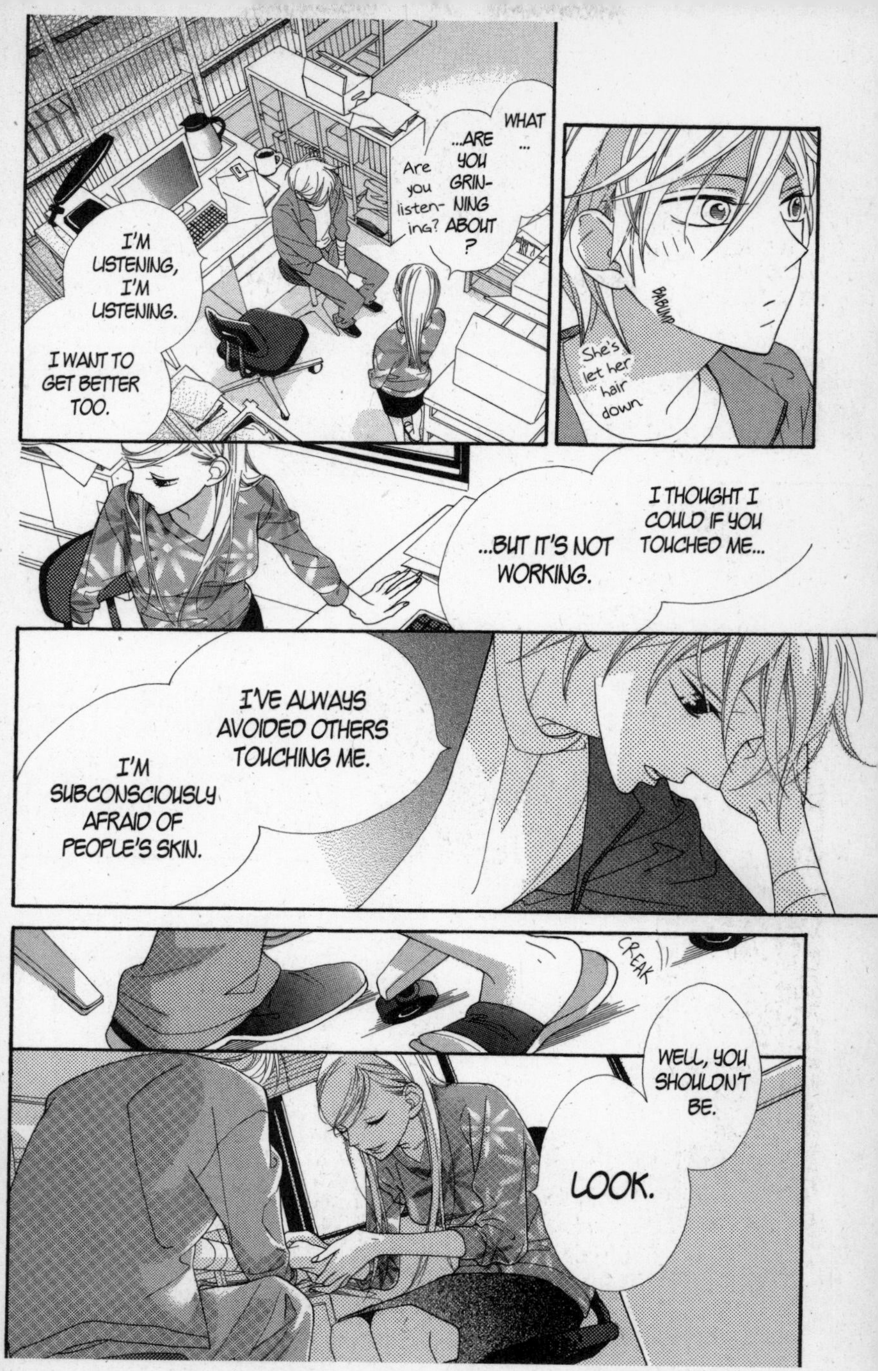
BABUMP
She's let her hair down.
WHAT ...
...ARE YOU GRIN-NING ABOUT ?
Are you listen-ing?
I'M LISTENING, I'M LISTENING.
I WANT TO GET BETTER TOO.
I THOUGHT I COULD IF YOU TOUCHED ME...
...BUT IT'S NOT WORKING.
I'VE ALWAYS AVOIDED OTHERS TOUCHING ME.
I'M SUBCONSCIOUSLY AFRAID OF PEOPLE'S SKIN.
CREAK
WELL, YOU SHOULDN'T BE.
LOOK.

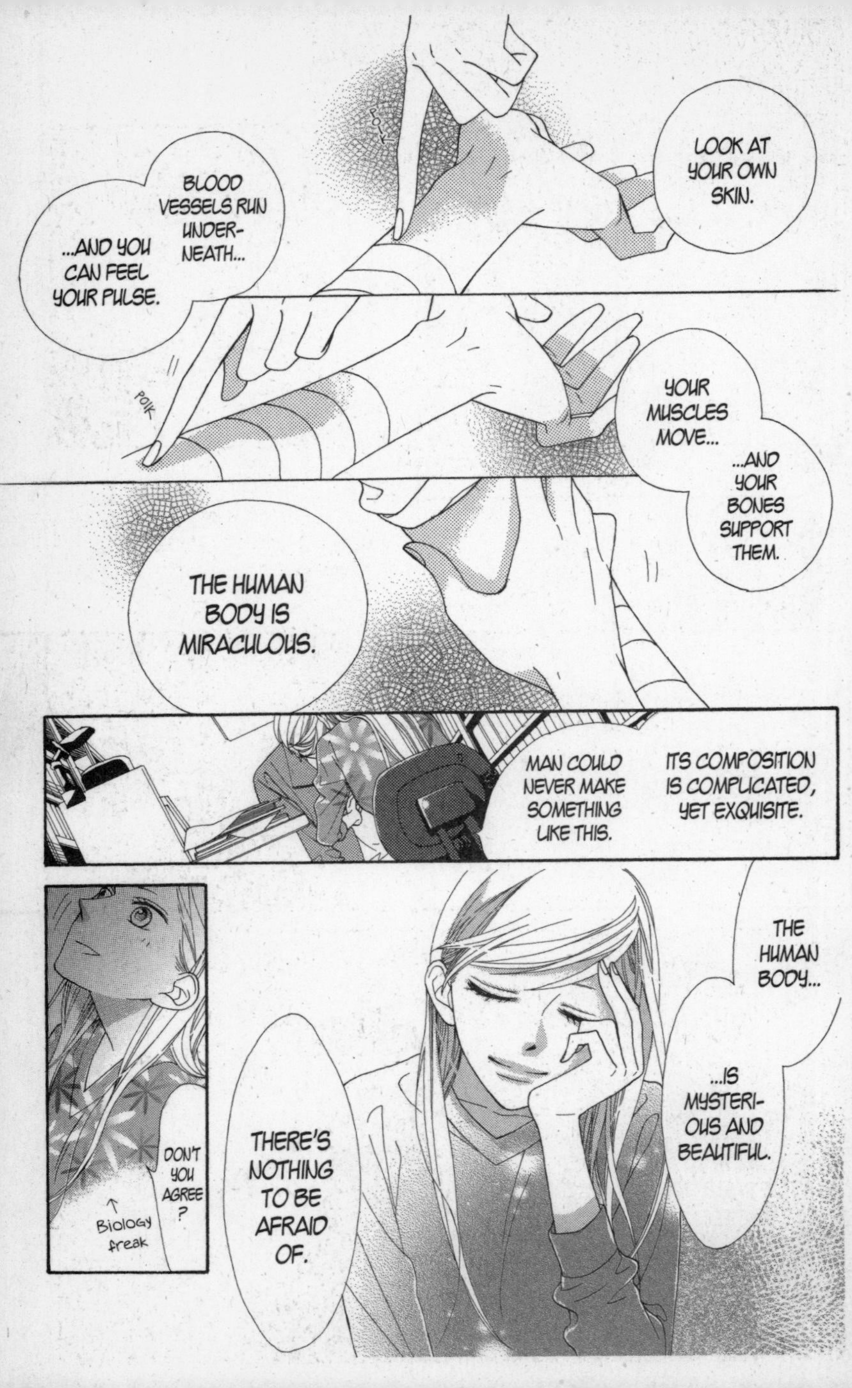
LOOK AT YOUR OWN SKIN.
POIK
BLOOD VESSELS RUN UNDER-NEATH...
...AND YOU CAN FEEL YOUR PULSE.
POIK
YOUR MUSCLES MOVE...
...AND YOUR BONES SUPPORT THEM.
THE HUMAN BODY IS MIRACULOUS.
ITS COMPOSITION IS COMPLICATED, YET EXQUISITE.
MAN COULD NEVER MAKE SOMETHING LIKE THIS.
THE HUMAN BODY...
...IS MYSTERI-OUS AND BEAUTIFUL.
THERE'S NOTHING TO BE AFRAID OF.
DON'T YOU AGREE ?
Biology freak

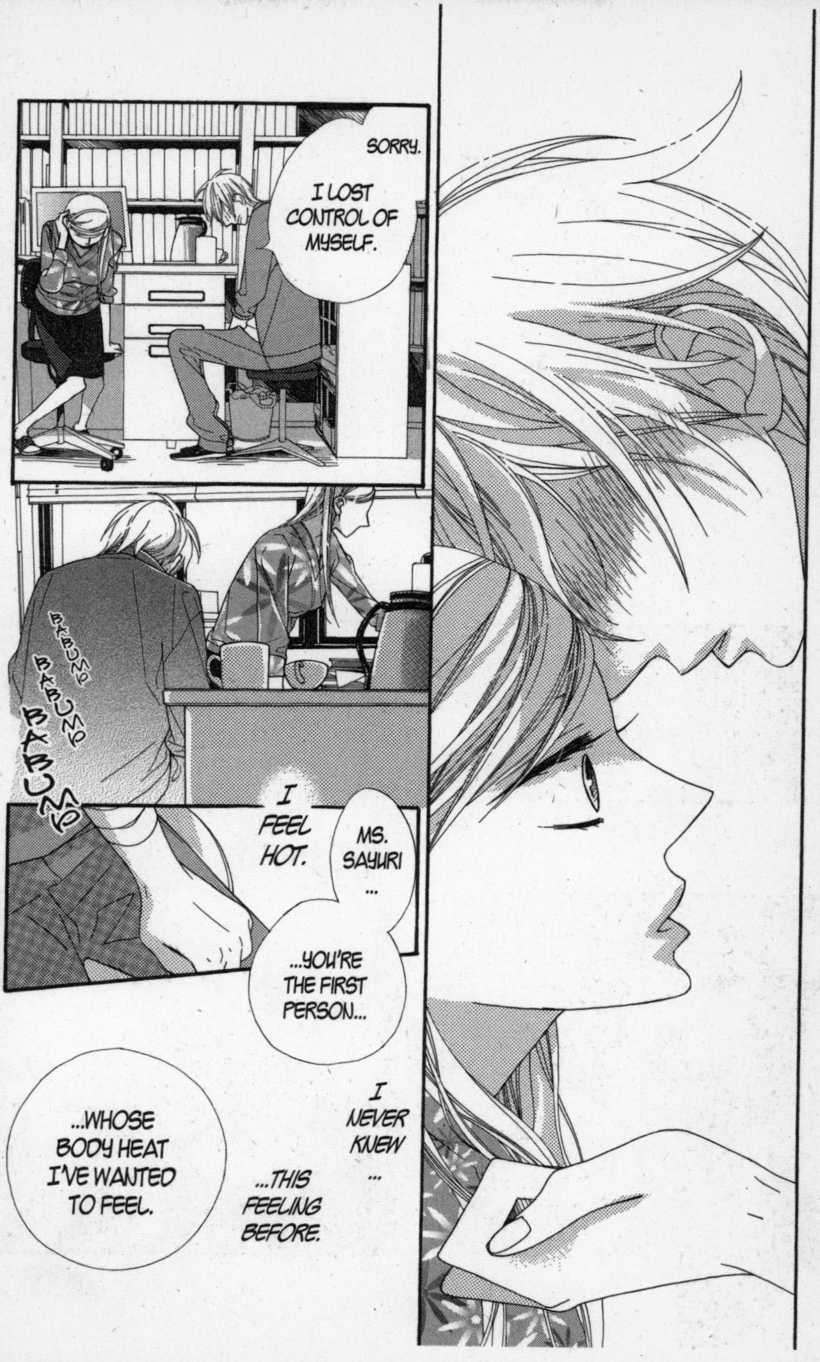
SORRY.
I LOST CONTROL OF MYSELF.
BABUMP
BABUMP
BABUMP
BABUMP
I FEEL HOT.
MS. SAYURI ...
...YOU'RE THE FIRST PERSON...
...WHOSE BODY HEAT I'VE WANTED TO FEEL.
I NEVER KNEW ...
...THIS FEELING BEFORE.

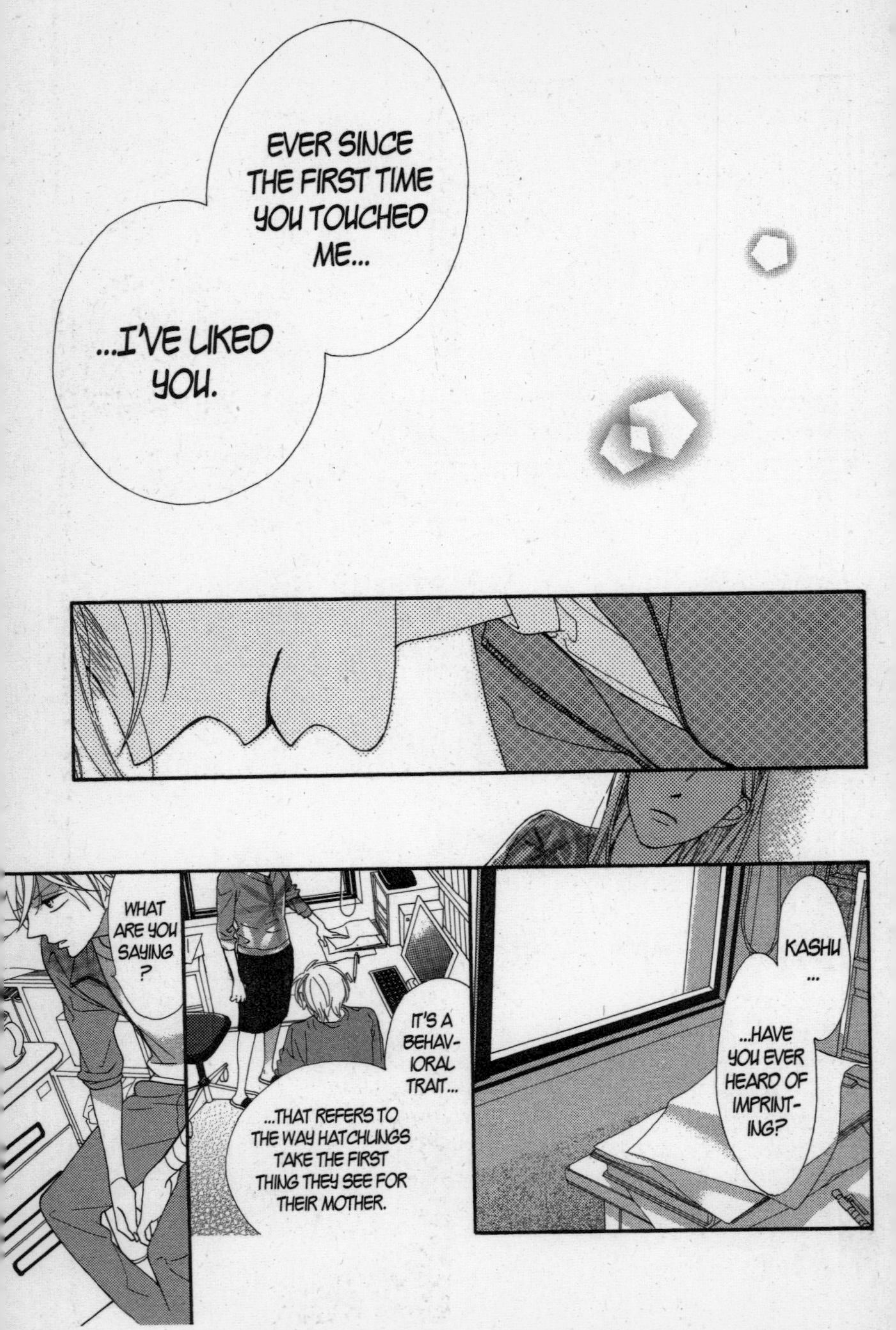
EVER SINCE THE FIRST TIME YOU TOUCHED ME...
...I'VE LIKED YOU.
KASHU...
...HAVE YOU EVER HEARD OF IMPRINTING?
IT'S A BEHAVIORAL TRAIT...
...THAT REFERS TO THE WAY HATCHLINGS TAKE THE FIRST THING THEY SEE FOR THEIR MOTHER.
WHAT ARE YOU SAYING?

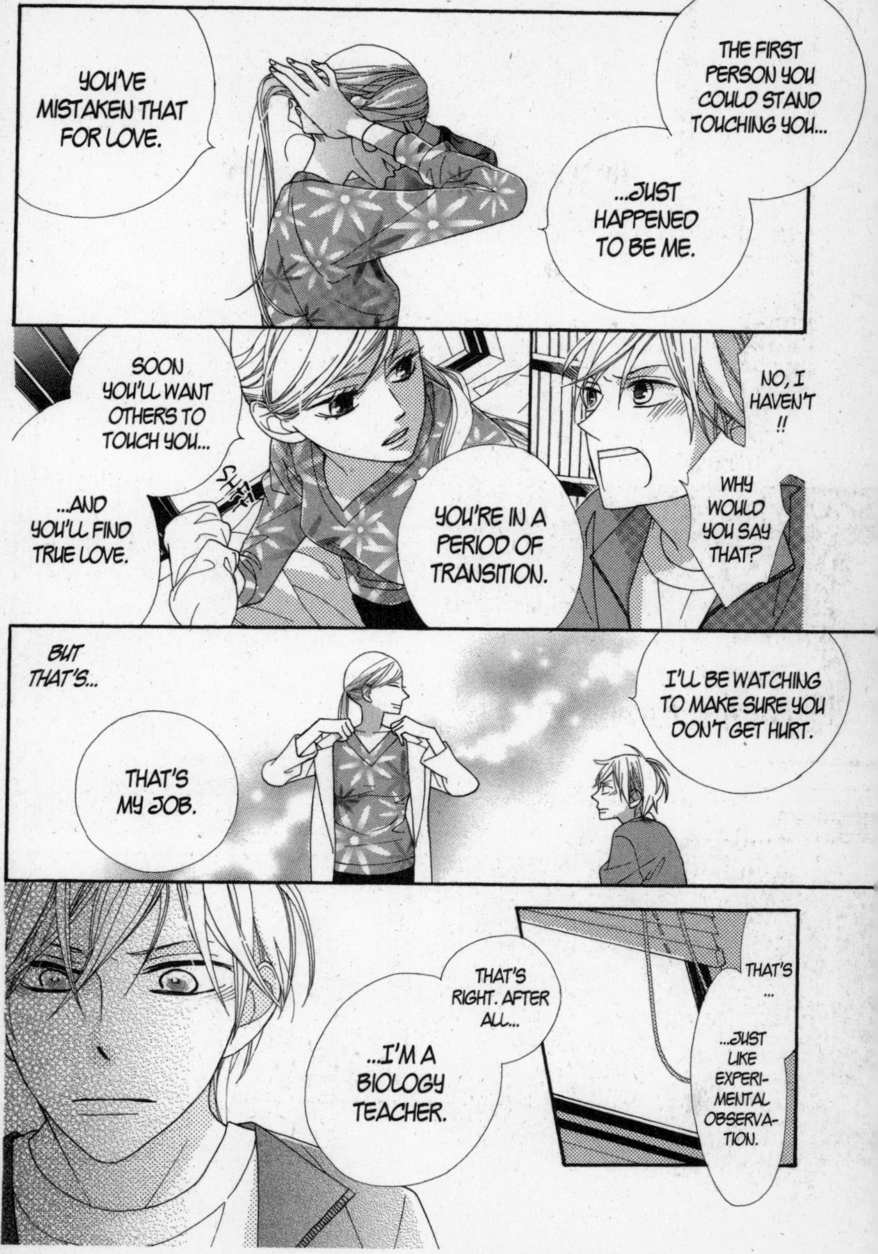

THE FIRST PERSON YOU COULD STAND TOUCHING YOU...
...JUST HAPPENED TO BE ME.
YOU'VE MISTAKEN THAT FOR LOVE.
NO, I HAVEN'T !!
WHY WOULD YOU SAY THAT?
YOU'RE IN A PERIOD OF TRANSITION.
SOON YOU'LL WANT OTHERS TO TOUCH YOU...
SHFF
...AND YOU'LL FIND TRUE LOVE.
I'LL BE WATCHING TO MAKE SURE YOU DON'T GET HURT.
BUT THAT'S...
THAT'S MY JOB.
THAT'S ...
...JUST LIKE EXPERIMENTAL OBSERVATION.
THAT'S RIGHT. AFTER ALL...
...I'M A BIOLOGY TEACHER.

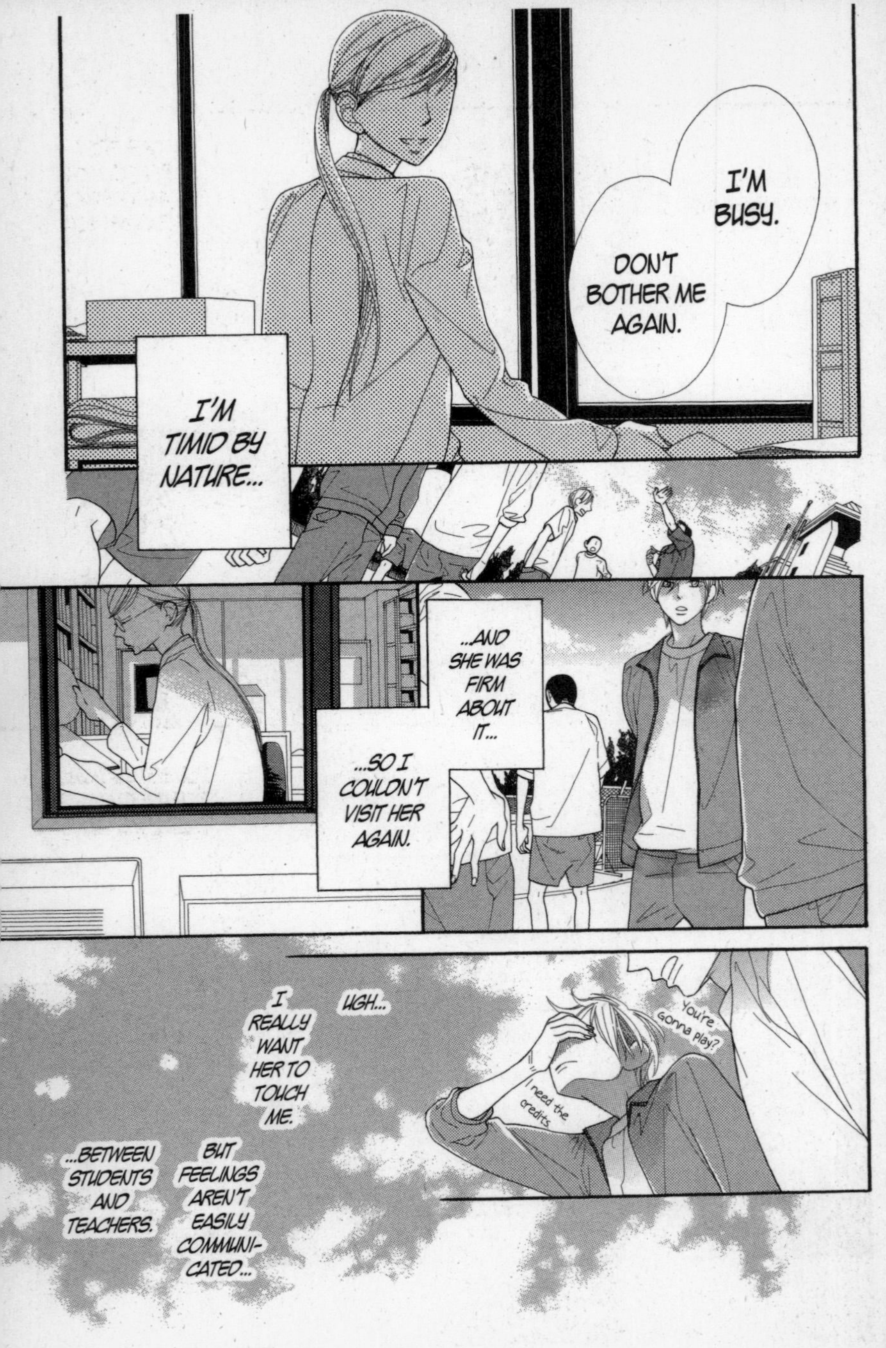
I'M BUSY.
DON'T BOTHER ME AGAIN.
I'M TIMID BY NATURE...
...AND SHE WAS FIRM ABOUT IT...
...SO I COULDN'T VISIT HER AGAIN.
You're gonna play?
I need the credits.
UGH...
I REALLY WANT HER TO TOUCH ME.
BUT FEELINGS AREN'T EASILY COMMUNI-CATED...
...BETWEEN STUDENTS AND TEACHERS.

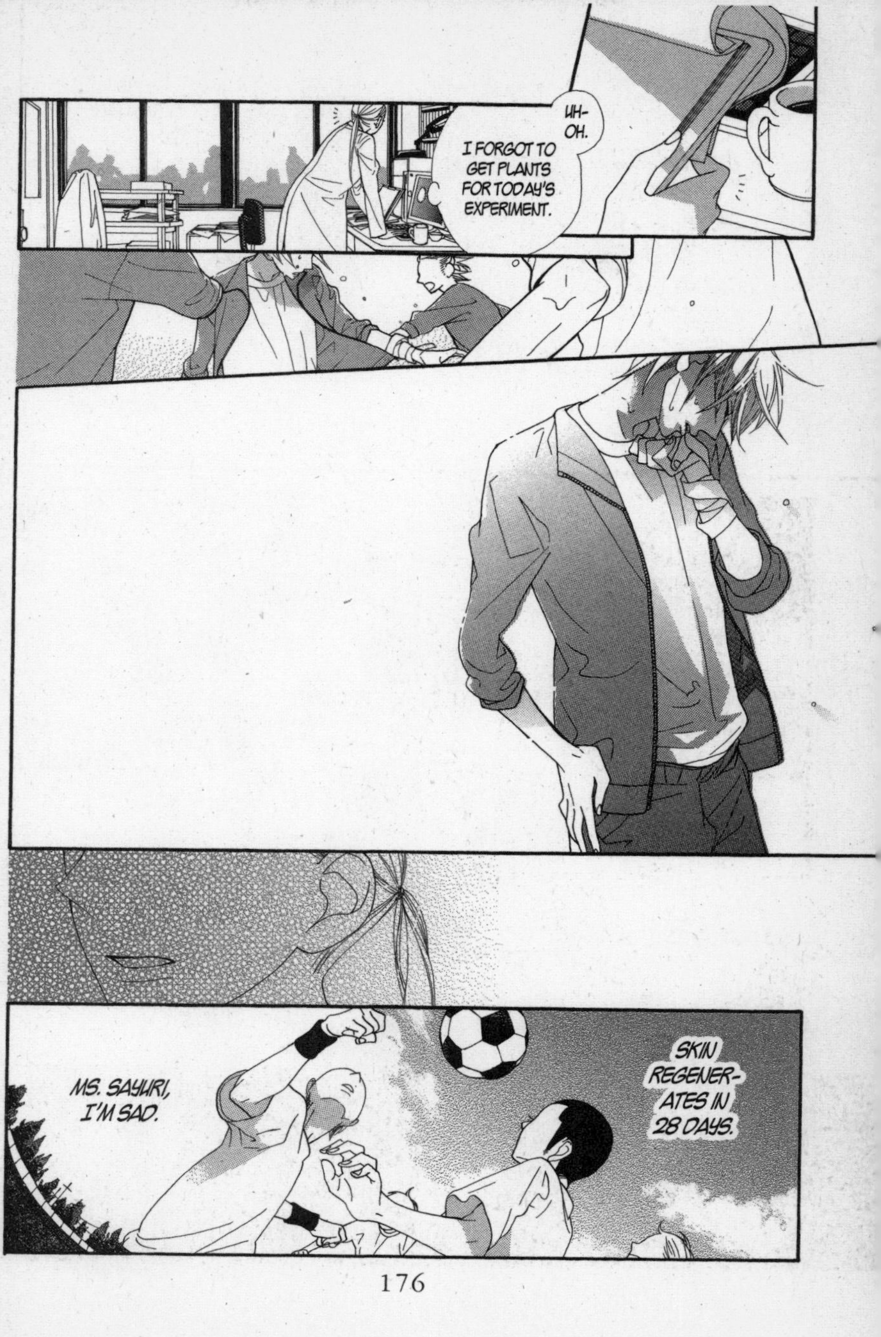
UH-OH.
I FORGOT TO GET PLANTS FOR TODAY'S EXPERIMENT.
SKIN REGENER-ATES IN 28 DAYS.
MS. SAYURI, I'M SAD.

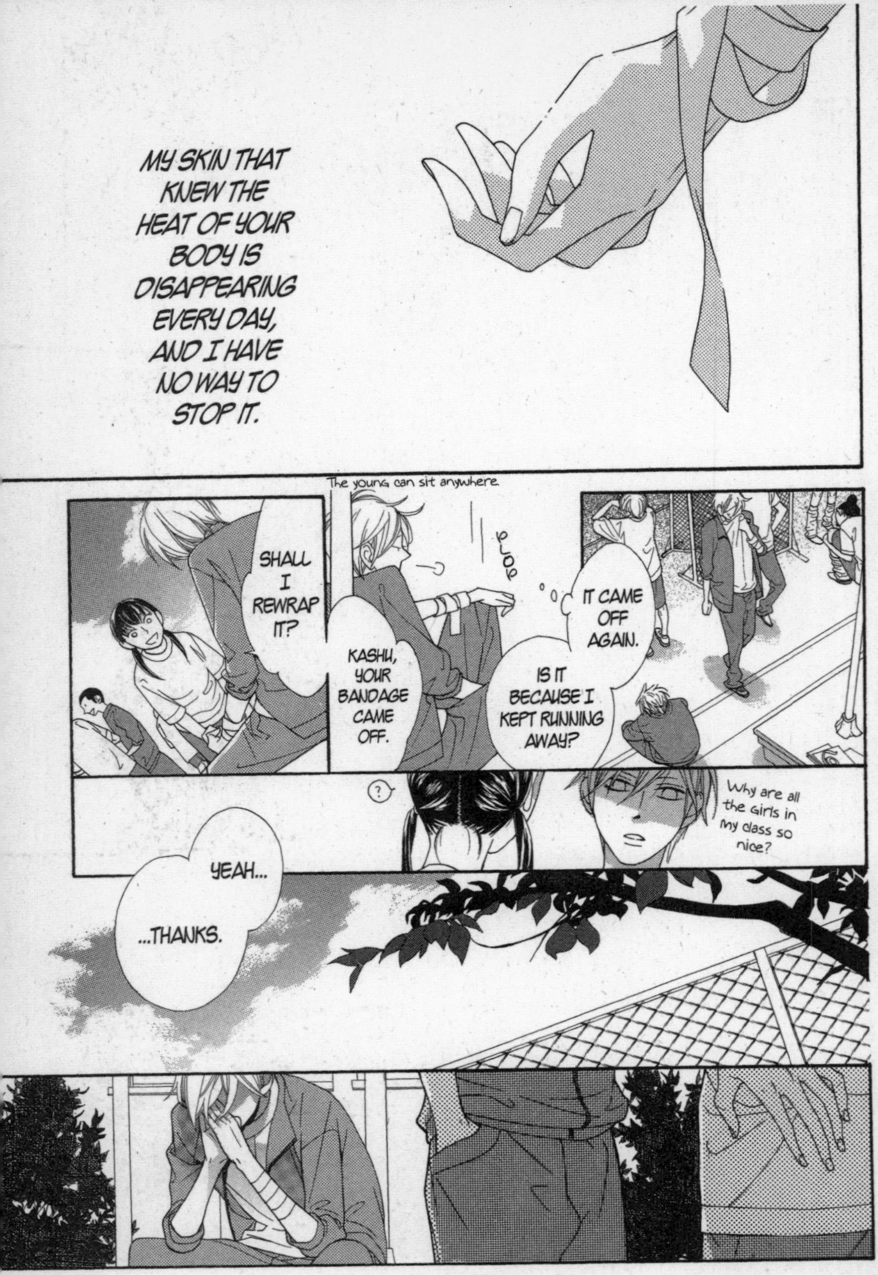
MY SKIN THAT KNEW THE HEAT OF YOUR BODY IS DISAPPEARING EVERY DAY, AND I HAVE NO WAY TO STOP IT.
IT CAME OFF AGAIN.
IS IT BECAUSE I KEPT RUNNING AWAY?
The young can sit anywhere.
plop
KASHU, YOUR BANDAGE CAME OFF.
SHALL I REWRAP IT?
Why are all the girls in my class so nice?
?
YEAH...
...THANKS.

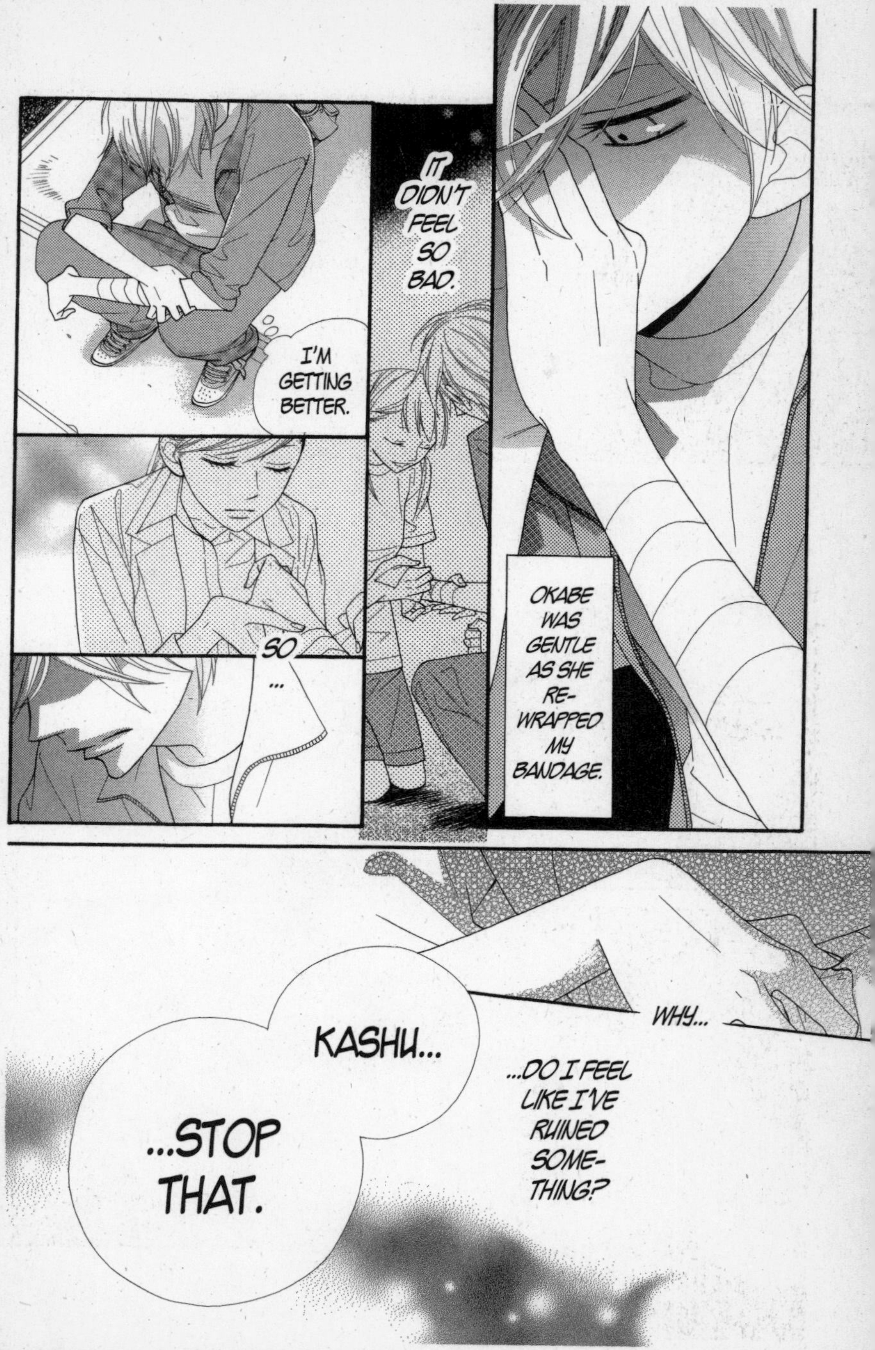
OKABE WAS GENTLE AS SHE RE-WRAPPED MY BANDAGE.
IT DIDN'T FEEL SO BAD.
I'M GETTING BETTER.
SO ...
WHY...
...DO I FEEL LIKE I'VE RUINED SOME-THING?
KASHU...
...STOP THAT.

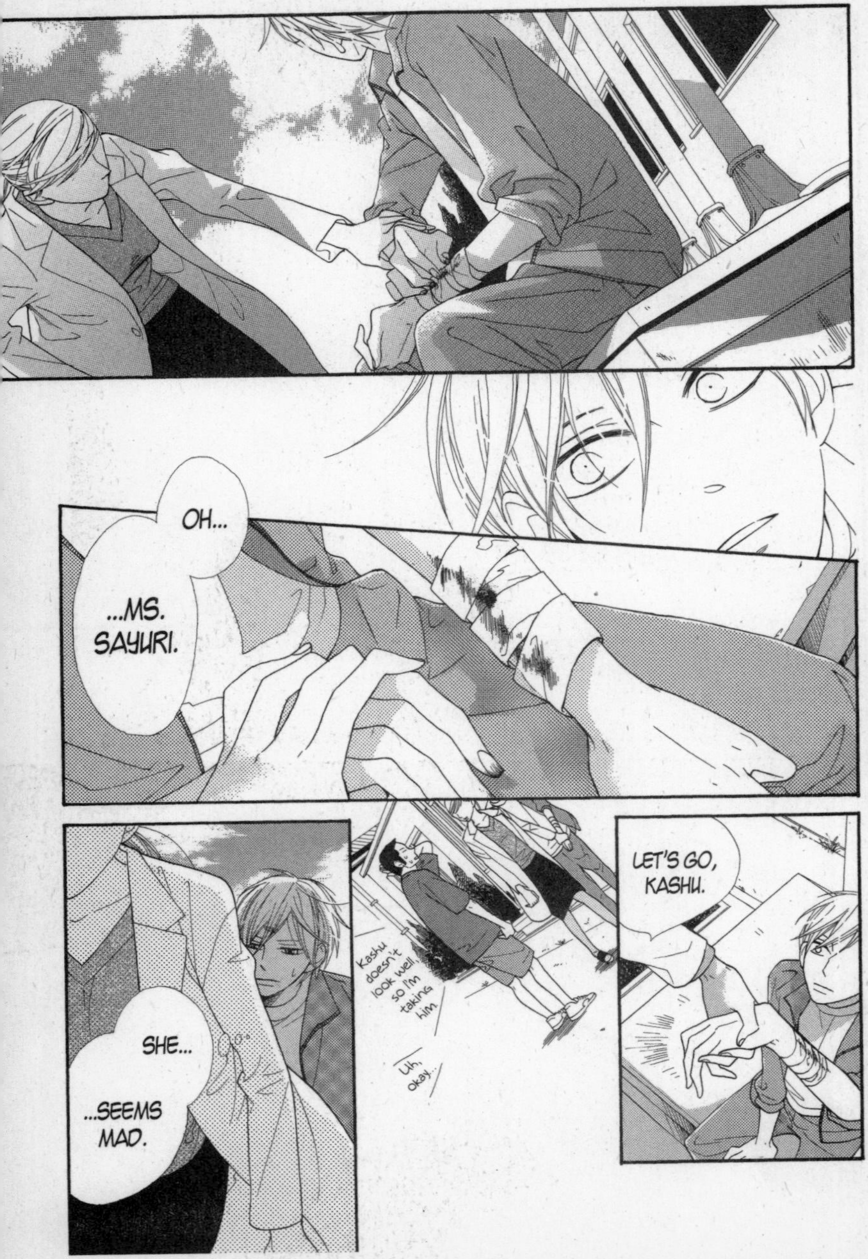
OH...
...MS. SAYURI.
LET'S GO, KASHU.
Kashu doesn't look well, so I'm taking him.
Uh, okay...
SHE...
...SEEMS MAD.

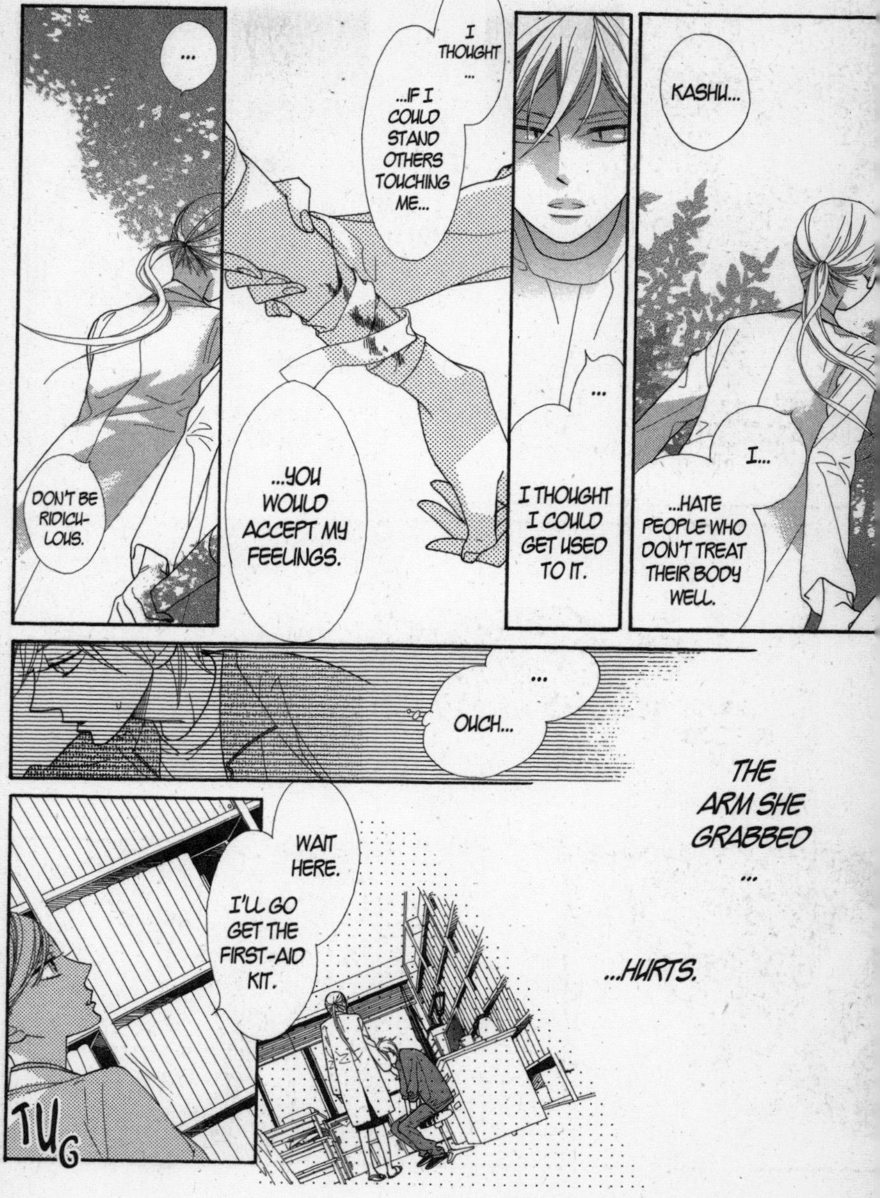
KASHU...
I...
...HATE PEOPLE WHO DON'T TREAT THEIR BODY WELL.
...
I THOUGHT I COULD GET USED TO IT.
I THOUGHT ...
...IF I COULD STAND OTHERS TOUCHING ME...
...YOU WOULD ACCEPT MY FEELINGS.
...
DON'T BE RIDICU-LOUS.
...
OUCH...
THE ARM SHE GRABBED ...
...HURTS.
WAIT HERE.
I'LL GO GET THE FIRST-AID KIT.
TUG

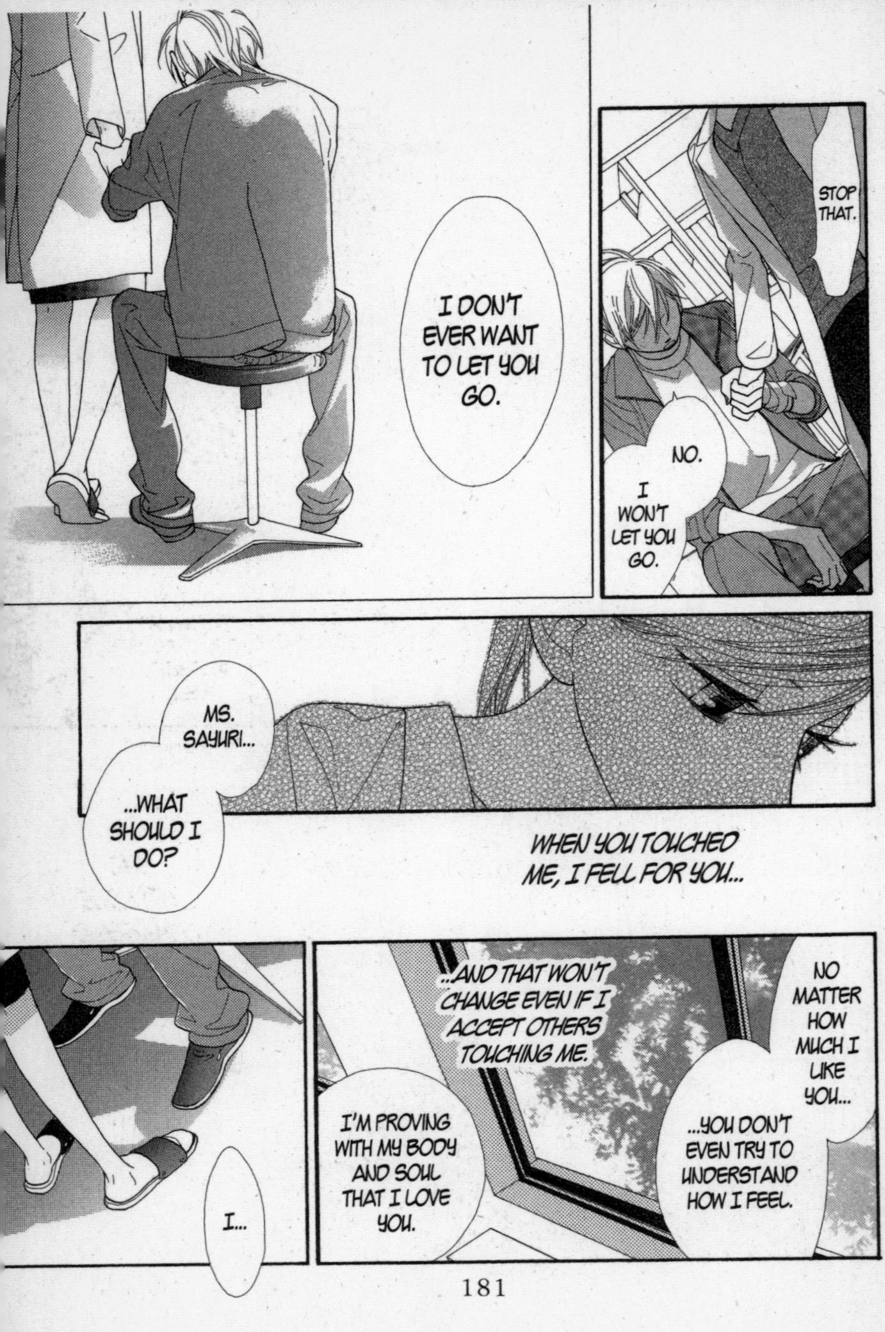
STOP THAT.
NO. I WON'T LET YOU GO.
I DON'T EVER WANT TO LET YOU GO.
MS. SAYURI...
...WHAT SHOULD I DO?
WHEN YOU TOUCHED ME, I FELL FOR YOU...
NO MATTER HOW MUCH I LIKE YOU...
...YOU DON'T EVEN TRY TO UNDERSTAND HOW I FEEL.
...AND THAT WON'T CHANGE EVEN IF I ACCEPT OTHERS TOUCHING ME.
I'M PROVING WITH MY BODY AND SOUL THAT I LOVE YOU.
I...

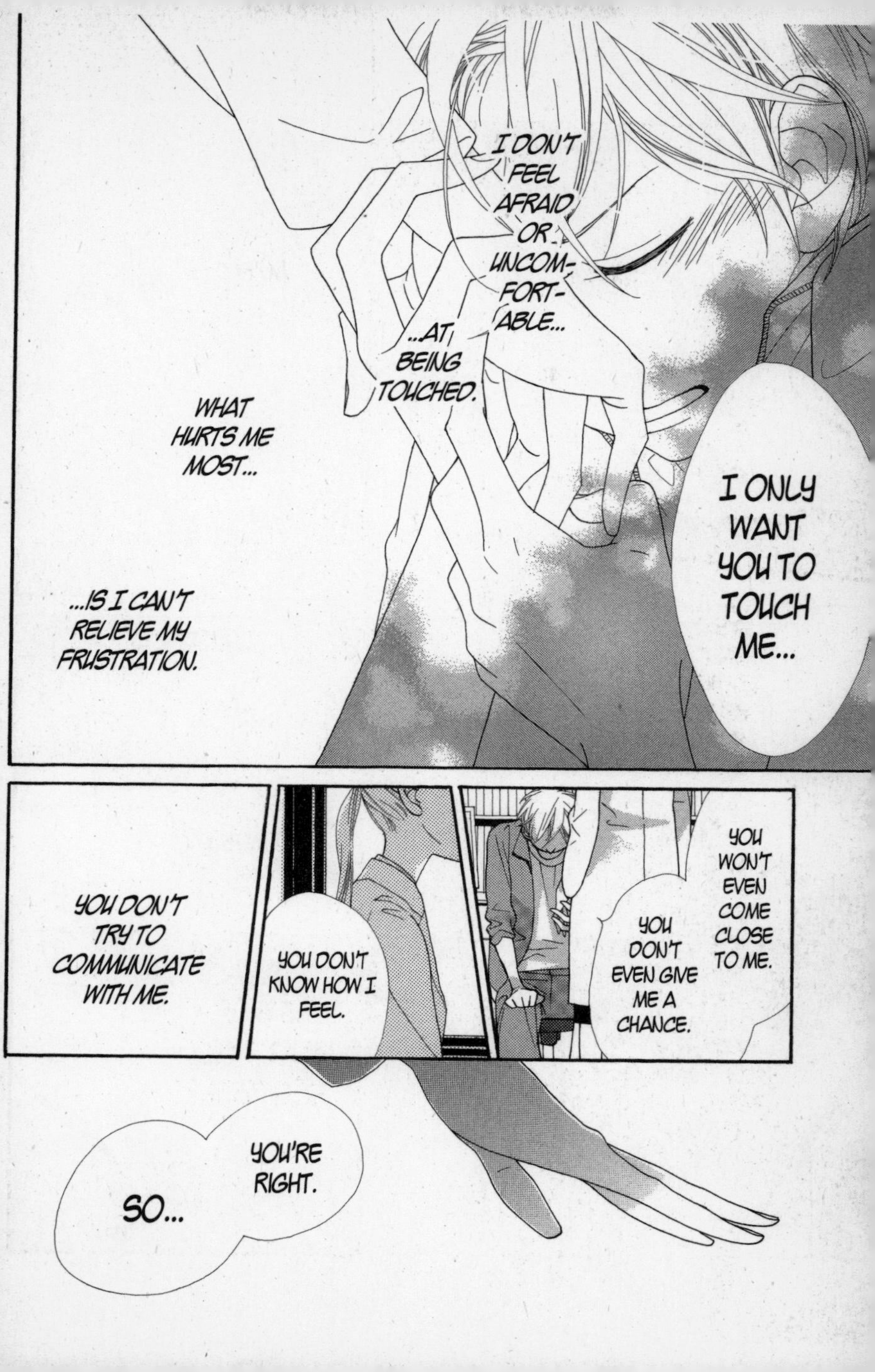
I DON'T FEEL AFRAID OR UNCOM-FORT-ABLE...
...AT BEING TOUCHED.
I ONLY WANT YOU TO TOUCH ME...
WHAT HURTS ME MOST...
...IS I CAN'T RELIEVE MY FRUSTRATION.
YOU WON'T EVEN COME CLOSE TO ME.
YOU DON'T EVEN GIVE ME A CHANCE.
YOU DON'T KNOW HOW I FEEL.
YOU DON'T TRY TO COMMUNICATE WITH ME.
YOU'RE RIGHT.
SO...

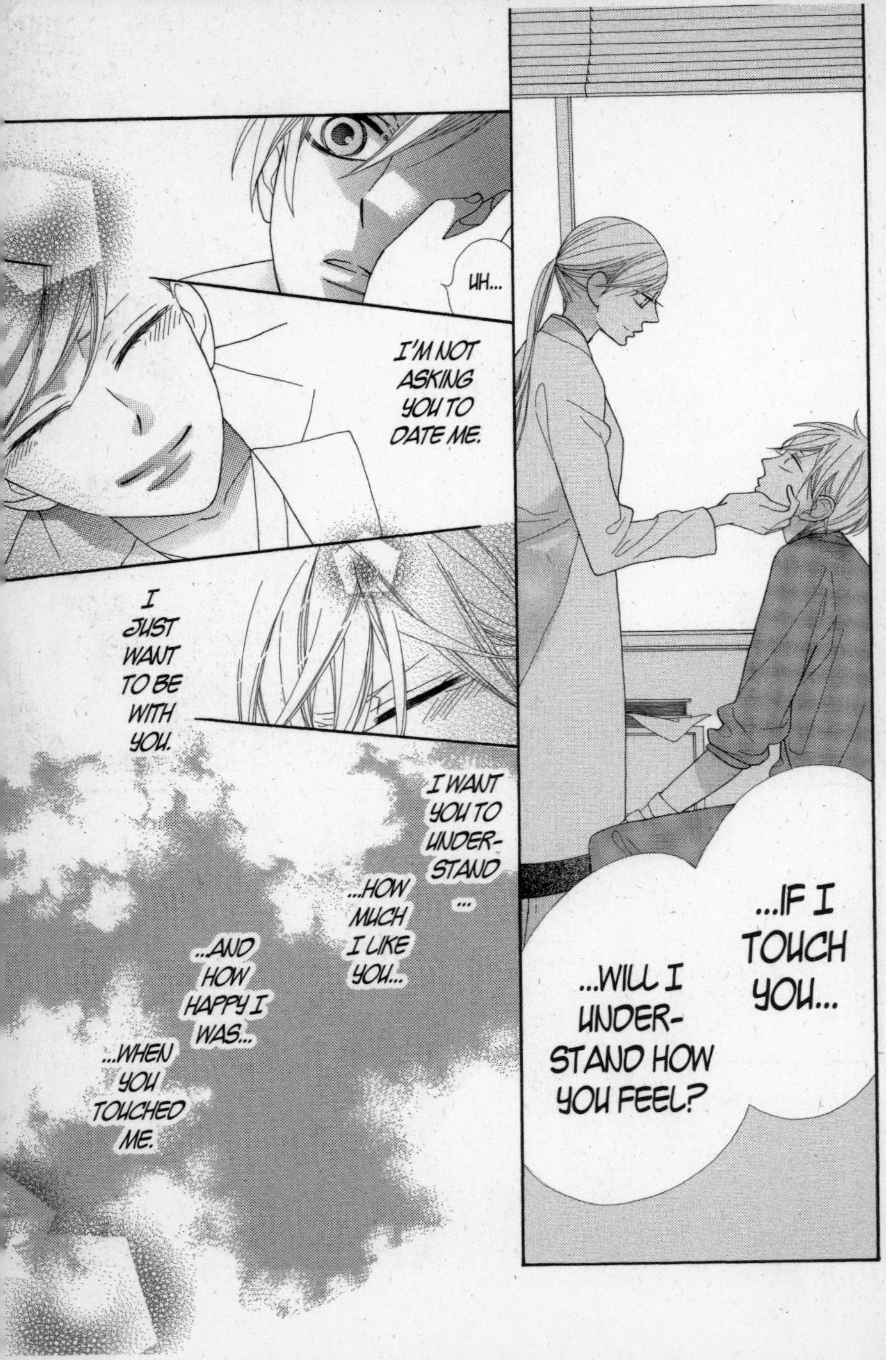
...IF I TOUCH YOU...
...WILL I UNDER-STAND HOW YOU FEEL?
UH...
I'M NOT ASKING YOU TO DATE ME.
I JUST WANT TO BE WITH YOU.
I WANT YOU TO UNDER-STAND ...
...HOW MUCH I LIKE YOU...
...AND HOW HAPPY I WAS...
...WHEN YOU TOUCHED ME.

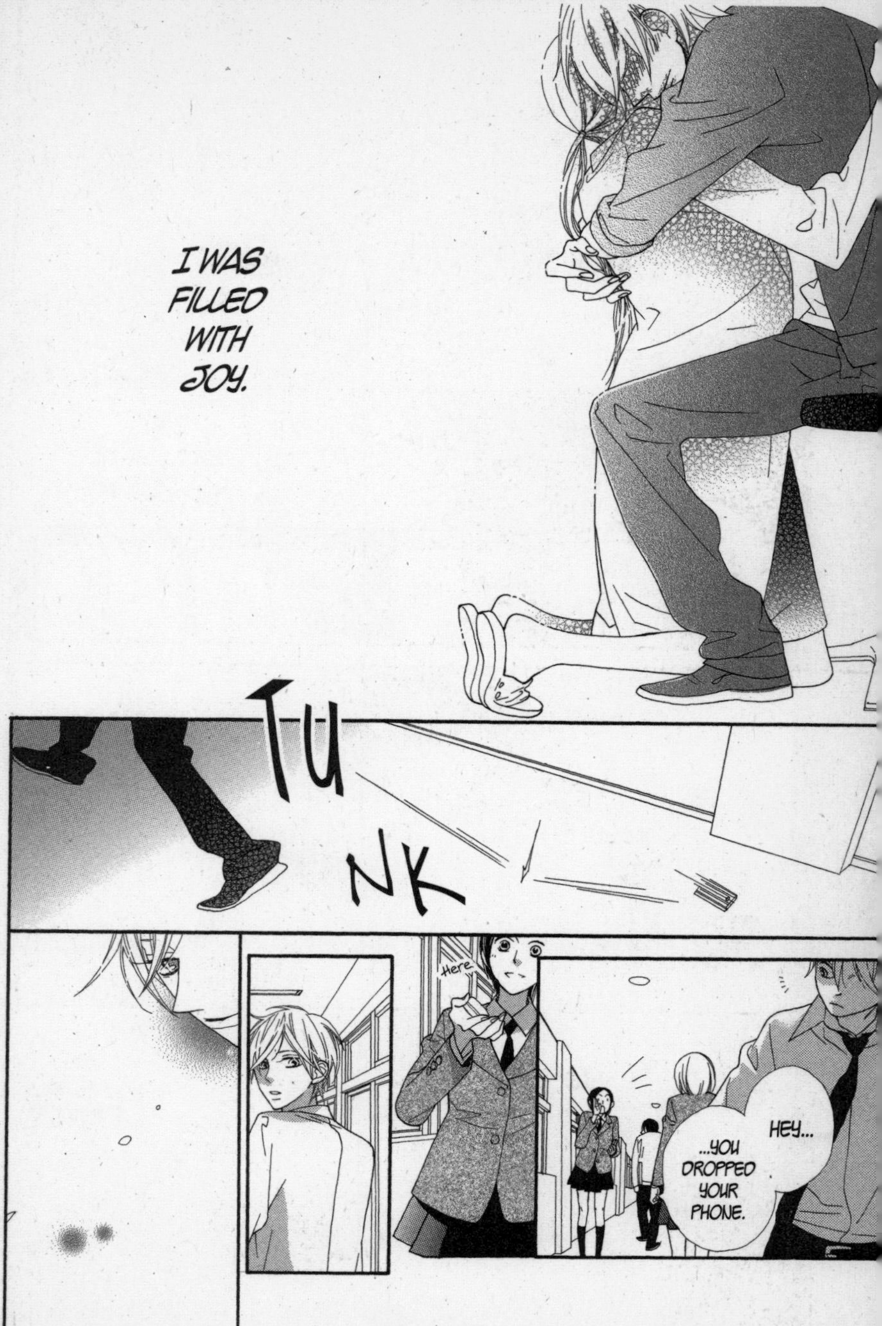
I WAS FILLED WITH JOY.
TUNK
HEY...
...YOU DROPPED YOUR PHONE.
Here.

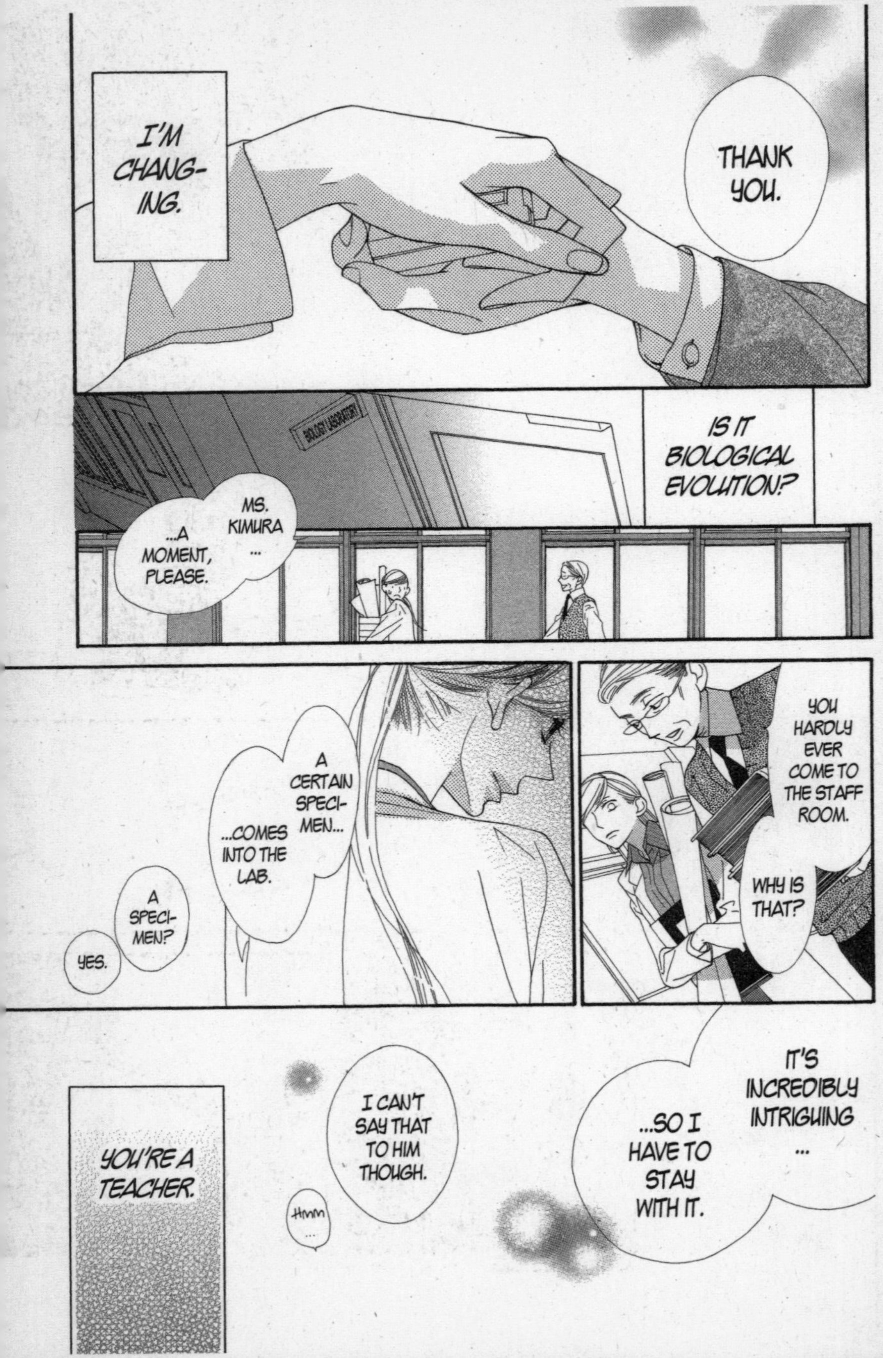
THANK YOU.
I'M CHANGING.
IS IT BIOLOGICAL EVOLUTION?
BIOLOGY LABORATORY
MS. KIMURA...
...A MOMENT, PLEASE.
YOU HARDLY EVER COME TO THE STAFF ROOM.
WHY IS THAT?
A CERTAIN SPECIMEN...
...COMES INTO THE LAB.
A SPECIMEN?
YES.
IT'S INCREDIBLY INTRIGUING...
...SO I HAVE TO STAY WITH IT.
I CAN'T SAY THAT TO HIM THOUGH.
Hmm...
YOU'RE A TEACHER.

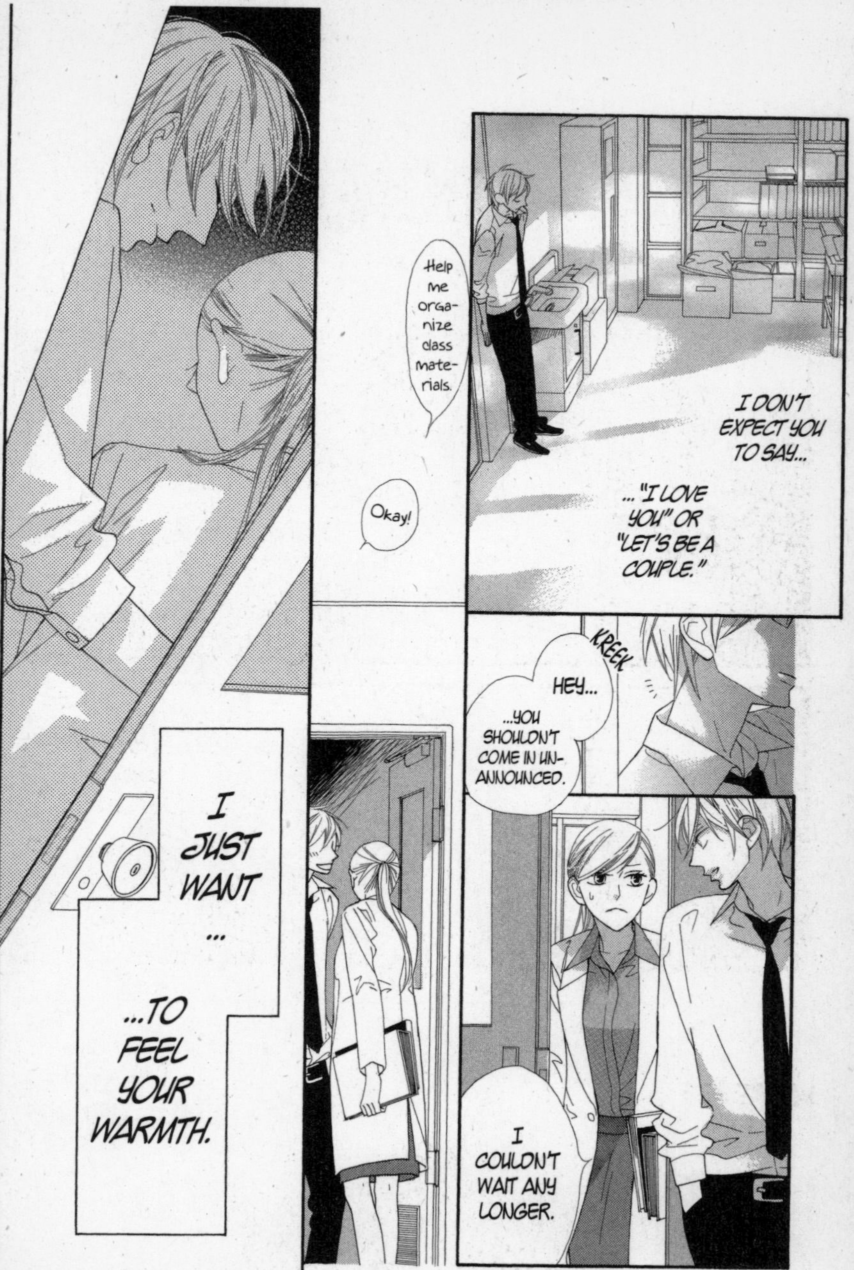

Help me organize class materials.
Okay!
I DON'T EXPECT YOU TO SAY...
... "I LOVE YOU" OR "LET'S BE A COUPLE."
KREEK
HEY...
...YOU SHOULDN'T COME IN UN-ANNOUNCED.
I COULDN'T WAIT ANY LONGER.
I JUST WANT ...
...TO FEEL YOUR WARMTH.

WARM TO THE TOUCH / END

BONUS STORM

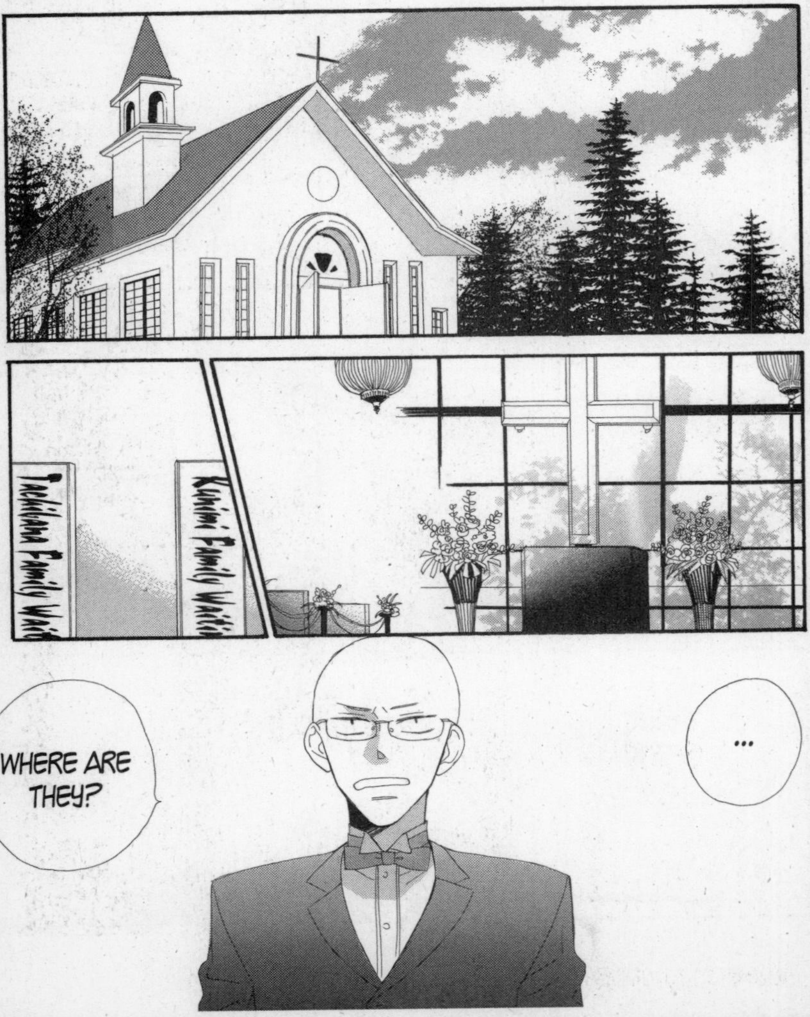
Kunimi Family Waiti
Tachibana Family Wait
...
WHERE ARE THEY?

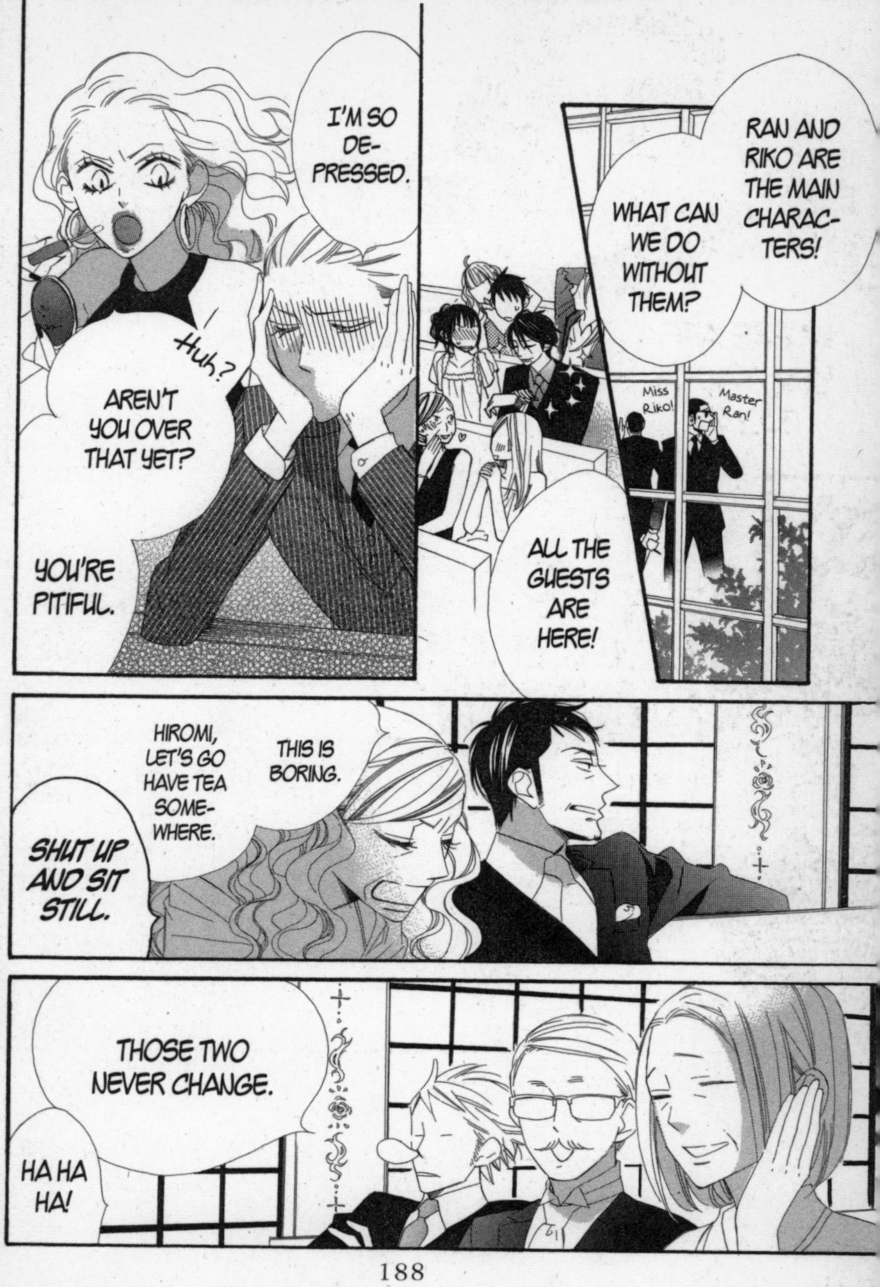

RAN AND RIKO ARE THE MAIN CHARACTERS!
WHAT CAN WE DO WITHOUT THEM?
Master Ran!
Miss Riko!
ALL THE GUESTS ARE HERE!
I'M SO DE-PRESSED.
Huh?
AREN'T YOU OVER THAT YET?
YOU'RE PITIFUL.
THIS IS BORING.
HIROMI, LET'S GO HAVE TEA SOME-WHERE.
SHUT UP AND SIT STILL.
THOSE TWO NEVER CHANGE.
HA HA HA!

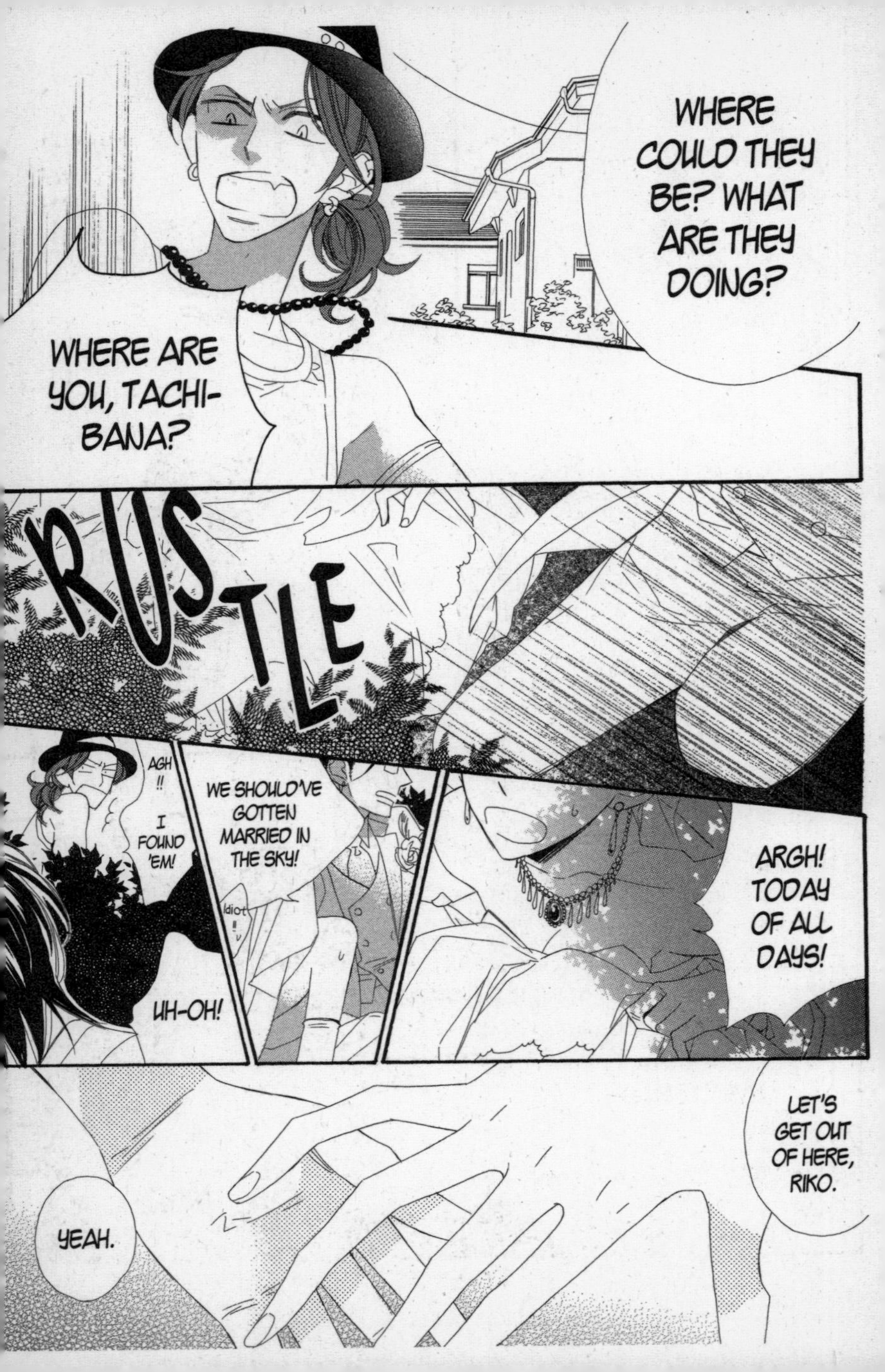
WHERE COULD THEY BE? WHAT ARE THEY DOING?
WHERE ARE YOU, TACHI-BANA?
RUSTLE
ARGH! TODAY OF ALL DAYS!
WE SHOULD'VE GOTTEN MARRIED IN THE SKY!
Idiot!!
AGH!! I FOUND 'EM!
UH-OH!
LET'S GET OUT OF HERE, RIKO.
YEAH.

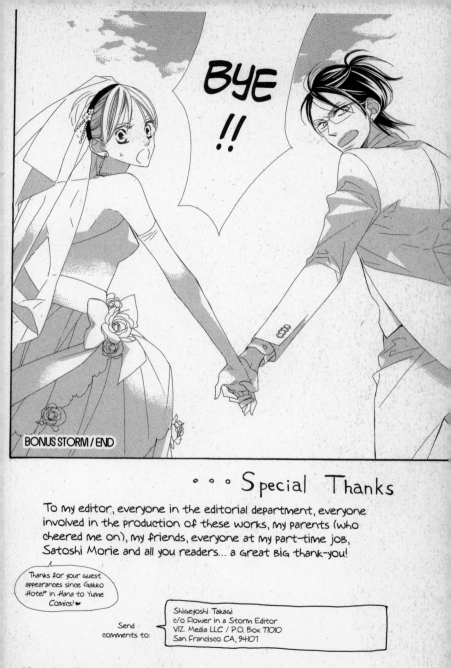

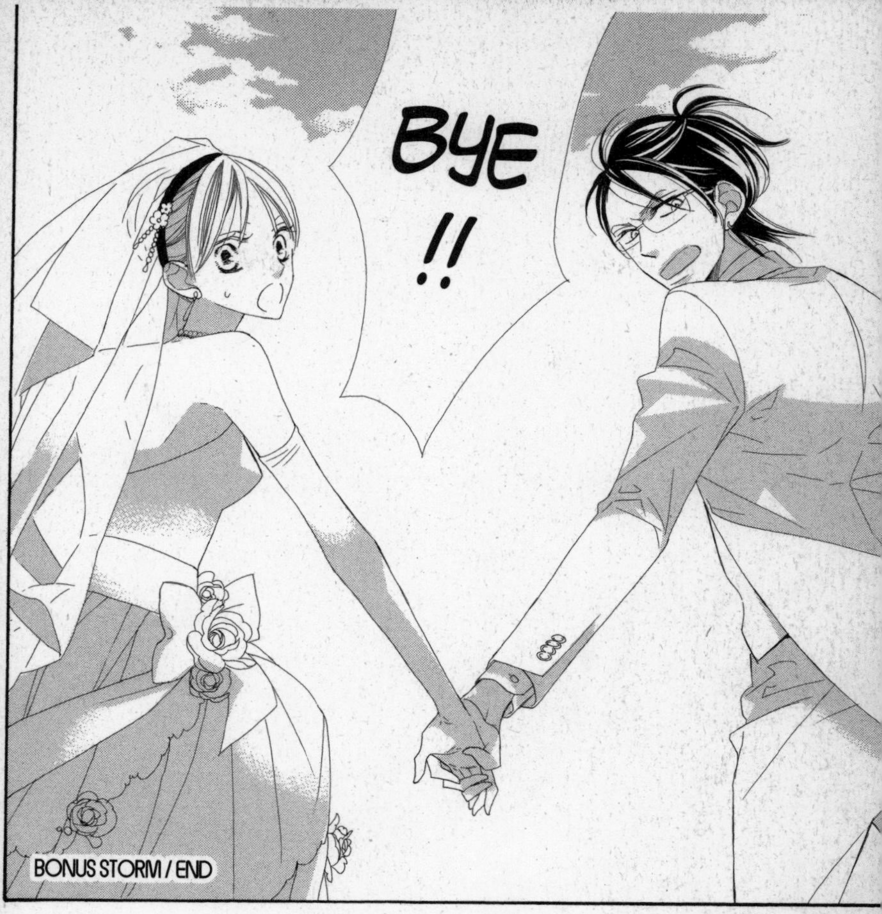
BYE !!
BONUS STORM / END

...Special Thanks

To my editor, everyone in the editorial department, everyone involved in the production of these works, my parents (who cheered me on), my friends, everyone at my part-time job, Satoshi Morie and all you readers... a great big thank-you!

Thanks for your guest appearances since Gakko Hotel* in Hana to Yume Comics!

Send comments to:

Shigeyoshi Takagi
c/o Flower in a Storm Editor
VIZ Media LLC / P.O. Box 77010
San Francisco CA, 94107

*Gakko Hotel (School Hotel) appeared in the magazine Hana to Yume Comics, Nos. 16, 22-24.

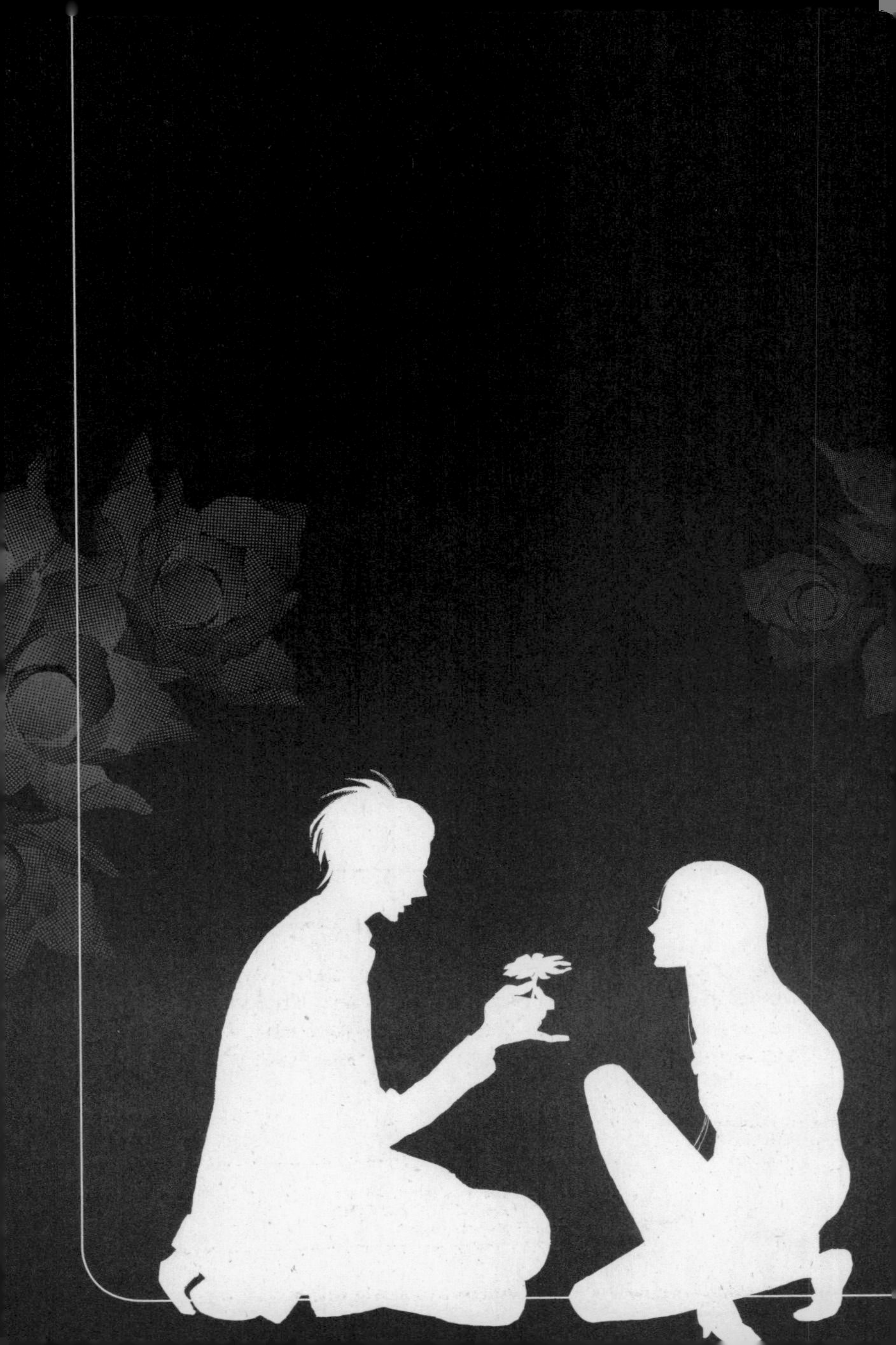

ABOUT THE AUTHOR

The author of *Flower in a Storm* uses the pen name Shigeyoshi Takagi. Her work has been published in the shojo manga anthologies *LaLa* and *LaLa DX* in Japan. *Flower in a Storm* is her first graphic novel.

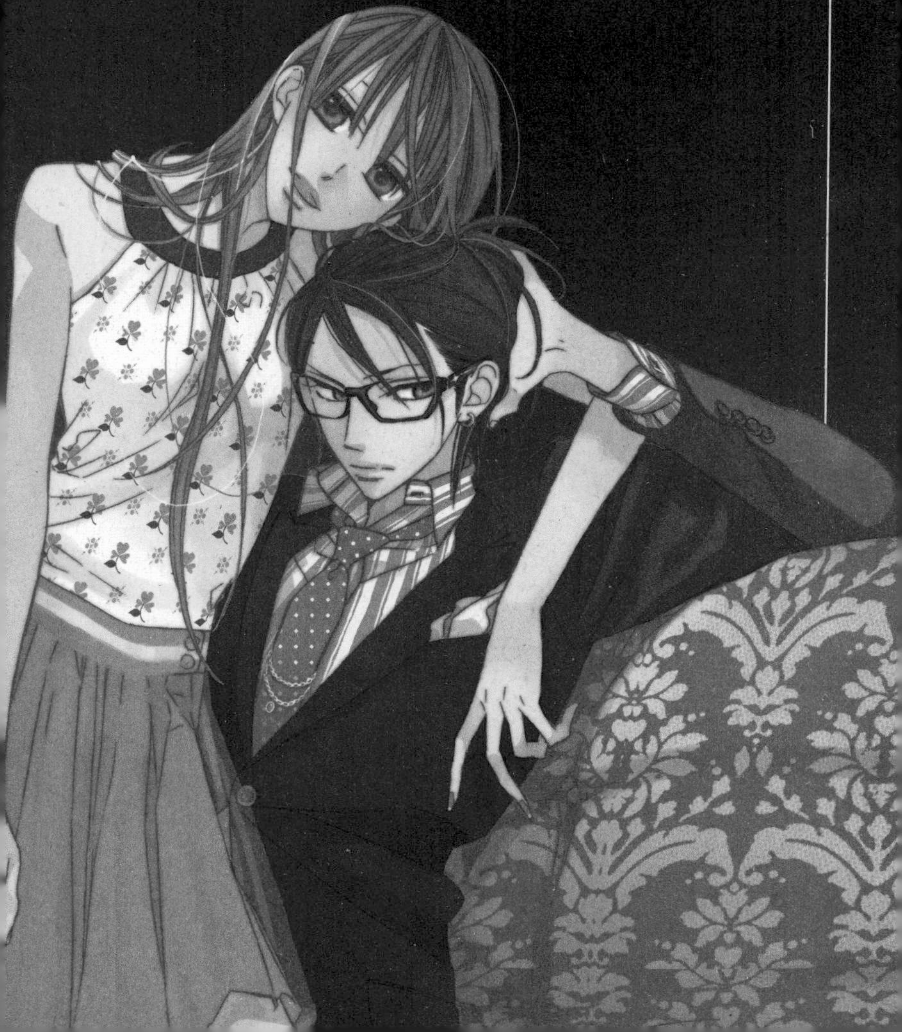

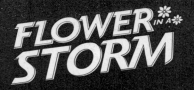

FLOWER IN A STORM

Volume 2

Shojo Beat Edition

Story and Art by Shigeyoshi Takagi

Translation HC Language Solutions, Inc.
Touch-up Art & Lettering Vanessa Satone
Design Frances O. Liddell
Editor Carrie Shepherd

VP, Production Alvin Lu
VP, Sales & Product Marketing Gonzalo Ferreyra
VP, Creative Linda Espinosa
Publisher Hyoe Narita

Hana ni Arashi by Shigeyoshi Takagi
© Shigeyoshi Takagi 2008
All rights reserved.
First published in Japan in 2008 by HAKUSENSHA, Inc., Tokyo.
English language translation rights arranged with HAKUSENSHA, Inc., Tokyo.

Printed in the U.S.A.

Published by VIZ Media, LLC
P.O. Box 77010
San Francisco, CA 94107

10 9 8 7 6 5 4 3 2 1
First printing, August 2010

Don't Hide What's *Inside*

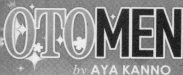

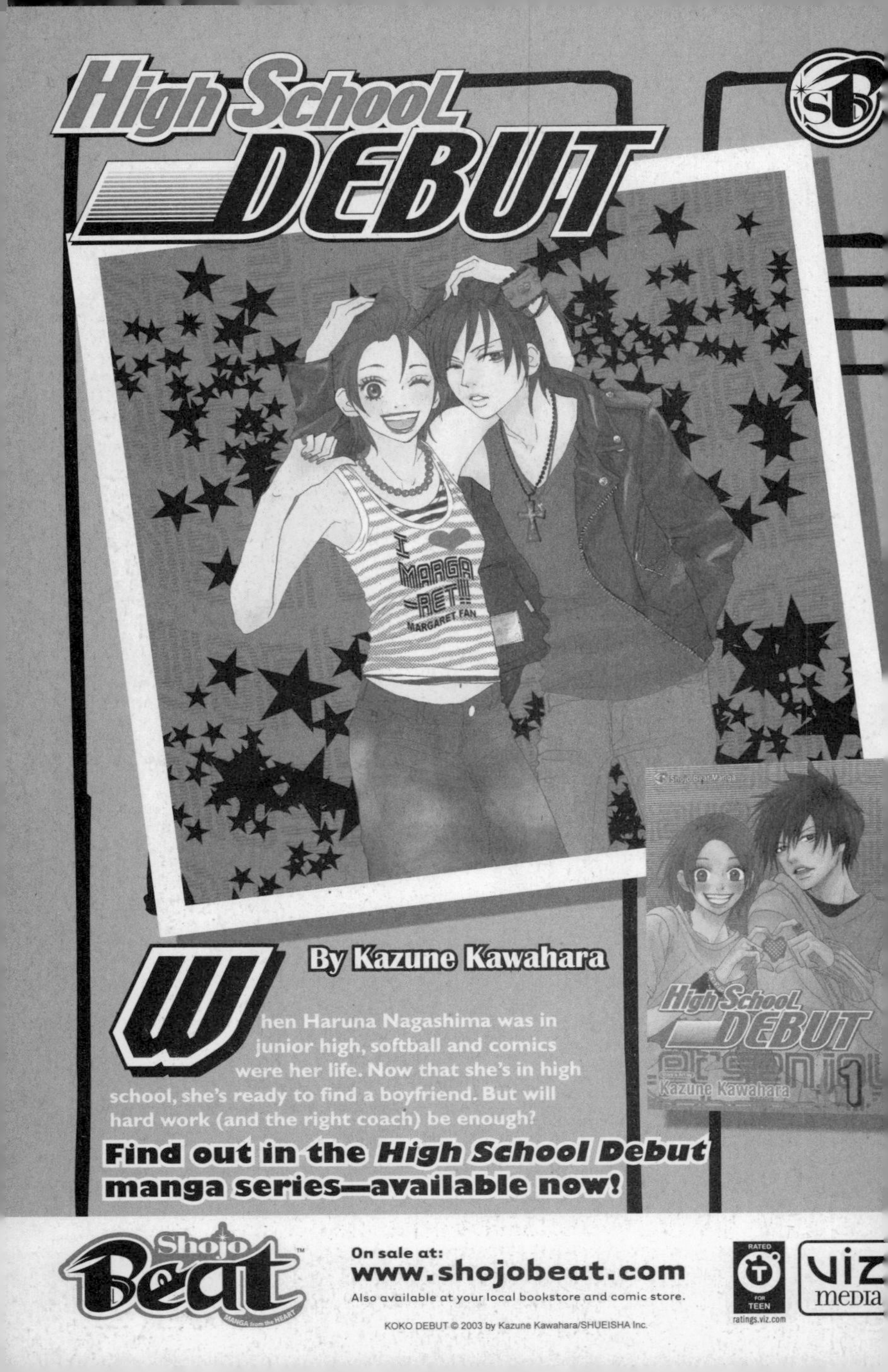
High School DEBUT
SB
Shojo Beat Manga
High School DEBUT
Kazune Kawahara
1
By Kazune Kawahara
When Haruna Nagashima was in junior high, softball and comics were her life. Now that she's in high school, she's ready to find a boyfriend. But will hard work (and the right coach) be enough?
Find out in the High School Debut manga series—available now!
Shojo Beat
MANGA from the HEART
On sale at:
www.shojobeat.com
Also available at your local bookstore and comic store.
RATED T FOR TEEN
ratings.viz.com
VIZ media
KOKO DEBUT © 2003 by Kazune Kawahara/SHUEISHA Inc.

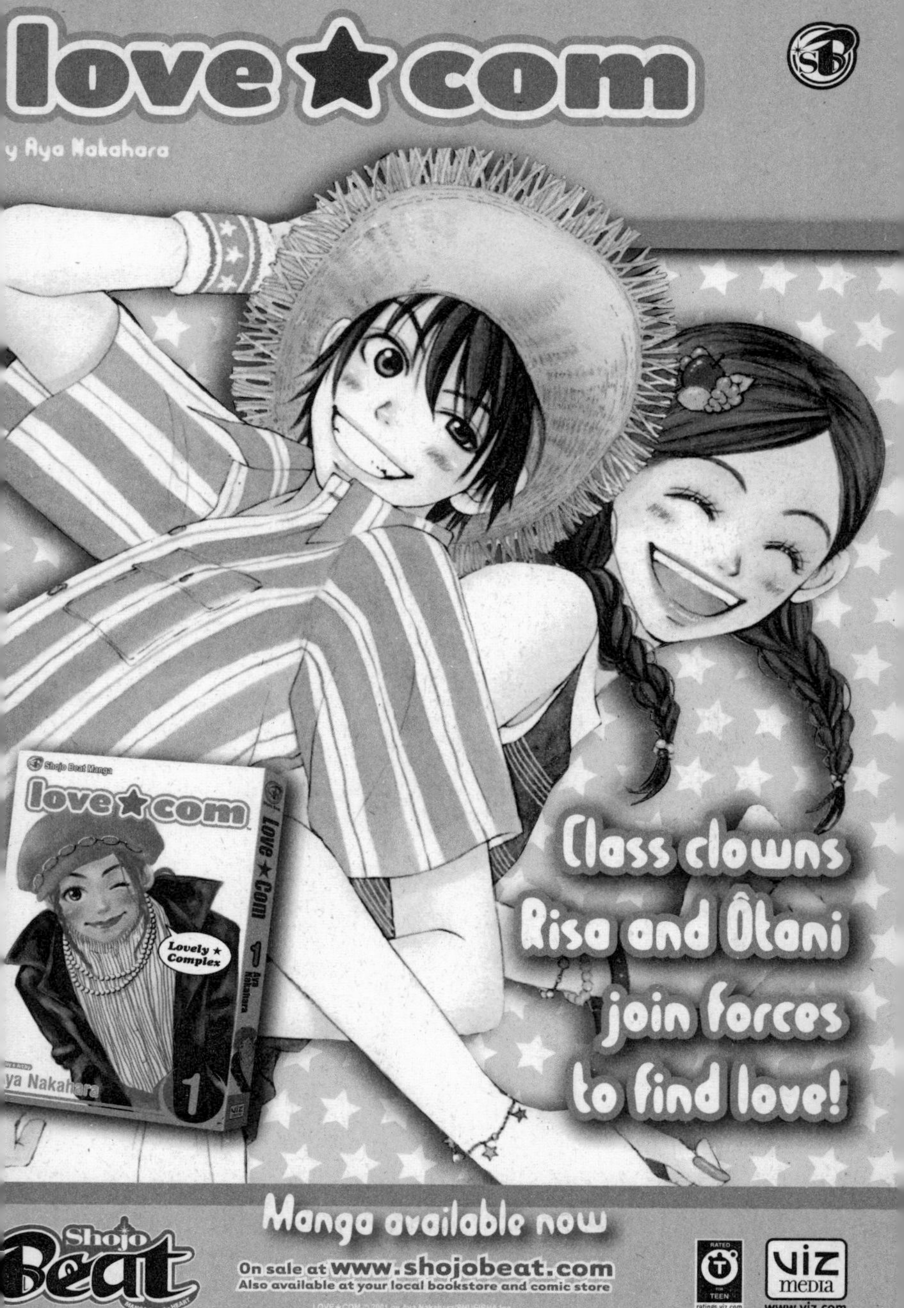

love★com
y Aya Nakahara
Shojo Beat Manga
love★com
Love★Com
1
Lovely ★ Complex
Aya Nakahara
Class clowns
Risa and Ôtani
join forces
to find love!
Manga available now
Shojo Beat
On sale at www.shojobeat.com
Also available at your local bookstore and comic store
LOVE★COM © 2001 by Aya Nakahara/SHUEISHA Inc.
RATED T FOR TEEN
ratings.viz.com
VIZ media
www.viz.com

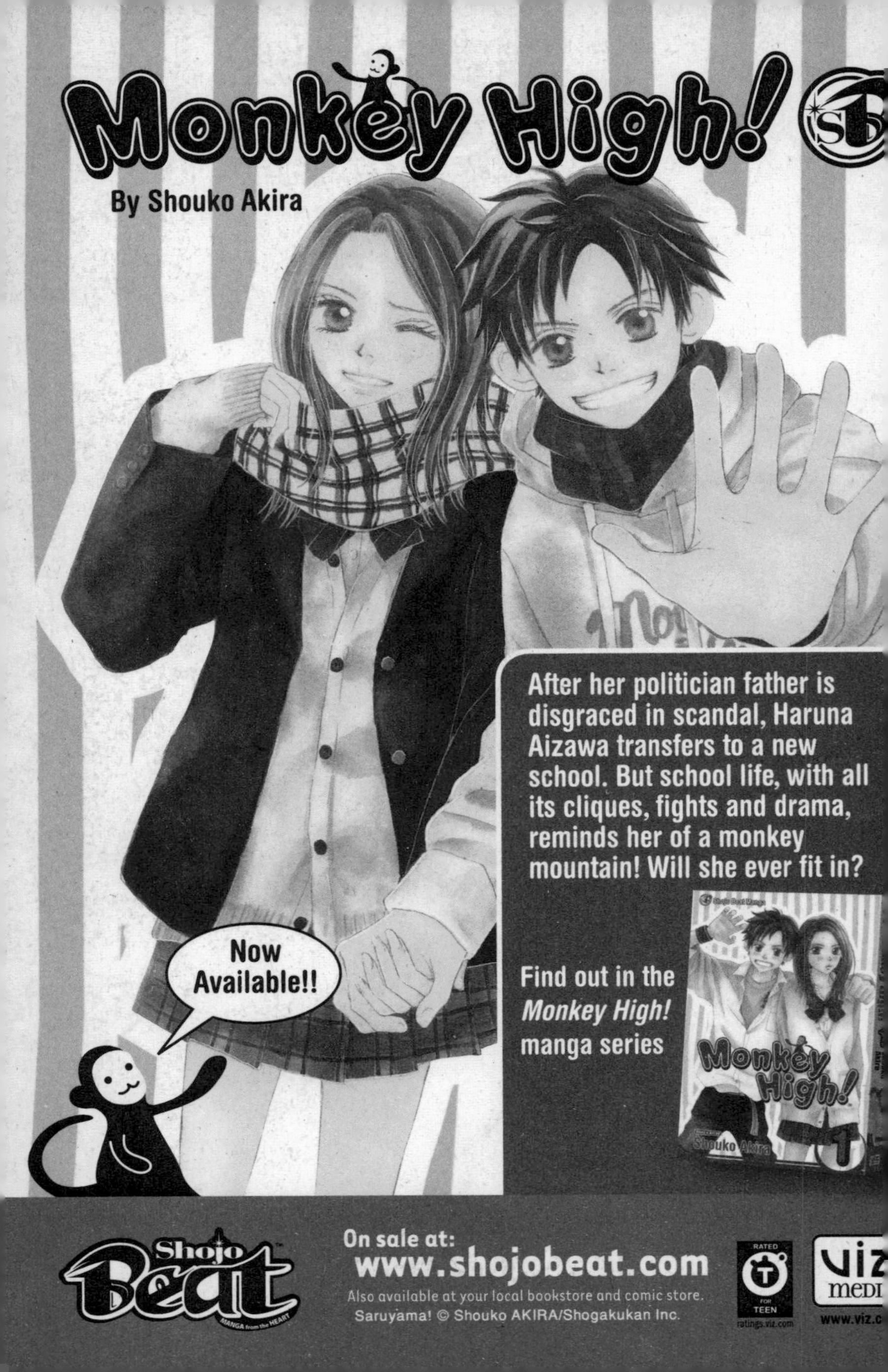
Monkey High!
By Shouko Akira
After her politician father is disgraced in scandal, Haruna Aizawa transfers to a new school. But school life, with all its cliques, fights and drama, reminds her of a monkey mountain! Will she ever fit in?
Now Available!!
Find out in the Monkey High! manga series
Monkey High!
Shouko Akira
Shojo Beat
On sale at:
www.shojobeat.com
Also available at your local bookstore and comic store.
Saruyama! © Shouko AKIRA/Shogakukan Inc.
RATED T FOR TEEN
ratings.viz.com

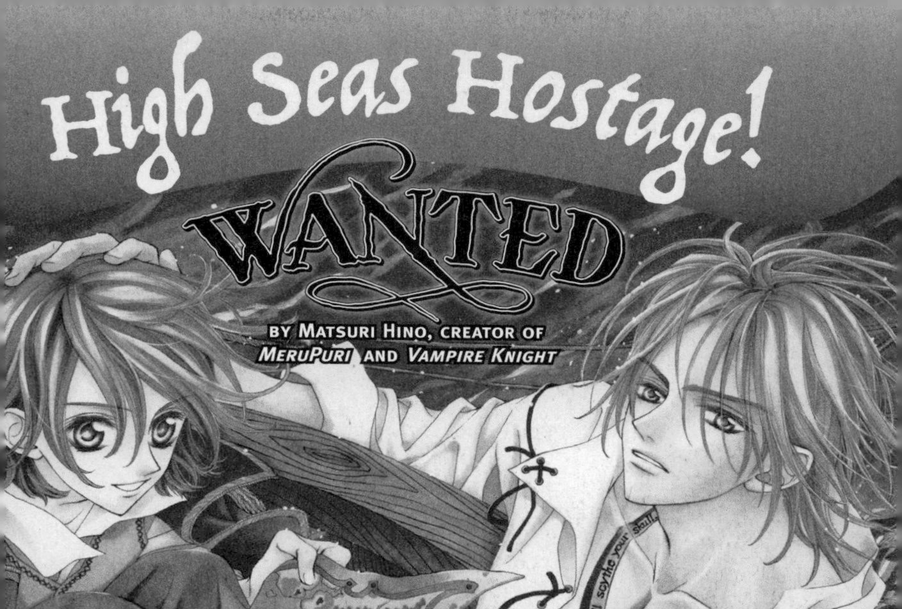
High Seas Hostage!
WANTED
BY MATSURI HINO, CREATOR OF
MERUPURI AND VAMPIRE KNIGHT
Death shall scythe your skull

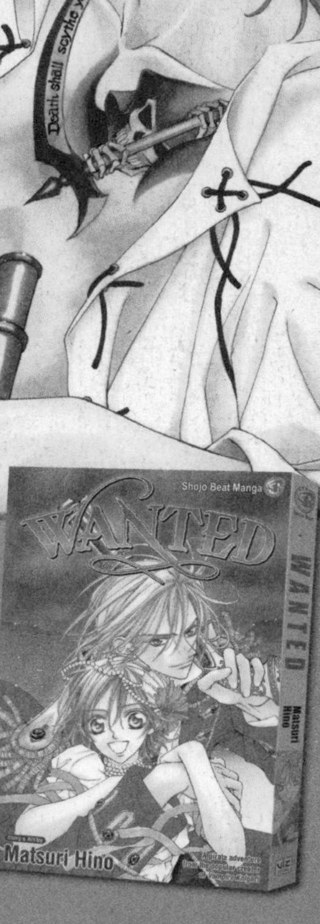
Shojo Beat Manga
WANTED
WANTED
Matsuri Hino
Matsuri Hino

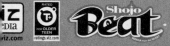

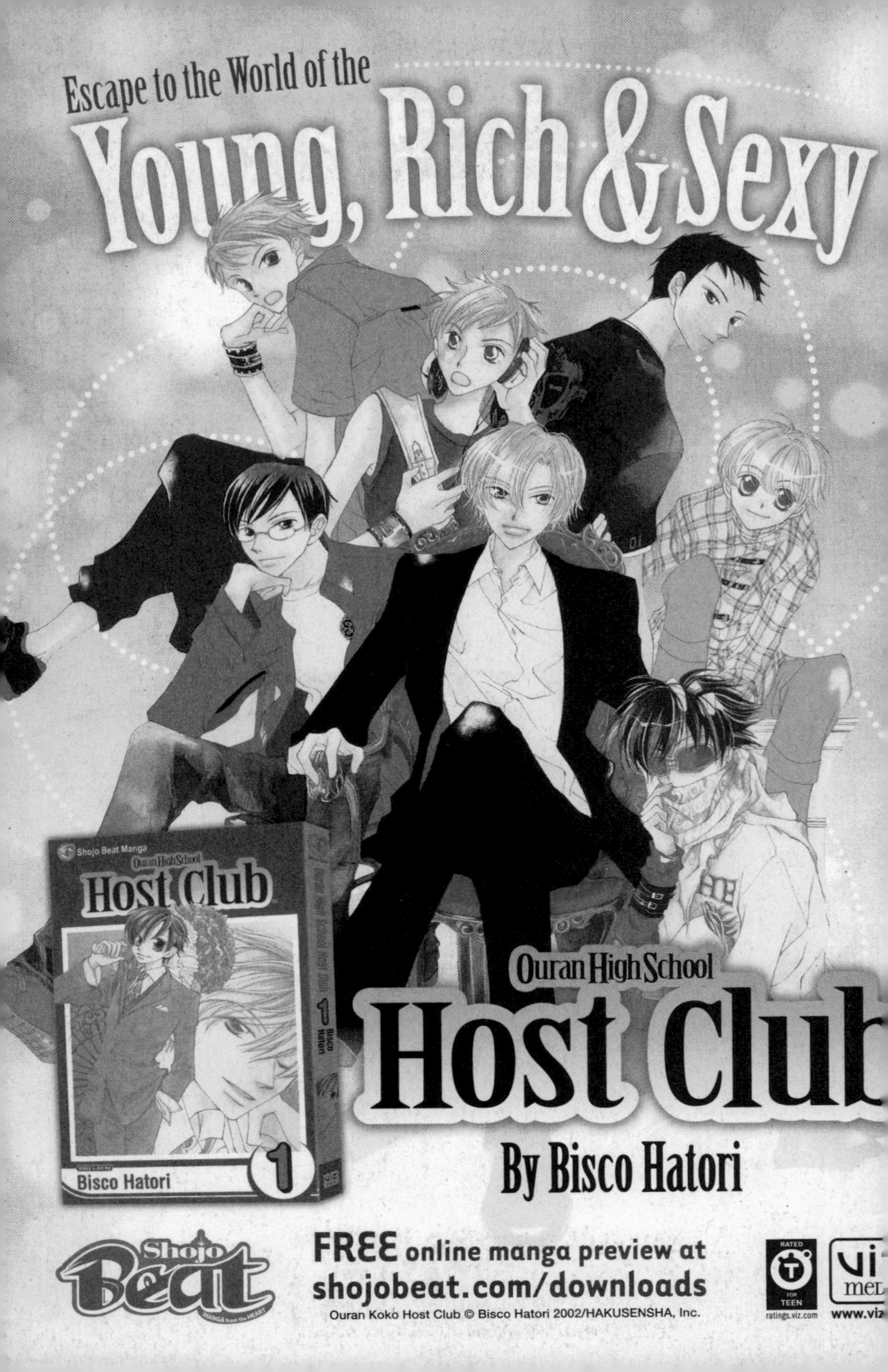
Escape to the World of the
Young, Rich & Sexy
Shojo Beat Manga
Ouran High School
Host Club
Bisco Hatori
1
Ouran High School
Host Club
By Bisco Hatori
Shojo Beat
MANGA from the HEART
FREE online manga preview at
shojobeat.com/downloads
Ouran Koko Host Club © Bisco Hatori 2002/HAKUSENSHA, Inc.
RATED T FOR TEEN
ratings.viz.com

MANGA from the HEART

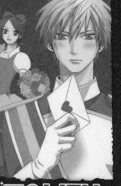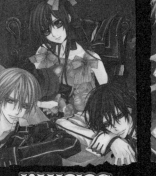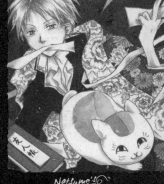

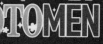TOMEN

STORY AND ART BY
AYA KANNO

VAMPIRE
KNIGHT

STORY AND ART BY
MATSURI HINO

Natsume's
BOOK of FRIENDS

STORY AND ART BY
YUKI MIDORIKAWA

Want to see more of what you're looking for?

Let your voice be heard!

hojobeat.com/mangasurvey

Help us give you more manga from the heart!

ya Kanno 2006/HAKUSENSHA, Inc.
alt © Matsuri Hino 2004/HAKUSENSHA, Inc.
ncho © Yuki Midorikawa 2005/ HAKUSENSHA, Inc.

ratings.viz.com

VIZ
MEDIA
www.viz.com